ETHNOGRAPHY UNBOUND

ETHNOGRAPHY UNBOUND

From Theory Shock to Critical Praxis

❖

Edited by

Stephen Gilbert Brown

and

Sidney I. Dobrin

STATE UNIVERSITY OF NEW YORK PRESS

Published by
State University of New York Press, Albany

© 2004 State University of New York

For information, address State University of New York Press,
90 State Street, Suite 700, Albany, NY 12207

Production by Marilyn P. Semerad
Marketing by Anne M. Valentine

Library of Congress Cataloging-in-Publication Data

Ethnography unbound : from theory shock to critical praxis / edited by Stephen Gilbert
Brown and Sidney I. Dobrin.
    p. cm.
Includes bibliographical references and index.
ISBN 0-7914-6051-7 (alk. paper) — ISBN 0-7914-6052-5 (pbk. : alk. paper)
    1. Ethnology—Methodology. 2. Ethnology—Philosophy. I. Brown, Stephen Gilbert. II.
Dobrin, Sidney I., 1967–

GN345.E783 2004
305.8'001—dc22

2003059513

10 9 8 7 6 5 4 3 2 1

In loving memory of Stew Merritt and Joan Brown

This one's for the Idyots.

CONTENTS

V. Texts and (Con)Texts: Intertextual Voices

ACKNOWLEDGMENTS

Stephen Gilbert Brown would like to acknowledge the work of Ralph Cintron (UIC) for providing the intellectual and theoretical spark in a presentation at CCCC (Denver 2000) that gave rise to this collection. He would also like to express his appreciation to Patricia Sullivan (University of Colorado) for underscoring the significant contribution of feminist discourse to critical ethnography. A word of thanks, as well, to Juan Guerra (University of Washington): though unable to contribute to this collection, his concept of "nomadic consciousness" helped sharpen our perception of the fluid and shifting subject positions inhabited in critical ethnography. A word of sincere appreciation goes out to colleagues at various institutions who have supported this project: Gary Olson and Lynn Worsham (University of South Florida), Jeff Klepfer and David Marcus (University of Tampa), John Irsfeld and Jim Frey (University of Nevada, Las Vegas). Additionally, I would like to thank colleagues in the English Department at UNLV. Finally, a special word of thanks to the research librarians, and to Priscilla Finley in particular, at University of Nevada, Las Vegas, for their tireless and friendly assistance with this project.

Sid Dobrin would like to acknowledge and thank Steve Brown for inviting me to participate in this fascinating project. Having not been deeply entrenched in the issues of critical ethnography, working on this collection has taught me much. I would also like to thank Carla Blount for her never-ending assistance and support. Thanks to Gary Olson and Lynn Worsham for their continuing encouragement. Thanks also to Anis S. Bawarshi, Christopher J. Keller, Raul Sanchez, Joe Hardin, Christian Weisser, and Julie Drew for the many conversations that help me see my work more clearly; they are magnificent colleagues and great friends. In particular, I want to thank and acknowledge Teresa Cocks who I seem to have forgotten to thank and acknowledge in *A Closer Look,* so I want to be sure to acknowledge her twice in this book. I am forever indebted to Teresa and am grateful for everything she does to support my work.

We would both like to extend our special thanks to Priscilla Ross at State University of New York Press for her guidance and support of this project from its inception. Her commitment, as well as the support of the manuscript reviewers and Editorial Board is sincerely appreciated.

Finally, we wish to express our gratitude to the contributors of this collection for their diligence in meeting production deadlines, for their patience in the review and revision process, and most of all for the provocative new directions of their writing research.

1

Introduction:
New Writers of the Cultural Sage

From Postmodern Theory Shock to Critical Praxis

STEPHEN GILBERT BROWN and SIDNEY I. DOBRIN

A RECENT BODY OF SCHOLARSHIP has questioned the assumptions, aims, and methods of traditional ethnography—to the point of rendering it impracticable. How ethnography has reinvented itself in the wake of this postmodern critique is one of the more interesting, not to say significant, events in recent composition studies. Moreover, the emergence of critical ethnography in this postpositivist moment not only evidences the resilience of ethnographic inquiry, but the efficacy of a truly dialectical engagement between theory and practice in general, and between postmodern theory and critical ethnographic praxis in particular. Furthermore, the emergent discourse of critical ethnography has important implications for composition studies and particularly for pedagogies of cultural change. Finally, the discursive engagement between postmodern theory and critical ethnography is evolving into a new dialectic whose effects are moving beyond the deterministic toward the protean—toward a new ethnographic praxis informed by postmodern theory, yet moving beyond the limitations of it.

As evidenced by its evolving, diversified response to this postmodern critique, critical ethnography is discovering new sites for praxis, occupying new theoretical topoi, developing new signifying practices, articulating a new ethnographic subject, redefining its goals, reinventing its methodologies, and revising its assumptions in what constitutes a radical ontological and epistemological transformation. In its emergent, postpositivist incarnation, critical ethnography is personalizing, politicizing, and socializing its praxis: it is politicizing the ends of ethnographic inquiry and socializing the process of ethnographic knowledge-making, while rediscovering its own critical voice with which it is beginning to "talk back" to postmodern theory to answer the fundamental questions the postmodern assault on traditional ethnographic practice raised.

The questions driving this new critical praxis have serious epistemological and ontological implications, and are deeply embedded with ethical and political connotations, as evinced by a selective recapitulation of them. Is ethnography possible in this postpositivist moment? Has postmodern theory rendered ethnographic practice obsolete, emptied it of all relevant content? Is the sign of positivist ethnography an empty signifier? What is the ethnographer's role in the wake of this postmodern assault? Can logos and ethos coexist in the ethnographic field? Can both inform praxis? What new goals, methods, and assumptions is ethnography evolving in response to the theoretical imperatives of this postmodern critique? How is it responding to the "crisis of representation," which of all of criticism's effects has been the most problematic? What role does signification play in the discursive power struggle between postmodern theory and ethnographic practice? To what extent is the practical being determined by the rhetorical? To what extent is the traditional field site being expanded to include the rhetorical in ethnographic inquiry? What does the discursive power struggle between theory and praxis reveal about the signifying practices of each? And, more important, what are the implications for composition studies in general, and for critical ethnography in particular? Can democracy long survive when the accumulation of power and the acquisition of knowledge are divested of ethos? Can critical ethnography contribute to the liberatory struggles of the oppressed for the democratic redistribution of power within and beyond U.S. borders? And finally, as Sharon Stevens asks, "what type of validity does our knowledge have?" (220).

As the ethnographies in this collection evidence, this discourse is emerging across a diverse range of field sites in the process redefining virtually every aspect of ethnographic research: our concept of a field site, of the ethnographic Self, of the relationship between ethnographer and participant, and of the desired outcomes of ethnographic inquiry. From urban schools in Great Britain to rural communities in Nebraska, from the signifying practices of stakeholders in the ecowars of the Sonoran Desert to cultural materialist analyses of the logic of the marketplace, critical ethnography is manifesting its protean relevance to pedagogies of cultural change. Having been placed under erasure for decades by positivist ethnographic assumptions, the ethnographic Self is finally beginning to sign itself into existence, to convert its pseudohier-archical absence into a dialectical presence not only with its readers but also with its participants. Furthermore, it now approaches participants as potential collaborators, not as exotic Others to be objectified by definitive scientific signs, as part of a reconfigured knowledge-making process that is social and whose ends are political. Additionally, critical ethnography is finally showing signs of recovering from the "theoretical anxiety" of the postmodern critique that temporarily disabled and almost permanently crippled it.

As it rediscovers its own theoretical and pedagogical legs, critical ethnog-raphy is beginning to move beyond the issues of the postmodern critique that gave birth to it, to move beyond its engagement with this theoretical critique to reimmersion in critical praxis: a praxis that is theoretically informed, methodologically dialectical, and politically and ethically oriented given its concerns for transformative cultural action. It is critiquing its critics, liberat-ing itself from the reductive, contradictory chains of postmodern signification, opening up new critical spaces for itself, evolving a critical praxis that is at once emergent and immersed.

Make no mistake about it, the postmodern critique of positivist ethnog-raphy was a catastrophic event in the history of that discourse. Having finally recovered from the shock of this theoretical and practical meltdown, critical ethnography is once again striking off in directions as innovative as they were unforeseen. A significant debt is nevertheless owed to postmod-ern theory for "clearing the way," and more important, for showing the way, for redirecting the critical gaze of ethnography away from science and toward politics, away from the interests of the ethnographic Self and toward a concern for altering the material conditions that determine the lived real-ity of the Other. Nevertheless, this critique, as is often the case in discursive power struggles, was guilty of theoretical and rhetorical overkill, its own analyses ironically flawed by faulty assumptions, reductive representations, and contradictory imperatives: inadequacies exposed by the countercritique of critical ethnography.

Insofar as this introduction constitutes a point of departure into this col-lection, we feel proffering a definition of *critical ethnography* is useful at this juncture. Beverly Moss provides a succinct and useful distinction between ethnography and critical ethnography: "While ethnography in general is con-cerned with describing and analyzing a culture, ethnography in composition studies . . . is concerned more narrowly with communicative behavior or the interrelationship of language and culture." Mary Jo Reiff concurs (*Ethnogra-phy and Composition* 156):

> Ethnography in rhetoric-composition, particularly as a pedagogical approach, is concerned not just with the lived experience or behavior of cultures (as in anthropology or sociology) but with the way in which this behavior manifests itself rhetorically—what Dell Hymes calls "ethnography of communication."

Lance Massey endorses Reiff's view, observing that the focus of critical ethnography is an "adequate account of the literate practices of others." Robert Brooke and Charlotte Hogg proffer an equally useful, if more nuanced, definition of critical ethnography:

> We understand critical ethnography as a research practice, primarily related to education, whose purpose is to use dialogue about a cultural context to develop critical action, while remaining highly attuned to the ethics and politics of representation in the practice and reporting of that dialogue and resulting actions. (161)

The origins of critical ethnography are partially rooted in the theories and fieldwork of Paulo Freire, "and moves through Ira Shor and Henry Giroux in contemporary American education" (161).

The ethical, political, and social turn in critical ethnography derives not only from Freirean praxis, however, but from the intellectual tradition of academic feminism, whose "interest in ethics," as Mortensen and Kirsch observe, "arises from frustration with a kind of ethical relativism that has often overtaken—and paralyzed—discussions of subjectivity and agency in postmodern theories of culture" (xxi). Feminists' concerns with agency, the ethics of representation, the emancipatory ends of research ("for women rather than on women"), and the "multiple and shifting subject positions we inhabit" (xxi) prefigure the postmodern paradigmatic shifts in critical ethnography. The questions driving feminist inquiry similarly anticipate the postmodern interrogation of positivist ethnographic practice: "Who benefits from the research? Whose interests are at stake? What are the consequences for participants?" (xxi). Mortensen and Kirsch continue:

> As a consequence of feminist interventions, as well as (sometimes conflicting) contributions from poststructural and postcolonial theorists, we have come to recognize how hierarchies and inequalities (marked by gender, race, class, social groupings, and more) are transferred onto and reproduced within participant-researcher relations. (xxi)

In other words, critical ethnography lives in the dialectical relationship between the Word and the World: a dialectic that it seeks to regenerate, operating from an assumed faith in the procreative power of any dialectic. Here is where Giroux's theories on the dialectic between education and culture, particularly as enunciated in *Theory and Resistance in Education,* prove most useful. Critical ethnography, then, is but one of several discourses that seeks to extend Freirean theory and praxis into American contexts by combining radical pedagogy and writing research. As Brooke and Hogg observe, *"critical ethnography* emerges from an extensive body of work in critical pedagogy in which the goal of teaching is to engage the students (or other groups of learners) in the dialogic work of understanding their social location and developing cultural actions appropriate to that location" (161). Building on this Freirean tradition, scholars such as Bruce Horner theorize critical ethnography under the sign of "labor" and "work" to emphasize the intrinsically social and collaborative nature of it.

Unlike traditional ethnographic practice, critical ethnography shifts the goal of praxis away from the acquisition of knowledge about the Other (either for its own sake or in the service of the ethnographer's career) to the formation of a dialogic relationship with the Other whose destination is the social transformation of material conditions that immediately oppress, marginalize, or otherwise subjugate the ethnographic participant. This reconfigured praxis seeks to actualize both aspects of the Freirean educational dialectic, in which critical analysis of localized and politicized problems is but a springboard into meaningful action to mitigate, legislate, or eliminate those problems. The activating agent for this analysis-into-action dialectic is the ethnographer-other dyad: is the emerging, peerlike partnership between ethnographer and participant in which the student-other is empowered as a coinvestigator of a problem that is critically analyzed in collaboration with the ethnographer as a precondition for evolving an action plan to meaningfully and effectively engage the problem. We believe the ethnographies in this collection eloquently signify the continuing relevance, resilience, and innovation of field-based research that is helping restore a protean dialectic between theory and praxis.

New Writers of the Cultural Sage

Ethnography Unbound commences with four ethnographies clustered under the signs of the *theoretical* and the *rhetorical.* In "Critical Ethnography, Ethics, and Work: Rearticulating Labor," Bruce Horner reinforces the protean dialectic between theory and practice in general, and between cultural materialist perspectives and critical praxis in particular. Horner's nuanced critique exposes the limitations of postmodern theory, particularly its reductive representation of the ethnographic Self under the sign of "the Lone Ethnographer." The sophistication of Horner's critique effectively situates his work at the cutting edge of critical ethnography. More important, however, is the liberatory effect his countercritique will have on critical praxis by freeing it from such disabling signifiers as the Lone Ethnographer and by foregrounding the inherently collaborative nature of all ethnographic writing.

Mary Jo Reiff's chapter, "Mediating Materiality and Discursivity: Critical Ethnography as Metageneric Learning," similarly foregrounds signifying practices and the rhetorical. Reiff situates ethnography as a "genre" that mediates between the ethnographer and the culture under observation, that mediates between the rhetorical and the social, that shifts ethnographic inquiry from the material to the symbolic—or rather, resituates it in the protean intersection between the cultural and the rhetorical: one that integrates texts and contexts. Her work, consequently, recuperates a generative dialectic between "lived experiences and lived textuality" (55).

In "The Ethnographic Experience of Postmodern Literacies," Christopher Schroeder models a classroom ethnography in which critical praxis is informed by postmodern theory and that evidences the usefulness of a cultural materialist approach in particular. As with Horner, Schroeder develops a nuanced analysis of the material conditions that influence and inform the construction of ethnographic knowledge, not only in the academy but also in the culture by which it is encompassed. Schroeder brings student voices into play perhaps more effectively than any chapter in this collection, in a "co-performance" that raises important questions about power and representation.

Gwen Gorzelsky, likewise, foregrounds the rhetorical, and particularly the figurative, in her chapter, "Shifting Figures: Rhetorical Ethnography." Gorzelsky foregrounds ethnography's solidarity with political struggles in a project that explores the useful intersections between figurative self-reflexivity, ethics, and social transformation. Informed by Bateson and Gestalt's theories, her analysis recuperates a metaphoric dialectic between participation and observation.

Lynée Lewis Gaillet also explores the symbiotic relationship between the ethnographic and the rhetorical in her chapter, "Writing Program Redesign: Learning from Ethnographic Inquiry, Civic Rhetoric, and the History of Rhetorical Education." In this chapter, Gaillet links ethnography to civic discourse, conjoining service learning and political controversies in a unified project that reinvigorates the eighteenth century and Isocratean ideal of the public intellectual. Gaillet establishes the efficacy of writing with a "civic tongue" to develop writing programs informed by civic rhetoric, grounded in the concept of *civitas*.

A second group of ethnographies are organized under the subheading "Place-Conscious Ethnographies: Situating Praxis in the Field." In "Open to Change: Ethos, Identification, and Critical Ethnography in Composition Studies," Robert Brooke and Charlotte Hogg reinvigorate the protean dialectic between theory and praxis. They theorize critical ethnography from a Freirean perspective, noting the contributions of Shor and Giroux. In a critique as nuanced as it is useful, Brooke and Hogg problematize Ralph Cintron's deployment of Aristotelean ethos, approaching ethos instead from a Burkean perspective. They theorize the constructed nature of ethnographic knowledge, envisioning the field site as emerging through the "crucial filter" of ethnography. This theoretical analysis is situated in two very site-specific projects that not only complete the dialectic between theory and praxis, but also evince the efficacy of community-based, project-oriented ethnographies in particular.

In "State Standards in the United States and the National Curriculum in the United Kingdom: Political Siege Engines against Teacher Professionalism?" John Sylvester Lofty similarly revitalizes the dialectic between theory and praxis, between theoretical texts and ethnographic contexts. Lofty brings two site-specific case studies into metaphoric juxtaposition to illustrate the effects of "legislated literacy" on teacher professionalism across national boundaries. Lofty's inquiry is at once a nuanced interrogation of hierarchical power relations, liberatory resistance, and identity politics as well as an articulate argument for the efficacy of teacher autonomy versus the educational determinants of state mandates.

Sharon McKenzie Stevens, likewise, models a "place-conscious" critical praxis that invigorates the dialectic between postmodern theory and ethnographic practice. In "Debating Ecology: Ethnographic Writing that 'Makes a Difference,'" Stevens successfully fuses two emerging discourses: ecocomposition and critical ethnography, creating in the process a new, metageneric discourse, ecoethnography. As is the case with Brooke and Hogg's inquiry, the field site here emerges through the filter of the ethnographer's interpretative stance. Stevens responds to the "crisis of representation" and the "implied ethical imperatives" of the postmodern critique of positivist ehtnography by personalizing and politicizing ethnographic inquiry: responses that will prove useful to critical ethnographers negotiating similar "crises" and "imperatives." Stevens draws on Donna Haraway's concept of "diffraction" to capture the dialogic nature of the relationship between field site and ethnographer in a manner that resonates with Brooke and Hogg's use of the sign *filter*. Stevens's inquiry similarly emphasizes the "relational" nature of critical ethnography, foregrounding the assertion that knowledge-making is a function of a "web of relations," of a "relationship-conscious ethnography."

A third group of critical ethnographies is organized under the sign of "the ethnographic Self," insofar as they depict the "reorganization of the self in the field." In "Critical Auto/Ethnography: A Constructive Approach to Research in the Composition Classroom," Susan S. Hanson joins the effort to open up a new "space within ethnography to locate the self" (257) by fusing autobiography and ethnography into a new genre: critical auto/ethnography: one that is deeply informed by the discourses of feminist autobiography and postcolonial theory.

Christopher Keller similarly situates his argument in the debates swirling around the ethnographic Self. In "Unsituating the Subject: 'Locating' Composition and Ethnography in Mobile Worlds," Keller evidences the critical role signifying practices play in the postpositivist ethnographic moment. Keller interrogates the usefulness of ethnography for composition studies in an effort to embed it more meaningfully within that discourse. To date, it has floated too freely beyond the disciplinary bounds of composition, gravitating toward anthropology. To solve this dilemma, Keller argues the efficacy of evolving a new research methodology, of enacting a new genre: one that is situated more meaningfully within the domain of composition. He articulates this methodology under the sign of psychography in a provocative illustration of the way critical ethnographers are reinventing signifying practices to reinvent critical praxis. Keller's argument explodes the hierarchical binary between ethnography and composition, liberating composition into its own ethnographic terrain.

Issues of self-reflexivity also comprise the focus of Janet Alsup's chapter, "Protean Subjectivities: Qualitative Research and the Inclusion of the Personal." Alsup critiques the recent trend toward the personal in ethnographic research, enunciating a more nuanced, "thoughtful, purposeful, reasoned" inclusion of it. Her interrogation of disciplinary authority problematizes the acquisition of knowledge as an end in itself, privileging instead a praxis that uses knowledge as a collaborative means to political ends, that situates the ethnographic Self in social solidarity with the Other, as part of a knowledge-making dialectic that favors a "reciprocal, nonunitary subjectivity." The sociopolitical orientation of Alsup's research anticipates the final two chapters in this collection.

A fourth group of critical ethnographies is situated under the subhead, "Ethnographies of Cultural Change." A concern for the political ends of praxis characterizes these inquiries, which shifts ehnographic praxis away from the realms of a self-serving science to the Other-oriented domain of the political. In "Changing Directions: Participatory-Action Research, Agency, and Representation," Bronwyn T. Williams and Mary Brydon-Miller foreground the necessity of linking ethnographic analysis to cultural action. As do Horner, and Brooke and Hogg, they situate "participatory-action research" within the tradition of Freirean praxis, as evidenced by their emphasis of "social reflexivity" and "social justice." Williams and Brydon-Miller elaborate a critical ethnography that is not the by-product of a fixed, unified discourse, but the site of multiple discourses dispersed across a field of signification ranging from the personal to the political, the symbolic to the material, the urban to the rural, and the corporeal to the virtual.

Lance Massey, similarly, foregrounds the political in his work, "Just What *Are* We Talking About? Disciplinary Struggle and the Ethnographic Imaginary." Responding to the postmodern attack on the goals of positivist ethnography, Massey articulates a new set of outcomes, privileging agency, empowerment, and transformative action over a pseudoscientific, self-serving, apolitical "knowledge" producing apparatus. Massey provides a useful and nuanced analysis of "theoretical anxiety," of the postmodern theory shock that temporarily disabled ethnographers by virtue of the critical binds and seemingly contradictory imperatives to which it subjected them. As with many ethnographies in this collection, Massey's recuperates the protean dialectic between theory and praxis, advocating a praxis that is not only informed by theory but in which the pragmatic is oriented toward the political.

Our collection closes with two "response" pieces, coupled under the heading, "Texts and (Con)texts: Intertextual Voices." In "The Ethics of Reading Critical Ethnography," Min-Zhan Lu responds to many of the ethnographers in this collection, using their arguments to inform her own. Of the many debates being contested in the discourse of critical ethnography, perhaps none is more lively than the debate over ethics. Min-Zhan's chapter not only evidences the centrality of this debate, but also shifts it into new, unexamined terrain: arguing not just for an ethics of writing, but for an ethics of reading. She challenges readers of ethnographic discourse to evolve a self-reflexive ethos as rigorous as the ethics they expect of ethnographers. Moroever, she innovatively posits the construction and practice of an ethnographic ethos as an enabling dialectic between ethnographers and readers, in which an ethics of reading complements an ethics of praxis, in which readers participate in the making and practice of ethnographic ethics. Her critique of postmodern interrogations of ethnography is grounded in a nuanced analysis of the material conditions that influence the production of ethnographic texts and discourse, that "enable and constrain disciplinary knowledge production."

In "Beyond Theory Shock: Ethos, Knowledge, and Power in Critical Ethnography," Stephen Gilbert Brown analyzes the responses of the critical ethnographers in this collection to the postmodern critique of positivist ethnography. Brown focuses on five aspects of ethnography's critical response to postmodern theory in this postpositivist moment: its liberatory countercritique; the politicization of its goals; the socialization of its methods; the personalization of its voice; and the reinvention of its rhetorical strategies. Additionally, he assesses the implications of these critical responses, not only for critical ethnography, but also for all pedagogies of cultural change.

WORKS CITED

Mortensen, Peter, and Gesa E. Kirsch. *Ethics and Representation in Qualitative Studies of Literacy* Fwd. by Andrea Lunsford. Intro. by Mortensen and Kirsch. NCTE (1996): i–xxxiv.

Moss, Beverly. "Ethnography and Composition: Studying Language at Home." *Methods and Methodologies in Composition Research*. Ed. Gesa Kirsch and Patricia Sullivan. Carbondale: SIUP, 1992. 153–71.

PART I

Theoretical and Rhetorical Perspectives

2

Critical Ethnography, Ethics, and Work

Rearticulating Labor

BRUCE HORNER

IN THIS CHAPTER, I argue that a cultural materialist perspective on the work of critical ethnography in composition studies can provide a useful framework that accounts for and can help to resolve some of the significant ethical dilemmas to which recent critiques of critical ethnography in composition have pointed (Cintron, Cushman, Kirsch, Kirsch and Ritchie, Lu and Horner, Mortensen and Kirsch). My argument is aligned with, and intended to further, the materialist emphasis of those critiques. Responding to the limitations of traditional ethnographic practices, those critiques resituate the work of ethnography in the material social circumstances of its enactment to take into account the power relations among those involved in such work and the material consequences for those living at the research "site." But this has led to calls for a seemingly endless series of ethical strictures on the direction, conduct, outcome, and writing of critical ethnographies that, in their overwhelming number and sometimes conflicting recommendations, can appear to place an impossible set of responsibilities on the shoulders of the critical ethnographer. This results, I argue, not from the materialist emphasis of these critiques but by their failure to be materialist enough in their conception of the work of ethnography. By challenging how such critiques define the work, workers, and the production of value through such work, and by locating that work more insistently in the material realm, a cultural materialist perspective, although not eliminating the ethical demands on critical ethnography, can redefine by redistributing more broadly the meanings and means of addressing such demands as indeed demands, not dilemmas.

I begin by describing recent critiques of ethnography in composition studies, highlighting the model of academic work to which such critiques respond but that remain in the recommendations emerging from these critiques. I go on to describe how a cultural materialist view of academic work redefines the dilemmas addressed in such critiques from being understood as strictly ethical dilemmas to being understood as challenges arising out of material social conditions and therefore to be addressed in terms of such conditions. To demonstrate the aptness of such an understanding for critical ethnography in composition, I revisit some of the critiques of ethnographic work to consider alternative strategies for responding to the dilemmas these critiques identify.

Recent critiques of ethnography have complicated not simply researchers' understanding of ethnography but also their research practice as well. Researchers now must ask themselves a host of new questions as they design, conduct, and report on their research. These questions respond to feminist, postcolonial, and poststructuralist perspectives on experience and knowledge that highlight the partiality and historicity of knowledge and experience—importantly, not only the "informant's" but also the researcher's—and consequently call for reimagining research projects as "praxis," responsive to the local research site and those residing there in its origination, implementation, and representation (Kirsch and Ritchie 25 and passim; Lu and Horner 261–63). Knowledge and experience are approached as "partial" in all senses: neither complete, fixed, disinterested, universal, nor neutral but instead situated, local, interested, material, and historical.

To ensure a socially just response to the partiality of knowledge and experience in the practice of ethnography, greater attention is paid to asymmetrical power relations between researcher and informant, researcher and researcher, researcher and community, institutional site and researcher, and funding agency and researcher as these affect the definition, conduct, outcomes, and reporting of the ethnographic project. Put crudely, given inevitably asymmetrical relations of power between these parties, and given the partiality of knowledge and experience, researchers are now expected to ask themselves what would constitute ethically responsible ways of defining, initiating, carrying out, and reporting on their research. Those asking such questions have produced myriad recommendations, but I will focus on the three that have garnered the most attention and that are most germane to questions of materiality: an emphasis on collaboration, on multivocality, and on self-reflexivity. Although each of these challenge the traditional model of academic work, my argument will be that they are not materialist enough in the framework by which they understand that model, and so the recommendations they present remain insufficient.

❦

> Once upon a time, the Lone Ethnographer rode off into the sunset in search of "his native." After undergoing a series of trials, he encountered the object of his quest in a distant land. There he underwent his rite of passage by enduring the ultimate ordeal of "fieldwork." After collecting "the data," the Lone Ethnographer returned home and wrote a "true" account of "the culture." (Rosaldo, 30)

Renato Rosaldo's satiric depiction of the ideal of traditional ethnography is telling especially for what that ideal omits from consideration. The traditional model of academic work is closely tied to the ideal of academic professionalism. In that model, the researcher serves his (*sic*, in the ideal) discipline, rightly oblivious to the material social realm, which always threatens to corrupt his work. In Rosaldo's satiric depiction, the Lone Ethnographer produces his ethnography as a result of a quest that seems to be self-defined, "his," not the result of any set of social or historical circumstances. In producing his "true" account, "professional" standards for conducting, reporting, and evaluating research are used to guard against corruption from such circumstances and to ensure the "quality," objectivity, and neutrality of the researcher. In ethnography, for example, triangulation is intended as a means of verifying that data are evaluated accurately. More generally, practices such as peer review of manuscripts are intended to guarantee both the quality and legitimacy of academic scholarship.

The divorce of the researcher's research agenda from the material social realm is mirrored in the imagined divorce of the location of the work of research from that same realm. First, the work produced is imagined as the researcher's own, arising out of and testimony to his own genius. Rosaldo's Lone Ethnographer is "lone," makes "his" quest to find "his" native, makes his trip alone and apparently by his own means, and writes his "'true' account" all by himself and for himself and others like him. Or, as Rosaldo puts it, these accounts were produced "by and for specialists," treated as "storehouses of purportedly incontrovertible information to be mined by armchair theorists engaged in comparative studies" (32). Second, although the work of ethnography, like all other work, is made possible by particular social and material conditions (for example, an elaborated educational system [the "academy"], funding agencies, informants, libraries, clerical support, academic departments, journals, research assistants, university presses and the editors and others that work for them), the contributions of these to the work produced is largely dismissed, relegated at best to notes of acknowledgement by the work's "author." The materiality of ethnographic work—its demands of time; bodily health; equipment; money to pay for equipment, salaries, and travel, and so forth—is ignored as necessary but having nothing to do with the actual production of the ethnographic work, imagined as strictly "the product of the Lone Ethnographer's labors" (31). Third, it is understood that although "fieldwork" is crucial, the "field" is imagined as untouched by the researcher's work there; the researcher instead is imagined to observe the field from a privileged location of "'detached impartiality'" above the field, his observations having no impact on, while accurately identifying truths of, the field (30). Finally, the value of the work, located in the textual product, is attributed not to the labor of all these participants but to features of the text itself as a commodity. The Lone Ethnographer's account is admired as an "artifact worthy of being housed in the collection of a major museum" (31).

In its insistence on collaboration, multivocality, and self-reflexiveness on the impact of power relations on the ethnographic project, critical ethnography begins to contest this traditional ideal vision of ethnographic work. It recognizes the contributions of others in addition to the Lone Ethnographer to the work produced; it calls for their voices and interests to be included in the definition of the project, and it insists that the Lone Ethnographer remove what Rosaldo terms his "mask of innocence" to confront the asymmetrical power relations with which his work is complicit (30). However, as I will suggest, a residual idealism limits the challenges critical ethnography poses to this model. By framing the problems with traditional ethnography in terms of ethics, critical ethnography continues to identify the work and the responsibility for it as the Lone Ethnographer's, even in those arguments that appear to call for recognizing the sociality of ethnographic work. Thus, new burdens of ethical responsibility are simply added to the traditional ideal of the Lone Ethnographer, leading to seemingly tortuous dilemmas.

COLLABORATION

Critical ethnographers, along with many others, frequently recommend some form of collaboration, whether between researcher and informant, fellow researchers, researchers and communities, researchers and institutions, or some or all of these. First, collaboration with informants is understood as a means of contesting the hierarchical relationships between "researcher" and "informant," indeed rendering such distinctions somewhat arbitrary as both take on the role of researching and informing. In collaborative arrangements, at least in theory, both parties have a say in the design, implementation, and writing of the ethnography so that both parties, and not just the researcher or research community, can benefit from the project. As Cheri L. Williams observes,

> When research is truly collaborative, the researcher and the informants participate as a team; they become co-researchers who explore an issue of common interest and concern. They co-author the research questions, co-collect, co-analyze, and co-interpret the data, and they co-construct the final products (e.g., written reports, public presentations). The researchers develop an interactive, dialogic, reciprocal relationship that mitigates the strictures of traditional, imperialistic hegemony. They learn to respect one another's perspective and honor one another's trust. (51)

Gesa Kirsch and Joy Ritchie advocate collaboration as a means of reducing the distance between researcher and informant and the marginalization of the latter that mark the difference between the Lone Ethnographer and "native" in traditional ethnography (22). From the standpoint of an "ethic of care" for which they argue, unequal power relations between researcher and informants require that research be used as "'praxis' to help those who participate with [researchers] in research to understand and change their situation, to help those who have been marginalized to speak for themselves" (25).

Second, as Kirsch and Ritchie observe, through collaboration between researchers and participants, "[r]esearchers can gather additional insights by getting to know participants in the context of their daily lives, and participants can gain new knowledge about themselves and their lives through the research project (14; see also Blakeslee et al. 142; Cushman, "Public" 332; Sullivan 109). In counterdistinction to the Lone Ethnographer, knowledge from the research is imagined to accrue not simply to the Lone Ethnographer and his fellow specialists and armchair theorists, but also to the "natives." Furthermore, the ethnographer, no longer "lone," is imagined to gain even more knowledge through working more collaboratively with "his native" than he might otherwise gain—in Kirsch and Ritchie's words, researchers "can gather additional insights" through collaboration. But the motivation for collaboration is not simply to increase knowledge and benefit or to make these reciprocal. Collaboration is also seen as methodologically more consistent with critical ethnographers' belief in the social construction of knowledge. As Jennie Dautermann argues, "[I]f we are serious about social construction of knowledge, it is important to authorize and practice collaborative methods for analyzing and reporting our research as well as for collecting it (257; see also Durst and Stanforth 60; Sullivan 109).

It is thus that, as Russel Durst and Sherry Stanforth remark, the literature on collaboration in research portrays collaborative research as both "politically progressive" and "beneficial to learning" (60). However, as Durst and

Stanforth themselves, as well as others, report, this collaborative ideal seems frequently to become problematic in practice, the ideal creating friction in its encounters with the material social realm. First, the ideal assumes that others—that is, the "natives"—share the academics' interest in research. But as several researchers warn, many "participants" may in fact have little or no interest in ethnographic research (Blakeslee et al. 146; Brueggemann 33; Kirsch and Ritchie 15–16). The ideal that Williams (as well as others) heralds of participants as coresearchers may simply be unappealing to many. Second, differences in the social positioning of "participants" complicate the ideal. In a report on their research experience, Durst and Stanforth note that published discussions of collaborative research do not often articulate the complexity they themselves experienced as collaborators, instead presenting "exceedingly sanguine" accounts of its benefits, emphasizing its "positive, feel-good aspects" (60). Whereas both Durst and Stanforth were academics in composition studies and so could be expected to share an interest in composition research, their very different positioning in the academic hierarchy—Durst was a tenured male professor and writing program director, Stanforth a graduate student in composition studies for whom Durst was teacher, academic advisor, and job supervisor—significantly complicated the agenda, conduct, and interpretation of their research, transforming it from a study of composition instruction to "an examination of the politics of studying scenes of instruction" (60–61).

Where those involved include nonacademics, interests may collide more significantly. Dautermann reports that in her study of hospital writing practices, a hospital administrator did not want the hospital's investment in Dautermann as a writing consultant to fund her dissertation (245). Ruth Ray warns that in research collaborations between university and primary- or secondary-school teachers, each party may be pursuing conflicting goals masked under the "research" rubric: "[t]eachers conduct research because of its transformative potential for themselves and their classrooms; [academic] researchers conduct research because of its transformative potential for their fields" (292; see also Dale 82). More pointedly, researchers have reported conflicts between the researcher's desire to present a full account and participants' desire not to disclose personal information, and between researchers' and informants' religious and political beliefs. How, for example, does a researcher committed to fighting homophobia "honor" a fundamentalist Christian informant's desire not to disclose her lesbian past (see Kirsch and Ritchie 17)? How does a feminist researcher report on the experiences of a woman who explicitly rejects feminist accounts of her experience (Kirsch and Ritchie 19)? Or how does the ethnographer "fairly" represent a teacher's literacy pedagogy when it collides with the researcher's own beliefs about such pedagogy (Williams 48–49)?

Finally, even in instances where the researcher and the participant-informant share research and political commitments, material barriers can intrude.

Helen Dale describes the difficulties she encountered collaborating with Carol, a ninth-grade English teacher, in researching student coauthoring. Carol shared Dale's interest in the research and invited her to coteach for a quarter, and the two developed a plan for Dale to coteach the class and for the two to collaborate on conducting the research. However, Dale found that although she had hoped "to work with Carol on all ongoing aspects of teaching and research, . . . that was not possible because Carol did not have time to collaborate with me so fully" (79). Although Carol was very excited at the prospect of "'talking about teaching English, getting ideas,'" especially "'because in a typical public school teacher's [sic] day, you know, there's so little time to talk about teaching,'" as the project developed, Carol ended up having no time to devote to it (Dale 80, 81). In hindsight, although "frustrating for both," this was perhaps inevitable, given the very different situations of the two: Dale was a researcher working on her doctoral dissertation; Carol was a ninth-grade schoolteacher responsible for teaching five classes and serving as faculty advisor for the student newspaper (83–84). "Carol," Dale observes, "was understandably more concerned with her daily class schedule, the yearly curriculum, and the various demands on her time and attention" than with the progress of the research, despite her initial enthusiasm for the ideal of such research and the promise it held for her own teaching (79).

These conflicts point to a residual attachment to the ideal—that is, non-materialist—model of ethnographic work in conscious critiques of and attempts to engage in practices counter to it. From the idealist perspective of the Lone Ethnographer, research to add to the universal fund of knowledge is in itself valuable and something that all, if possessed of sufficient genius, would want to participate in conducting. No disputes would arise about whose interests would be served, or hurt, by the knowledge gained by such research; its im-partiality would guarantee universal acceptance of the project of its production and dissemination. Who, after all, could object to the discovery and spread of Truth? Furthermore, in pursuit of such a goal, all would presumably be cooperating freely as independent agents, contributing their mite to the Discovery of Truth (without, of course, demanding recognition for such contributions from the Lone Ethnographer). Finally, given the worthiness of the goal, no possible barriers of time or competing demands would interfere with its pursuit.

In contrast, the difficulties the researchers described demonstrate the crucial role of social material positioning in determining individuals' perspectives on, interests in, and abilities to participate in ethnographic research, and the significance of the material facticity of the work itself (for example, its location in and demands on time) in shaping that work. In a curious way, the perpetual praise researchers give to the generosity of their informants and anonymous or pseudonymed participants, and the qualms they express about the ethical status of their decisions, points to the residual idealism that frames their accounts of these difficulties. That is to say, rather than understanding these difficulties in terms of material barriers to be addressed as such—in the case of Dale's research, for example, through giving "Carol" release time to devote herself more thoroughly to the project to which she appeared to be so committed—they come to be understood in terms of ethical dilemmas whose resolution depends on the good character (ethos) of the researcher and participants—questions of "fidelity," "empathy," "generosity," "betrayal," "honesty," "guilt," "willingness," or "cooperativeness" (see Dale, Newkirk, Kirsch and Ritchie, Williams, Dautermann). Obviously, honesty, generosity, fidelity, empathy, and team spirit can be good things. And, less obviously, as writers such as those cited earlier argue persuasively, determining what constitutes behavior that demonstrates such qualities in given situations can be quite complicated. At the same time, some of these dilemmas arise specifically from understanding the demands of the research from the start in terms of idealist ethics rather than in terms of material conditions, in terms of good character rather than relations of labor.

We might, in this regard, consider an alternative perspective on calls for collaboration emerging in the field of industrial relations. Philip Kraft, in a critique of new management theories like Total Quality Management (TQM) and Business Process Reengineering (BPR), argues that such theories "are about systematically appropriating ideas and knowledge from all workers" (25). Unlike Taylorism, which attempted to rationalize work to reduce agency from workers, "TQM and BPR encourage employees to 'surface' tacit knowledge in order to systematically incorporate it into 'rational' processes," a process managers call *"empowerment"* (28). In this system, "[p]ower and control are usually given labels like flexibility and cooperation" (29). Workers, "newly empowered on self-directed multifunctional work teams, are informed they are engaged in a 'win-win' quest with their employers," if only they will agree to cooperate (29). As Kraft warns, such calls for cooperation and flexibility easily lend themselves to arguments against unions as uncooperative and adversarial (29). Equally ominously, the invocation of "teamwork" can "get team members to reveal their attitudes and opinions, to confess their individual sins and seek forgiveness from the group" (29).

Joan Greenbaum, in an analysis of recent changes in the design and organization of white-collar work, notes that the move to integrate rather than separate tasks and to broaden rather than specialize job responsibilities has required greater flexibility from workers (80–81). However, "the new, so-called flexibility of workers to do more tasks and use more skills does not imply increased wages or improved working conditions." Instead, "integrating tasks and broadening jobs have . . . increase[d] the pace and intensity of work" (81). These intensified work practices are internalized under the rubric of professionalism, which is used "to cloak the fact that work intensification is not being linked with increased wages" (88, 90).

In a critique of the discourse of "fast capitalist texts" advocating TQM and the like, James Paul Gee et al. warn that such texts "grab us" because they use:

> words that name things which nearly all of us like but which, on reflection are seen to mean slightly (and sometimes *very*) different things in fast capitalist texts than they might mean to many of us: words like "liberation," "empowerment," "trust," "vision," "collaboration," "teams," "self-directed learning," "quality," and many more. (29)

Gee et al.'s warning works two ways: on the one hand, it warns against being seduced by the attraction words such as *collaboration* have into giving up things such as job security and decent wages and working conditions. (Think of the deeply conflicting meanings associated historically with the term *collaborators*.) On the other, it can also be read as a warning against the unintended consequences of our own use of such words to name, and think about, what we do in our work and the work we conduct with others. Gee et al. direct their warnings both ways: at the discourse of fast capitalist texts and at the disturbing alignments of educators in their theorizing and pedagogies with that discourse (see Gee et al. chap. 3). Without denying the potential value to be gained by educators in promoting some forms of empowerment, collaboration, self-directed learning, and even teams, they caution against the cooptation of these by new capitalism for its own aims, in service of its own values and politics (67, 71).

Such a threat may seem remote from the situation facing the Critical Ethnographer, who is neither alone nor impartial but part of a team deeply committed to working collaboratively with her participant-informants for the empowerment of all. But such a view again assumes a removal of the work of ethnography from the material social realm. As the difficulties the researchers cited earlier suggest, unexpected questions of labor, value, and capital (symbolic and otherwise) surface insistently in issues of who will do what work, determined by whom, to produce what use value and exchange value realized by and for whom, paid for how, on whose time, by what means. These questions arise in part because the work is imagined not as "work"—in the sense of labor—at all but in terms of professional duty: a matter of professional commitment to the field, which motivates the research in the first place, and of professional standards of ethical conduct toward those living at the research site. If, alternatively, we imagined critical ethnographic work in terms of labor, in the sense of material practices aimed at altering the physical and social environment, then questions of time and commitment and pay and results would be at the forefront in how research is planned and conducted.

In the introduction of ethnographic work into the composition class-room, the same issues would operate. If we think of the work composition students do as work, that is, again, the expense of energy to produce, repro-duce, and alter both students' material social environment and, simultane-ously, themselves, then ethnographic projects in the composition classroom involve students, wittingly or not, as participants in the production of such projects. This is counter to many discussions about collaborative classroom research in which the asymmetrical relations of power complicating the col-laboration are understood exclusively as those between researcher and teacher (as coresearcher) rather than among researcher, teachers, and students (as all three in some ways researchers and teachers of each other; see Lu and Horner). This is not to call for issuing blanket invitations to composition stu-dents to join us in collaborating on ethnographic research. To do so would be to ignore asymmetrical power relations between students and teachers and differences between the material and social positions and, consequently, interests of students *as* students (and teachers as teachers). But it is to insist on recognizing the classroom, the students populating it, and the institu-tional pressures on the students and teachers as agents operating in, and on, the composition classroom ethnographer's research site. Thus, although, as some have suggested, in some ways ethnographers of composition classrooms would seem to be ideally situated, as also composition teachers, to conduct the collaborative sort of inquiry for which postmodern ethnography calls (see Kirsch and Ritchie 14, Sullivan 109), we need to recognize and confront the material differences at the research site among the researchers and researched rather than assume an ideal of shared interest among equal partners, and we need to recognize the labor all contribute, and factor in the values to be accrued through such labor and how such values are realized, in planning and taking up such inquiry.

MULTIVOCALITY

To bridge the hierarchical divide between researcher and informants, high-light the partiality of the researcher's perspective, and give voice to those often silenced or marginalized—the research*ed*—critiques of ethnography have called for multivocality in research texts. Patricia A. Sullivan poses the issue thus:

> How can we get at and represent an other, and not the self, in the act of writ-ing? How do we allow the other to speak itself, to speak on and in its own terms, rather than reconstitute the other in our own likeness? How can we create textual conditions that will allow others to speak in and through our

texts with their own powers of recognition, representation, and persuasion intact? And lastly, how can we write not only about the other but for the other? How can we write ethnographies that not only exist for the sake of knowledge but that can be put to good use? (106)

Multivocality is understood as one strategy by which to answer these questions. The "other" can now speak in the text rather than being "spoken about" by the ethnographer. Thus perspectives other than the ethnographers', and the contributions of these others—in short, the collaborative role of participants in ethnographic work—can be made manifest. As Ann Blakeslee et al. suggest, to address the concern with "unsilencing" subjects, feminists have proposed a variety of approaches in producing texts "to include subjects' voices . . . consistent with a participatory approach to situated inquiry." These include "writing collaboratively with subjects, . . . [h]aving subjects read the research to see whether they hear and recognize their voices in the work, . . . [and] negotiating and modifying those parts of the texts that subjects find questionable or inaccurate" (147).

Strikingly, in these arguments, the dilemma is often framed in terms of written conventions, of creating "textual conditions." That is to say, both the provisionality of the researcher's knowledge and the marginalization of groups being studied are to be addressed through breaking from the univocality of the research text. Marginalization is understood as "silencing," and the provisionality of knowledge is linked to particular discursive conventions. Thus, critics have focused their energies on producing multivocal texts that accentuate a plurality of voices and perspectives, a plurality that itself is intended to highlight the provisionality of any one of those perspectives (see Kirsch and Ritchie 24–25). Doing so is expected to enable researchers to conform in their work to the ethical and epistemological principles of emancipatory critical ethnography. As Kirsch and Ritchie observe,

> an ethical stance . . . suggests that we encode in our research narratives the provisional nature of knowledge that our work generates and the moral dilemmas inherent in research. We need to reconsider our privileging of certain, coherent, and univocal writing and include multiple voices and diverse interpretations in our research narratives, highlighting the ideologies that govern our thinking as well as those that may contradict our own. (24)

Multivocal, innovative forms of writing "highlight rather than suppress the problems of representation in our writing, and expose the multiple, shifting, and contradictory subject positions of researchers and participants" (Kirsch and Ritchie 25).

In identifying the work of ethnography with the written text, this emphasis on multivocal, innovative forms of writing closely aligns critical ethnography with the traditional definition of academic professional work as synonymous with academic texts (rather than, say, teaching).[1] More particularly, attention to the particular discursive forms the text takes as a means of manifesting particular research stances and practices instances commodity fetishism. Commodity fetishism occludes the labor involved in the production of value—here the labor of researching and writing and distributing the text (and the labor of all those involved in these activities) and the labor of reading it.

In short, just as calls for collaboration gloss over the labor involved in such work and the material social positionings of those called to take it up, calls for multivocal writing can gloss over the facticity of writing and reading as material social practice. So, for example, although it may seem ethically mandatory for researchers to ask subjects to write collaboratively with them, those subjects may have no interest in the research, may lack the necessary time or other means to write, or may have notions of writing that collide with those of the researcher. As several researchers have reported, many participants, for a variety of reasons, decline the invitation to "participate" in the production of research texts, despite the researchers' strong desire for their participation as a means of conforming to the ethical strictures of critical ethnography (see for example, Williams 50–51; Dale). However, as Brueggemann observes, "We [researchers] cannot make [participants] participate if they only want to observe. We cannot require them to speak if they only want to remain anonymous or silent" (33). In other words, when viewed strictly in terms of ethics, the ethnographer is caught in a dilemma, restricted by ethical strictures of respecting participants' wishes from following the ethical stricture to require collaborative writing. Alternatively, were the issue understood in terms of material social conditions, ethical issues, although not eliminated, would be addressed differently. Instead of calling on, hoping for, or regretting a failure in the generosity of participants, for example, such participation would be understood in terms of labor and compensation for it, perhaps issues to be addressed in the funding for the research and the negotiation of participant "consent."

But calls for multivocality gloss not only the labor participants are expected to contribute to writing the research but also the labor of reading the texts that result. Instead, appeals are made for greater tolerance for innovative writing from editors and readers. Kirsch and Ritchie, for example, while calling for such texts, note that such a call "challenges scholars to find new ways of representing research, challenges journal editors to develop a greater tolerance for ambiguity and unconventional forms of discourse, and challenges readers to learn new ways of reading and interpreting texts" (25). Dautermann warns that we need to become "better writers *and* readers of qualitative research" (257). The assumption behind the issuing of such challenges would seem to be that the value of such texts resides in their innovative forms and that therefore editors, and ultimately readers, perforce must learn to appreciate such values by changing their reading practices.

However, as Gesa Kirsch warns in a subsequent essay, the emancipatory aims behind such texts can be stymied by the very textual forms produced to achieve them:

> These new textual practices have a number of serious limitations in terms of readability, accessibility, and interpretation. They can disguise writers' continuing authorial control, they can fail to provide the theoretical framework and cultural context necessary for understanding the multiple voices merging in a single text, they make new and difficult demands on readers, they require tolerance for ambiguity and contradictory claims, and they easily become elitist and exclusionary. (193–94)

Thus, she argues, before embracing such writing, "we need to examine our motivations for creating (and celebrating) these new forms of discourse, we need to anticipate their effects on different communities of readers, and we need to make conscious, deliberate decisions about when to write (and when to avoid writing) multi-vocal texts" (194).

One clear problem is that the exclusionary effects of such texts contradict the politically emancipatory aims of the writers. This dilemma arises, again, from identifying the value of the work with the text as commodity, occluding the role that labor—here, the labor of readers—contributes to the production of particular values through interaction with the text. And it arises from then eliding the material conditions necessary for particular kinds of labor to be performed on the text to produce the intended value. Ralph Cintron, in a review of such textual experimentation, notes that only those writers who "need not answer to institutions that are significantly controlled by 'bottom-line' economics," who instead "have the luxury to experiment," can legitimately engage in such experimentation (401). Similarly, we may say that only those readers who have the necessary conditions to luxuriate in the difficulties multivocal texts pose are likely to develop and engage in the kinds of reading practices that would yield the values their authors hope for. As Cintron argues, "the discourses of postmodern ethnographers and critical ethnographers have a limited audience, namely, an academic one" (403). Conversely, "the audience for writing research imposes on researchers a normative discourse that lacks elasticity." As he explains, "Teachers, principals, school boards, government agencies, the public, and even the media want to know what the language situation is and how to deal with it. They need to know how well their programs are working or how well their money is being spent" (401; see also Kirsch 197). In short, the specific material social conditions of the audience for whom much writing research is intended places particular demands on its reading practices. For example, "it is hard," Dautermann observes, "to imagine many readers willing to tolerate the 2,000–plus pages of some qualitative research reports" (255).

What such writing demonstrates above all is a privileging of the exchange value of the textual commodity over any potential use value. In her essay questioning the value of multivocal texts, Kirsch describes the reaction to them as a "rush to celebrate these new textual practices" and their authors and publishers as "brave" (191). That is, the texts are admired less for what readers might learn from them about their putative subjects than for their forms and for what those forms say about their authors and publishers. Status is garnered either for the authors' daring or for display (and thereby confirmation) of the privileged position the authors occupy, a position that enables them to engage in such daring—for what the texts represent about the authors and their writing *as* writing rather than about the subject they ostensibly address *in* their writing. But as Ray observes, we need to bear in mind "the crucial difference between representational issues that arise out of a desire to be politically and intellectually current"—that is, out of a concern for the ethical or professional status of the ethnographer author—and "representational issues that arise out of a desire to change the way people read, write, and act in the world" (299). In contrast to a call for the production of a single text that offers displays of multivocality, Ray calls on researchers to produce a multiplicity of types of texts, including "speeches to the school board, inservice *[sic]* presentations, and articles in newsletters and newspapers that reach students, parents, teachers, administrators, and community organizers" (298). This list would, presumably, not exclude multivocal texts but would recognize that the question for ethnographers to ask is, as Kirsch puts it, "when to write (and when to avoid writing) multi-vocal texts" (194), rather than assuming that such texts in themselves carry specific values for all.

SELF-REFLEXIVITY

The feminist, postcolonial, and poststructuralist perspectives on experience and knowledge that insist on the partiality and historicity of knowledge and experience have fueled a heightened stress on researchers to practice self-reflexivity. In place of the Lone Ethnographer pursuing his quest without question, the Critical Ethnographer is expected to constantly question her motives, practices, and interpretations to avoid the colonizing discourse of traditional ethnography (see Brueggemann 19). Indeed, Elizabeth Chiseri-Strater claims that "[i]n ethnography . . . a major goal of the research process *is* self-reflexivity—what we learn about the self as a result of the study of the 'other'" (119, emphasis added). Kirsch and Ritchie, for example, call for "rigorously reflexive examination of ourselves as researchers that is as careful as our observation of the object of our inquiry" (9), and they tell researchers they need to "examine deeply held assumptions" (19), "interrogate their relations with the people they study and the power they hold over them" (20), "open themselves to change and learning, to reinterpreting their own lives, and to reinventing their own 'otherness,'" "attempt to identify what may be repressed and unconscious in their own experiences, and to claim their own contradictory social and gendered identities" (22), and conduct "rigorous on-going scrutiny of [their] motivations and methods" (24).[2]

The practice of such reflexivity is intended as a professional safeguard against taking one's own perspective as universal rather than local and personal, and against rewriting the experiences of those researched in one's own terms. Again, it is difficult to argue against these as ethical strictures: rigorous and continual self-examination is what professionals are expected to do to counter tendencies toward professional arrogance. At the same time, precisely because they point to an ideal of academic professionalism, such calls tend to obscure the material social conditions of ethnographic work. As a result, what is intended as a cautionary practice can become a textually commodified guarantor of professional purity. Like the call for multivocality in texts, a concern about research practice can be transformed into a demand for a particular kind of product as evidence of professional worthiness.

In a critique of the reception of postmodern notions of the inevitability of ideology, Patricia Bizzell notes that some have taken such notions as a reason to view the scholar who avows ethical commitments with "embarrassment": "enmeshed in ideologies, we see ethical commitments as just another ideological construct, ratified by no transcendent authority or by no match with transcendent truth" (55). However, as Bizzell argues,

> our embarrassment about ethical commitments indicates a real nostalgia for the transcendent ratification that we in theory reject. For if we were utterly convinced of the inevitability of ideology, we would not feel uneasy about seeing the world through ideological interpretations . . . any more than we feel embarrassed about needing to eat or drink. (55)

Ethnographers' admissions of the ideological character of their work can seem like attempts to ward off such embarrassment and achieve transcendence. In such instances, explicit self-reflexivity about one's ideology can be employed as a kind of paradoxical strategy for innoculating oneself from the effects of that ideology: by acknowledging (confessing?) one's own imprisonment in ideology, one can achieve a kind of absolution. Cintron appears to recommend such a strategy when he suggests that "[m]aking anthropologists more aware of their rhetoric and how ideological positions are embedded inside particular rhetorics may indeed further anthropology's ability to tell us something 'real' about how others live their lives" (376). Similarly, when

Kirsch and Ritchie propose "that composition researchers theorize their locations by examining their experiences as reflections of ideology and culture, by reinterpreting their own experiences through the eyes of others, and by recognizing their own split selves, their multiple and often unknowable identities" (8), the intention appears to be that such theorizing will enable researchers to guard against "being blinded by [their] own culturally determined world views" (8). However, if we take Bizzell's point, such "blindness" is in a sense unavoidable. Removal from one set of ideological blinders does not preclude blindness; rather, one ideological set is simply replaced by another—in this case, an ideology holding that we are all enmeshed in ideologies. As Kirsch and Ritchie later acknowledge, "[W]e can never fully step outside our culture in order to examine our assumptions, values, and goals." Indeed, "no attempt at analyzing our assumptions is neutral or value-free; it is always a culturally and politically charged activity" (10). The value placed on self-reflexivity, in other words, is itself evidence of a particular ideology, one I have been identifying with beliefs about academic professionalism.

When self-reflexivity comes to be accepted (ideologically, of course) with such professionalism, then we can expect to see its value shift from having particular use value for researchers (and others) to having exchange value as an identifier of the researcher's status as a professional and as someone savvy about postmodern understandings of ideology. A concern with the exchange value of self-reflexivity then displaces the concern with the potential use value of textual conventions for exhibiting self-reflexivity, as several researchers suggest in questioning the value of self-reflexivity in research texts. In other words, although we can embrace the call to self-reflexivity as valuable for researchers, that is not the same as requiring textual gestures of self-reflexivity.

Two confusions about the place of self-reflexivity in ethnographic work are in operation here. First, there is a conflation of ethnographic work with a text, leading to the fetishizing of textual gestures of self-reflexivity, such as the "facile statements" with which Kirsch and Ritchie note many research articles begin (9). Self-reflexivity comes to be understood as an inherently valuable attribute of the textual commodity. Again, this removes the writing from the social material practices that might, indeed, involve self-reflexivity on the part of any number of actors—researchers, participants, editors, readers—that have the effect of realizing any number of specific use values. Instead, it locates self-reflexivity in the text as a commodity characteristic that adds to its inherent exchange value in the economy of high status ethnographic texts (ostensibly authored by high status ethnographers). Secondly, just as self-reflexivity is treated as a textual commodity, thereby occluding the labor of actors in realizing particular use values from it, so it is often treated as an ethical characteristic of individuals, a matter of ethos, not praxis—individuals are encouraged to be self-reflective rather than to reflect. In making self-reflexivity a character trait, the material conditions under which individuals might engage in self-reflection are elided, as are the purposes for such engagements, hence the tendency of demands for self-reflexivity to resemble demands for researchers, on their own, to be "good."

These confusions risk the production of textual commodities that display authorial self-reflexivity, warranted or not, regardless of whether the writing emanates from, or encourages in readers, a reflexivity that serves particular purposes with which we might align ourselves. Attention is directed, instead, to the author as subject. As Brueggemann complains, self-reflexivity that turns on issues of representation as an antidote to the colonizing discourse of traditional ethnography "risks turning representation into a solipsistic, rhetorical position in which the researcher (the self)—ah, once again—usurps the position of the subject (the other). For in being self-reflexive, we turn the lens back on ourselves, put ourselves in the center of representation" (19). Sullivan argues similarly that in efforts to avoid the "transcendent epistemology" of traditional ethnography that purported to present a "view from nowhere" by bracketing the authorial self, we risk introducing what R. S. Khare describes as "'a self-reflexivity that dwells more on "ours" and "us" than on a genuinely power-sharing discourse with the Other'" (Sullivan 102, quoting Khare 12).

Rather than imagining self-reflexivity as requisite display in ethnographic texts, we might ask, as Chiseri-Strater, does, "How much self-reflexivity is valuable to readers as a way of understanding the ethics and methodology of the research context?" (119). We can address this in part by distinguishing among readers. If indeed the reader for a particular text—say an ethnographer's diary—is the ethnographer herself attempting to understand her material social location better, then for that text and that reader, it might indeed be the case that, as Chiseri-Strater earlier states, "a major goal *is* self-reflexivity—what we [ethnographers] learn about the self as a result of the study of the 'other'" (119, emphasis added). That is, if the "we" are the ethnographers, then it may be fully appropriate for "us" to use some kinds of writing to better understand "ourselves."

But we can distinguish the purposes, audiences, and uses to be realized from such texts with the purposes, uses, and audiences for other texts produced, such as reports. Secondly, we can distinguish self-reflexivity as an activity from self-reflexivity as an attribute of textual production altogether. While it may well be the case that the practice of writing can be used to engage in self-reflection, it does not and need not always do so, and, conversely, self-reflection may be practiced without involving writing. The conflation of ethnographic work with the production of textual commodities blinds us to such possibilities.

Third, critical ethnographers can avoid the potentially paralyzing effects of self-reflexivity by recognizing that they are not alone but part of the social. Insofar as critical ethnographers recognize that their self-reflexivity has ideological limitations, they can use those limitations as an acknowledgement that the limitations of the accounts they produce can and will likely be noted by others—not because they have been "unprofessional" but because of the inevitability of ideological blinders. Readers may and will realize meanings and values from accounts that differ from those their putative "authors" intended. That is to say, ethnographers can recognize the contributions that readers as participants make through the labor of interpretation to the meanings realized from their encounters with texts. This is not a call for abandoning responsibility in writing but for acknowledging, and acting on, the fact of shared responsibility for meanings from the texts that result from their work, in their work as both researchers and writers.

Finally, if we redefine self-reflexivity as a material social practice with specific potential use values, then we must perforce revise the imperative for ethnographers to "be self-reflective" to the imperative to secure the material conditions that would allow ethnographers and their participants to self-reflect. Ellen Cushman, describing the practice of "activist" research, argues that in such research "researchers and participants fluidly negotiate power relations together as they try to facilitate each other's goals." This statement, she acknowledges, "presumes that participants have the critical reflexivity necessary in order to openly and carefully negotiate the terms of the ethnographic relation" (*Struggle* 23). Although part of her argument is to insist on a relationship of reciprocity between researcher and participants (27–31), the part most relevant here is that ethnographers often underestimate the ability of subordinate groups to resist dominant ideology in their daily practices, assuming instead, from attending only to accounts by the dominant, that subordinate groups share the dominant ideology (24–25).

Cushman's argument is a useful corrective to what Anthony Giddens identifies as social theorists' *"derogation of the lay actor,"* in which subordinate groups "are regarded as cultural dopes or mere 'bearers of a mode of production, with no worthwhile understanding of their surroundings or the circumstances of their action" (71). At the same time, we need to recognize as well that reflection is a material practice that as such requires particular conditions for its sustenance—most obviously, time. In other words, ensuring that research participants achieve Cushman's activist research ideal of being able to "openly and carefully negotiate the terms of the ethnographic relation" will require not only the presumption that participants *"have* the [necessary] critical reflexivity" (emphasis added), but also that they are afforded the means to *practice* that reflexivity in ways that benefit them. As Cushman observes in describing her research, "I needed a methodology that *provided room* for reflexively communicating the give-and-take terms of the relations community members and I developed" (*Struggle* 26, emphasis added).

☙❦❧

Recent critiques of traditional ethnography in composition studies have challenged the Lone Ethnographer's pretensions to innocence, neutrality, and objectivity, insisting that Critical Ethnographers acknowledge instead their partiality, the effect of their work on the lives of those at the research site, and the rights of participants to have a say, and a hand, in the nature and direction of that work. These critiques have led ethnographers to be sensitive to the impact of research on the lives of those researched, to recognize the rights of "participants," and to create forums for giving voice to individuals and perspectives historically silenced. As a consequence, there has been a significant increase in the understanding and knowledge of all concerned—researchers, participants, and readers of ethnographic texts. To safeguard the continuation of such benefits, I have been arguing that we need to face more fully the material sociality of ethnographic work as *work* performed on, with, and in the social and material in our design, practice, and writing about such work. Although recent calls for ethical strictures on ethnography have in some ways furthered such recognition, they often carry the residue of the model of the academic professional as, once again, "lone": isolated from the material social realm even in pursuit of multivocality and collaboration, the professional's work understood not as labor in and with material and the social but, in its extreme forms, as commodified, disembodied discourse.

Furthering the critique of the Lone Ethnographer thus requires moving from efforts to define professional ethics for ethnographers to articulating the ethics of labor in ethnography, understood as work on and with the social—as cultural material practice. As I have been suggesting, addressing questions of ethnographic practice from a cultural materialist frame does not eliminate many or even some of the significant difficulties facing critical ethnographers. The concerns that critiques such as those discussed have usefully raised all remain in place. However, addressing these from a cultural materialist framework can help to redefine these difficulties from being understood as "dilemmas" to challenges. What might otherwise appear to be impossible demands on ethnographers in their research and writing to be fully collaborative, multivocal, and thoroughly self-reflexive can be understood instead as challenges to consider who might best want to participate in defining and carrying out particular research projects, through what material means, with what "room" and forums for reflection, to be reported on through what different venues and genres to achieve what various purposes for which readers on which occasions. Rather than aiming at the development of a uniform code of professional ethics, this framework would have us consider and develop a multiplicity of strategies, each appropriate for different circumstances, to be used by researchers and research participants to define, pursue, and achieve their common projects.

NOTES

1. This results not from any lack of commitment among faculty to teaching or other activities but to the commodification of their work and social relations under which they can acquire exchange value primarily through production ("authorship") of research texts, not through teaching (Horner 4–7).

2. Similarly, composition teachers pursuing pedagogies informed by critical ethnographic perspectives have been asked to engage in significantly greater self-reflection on both their theoretical positions and classroom practices. For example, in "The Problematic of Experience," Min-Zhan Lu and I call on theorists of critical pedagogy to "reflect on their practice as theorists" (268) and for those enacting and interpreting critical projects in research and teaching researchers to "reflect, and reflect on, the tension [they] experience between the researcher's desire to produce knowledge about the student and the teacher's desire to bring about change in the student" (271).

WORKS CITED

Bizzell, Patricia. "Marxist Ideas in Composition Studies." *Contending with Words: Composition and Rhetoric in a Postmodern Age.* Ed. Patricia Harkin and John Schilb. New York: MLA, 1991. 52–68.

Blakeslee, Ann M., Caroline M. Cole, and Theresa Conefrey. "Constructing Voices in Writing Research: Developing Participatory Approaches to Situated Inquiry." *Ethics and Representation in Qualitative Studies of Literacy.* Ed. Peter Mortensen and Gesa E. Kirsch. Urbana, IL: NCTE, 1996. 134–54.

Brueggemann, Brenda Jo. "Still-Life: Representations and Silences in the Participant-Observer Role." *Ethics and Representation in Qualitative Studies of Literacy.* Ed. Peter Mortensen and Gesa E. Kirsch. Urbana, IL: NCTE, 1996. 17–39.

Chiseri-Strater, Elizabeth. "Turning In upon Ourselves: Positionality, Subjectivity, and Reflexivity in Case Study and Ethnographic Research." *Ethics and Representation in Qualitative Studies of Literacy.* Ed. Peter Mortensen and Gesa E. Kirsch. Urbana, IL: NCTE, 1996. 115–33.

Cintron, Ralph. "Wearing a Pith Helmet at a Sly Angle: or, Can Writing Researchers Do Ethnography in a Postmodern Era?" *Written Communication* 10 (1993): 371–412.

Cushman, Ellen. "The Public Intellectual, Service Learning, and Activist Research." *College English* 61 (1999): 328–36.

———. *The Struggle and the Tools: Oral and Literate Strategies in an Inner City Community.* Albany: State U of New York P, 1998.

Dale, Helen. "Dilemmas of Fidelity: Qualitative Research in the Classroom." *Ethics and Representation in Qualitative Studies of Literacy.* Ed. Peter Mortensen and Gesa E. Kirsch. Urbana, IL: NCTE, 1996. 77–94.

Dautermann, Jennie. "Social and Institutional Power Relationships in Studies of Workplace Writing." *Ethics and Representation in Qualitative Studies of Literacy.* Ed. Peter Mortensen and Gesa E. Kirsch. Urbana, IL: NCTE, 1996. 241–59.

Durst, Russel K., and Sherry Cook Stanforth. "'Everything's Negotiable': Collaboration and Conflict in Composition Research." *Ethics and Representation in Qualitative Studies of Literacy.* Ed. Peter Mortensen and Gesa E. Kirsch. Urbana, IL: NCTE, 1996. 58–76.

Gee, James Paul, Glynda Hull, and Colin Lankshear. *The New Work Order: Behind the Language of the New Capitalism.* Boulder, CO: Westview, 1998.

Giddens, Anthony. *Central Problems in Social Theory: Action, Structure and Contradiction in Social Analysis.* Berkeley: U of California P, 1979.

Greenbaum, Joan. "Spread over Time and Place: Redivided Labor and the Role of Technical Infrastructure." *Rethinking the Labor Process.* Ed. Mark Wardell, Thomas L. Steiger, and Peter Meiksins. Albany: State U of New York P, 1999. 79–92.

Horner, Bruce. *Terms of Work for Composition: A Materialist Critique.* Albany: State U of New York P, 2000.

Khare, R. S. "The Other's Double—The Anthropologist's Bracketed Self: Notes on Cultural Representation and Privileged Discourse." *New Literary History* 23 (1992): 1–23.

Kirsch, Gesa E. "Multi-Vocal Texts and Interpretive Responsibility." *College English* 59 (1997): 191–202.

Kirsch, Gesa E., and Joy S. Ritchie. "Beyond the Personal: Theorizing a Politics of Location in Composition Research." *College Composition and Communication* 46 (1995): 7–29.

Kraft, Philip. "To Control and Inspire: U.S. Management in the Age of Computer Information Systems and Global Production. *Rethinking the Labor Process.* Ed. Mark Wardell, Thomas L. Steiger, and Peter Meiksins. Albany: State U of New York P, 1999. 17–36.

Lu, Min-Zhan, and Bruce Horner. "The Problematic of Experience: Redefining Critical Work in Ethnography and Pedagogy." *College English* 60 (1998): 257–77.

Mortensen, Peter, and Gesa E. Kirsch, eds. *Ethics and Representation in Qualitative Studies of Literacy.* Urbana, IL: NCTE, 1996.

Newkirk, Thomas. "Seduction and Betrayal in Qualitative Research." *Ethics and Representation in Qualitative Studies of Literacy.* Ed. Peter Mortensen and Gesa E. Kirsch. Urbana, IL: NCTE, 1996. 3–16.

Ray, Ruth E. Afterword. "Ethics and Representation in Teacher Research." *Ethics and Representation in Qualitative Studies of Literacy.* Ed. Peter Mortensen and Gesa E. Kirsch. Urbana, IL: NCTE, 1996. 287–300.

Rosaldo, Renato. *Culture and Truth: The Remaking of Social Analysis.* Boston: Beacon, 1989.

Sullivan, Patricia A. "Ethnography and the Problem of the 'Other.'" *Ethics and Representation in Qualitative Studies of Literacy*. Ed. Peter Mortensen and Gesa E. Kirsch. Urbana, IL: NCTE, 1996. 97–114.

Wardell, Mark, Thomas L. Steiger, and Peter Meiksins, eds. *Rethinking the Labor Process*. Albany: State U of New York P, 1999.

Williams, Cheri L. "Dealing with the Data: Ethical Issues in Case Study Research." *Ethics and Representation in Qualitative Studies of Literacy*. Ed. Peter Mortensen and Gesa E. Kirsch. Urbana, IL: NCTE, 1996. 40–57.

3

Mediating Materiality and Discursivity

Critical Ethnography as Metageneric Learning

MARY JO REIFF

INTRODUCTION

IN HIS WELL-KNOWN OVERVIEW of methodological communities comprising the field of rhetoric-composition, *The Making of Knowledge in Composition*, Stephen North contends that "Ethnographic studies can hardly be said to have taken Composition by storm" (272). Fifteen years later, the field's interest in ethnography has evolved, challenging North's critique of ethnography's methodological integrity and his prediction that "the future of the embattled Ethnographic community cannot be all that bright" (313). Responding to challenges to the authority of ethnography as a research method, several ethnographic studies have been published in the field over the past decade, and books on research methods and methodologies in the field of rhetoric-composition regularly include sections on ethnographic methods, with a few whole texts devoted to the subject, such as Wendy Bishop's *Ethnographic Writing Research*, among others.[1]

Despite the increased interest in ethnography over the past decade, however, it remains fairly solidly in the realm North assigned to it fifteen years ago—within the community of "Researchers"—and has made few inroads into the communities of either "Scholars" or "Practitioners." There are positive signs that ethnography is gaining ground as a pedagogical method with the incorporation of ethnography into writing program curricula and with more frequent discussions of the subject at professional conferences (such as the preconference workshop on "Ethnography in Undergraduate Writing" at the 2001 Conference on College Composition and Communication).[2] Still, the lack of widespread validation in the field is evident in the scarcity of composition textbooks that integrate ethnography with the notable exception of Elizabeth Chiseri-Strater's and Bonnie Stone Sunstein's *Fieldworking: Reading and Writing Research.*

One reason that ethnography is not fully embraced as a pedagogical method is that it remains relatively undertheorized in the field of rhetoric-composition. Although rhetoricians have called for the convergence of rhetoric studies and ethnographic studies (Cintron) and for the convergence of ethnography and pedagogy (Lu and Horner, Zebroski), these calls have mostly gone unheeded. This article attempts to fill the gaps in our field's focus on ethnography by exploring the intersection of contemporary rhetorical genre studies and critical ethnography and by exploring the implications for teaching. Rhetorical theories of genre—which reconceptualize genres as culturally embedded actions—can be brought into fruitful dialogue with ethnography. I argue that ethnography, as both an academic research genre and a mode of genre analysis, mediates materiality and discursivity and gives researchers and students more direct access to the material interactions of social groups, a material access that has methodological and pedagogical implications for the study and teaching of writing.

INTERSECTIONS: RHETORICAL GENRE STUDIES AND CRITICAL ETHNOGRAPHY

In their detailed ethnography examining the relationships between writing in academic and workplace settings, Patrick Dias, Aviva Freedman et al. draw on the "comprehensively rhetorical character" of recent genre studies as the main framework for their study of situated discourse. According to the authors, "The most developed and comprehensive rhetorical theory to address writing in recent times goes by the misleadingly limiting name of genre studies" (18). The concept of *genre* is indeed limited by its traditional definition as a formal classification system or tool for categorizing texts. However, redefinitions of *genre* have been developing within the field of rhetoric-composition since the 1980s, beginning with Carolyn Miller's groundbreaking article "Genre as Social Action." Challenging views of genres as static forms or artificial classifications of discourse, Miller reenvisions genre's formal conventions as "typified rhetorical actions based in recurrent situations" (159). The textual regularities of genres, rather than seen as defining features, are seen as responses to repeated actions—the typical ways in which groups of writers engage rhetorically within repeated situations.

In addition to their pragmatic function as rhetorical strategies used to participate in and carry out the social actions of a group, genres—through their repeated actions—embody the ideologies of the group's repeated actions—their particular knowledge and beliefs and the roles and relationships of the participants in the social practices. As a result, contemporary rhetorical theorists have redefined *genres* as "sites of social and ideological action" (Schryer 208)—environments within which familiar social actions are rhetorically enacted and reproduced. Genres, then, function both pragmatically and epistemologically—both as sites of material interaction within groups and as tools for understanding and interpreting these interactions. Charles Bazerman further clarifies the complex functioning of genres, which both construct and are constructed by their settings of use:

> Genres are not just forms. Genres are forms of life, ways of being. They are frames for social action. They are environments for learning. They are locations within which meaning is constructed. Genres shape the thoughts we form and the communications by which we interact. Genres are the familiar places we go to create intelligible communicative action with each other and the guideposts we use to explore the unfamiliar. (19)

Genres are more than stable forms that contain meaning; they are dynamic discursive formations used to carry out particular social actions, language practices, and interpersonal relations. As the embodiments of these social actions, they are also tools for accessing cultures.

As "guideposts we use to explore the unfamiliar," genres clearly have relevance to ethnographic study. Miller demonstrates this relevance when she defines genres as "cultural artefacts"—the data that ethnographers use to compile their written representations of a culture. Just as anthropologists gather material artifacts, which are seen as vestiges of a culture's history, values, and beliefs, ethnographers can examine the "cultural artefacts" or genres—the living textual representations of a culture's knowledge, values, and beliefs. Cultures or communities use genres to engage in rhetorical action and to carry out social purposes, and their use of genres reproduces the social values and ideologies embedded in the genres. As a result, the repeated patternings of behavior can tell us much about a culture or, as Miller notes, "As recurrent patterns of language use, genres help constitute the substance of cultural life" (163). Genres, as social actions, give shape and substance to cultural sites and in turn enable and enhance the communicative actions of the participants in that site. This reciprocity enables ethnographers to gain access to material sites of cultural interactions as well as to the cultural beliefs and ideologies reproduced in these sites of generic interaction.

The reciprocity of ethnography and rhetoric is the subject of Ralph Cin-tron's recent call for "a fusion of ethnography and rhetoric where each exists as an inquiry into the other" and in which "rhetoric has dissolved the boundary between the discursive and nondiscursive" ("Ethnography"). Ethnography's retreat from traditional realist approaches based purely on the nondiscursive and genre's retreat from traditional definitions based purely on the discursive have already begun dissolving the boundaries between the discursive and nondiscursive, resulting in the convergence of critical ethnography and rhetor-ical genre studies. Classic realist models of ethnography posit a direct corre-spondence between observable actions in the real world and their cultural meanings, a flawed model as later theorists, encouraged by the influence of poststructuralism and postmodernism, point out. According to Martyn Ham-mersly, "One of the effects of the growing influence of anti-realism has been increased scrutiny of ethnographic accounts as texts, looking at the rhetorical devices that are used to create the world portrayed" (17). Although traditional ethnography takes this "rhetorical turn" toward the text, the traditional view of genre turns away from the definitions of genres as textual features and instead takes as its starting point the context of production and interpretation of texts. As ethnographic studies and genre studies converge and the boundary between the discursive and nondiscursive dissolves, how is it that critical ethnography and rhetorical genre studies can each function as an inquiry into the other?

Through its inquiry into genre studies, ethnography can further subvert the realist agenda. Cultural anthropologists and sociologists characterize the antirealist moment in ethnographic studies as a "crisis of representation," a cri-sis that prompts an acknowledgement of the constructedness of ethnographic accounts and their inability to capture lived experience fully. Because the lived experiences and material actions of a social group are always produced and reproduced by genres—by the group's lived textuality or rhetorical actions— genre integrates text and context, the rhetorical and social, the discursive and the nondiscursive. Miller argues that genre is located between microlevel analysis (of the materiality of language processing and language exchange) and macrolevel analysis (of cultural systems). Genre, then, as symbolic action, mediates between individuals and their collectivities and establishes a critical middle ground that encompasses both the particular material actions and the symbolic representations of the shared values and ideologies of a culture. Nor-man K. Denzin clarifies this dialectical relationship between genre ("lived tex-tuality") and ethnography ("lived experience"):

> Lived textuality transforms lived experience. Real-life experiences are in turn shaped by prior textual representations. These experiences are in turn shaped by understandings gained from participating in the performances of oth-ers—performances turned into texts. (33)

Genres constitute the lived textuality—the rhetorical performances that both shape and are shaped by lived experiences. Genre, then, is a critical ethnographic method for gaining access to a culture's material and linguistic actions. In addition, because critical ethnography "deals overtly with the ideological dimensions of meaning making" (Cintron 407), genres, which embody a group's ideologies, can give ethnographers a way to organize and interpret patterns of cultural experience (and disruptions of these patterns) and to access the ideological beliefs revealed through these repeated rhetorical and social behaviors. By studying genres, ethnographers can gain access to both the production and reproduction of an organization's knowledge, power, and cultural perspectives.

Min-Zhan Lu and Bruce Horner have argued that critical ethnography must "sustain the tension between experience and discursive understanding" (259). Genre is one way to sustain this tension, both for the researcher's examination of the culture's "lived experience" as it interacts with "lived textuality" and for the researcher's own experience as a participant in the culture and formulation of rhetorical strategies for representing lived experience. Genre, by drawing into tension the material interactions of the community and the researcher's discursive understanding, promotes a self-reflexivity that is necessary to critical ethnography, "a concern with how the selves and identities of the researcher and researched affect the research process" (Brewer 126). Ethnography is mediated by the multiple subject positions of the researcher who must be aware of his or her discursive positions when interpreting or representing the experience of the cultural participants. This reflexivity includes an awareness of the social processes influencing the data. Because genres are embedded in cultures—are always already situated—and embody the values and ideologies of those cultures, ethnographers who use genres to gain access to communities will always already have a heightened awareness of the social functioning of language use. In addition, genres—as social actions—are always evolving, never stabilized, and always resisting interpretation, lending a critical perspective to ethnographers who would find a direct correspondence between a culture's actions and the meaning of those actions. Both as participants in the culture under study and participants in the ethnography (a genre belonging to their research community), ethnographers occupy various subject positions and produce situated knowledge that is partial and contingent.

Whereas ethnography's inquiry into genre brings into play the dialectical relationship between the material and the symbolic, genre's inquiry into ethnography can further dissolve the boundary between the discursive and nondiscursive. Just as genre situates the social actions of a group, ethnography situates the study and observation of these actions. Genres, after all, not only give ethnographers access to sites of cultural production and reproduction, but ethnographers themselves participate in genres within their disciplinary cultures and are themselves situated—not only in the culture they are studying but also in their disciplinary culture. Ethnographers undertake their own typical rhetorical actions (genres) to study the typical rhetorical actions, or genres, of others (the next section focuses on this metageneric aspect of ethnography).

Critics of genre analysis, particularly as it is used pedagogically, question its ability to maintain a dialectic between the discursive and nondiscursive. In her introduction to a series of articles debating the pedagogical implications of genre theory, Freedman poses the following question: "Can the complex web of social, cultural and rhetorical features to which genres respond be explicated at all, or in such a way that can be useful to learners?" (225). Freedman's concern is with studying genres outside the contexts that they function for—with abstracting genres from the complex and dynamic social and cultural contexts that shape and are shaped by them. David Bleich shares her concern. In his recent discussion of materiality and genre, he argues that genres—like all language use—cannot be abstracted from the material conditions of their use. According to Bleich, "The process of study lies always within the language-using society. There is no sense in which the language one tries to understand can be thought of as located outside the living situation in which the thinker (who is all the while using the language) is working" (122). Studying genres within the actual contexts of their use—within real human groups—requires "insider" research, a type of research that can be accomplished through a particular genre, the genre of ethnography. With its emphasis on participant/observation research and hands-on exploration of communities, ethnography enables students to examine communicative actions within "living situations" (120) and to see firsthand how communities use genres to carry out social actions and agendas.

To understand genres as situated actions, Miller has advocated what she calls an "ethnomethodological" approach, one that "seeks to explicate the knowledge that practice creates" (155)—knowledge rooted in the materiality of circumstances and conditions of actual use of genres. Similarly, Bazerman has argued that "by forging closer links with the related enterprise of . . . ethnomethodology," genre analysis can play a "major role" in investigating communication within social organizations (23). The genre of ethnography, with its emphasis on "explicating" the community's practices and knowledge through observation of and participation in the social actions of the group, can create more authentic contexts for learning. The next section explores how ethnography, as both an academic research genre and a mode of genre analysis, can provide more authentic language tasks within the classroom context while simultaneously giving students access to real contexts for language use beyond the classroom.

CRITICAL ETHNOGRAPHY AS METAGENERIC LEARNING

Ethnography, as discussed in many cultural anthropology and sociology texts, is said to have had its origins in travel writing, dating back to Herodotus and his exploration of the western provinces of the Persian Empire. These travelers to foreign lands attempted to capture the essence of a culture and to translate their understanding to those unfamiliar with the culture, resulting in "traveler's tales" that comprised some of the earliest known ethnographies. Ethnography's origins in travel writing is interesting considering that genres are often described using travel metaphors. If ethnographies are accounts of unfamiliar lands, genres are the road maps that writers and researchers use to navigate "discursive landscapes" (Bazerman 19). Because genres are the rhetorical manifestations of a group's actions, they function as rhetorical maps that ethnographers can use to chart familiar behaviors or frequently traveled communicative paths; in addition, genres can assist ethnographic travelers entering into unfamiliar cultures by providing signposts as they adapt to new terrains and explore new territories. Genres, then, are a significant ethnographic methodology, the signposts for navigating an unfamiliar community or culture.

If ethnographies are studies of communities and their social actions and genres are the rhetorical manifestations or maps of a community's actions, then genre analysis becomes a critical component of ethnography—a significant ethnographic methodology. To investigate a community's social motives and actions, ethnographers can examine the rhetorical manifestations of these actions, the group's genres, by gathering samples of the genre and analyzing what the rhetorical patterns reveal about the community—its purpose, participants, and the group's values, beliefs, and ideologies. Ethnography, then, functions as a "metagenre," as both a genre (a research narrative) and a mode of genre analysis—a research methodology used to grasp cultural beliefs and behaviors, often through the examination of genres, which are "frames for social action" (Bazerman 19). Ethnography is both "act" and "action," subject and verb, process and product. It refers both to the written genre or rhetorical performance whose typified patternings reflect and reveal the investigative purposes of a community of researchers and to the research methods or "actions" that give rise to this genre, requiring researchers to observe and participate in the actions of the community being investigated. Insofar as the ethnographer interprets the culture, both inscribing and describing, rendering it more familiar and materially accessible, he or she must explore the genre activity—the rhetorical enactments of the community's goals, values, and ideologies that act as a framework or site for studying the group's material exchanges.

In "Observing Genres in Action: Towards a Research Methodology," Anthony Paré and Graham Smart propose a research methodology that encompasses both ethnographic inquiry and genre analysis. Defining *genre* as "a rhetorical strategy enacted within a community," they argue that "a full appreciation of the part that [social] roles play in the production and use of generic texts can only be gained by observing an organization's drama of inter-action, the interpersonal dynamics that surround and support certain texts" (149). Ethnographic observation of a community that foregrounds genre analysis allows researchers to explore more fully the complexity of the group's social roles and actions, actions that constitute the community's repeated rhetorical strategies or genres.

Because ethnography functions as a research genre—one that dynami-cally enacts rhetorical and social analysis of language use in communities—it is an ideal instructional genre for composition courses at all levels. As a genre (a situated action within a research community) that itself entails genre analy-sis (study of another community's situated actions), ethnography entails meta-generic learning. Marilyn Chapman, in her exploration of the significance of genre to learning, identifies three main instructional goals:

1. learning genres, or widening students' genre repertoires;
2. learning about genres, or fostering awareness; and
3. learning through genres, or using genres as tools for thinking and learn-ing in particular situations. (473)

Using ethnography in the classroom would have students learn one genre, the genre of ethnography, while they simultaneously use ethnographic methodologies to learn about and through other genres. As a genre that itself entails genre analysis, ethnography as a classroom genre would accomplish the metageneric learning goals defined earlier, giving students access to the material practices of both the classroom community as well as communities beyond the classroom.

Learning Genres

When students are assigned ethnographies, they learn a new genre to add to their repertoire, a research genre that, true to recent reconceptualizations of genre, is defined less by its formal conventions than by its rhetorical actions—its purposes, participants, and subjects. According to Beverly Moss, the main purpose of the ethnographic genre is "to gain a comprehensive view of the social interactions, behaviors, and beliefs of a community or a social group" (155). This purpose casts student researchers, as users of the genre, into dual roles as both participants in the community and observers of the community's interactions. James Spradley explains how this genre embeds and enacts the roles and purposes of its users: "the participant observer enters a social situation for two purposes: to engage in activities appropriate to the situation and to observe the activities, people and physical aspects of the situation" (55). By carrying out the purposes of this genre and assuming the participant-observer role that the genre entails, the ethnographer is much like a photographer who both "takes pictures of the community" and is "in the picture at the same time" (Moss 154). The process of inquiry and first-hand participant observation entailed by this genre encourages critical and reflective thinking as students consider how best to portray their interpretation (deciding on what to include and what to leave out); how to portray the processes that produced that interpretation (descriptions of the data collection methodology, explanations of the data); and how best to portray themselves to an audience. These strategies promote reflexivity and critical inquiry based on the experiential knowledge of the researcher as it relates to the experiences of the culture under study. Grant and Buford note that students who are learning ethnography are encouraged "to reflect carefully on communicative and interpretive practices that are taken for granted in other forms of social research" (558).

The rhetorical strategies related to purpose, audience, and persona give rise to several varying rhetorical features and conventions. While the how-to literature of ethnography in anthropology, sociology, and rhetoric point to general recurrent features, ethnographies are based in rhetorical situations that are multiple and complex. Not only are the social contexts that they represent multiple (for instance, students might study academic settings, workplace organizations, or any variety of public settings or cultural sites), but also the academic contexts within which ethnographies function are also multiple and cross disciplinary boundaries. According to Grant and Buford's recent survey of ethnographic writing in the academy, ethnography is experiencing "newfound popularity" in a wide range of academic specializations including disciplines such as political science, clinical psychology, women's studies, ethnic studies, social work, nursing, journalism, ecology, and business. Ethnography is what Debra Journet has labeled a "hybrid genre," a form of intergeneric discourse that blurs disciplinary boundaries and recasts the values of one discipline into the language and discourse forms of the other. Wendy Bishop and others distinguish between the general research method of ethnography as a broad study of culture and ethnographic writing research, which usually explores particular sites of literacy or particular literacy practices. Clarifying this distinction, Beverly Moss notes, "While ethnography in general is concerned with describing and analyzing a culture, ethnography in composition studies is . . . concerned more narrowly with communicative behavior or the interrelationship of language and culture" (156). Ethnography in rhetoric-composition, particularly as a pedagogical approach, is concerned not just with the lived experience or behavior of cultures (as in anthropology or sociology) but with the way in which this behavior manifests itself rhetorically—what Dell Hymes calls the "ethnography of communication."

Students not only gain access to a valuable research genre that functions for various academic communities, but they also learn a genre that is fluid and dynamic rather than the often-rigid and stabilized genres of the writing classroom. Ethnography has been labeled a "postmodern genre" due to its transgression of rigid conventions and its fluid generic boundaries. Because ethnographies participate in multiple disciplinary contexts and social contexts, they are always evolving and changing as situations change. According to Amy Devitt, "Since genres and texts truly participate simultaneously in multiple genres, multiple functions, and multiple situations, generic identity, function, and situation are necessarily unstabilized—forever" (714). The genre of ethnography can contain multiple discourses, discourses that will be shaped by the community studied. Ethnographies can take the form of narratives, research reports, memoirs, and even poetry—or they can be multigenre texts that combine various traits of these genres. As a dynamic, shifting genre, ethnography resists calcification in the classroom and challenges the notion that there is one correct way to compose ethnographies.

By incorporating ethnography into the classroom, we also provide students with tools engaging the material site of the classroom. When students carry out ethnographies, they participate in hands-on research that transforms them into knowledge-makers, social actors who are both participating in and observing social actions—observing firsthand how knowledge is socially constructed while participating in the social construction of knowledge themselves (as researchers/ethnographers). Shifting the usual teacher/student dynamic, students assume the role of experts, investigators who speak from their own authority as researchers. As a result, the classroom is transformed from a community of student/learners to a community of researchers/knowledge producers. The genre of ethnography creates a culture of inquiry—inquiry into the social actions, rhetorical performances, and conflicts within communities and analysis of the relationship between a community's discourse and their agendas.

Learning about Genres

The second goal, learning about genres and fostering genre awareness, is also accomplished through the genre of ethnography. Because the main goal of an ethnographer, according to Moss, is to gain "increased insight into the ways in which language communities work" (170), it follows that the oral and written genres of groups will play a central role in the investigation of the social context of language use. Clifford Geertz defines ethnographies as "interpretations of interpretations" (9), meaning that students must study the genres that community members use to interpret their contexts to understand fully and themselves interpret the community. Similarly, if ethnography, as Hymes contends, is "mediated between what members of a given community know and do" (75), then genres—as the rhetorical, material manifestations of social action—give us access to a community's knowledge and actions.

Catherine Schryer argues that to understand the community's behavior, the "researcher must consult the interpreters of both the genre and the situation" (207). The genre activity of a group, then, becomes central to any study of a group's knowledge and practices. Indeed, Schryer's six-month ethnographic study of literacy at a veterinary college illustrates this point. The study centered on the analysis of medical records, revealing a great deal about the social roles, ideologies, and social actions of this community's members. Through her participation in the community and examination of its genres, Schryer found that the new system of record keeping mirrored the way that practitioners solved complicated medical problems and coordinated social action as other staff members added to the records. In addition, by comparing competing genres—comparing the new system of records to the former system—Schryer was able to discern varying social purposes and values implicit in these two genres, divergences that revealed tensions between researchers and practitioners in the college. Schryer's ethnographic study confirms what Paré and Smart point out: that genre can "serve as a lens for naturalistic research" (149) of communities.

Although students do not have six months to carry out ethnographic studies as Schryer did, they can carry out what Bishop has labeled "mini-ethnographies," more focused studies that explore a particular event or a single phenomenon in a community. Genre analysis, which limits the focus on the functioning of a particular typified response or typified way of communicating, can help delimit the topic and focus the ethnographic study more narrowly. Unlike textual analysis, genre analysis examines the dynamic interaction of text and context, asking students to simultaneously examine the recurrent features of genres and the disruptions of these repeated rhetorical actions as well as to interpret and analyze the ways in which these features reflect and reveal their situations. By focusing on a group's repeated rhetorical behaviors (and disruptions in that behavior), students can find ways to anchor their observations of cultural sites. Zebroski notes that his students—who carried out ethnographic studies of groups such as nursing homes, church groups, day-care centers, athletic groups, and various businesses—encountered problems with focusing their study and finding patterns in all the data they had collected. However, making genre analysis the focal point of ethnographic inquiry—having students examine the church group's newsletter or the employee handbook at a business—ties communicative actions to their contexts and can illustrate to students how patterns of rhetorical behavior are inextricably linked to patterns of social behavior.

For example, a prelaw student in my advanced composition class, who I'll call "Susan," carried out a mini-ethnography on the law community. To find out how novice members of the community become socialized to the values, beliefs, and knowledge of the community, Susan explored the genre activities of the community, such as opinions, wills, deeds, and contracts, and focused her study on the genre of case briefs. She began by collecting samples of constitutional law briefs, which she found "illustrated the legal community's shared value of commitment to tradition, as well as the need for a standard and convenient form of communicating important and complex legal concepts." Although Susan employed other ethnographic methodologies, such as interviews and observation of lawyers in a small local firm, the genre analysis formed the central focus of her analysis and gave her access to the habits and traditions of the law community. She not only learned about the genre features of case briefs—such as the technical terminology, rigid format, and formal style—but she also became more aware of how these formal patternings reflected and reinscribed the goals of the community. Recognizing that all the briefs follow the same format of presenting sections labeled "case information," "facts of the case," "procedural history," "issue," "holding," and "court reasoning," she surmised that, "even the rigid structure of the format can help with our analysis by suggesting the community's emphasis on logic and order, which are two esteemed values of the profession." For students such as Susan, using genre as a site for ethnographic inquiry cultivates a consciousness of the rhetorical strategies used to carry out the social actions of a community, thus making that community more tangible and accessible.

Learning through Genres

In addition to developing genre awareness, the third genre-related instructional goal is learning through genres, using genres as tools for thinking and learning in particular situations. Ethnography gives students experience not only with genre analysis but also in the production of additional genres in this research process. As ethnographers seek to describe a community, they use various genres as tools for research. Before beginning the study, students may write letters to seek permission to observe groups, or they might write proposals for their research or research plans and agendas. During the research, they draw on several generic tools such as field notes, journals or activity logs, project chronologies or summaries, progress reports, interview transcripts, even maps. And once the research is completed, they may practice additional genres that the situation warrants such as thank you notes, self-assessments, peer assessments, or abstracts. Class time might be spent discussing the genre of the interview or the different purposes of descriptive versus analytic field notes. These genres act as tools of ethnography, resources for supporting or extending thinking as students participate in this genre. So not only do students learn a genre (ethnography) that entails genre analysis but also one that employs other genres as tools for inquiry.

CONCLUSION

The fusion of critical ethnography and rhetorical genre studies has implications for rhetorical instruction. Students' participation in the genre of ethnography and their use of genre analysis as ethnographic method make visible the rhetorical actions of the classroom community a well as the actions of the community under investigation, thus reinforcing the dialectical interplay between experience and discursive understanding. Genres rhetorically embody and mediate the complex material relations and practices that define a culture; as a result, they give students access to the group's practices as well as the values and ideologies embedded in these practices.

Just as genre situates material language exchanges and interactions, ethnography situates language study—the study of these interactions. For students, this fusion of genre and ethnography brings into tension—a productive tension—their material experiences as student researchers as well as their discursive understanding of the lived experiences of cultures that they observe. Students can learn to critique their materialist conditions as writers through ethnography, which encourages reflexive awareness of their roles as researchers, their methods, their evaluation of data, and the challenges of rhetorically representing lived experience. Describing his use of ethnography in the first-year writing classroom, Zebroski finds that students begin to reenvision their role as participants in the classroom community and recognize the part they play in constructing meaning: "[Students] don't transmit information about the world so much as they create new worlds. Writers produce knowledge in the process of transmitting it" (41). Students working with genres and within the genre of ethnography develop a heightened awareness of both the possibilities and limits of representing lived experience. As teachers, we can further this self-reflexiveness by asking students to reflect on their work as an ethnographer and to keep logs not only on the activity of the group but also on their activity as researchers. We might also ask students to analyze the genre of ethnography in addition to the genres that constitute the culture they are studying. In this way, they study not just the contexts of language use but cultivate an awareness of their own situatedness as language users. The fusion of genre and ethnography gives students access to rhetorical performances of others while focusing attention on their own rhetorical performances as participants in the genre of ethnography.

Through their participation in the genre of ethnography and their implementation of genre analysis as ethnographic methodology, students simultaneously carry out the goals of the classroom community while observing "meaningful discourse in authentic contexts," thus accomplishing what Freedman defines as the two necessary criteria for effective writing instruction: the "exposure to written discourse" combined with "immersion in the relevant contexts" (247). Ethnography is a genre that requires its users to immerse themselves in the culture being studied, demanding that the relevant contexts be a part of the study of discourse. With its emphasis on participant/observation research and hands-on exploration of communities, ethnography enables students to examine communicative actions within "living situations" and to see firsthand how communities use genres to carry out social actions and agendas. Through their examination of authentic language acts within authentic situations, student ethnographers are able to study language use and genre use within real contexts of use—situations in which "speakers are alive, functioning, changing and interacting" (Bleich 120).

Ultimately, the fusion of rhetorical genre studies and critical ethnography gives students access to the material practices of both the classroom community as well as communities beyond the classroom. Bruce Horner calls for teachers to acknowledge the material locations of students and to find ways to help students "critically engage the material location of the composition classroom in the process of writing and reading both within and outside that location" (71). By organizing and constructing the social and rhetorical conditions comprising communities, genres allow student ethnographers to recognize, observe, and access communities and the various material interactions that take place within them. At the same time, ethnography situates students' study of a group's genre activity, calling attention to their own situatedness as participants in the cultural sites of classrooms and their construction of meaning. This interactive reciprocity between language use and the material situations of its use dissolves the boundary between the discursive and nondiscursive. The genre of ethnography makes visible the rhetorical actions of the classroom community—which becomes a research community, a culture of inquiry—as well as enacting and embodying the actions of communities and cultures under investigation. As a result, the genre of ethnography, using genre analysis as a critical methodology, mediates materiality and discursivity.

NOTES

This article is an expanded and revised version of a paper presented at the 2001 Conference on Composition and Communication.

1. Book-length ethnographic studies include, for example, Wendy Bishop's *Something Old, Something New* (1990), Ralph Cintron's *Angels' Town* (1997), Emily Decker

and Kathleen Geissler's *Situated Stories* (1998), Patrick Dias et al.'s *Worlds Apart* (1999), Anne DiPardo's *A Kind of Passport* (1993), Christian Knoeller's and Sarah Warshauer Freedman's *Voicing Ourselves* (1998), and Howard Tinburg's *Border Talk* (1998). Whereas few whole texts in rhetoric-composition devote themselves to ethnographic methods, several texts focus on classroom ethnographies or "teacher-research," including Glenda Bissex and Richard Bullock's *Seeing for Ourselves* (1987) and Ruth Ray's *The Practice of Theory: Teacher Research in Composition* (1993).

2. Syracuse is one such writing program that includes an ethnography unit as part of the curriculum. See "A New Teacher's Guide to Teaching Ethnography" at http://odyssey.syr.edu/survivalguide.html for more information on the theoretical justification for teaching ethnography and the pedagogical approaches recommended for new teachers.

WORKS CITED

Bazerman, Charles. "The Life of Genre, the Life in the Classroom." *Genre and Writing: Issues, Arguments, Alternatives.* Ed. Wendy Bishop and Hans Ostrom. Portsmouth, NH: Boynton/Cook, 1997. 19–26.

Bishop, Wendy. *Ethnographic Writing Research: Writing It Down, Writing It Up and Reading It.* Portsmouth, NH: Boynton/Cook, 1999.

——. *Something Old, Something New: College Writing Teachers and Classroom Change.* Carbondale, IL: Southern Illinois UP, 1990.

Bleich, David. "The Materiality of Language and the Pedagogy of Exchange." *Pedagogy: Critical Approaches to Teaching Literature, Language, Composition, and Culture* 1 (Winter 2001): 117–41.

Brewer, John D. *Ethnography.* Philadelphia: Open UP, 2000.

Bullock, Richard H., and Glenda Bissex. *Seeing for Ourselves: Case Study Research by Teachers of Writing.* Portsmouth, NH: Heinemann, 1987.

Chapman, Marilyn L. "Situated, Social, Active: Rewriting Genre in the Elementary Classroom." *Written Communication* (October 1999): 469–90.

Chiseri-Strater, Elizabeth, and Bonnie Stone Sunstein. *Fieldworking: Reading and Writing Research.* Englewood Cliffs, NJ: Prentice-Hall, 1997.

Cintron, Ralph. *Angel's Town: Chero Ways, Gang Life, and the Rhetorics of Everyday.* Boston, MA: Beacon Press, 1997.

——. "Ethnography and Rhetoric." *Research Network Forum, Conference on College Composition and Communication, Chicago, IL, 1 April 1998.*

——. "Wearing a Pith Helmet at a Sly Angle, or, Can Writing Researchers Do Ethnography in a Postmodern Era?" *Written Communication* 10 (July 1993): 371–412.

Decker, Emily, and Kathleen Geissler. *Situated Stories: Valuing Diversity in Composition Research.* Portsmouth, NH: Boynton/Cook, 1998.

Denzin, Norman K. *Interpretive Ethnography: Ethnographic Practices for the 21st Century.* Thousand Oaks, CA: Sage, 1997.

Devitt, Amy J. "Integrating Rhetorical and Literary Theories of Genre." *College English* 62 (July 2000): 696–718.

Dias, Patrick, Aviva Freedman et al. *Worlds Apart: Acting and Writing in Academic and Workplace Contexts.* Mahwah, NJ: Erlbaum, 1999.

DiPardo, Anne. *A Kind of Passport: A Basic Writing Adjunct Program and the Challenge of Student Diversity.* Urbana, IL: NCTE, 1993.

Freedman, Aviva. "Show and Tell? The Role of Explicit Teaching in the Learning of New Genres." *Research in the Teaching of English* 27 (October 1993): 222–51.

Geertz, Clifford. "Thick Description: Toward an Interpretive Theory of Culture." *The Interpretation of Cultures.* New York: Basic Books, 1973.

Grant, Linda, and Reuben Buford. "The Promises and Perils of Ethnography in the New Millennium: Lessons from Teaching." *Journal of Contemporary Ethnography* (October 1999): 549–60.

Hammersley, Martyn. *Reading Ethnographic Research.* New York: Longman, 1998.

Horner, Bruce. *Terms of Work for Composition: A Materialist Critique.* Albany: State U of New York P, 2000.

Hymes, Dell. "Ethnographic Monitoring." *Language Development in a Bilingual Setting.* Ed. Eugene J. Briere. Los Angeles: National Dissemination and Assessment Center, 1979. 73–88.

Journet, Debra. "Boundary Rhetoric and Disciplinary Genres: Redrawing the Maps in Interdisciplinary Writing." *Genre and Writing: Issues, Arguments, Alternatives.* Ed. Wendy Bishop and Hans Ostrom. Portsmouth, NH: Boynton/Cook, 1997.

Knoeller, Christian, and Sarah Warshaver Freedman. *Voicing Ourselves: Whose Words We Use When We Talk about Books.* Albany: State U of New York P, 1998.

Lu, Min-Zhan, and Bruce Horner. "The Problematic of Experience: Redefining Critical Work in Ethnography and Pedagogy." *College English* 60 (March 1998): 257–77.

Miller, Carolyn R. "Genre as Social Action." *Quarterly Journal of Speech* 70 (1984): 151–67.

Moss, Beverly. "Ethnography and Composition: Studying Language at Home." *Methods and Methodologies in Composition Research.* Ed. Gesa Kirsch and Patricia Sullivan. Carbondale, IL: SIUP, 1992. 153–71.

North, Stephen M. *The Making of Knowledge in Composition: Portrait of an Emerging Field.* Portsmouth, NH: Boynton/Cook, 1987.

Paré, Anthony, and Graham Smart. "Observing Genres in Action: Towards a Research Methodology." *Genre and the New Rhetoric.* Ed. Aviva Freedman and Peter Medway. Washington, DC: Taylor & Francis, 1994. 146–54.

Ray, Ruth, *The Practice of Theory: Teacher Research in Composition*. Urbana, IL: NCTE, 1993.

Schryer, Catherine. "Records as Genre." *Written Communication* 10 (April 1993): 200–34.

Spradley, James. *Participant Observation*. New York: Holt, 1980.

Tinberg, Howard B. *Border Talk: Writing and Knowing in the Two-Year College*. Urbana, IL: NCTE, 1997.

Zebroski, James. *Thinking through Theory: Vygotskian Perspectives on the Teaching of Writing*. Portsmouth, NH: Boynton/Cook, 1994.

4

The Ethnographic Experience of Postmodern Literacies

CHRISTOPHER SCHROEDER

Ethnography is enmeshed within the ideological practices of the academy. Many of these practices establish standards that are in direct opposition to the concerns of ethnographers. A few of these include: the need to truncate narratives and the voices of others to fit within the limited pages of refereed journals; social scientific standards for publication, and the need to publish as many short articles as possible or perish within the archaic academic power relations of the tenure process; and the deprivileging of personal experience narratives.

—James T. West, "Ethnography and Ideology"

A postmodern ethnography is a cooperatively evolved text consisting of fragments of discourse intended to evoke in the minds of both reader and writer an emergent fantasy of a possible world of commonsense reality, and thus to provoke an aesthetic integration that will have a therapeutic effect. It is, in a word, poetry—not in its textual form, but in its return to the original context and function of poetry, which, by means of its performative break with everyday speech, evoked memories of the *ethos* of the community and thereby provoked hearers to act ethically....

—Stephen Tyler, "Post-Modern Ethnography"

THE 1980S WILL BE REMEMBERED for more than Reagan rock and big hair, at least in terms of culture and literacies. Early in the 1980s, John Szwed argued that ethnographies—field observations of literacy events and literacy autobiographies—are the best way of studying the multiple literacies in contemporary society. At nearly the same time, Shirley Brice Heath published her landmark study of literacies in social and cultural contexts, which she called *Ways with Words,* and shortly thereafter, James Clifford and George Marcus edited a collection of essays, *Writing Culture,* that foregrounded the relationship among culture, writing, and postmodern ethnographies, particularly the extent to which researchers authorize interpretations of culture through the ways they write (about) it.

Such was the beginning of a long-term affair between ethnography and literacy. For instance, those who were involved in what became known as the New Literacy Studies applied the self-critiques and perspectives that originated in anthropology with Dell Hymes and Clifford Geertz as they began to challenge *the literacy myth,* or the belief that a functional ability to read and write, would bestow significant and substantial cognitive, economic, and social advantages. From this point forward, the study of literacy began to exhibit distinctly ethnographic dimensions, eventually generating new genres, which Linda Brodkey called *critical ethnographic narratives,* whose purpose is to challenge "cultural hegemony" in order to transform local institutions, including schools (67).[1] Even in the more limited focus of literacies in college classrooms, ethnographic approaches in both composition classrooms and across the curriculum[2] have produced methodologies and genres, including *teacher-research* or *action research* and *classroom ethnographies,* that, their proponents suggest, challenge hierarchical social structures despite a lukewarm disciplinary welcome.[3]

This affair between ethnographies and literacies has not been complete bliss. In general terms, some have questioned the extent to which contemporary ethnographers have misrepresented cultures and themselves, and others have questioned the extent to which ethnographers situate the researcher as the sole source of interpretive authority and establish scholarly objectivity as the goal of ethnographic reports (for example, West, Miller). In a similar way, some in literacy studies have challenged the ways that researchers have ignored larger social contexts, and others in composition studies have argued that ethnographies have focused on too few subjects over too short a time and have engaged in hypothesis-testing instead of hypothesis-generating (for example, Prendergast, Rhodes).

As the existence of this volume attests, the postmodern context marks a different stage in the relationship between ethnographies and literacies. In fact, some have questioned whether researchers can actually conduct ethnographies in a postmodern world (Kleine). According to Ralph Cintron, the debates between conventional and postmodern ethnographies, which coalesce around the usual issues, including language, knowledge, truth, culture, society, authority, reflexivity, and textuality, have largely been staged and can be traced to disagreements over language, texts, and text-making (376–81). In many ways, the nexus of these disagreements is the legitimization of experience, a culturally and materially contested space. On the one hand, ethnographic methodologies provide evidence from experience, not from experiment, which Cintron points out (371 ff), thereby making it particularly amenable to literacy studies and composition studies. On the other, ethnographic methodologies involve someone who is defining experience for another. If, according to Min-Zhan Lu and Bruce Horner, we problematize experience, we discover powerful questions (what counts as experience? who represents it? to whom? in what ways and to what ends?) whose answers necessitate rereadings of ethnographic meanings. Regardless, ethnographic meanings, in the end, are always contingent, as Robert Brooke has powerfully illustrated in his rereading of his own earlier ethnographic research ("Ethnographic").

For my interests in culture and literacy, postmodern ethnographies offer an accepted way of talking about the experience of literacy events and literacy acts. Specifically, the assumptions that we make about literacy experiences, including assumptions about texts and communities, lead to fixed interpretations of these events and acts, as well as to versions of the world that have implications for what we do and how we live. Despite the theoretical challenges of postmodernism, research in both literacy studies and composition studies has largely relied on versions of static literacies, monologic discourses, and homogeneous communities. A good example is David Bartholomae's Inventing the University model:

> The student has to appropriate (or be appropriated by) *a specialized discourse,* and he has to do this as though he were easily and comfortably *one with his audience,* as though he were *a member of the academy* or a historian or an anthropologist or an economist; he has to invent the university by assembling and mimicking *its language* while finding some compromise between idiosyncrasy, a personal history, on the one hand and the requirements of convention, the history of a discipline, on the other hand. He must learn to speak *our language.* Or he must dare to speak it or to carry off the bluff, since speaking and writing will most certainly be required long before the skill is "learned." And this, understandably, causes problems. (135, emphasis added)

One of the biggest problems, I maintain, is the extent to which such theorizing authorizes static models of literacy, models that lead people, such as J. Elspeth Stuckey and even Bartholomae, elsewhere to characterize these experiences and events as acts of violence.

Although such versions of literacy, with their self-serving arrangements between insiders and outsiders, have been criticized,[4] recent research in literacy, such as the work of Alessandro Duranti and Elinor Ochs or the work of the Multiliteracies Project (Cope and Kalantzis), has begun to legitimize more dynamic models of literacy, discourse, and communities. Such is my interest in this project. When I encountered the Call for Papers for this collection, I had recently published *ReInventing the University*, in which I speculate about negotiated literacies, or models of literacy, in which literacy acts amounted to navigating among competing cultural and discursive contexts. At the time I had just started a new semester, and I was again teaching cultural linguistics. Wouldn't it be interesting, I thought, riding the bus home on a surprisingly seasonal September evening, to look at experience and literacies in this cultural linguistics classroom? To see how assuming that people do, in fact, negotiate among discursive and cultural differences as they construct their own literacy acts changes the way (they and) I make sense of their literacy experiences? Already, the issues of experience and language were foregrounded as the content of this course. As the students and I discussed the influence of culture and language on meaning, they, and we, would be the object of study, in much the same way that the lived experience of graduate students was also the object of study in Gail Stygall's research on the ways that the discursive practices of students and teachers of English construct basic writers.

๑๖๏

As I explain in *ReInventing the University*, dissatisfying experiences as a student were primarily the reason that I began working with alternative literacies. The longer I stayed in school, the more I began to connect my experiences as a white, middle-class male to the larger critiques of education that many, including bell hooks, Jean François Lyotard, Neil Postman, and Bill Readings, have made. From my perspective, I began to wonder whether what critics had conventionally called *crises in literacy* would be more usefully seen as crises in legitimacy. Many, including Lester Faigley, Marcia Farr, John Trimbur, and others, have argued that the practices of academic literacies are largely those of essayist literacies, which Ron and Suzanne B. K. Scollon define as elaborated syntactical and sequential information, large amounts of new information, and absolute truths rather than contingent meanings (41 ff). Perhaps more important, these specific textual and discursive practices authorize particular versions of the self and the world—as essentialized (Western) rational minds communicating with other rational minds and a completely accessibly reality that is entirely expressible in texts—that challenge the contingency of postmodern experience. As such, being academically literate entails not only being able to engage in these elaborated discursive practices but also to do so in such a way that demonstrates an allegiance to these culturally specific definitions of experience. In this way, academic literacies are particular cultural literacies, ones that legitimize particular versions of experience.

Central to *ReInventing the University* was the belief that these versions of experience increasingly lack widespread legitimacy in a culturally differentiated postmodern world. At best, this lack of legitimacy will only increase. From 1995 to 2015, the combined undergraduate population in the United States is expected to increase 19% from 13.4 million students to 16 million students. Of the additional 2.6 million students, more than 2 million of them will be minorities—African American, Hispanic, Asian, Pacific Islander, and so forth—thereby increasing the total number of minority students from 29.4% in 1995 to 37.2% in 2015 (Educational). For these students, conventional literacies will represent obstacles to overcome or threats to resist, depending on whether, to use John Ogbu's distinction, they are immigrant (that is, voluntary) or involuntary minorities. At the same time, more and more mainstream students, I believe, will be forced to confront this legitimacy crisis, although not in the same way, because as Peter Elbow, Jacqueline Jones-Royster, Victor Villanueva, and others have pointed out, academic discourse has never been anyone's mother tongue and, I believe, is becoming more different from the discourses into which people are born.

ReInventing the University argues that if we are to do more than insist that this legitimacy crisis is actually a literacy crisis, then we will need to authorize alternatives for experience. One way to do so is negotiated literacies. According to such a theory of literacy, becoming literate is less the mastering of a stable, homogeneous discourse and more negotiating among competing discourses and overlapping, and often conflicting, cultures. As a legitimate alternative, negotiated literacies both recognize the cultural limitations of conventional academic discourses, as well as the opportunities of other discourses, and enable third spaces for competing discourses.

⊙✢⊚

An amenable place to study negotiated literacies, I thought, was the cultural linguistics course because we would already be examining the ways that experience is shaped by language and culture. Originally, we had been assigned to meet in Humanities 109, a spacious classroom with dirty yellow walls and rows of loosely organized desks that were stretched along two large windows that opened on an expansive lawn, which, campus lore maintains, was the golf course of a wealthy cereal manufacturer heiress when the campus was still her exclusive estate. In addition to this room, I had reserved a computer lab, a tiny space of fixed computers, two terminals on each desk, which were arranged in two tight columns and not enough rows.

Generally, the cultural linguistics course was cross-listed as an education course, an English course, and a foreign language course (that is, linguistics) course, but in the fall of 2001, it was listed only as an education course. We were scheduled to meet for two hours each week on Tuesday nights over a span of sixteen weeks from September to December. In addition, we also came together through an electronic list, <LINGUISTICS>, which I had established for this class.

Of the twenty-one graduate students in this cultural linguistics course, all of them were there to earn graduate degrees in education. Nineteen of them were earning master's degrees in TESOL (teaching English to speakers of other languages), and the other two were specializing in bilingual education and elementary education. Most were relatively experienced graduate students with more than one-half having completed twelve or more of the required thirty hours toward their master's degrees before starting this course. Only five of them were embarking on their first semester in their programs. In a similar way, most of them were familiar with classrooms from both sides of the desk. Fifteen were employed throughout this particular semester as teachers or teacher's aides. Four were full-time graduate students. The other two, a social worker and an insurance fraud investigator, were returning to obtain teaching credentials to change their careers.

To our classroom, they brought a range of cultural experiences. All of them were women, ranging from Nicki, a nineteen-year-old new college graduate to students in their late forties and early fifties who were returning for second and third careers. Nine of them were identifiable as racial or ethnic minorities, including Ecuadorian, El Salvadorian, Korean, Italian, and Puerto Rican, as well as African American, and three others had either lived or studied abroad. At least eleven of them were bilingual or multilingual, including Spanish, Korean, Italian, and Portuguese, and their communities or life circumstances reflected this diversity of experience. For instance, two of the Hispanic students had married European Americans. Geographically, the students brought a range of experiences, as well. Two of them lived in the boroughs of New York City, and others worked there, and at least for some, had grown up there before moving to the suburbs. The rest lived on Long Island, which is divided by I-495 into a North Shore, where generally more affluent people live and where our campus was located, and a South Shore, where more lower-middle-class and working-class people live. Our campus was one of several in what the administration often billed as the eighth largest private university in the country, and the cost of tuition and fees reflected the inflated New York metropolitan cost of living. Nevertheless, many of the students report that they begrudgingly pay private school tuition for a variety of pragmatic reasons, such as to avoid a long commute or to complete their degrees more quickly.

Throughout the semester, I collected data, including texts and e-list posts, as well as field notes both during and after class. At the end of the semester, I supplemented an institutionalized evaluation form with my own self-administered evaluation that asked the students to assign a letter grade to the course and to explain their assessments, which one of the students collected and delivered to the chairperson of the English Department, who retained them until I had submitted grades after the semester had ended. Also, I distributed consent forms, which had been approved by the Institutional Research Board (IRB), detailing the focus of this project, the voluntary nature of their participation, the option not to have their work included, the opportunity for access to drafts of this report, and the contact information for the chairperson of the English Department, the secretary of the IRB, and me. After the semester ended, I followed up both in person and online with those who had agreed to participate, and after I had produced an early draft, I invited everyone from the class, regardless of whether they had agreed to participate, to respond, as well as circulating it among colleagues and friends whose perspectives I value.

Obviously, being a participant-observer in my own classroom raises some interesting questions about the legitimacy of experience. Many, including Min-Zhan Lu and Bruce Horner, Richard Miller, Renato Rosaldo, and others, have challenged the primacy of the researcher's experience, which is often the ultimate, if not the only, basis for meaning. Generally, their challenges have questioned the boundary between *participant* and *observer*. In being situated between these, my simultaneous position of teacher and researcher established both access to and alienation from the community I was studying, a condition that A. Suresh Canagarajah and others acknowledge is always a part of classroom ethnographies (606). By definition my status as the instructor separated me from the students, and the role of teacher enabled me to unobtrusively collect artifacts and data that are particularly useful for this project in the normal course of teaching, particularly because the focus of the course was already culture, language, and meaning. As such, this situatedness raises significant challenges to conventional ethnographic expectations about the experience of researchers. To a large extent, it complicates the expectation that Karen Ann Watson-Grego and others have for ethnographic work that is "systematic, detailed, and rigorous rather than anecdotal or impressionistic" (588). First, systematicity, details, and rigor are not mutually exclusive with anecdotes and impressions. Second, systematic rigor often ensures that researchers authorize predictable experiences and legitimize the cultural capital of the academy.

My situatedness offered an unusual perspective on the traditional methodological distinction between object and subject, one that became an *intersubjectivity*. At the same time, this situatedness left me in a particularly powerful position to shape the experiences of participants in this project. For example, the first half of the semester would be taught by me alone, during which I would introduce key ideas, such as *situated meanings* and *cultural models*, within the context of *academic cultural literacies*. As explained in the syllabus, the course would explore the interrelations of language, discourse, and communication in cultural contexts. Students would read several books and articles, post to the class e-list, produce a cultural literacies narrative and a project proposal, submit a portfolio, and complete a final exam. The second half of the semester, during which we would explore areas of interest from their projected proposals, would be cotaught by the students and me. Due to the tragic events of 9/11, the university closed the campus on what was to be the second meeting of the class, which meant that along with the original religious holidays that were to be the third and fourth meetings, four weeks elapsed between our first class and our second class. As a result, I distributed a revised course schedule in which I not only deleted the project proposal but also refocused the second half of the semester to juxtapose the academic cultural literacies, which we had used to contextualize our discussions during the first half of the semester, with African-American cultural literacies. Instead of readings that the students proposed based on their research, I assigned ten articles that examined the linguistic, discursive, and social dimensions of African-American discourses, including syntactic analyses of African-American English, sociocultural descriptions of African-American discursive practices and discourse communities, and educational arguments for and against Ebonics.

For the most part, the students indicated on my course evaluations at the end of the semester that they thought that the semester had been successful. On retrieving their responses after submitting their grades, I learned that the average grade that they had assigned this course was an A–. In explaining their evaluations, students wrote:

- Taught on a high, academic level—the way in which a graduate course should be taught.
- I think it is obvious that we have all come a long way since day 1. We have learned to think outside of the box and have developed an awareness about language and culture that we did not have before.
- This was the most thought provoking and interesting class I have ever taken. It was dope :) to see all the ways discourse affects us in our lives, and interesting and thought provoking—expert instruction and content knowledge—looked forward to class each week.[5]

The question, however, is the extent to which these experiences were the results of negotiations among cultures and discourses.

☙❧

Current theories of static literacies and monologic discourses define literacy as learning to control the standard discourse, thereby providing an orderly theory of socialization into dominant communities. Dynamic theories of literacy, on the other hand, suggest that becoming literate involves negotiating among competing discourses and cultures moment by moment, a perspective that foregrounds material conditions. What was once seen as socialization into standard discourses, such as appropriating or being appropriated of Bartholomae's Inventing the University model, becomes approximate performances based on interpretations and perceived expectations, which are conducted within the multiple contexts, subject positions, and material conditions surrounding specific literacy events.

The question of communities is central to the study of literacies. For example, some believe that classrooms cannot be discourse communities (for example, Cintron). Others argue that classrooms are, or at least can be, discourse communities (for example, Elasser and Irving). Still others advocate for the relative autonomy for classrooms as communities (for example, Canagarajah). At least for negotiated literacies, a more useful understanding of community is the one offered by Joseph Harris, Bruce Horner, and others, in which communities are seen as comprised of the materialist conditions in which they exist. Moreover, such a version of community would acknowledge significant cultural and material dimensions that are often overlooked or ignored. For example, loose affiliations and allegiances were created even within the physical and intellectual spaces of the classroom that affected the experiences that the students had in the course. Almost one-fifth of the students had taken a graduate sociolinguistics course immediately before they took this cultural linguistics course. Another student, who had dropped the sociolinguistics course after the first meeting, promised on the first night of the cultural linguistics course that she was not going to drop this course. Predictably, these students invoked these previous experiences, both publicly in class and on <LINGUISTICS> list and privately in conversations and e-mails, as part of their negotiations of their present experiences, comparing the semesters and the courses as a way of negotiating their interpretations of policies or assignments and, in so doing, establishing a history and solidarity with each other and with me. In a similar way, other students, and not necessarily the same ones who had taken the sociolinguistics course, had taken other classes together or were currently taking the same courses with other instructors, which enabled them to bring other experiences and alignments to our conversations.

Within these complex communities, the students were most noticeably engaging in cultural negotiations on the e-list. In many ways, e-mail offered spaces in which students could negotiate a cross-border legitimacy within their own historical, social, and cultural contexts. For the most part, the literacy events online were more dynamic, conflicted, and overlapping, which Terry Craig,

Leslie Harris, and Richard Smith argue is characteristic of e-mail in classrooms generally. When research on e-mail first began to appear, critics and theorists, such as Gail Hawisher and Charles Moran, suggested that e-mail as a discursive practice would challenge conventional discursive practices with a grammar of the screen, different expectations for discursive organization, and new conventions (including flaming and interinsulating), as well as a renewed need for audience awareness, an accelerated process, potentially revealing perspectives on cultural aspects of literacy events, and increased accessibility and interactivity. More recently, Michael Spooner and Kathleen Yancey, in attempting to "narrow the focus" of e-mail, a "floating signifier of the worst kind," distinguished among five e-mail genres—e-mail simple; e-mail on e-lists; e-mail in the classroom; e-mail as a resource; and e-mail-as-collaboration—before concluding that e-mail lacks a stable generic form.

In many ways, these virtual spaces provided spaces that were conducive for these cultural negotiations, sometimes even inducing a crisis that prompted these negotiations:

From: Jerri
To: <LINGUISTICS>
Subject: RE: heidi's request
Date: Thursday, October 20, 2001 4:30 PM

I am in complete agreement with Miriam about competing cultural literacies in the classroom. As soon as I read her email I thought, "she's right! and I never would have picked it out myself." The reason I feel this way or have felt in my classroom is not that my peronal Hispanic cultural model doesn't fit with yours, but I've never experienced the classroom in this way, let alone all of the work we do on the computer. Yes I find it intimidating and over-whelming, but only b/c it's something that I'm not used to. The computer has always been a HUGE part of my life, but never to this degree. Person-ally I find it difficult to keep up. I'm used to getting an assignment, reading or whatever, memorizing/learning and being done with it. I'm not saying one is better than the other, just different. As the classes go on I find myself speaking up more and getting used to all of these emails. We talk a lot, which I love, except for the uncomfortable silence. I think the silence has to do with people just not wanting to offend others and I don't blame them. In todays world, no matter how "far" we've come, you reallly have to be careful what you say so you don't hurt others. I can already tell in class who would be offended by what comments and then there are some people you think would be offended, but could [not] care less. So that puts us back to square one—do we go with what we think about certain cultures? do we assume things?, do we ask questions?, do we offend? . . .

Even within the confines of the e-list itself, some of the posts were what Spooner and Yancey call *email simple* (messages that function much like a letter with greetings, closings, and other epistolary conventions) whereas others were what they call *email as a resource* (electronic articles on language diversity or URLs of Ebonics Web sites) or *email-as-collaboration* (feedback about drafts or the final exam).

At the same time, a range of discursive styles appeared from different students. For example, Meg, an African-American student who had returned to school for her education certification after having studied art abroad and working in the fashion industry, attempted to approximate academic discourse, complete with academic claims and formal citations, whereas Kim, a young European-American student who had previously taught in Portugal and worked for the Coca-Cola company, regularly posted short, more succinct comments, often in response to others. Even within specific posts, students were exploiting the virtual spaces to negotiate among the various positions that they occupied:

From: Heidi
To: <LINGUISTICS>
Subject: Hip Hop Vs Standard English
Date: Thursday, November 08, 2001 10:59 PM

I love Hip Hop, Everything about it I love, My Bfrnd works for DEF JAM an African American record label, he's also a DJ who works with Funk Flex (hot 97 an AA [African American] radio station). So as you can imagine I am always around Hip Hop and it never bothered me until I started taking this class. I was at the studio w/ my BF and he was recording this new up and coming Hip Hop artist, I sat back and Chris you would have been proud if you could have heard the things running through my head, I was analyzing every little thing that they said. Within five minutes I am not kidding I heard 30 niggers, 55 yo's, and about 100 bitches. What is up with that? it isn't even the use of the words anymore it's the lack of vocabulary. I am all for BE [Black English] but I know for a fact it does not pertain to those three words alone. Not only this but then the song started and it was about a guy who didn't need his bitch no mo because his dick was 9 inches long and his niggers had his back. Does this make a statement? Does this song do anything other than rile up a bunch of guys and piss off a few girls? Isn't there anything other to rap about? The use of language although I must give him credit on his poetic style I can't complement [sic] his choice of theme or words? Why is the music I love now making me wonder what type of place some of these people come from? I understand everyone wants to bling bling and get high and chill at least this is the message they send, But what next? Where can we draw the line? Am I only offended because I looked beyond the phat beat and actually listened to this guy or is it because I am from a different Cultural Model? What do you think? Sometimes I think it's better when it's all beats then no ones offended.

Heidi

Much like the performances of students that Anne Haas Dyson and Tom Fox describe, Heidi's post demonstrates the extent to which she is negotiating among cultures—the culture of rap, with its connections to African-American communities; the culture of cultural linguistics, with its connections to the academy; and others—as she assembles a performance from the various positions that she occupies (teacher, student, girlfriend, rap enthusiast, and novice cultural linguist) and reconsiders the linguistic politics of all these worlds.

Beyond the e-list, these negotiations were also evident in more conventional literacy events. For her literacy narrative, Kim brought together the genres of the obituary and academic exposition. The final version she submitted had two columns on each page and used different fonts and styles depending on whether she was using academic or journalistic discourse. The rationale, I later learned, was to dramatize her experience:

> From: Kim
> To: Christopher
> Subject: RE:
> Date: Friday, 15 March 2002 9:42 PM
>
> Chris—
>
> Initially, I was very overwhelmed by your class. I knew you encouraged "alternative" ways of constructing literature and I honestly didn't know any other professor that did . . . so, I thought it might be the only opportunity I had to do something different. However, at the same time, I felt overwhelmed with the idea . . . I mean, writing a paper "APA style" is a no-brainer, so the idea of doing something "creative" was "killing me" in the sense that I was having a hard time coming up with an idea. I took my stress and the fact that I was having a hard time and decided to use that feeling to write my paper. It actually killed me, hence the obituary. I used it for the final version because it worked. I felt I was able to play with language and use it in way that I never thought I could. I think I said this once before but I even used a more formal language for the "obituary" part of the paper and a more informal language for the "academic" part of the paper . . . thus playing with language and language style.

If we trust Kim's account, then we can interpret her performance, using a dynamic theory of literacy, as a negotiation within a particular moment in space and time—her educational history in postsecondary institutions; her experiences producing "APA style" texts; her reading of our class and of me; even her stress of this negotiation—that manifests itself in discursive choices, from selecting particular genres to employing certain registers and so on.

Throughout the semester, I regularly encouraged the students to negotiate the terms for the course, including assignments and assessment criteria, yet they resisted in some unexpected ways. One of the most obvious examples was their learning contracts. At the beginning of the semester, I had asked them to generate learning contracts as means of assessment. I also provided them with sample contracts and a deadline of the midterm for completing these negotiations. However, most of the students simply accepted one of the sample contracts that I had distributed. Those who did negotiate their contracts limited themselves to haggling over minor variations, such as changing the acceptable number of absences from one to two or the required number of weekly e-posts from four to three. (Near the end of the semester, several of them wondered on the e-list why no one had engaged in any serious negotiations.) In the end, several of them failed to complete their negotiations by the midterm, and more than one of them attempted to negotiate their contracts up to and during the last week of the semester. Depending on the perspective, this resistance can be explained in multiple ways. One way is to attribute this situation to the coercive tendencies of the semester, particularly the ways that institutional structures accord power to particular positions regardless of whether the people occupying those positions want. In a similar way, I may be accorded power or status, regardless of what I might say, simply because I am a white, middle-class, European-American male. Or it may also suggest that legitimate negotiations, at least in educational settings, are limited by numerous factors, including the power relations among participants or the permeability of social institutions in which these negotiations are occurring.

When I asked the students whether they believed that negotiated third spaces were realistic, they were mixed in their perspectives. For example, Meg, the returning African-American student, insisted that these third spaces were not possible, at least not in schools, because the differences would inevitably create conflict, conflict that, she believed, might be subdued in universities that could appeal to rationality but that would be inconsistent with the function of elementary and secondary schools, whose primary function, she claimed, was to facilitate peaceful interactions. At the same time, Nicki, a European-American student who had studied in Costa Rica, argued that these third spaces would be realistic over time and that these would enable teachers to escape a standard-nonstandard binary. In contrast, Vanessa, a returning student who, as a child, had emigrated to Italy and who was the mother of a young, bicultural son, suggested that in the diversity that is contemporary social experience, the work of negotiating legitimate third spaces had already begun.

CONCLUSIONS

Already, the New Ethnography, with its shifts away from fieldwork in foreign lands, extended participant observations, elaborated life histories, and extensive questionnaires to language as the means of access to culture (Jenkins), so the connections that Szwed et al. make in the 1980s are not surprising. Given the political agendas of literacy studies, postmodern ethnographic methodologies are even more relevant. For instance, Dwight Conquergood defines *postmodern ethnography* as the formation of a critical cultural politics centered on the role of the body in meaning-making, the fluidity and permeability of boundaries, the importance of performance, and the need for self-consciousness about textual productions. As such, postmodern ethnography is useful for recent theoretical shifts in literacy studies. In this context, literacy events are sites of competing discourses and cultures, and literacy acts are efforts to navigate among these within specific social, material, and political contexts. Within the (constructed) self as the site of competing discourses and cultures, conventional understandings of boundaries as fixed demarcations among cultures, languages, and communities are reread as dynamic and fluid, shifting and changing depending on which matrix of variables is authorized at any given moment. Such perspectives go beyond recognizing the existence of multiple cultures within classrooms, as Kay Losey recommends, and other communities to acknowledging that individuals themselves are situated within overlapping, and often competing, cultures and spaces. Within these, participants in literacy events must negotiate among cultural variables, as well as their perspectives and interpretations of the other variables.

Such a perspective requires a shift from universalized interpretations of literacy events and absolute standards for literacy acts to context-specific practices and situations, parts of which are negotiated in interactions, as Ellen Barton illustrates, some of which have already been negotiated in previous interactions. In the give-and-take of these discursive performances, the negotiations of those involved encourage subtle and not-so-subtle shifts in subsequent choices.[6] At the same time, ongoing internal negotiations with previous experiences, past encounters, and preconceived expectations also shape the interaction regardless of how noticeable these are to those involved (or to participant-observers who might be watching them).

As I was reading and writing about these experiences, I found myself trying to negotiate among discourses and cultures. In doing so, I recognized the extent to which I occupy multiple positions simultaneously—teacher and researcher whose interests include cultures and literacies, whose perspectives are influenced by multiple cultures in my own home—that formed the context for my experiences. During the semester, these experiences rippled through my perspective, causing me to (re)negotiate both the course and my reading of it. At one point during the semester, I thought that the problem with class discussions was that I was dominating the conversations, so I began composing my comments before class and sending them to the e-list, thinking that in doing so, I would be minimizing my presence and opening space for others. However, I learned, as I was writing this report, that at least some of the students read these efforts as attempts to assert more control over the classroom, an interpretation that did not even occur to me at the time. In drafting early versions of this text, I experimented with a range of discursive practices, from academic exposition to mosaic and academic argument to scrapping,[7] and yet in trying to keep within the constraints of this collection, I was confined in the ways that I could connect and elaborate on these pieces, which I eliminated in the final version. These negotiations are significant contributions, as the epigraphs to this text suggest, cooperatively evolved texts that are, at the same time, enmeshed within the cultural practices of the academy.

And, it seems, I was not the only one who was negotiating the semester after it had ended. Shortly after submitting grades, I found this e-mail waiting for me:

From: Kim
To: Christopher
Subject: EDU 837
Date: Tuesday, December 18, 2001 9:41 AM

Hi Chris——
I just wanted to let you know that I really enjoyed your class. Unlike most professors at [ ], you required us to think and I really appreciate that because I love to think and find myself thinking all the time (. . . not just about class mind you). I also appreciate all the work that you've done . . . another thing the professors at [ ] don't like to do.

I guess you can say, as you do, "I got my money's worth!" . . . but that's not really what's important.

To be honest with you, I really HATED your class at first. I think it had a lot to do with the language that you use in class. Now I'm wondering exactly WHY do you do that? Is it because that's your cultural model and in an attempt for us to understand what it feels like to have a cultural model enforced upon us, you use language and make references to theo- rists/books/articles in passing speech to see just how much we "get"? At least, that's my take on it . . .

OR are you just showing that you are very well read? (unlike some of us :)

I get the feeling that you're more into publishing than teaching even though you are an excellent teacher . . . but I guess you need to teach in order to understand what's going on in the areas you're interested in and to have material for your books.

Anyway, I'm getting off the topic. Thanks for a great semester.

Kim

PS If you use any of my work in your future publications, can you use the pseudonym "Kim?" Thanks :)[8]

NOTES

1. See also, Canagarajah, Conquergood, LeCompte, Miller, and West

2. For ethnographic studies of writing both in composition classrooms and across the curriculum, see Aber; Bazerman; Bleich; Brooke, "Underlife"; Chiseri-Strater; Losey; McCarthy; Yager; and Zebroski and Mack

3. See North (312 ff) for the initial assessment of ethnographic methodologies in composition studies

4. See, for example, Bizzell, Fox, and Schroeder

5. In response to other questions, the students most often cited class discussions and the e-list as the most productive aspects of the course, and they most often identified the amount of work and, strangely, the e-list as the least productive aspects of the course When asked to explain the one change they would make to the semester, the students most often identified something about the readings and no changes.

6. As such, this process resembles the triangulation Thomas Kent, Sidney Dobrin, and others describe as *paralogic rhetoric*.

7. *Mosaic* and *scrapping*, as their names suggest, involve assembling a text from other pieces of text. For more, see Camitta (mosaic) and Gernes (scrapping).

8. I would like to thank Ann Dobie, Helen Fox, Michael Spooner, and the students from this Cultural Linguistics class for responding to various drafts of this text and Steve Brown and Sid Dobrin for their patience and interest. The data for this project were collected while I was working at Long Island University.

WORKS CITED

Aber, John. "Composition Teachers Need to Become Teacher-Researchers: Reflections Based on an Ethnography of Teacher Training Sessions." Bloomington, IN: ERIC Clearinghouse on Reading English, and Communication, 1988. *ERIC*. ED 293 134.

Bartholomae, David. "Inventing the University." *When a Writer Can't Write: Studies in Writer's Block and Other Composing Problems*. Ed. Mike Rose. New York: Guilford, 1985. 134–65.

Barton, Ellen L. "Literacy in (Inter)Action." *College English* 59.4 (1997): 408–37.

Bazerman, Charles. "What Written Knowledge Does: Three Examples of Academic Discourse." *Philosophy of the Social Sciences* 11 (1981): 361–87.

Bizzell, Patricia. "Hybrid Academic Discourses: What, How, and Why." *Composition Studies* 27.2 (1999): 7–22.

Bleich, David. "Ethnography and the Study of Literacy: Prospects for Socially Generous Research." *Into the Field: Sites of Composition Studies*. Ed. Anne Ruggles Gere. New York: MLA, 1993. 176–92.

Brodkey, Linda. "Writing Critical Ethnographic Narratives." *Anthropological and Education Quarterly* 18 (1987): 67–76.

Brooke, Robert. "Ethnographic Practice as a Means of Invention: Seeking a Rhetorical Paradigm for Ethnographic Writing." Kirklighter, Vincent, and Moxley 11–23.

———. "Underlife and Writing Instruction." *College Composition and Communication* 38.2 (1987): 141–53.

Camitta, Miriam P. "Adolescent Vernacular Writing: Literacy Reconsidered." *The Right to Literacy*. Ed. Andrea A. Lunsford, Helen Moglen, and James Slevin. New York: MLA, 1990. 262–68.

Canagarajah, A. Suresh. "Critical Ethnography of a Sri Lankan Classroom: Ambiguities in Student Opposition to Reproduction through ESOL." *TESOL Quarterly* 27.4 (1993): 601–26.

Chiseri-Strater, Elizabeth. *Academic Literacies: The Public and Private Discourse of University Students*. Portsmouth, NH: Boynton/Cook Heinemann, 1991.

Cintron, Ralph. "Wearing a Pith Helmet at a Sly Angle: Or, Can Writing Researchers Do Ethnography in a Postmodern Era?" *Written Communication* 10.3 (1993): 371–412.

Clifford, James, and George E. Marcus, eds. *Writing Culture: The Poetics and Politics of Ethnography*. Berkeley: U of California P, 1986.

Conquergood, Dwight. "Rethinking Ethnography: Towards a Critical Cultural Politics." *Communication Monographs* 58 (1991): 179–94.

Cope, Bill, and Mary Kalantzis, eds. *Multiliteracies: Literacy Learning and the Design of Social Futures*. London: Routledge, 2000.

Craig, Terry, Leslie Harris, and Richard Smith. "Rhetoric of the 'Contact Zone': Composition on the Front Lines." *Literacy Theory in the Age of the Internet*. Ed. Todd Taylor and Irene Ward. New York: Columbia UP, 1998. 122–45.

Dobrin, Sidney I. *Constructing Knowledges: The Politics of Theory-Building and Pedagogy in Composition*. Albany: State U of New York P, 1997.

Duranti, Alessandro, and Elinor Ochs. "Syncretic Literacy: Multiculturalism in Samoan American Families." *Research Report 16*. Santa Cruz, CA: National Center for Research on Cultural Diversity and Second Language Learning, 1997. 1–15.

Dyson, Anne Haas. "Coach Bombay's Kids Learn to Write: Children's Appropriation of Media Material for School Literacy." *Research in the Teaching of English* 33.4 (1999): 367–401.

Educational Testing Service. "Soaring Number of Qualified Minority Students Poised to Enter College." <http://www.ets.org/textonly/aboutets/news/00052401.html>. 20 November 2001.

Elasser, Nan, and Patricia Irving. "Literacy as Commodity: Redistributing the Goods." *Journal of Education* 174 (1992): 26–40.

Elbow, Peter. "Vernacular Rhetorics and Grammars in Teaching Writing: Probing the Culture of Literacy." Schroeder, Fox, and Bizzell 126–38.

Faigley, Lester. "Going Electronic: Creating Multiple Sites for Innovation in a Writing Program." *Resituating Writing: Constructing and Administering Writing Programs.* Ed. Joseph Janagelo and Kristine Hansen. Portsmouth, NH: Boynton/Cook Heinemann, 1995. 46–58.

Farr, Marcia. "Essayist Literacy and Other Verbal Performances." *Written Communication* 10.1 (1993): 4–38.

Fox, Tom. *The Social Uses of Writing: Politics and Pedagogy.* Norwood, NJ: Ablex, 1990.

Gernes, Todd S. "Recasting the Culture of Ephemera." Trimbur 107–27.

Harris, Joseph. *A Teaching Subject: Composition Since 1966.* Upper Saddle River, NJ: Prentice Hall, 1997.

Hawisher, Gail E., and Charles Moran. "Electronic Mail and the Writing Instructor." *College English* 55.6 (1993): 627–43.

Heath, Shirley Brice. *Ways with Words: Language, Life, and Work in Communities and Classrooms.* New York: Cambridge UP, 1983.

hooks, bell. *Teaching to Transgress: Education as the Practice of Freedom.* New York: Routledge, 1994.

Horner, Bruce. *Terms of Work for Composition: A Materialist Critique.* Albany: State U of New York P, 2000.

Jenkins, Evan. "The New Ethnography: Language as the Key to Culture." *Change* 10.1 (1978): 16–19.

Jones-Royster, Jacqueline. "Academic Discourses or Small Boats in Big Seas." Schroeder, Fox, and Bizzell 24–31.

Kent, Thomas. *Paralogic Rhetoric: A Theory of Communicative Interaction.* Lewisburg, OH: Bucknell UP, 1993.

Kirklighter, Cristina, Cloe Vincent, and Joseph M. Moxley, eds. *Voices and Visions: Refiguring Ethnography in Composition.* Portsmouth, NH: Boynton/Cook Heinemann, 1997.

Kleine, Michael. "Beyond Triangulation: Ethnography, Writing, and Rhetoric." *JAC: A Journal of Composition Theory* 10.1 (1990): 117–25.

LeCompte, Margaret D. "Bias in the Biography: Bias and Subjectivity in Ethnographic Research." *Anthropology and Education Quarterly* 18 (1987): 43–52.

Losey, Kay. "Describing the Cultures of the Classroom: Problems in Classroom Ethnography." Kirklighter, Vincent, and Moxley 86–94.

Lu, Min-Zhan, and Bruce Horner. "The Problematic of Experience: Redefining Critical Work in Ethnography and Pedagogy." *College English* 60 (1998): 257–77.

Lyotard, Jean-François. *The Postmodern Condition: A Report on Knowledge.* Trans. Geoff Bennington and Brian Massumi. Minneapolis: U of Minnesota P, 1979.

McCarthy, Lucille Parkinson. "A Stranger in Strange Lands: A College Student Writing Across the Curriculum." *Research in the Teaching of English* 21.3 (1987): 233–65.

Miller, Richard. *As If Learning Mattered: Reforming Higher Education.* Ithaca, NY: Cornell UP, 1998.

North, Stephen. *The Making of Knowledge in Composition: Portrait of an Emerging Field.* Portsmouth, NH: Boynton/Cook Heinemann, 1987.

Ogbu, John. "Minority Education in Comparative Perspective," *Journal of Negro Education* 59.1 (1990): 45–57.

Prendergast, Catherine. "The Water in the Fishbowl: Historicizing *Ways with Words.*" *Written Communication* 17 (2000): 452–90.

Readings, Bill. *The University in Ruins.* Cambridge, MA: Harvard UP, 1996.

Rhodes, Keith. "Ethnography of Psychography? The Evolution and Ethics of a New Genre in Composition." Kirklighter, Vincent, and Moxley 24–36.

Rosaldo, Renato. "From the Door of His Tent: The Fieldworker and the Inquisitor." Clifford and Marcus 77–97.

Schroeder, Christopher. *ReInventing the University: Literacies and Legitimacy in the Postmodern Academy.* Logan: Utah State UP, 2001.

Schroeder, Christopher, Helen Fox, and Patricia Bizzell, eds. *ALT DIS: Alternative Discourses and the Academy.* Portsmouth, NH: Boynton/Cook Heinemann, 2002.

Scollon, Ron, and Suzanne B. K. Scollon. *Narrative, Literacy, and Face in Interethnic Communities.* Norwood, NJ: Ablex, 1981.

Spooner, Michael, and Kathleen Yancey. "Postings on a Genre of Email." *College Composition and Communication* 47.2 (1996): 252–78.

Stuckey, J. Elspeth. *The Violence of Literacy.* Portsmouth, NH: Boynton/Cook Heinemann, 1991.

Stygall, Gail. "Resisting Privilege: Basic Writing and Foucault's Author Function." *College Composition and Communication* 45.3 (1994): 320–41.

Szwed, John F. "The Ethnography of Literacy." *Writing: The Nature, Development, and Teaching of Written Communication.* Ed. Marcia Farr Whiteman. Mahwah, NJ: Erlbaum, 1981. 13–23.

Trimbur, John. "Essayist Literacy and the Rhetoric of Deproduction." *Rhetoric Review* 9.1 (1990): 72–86.

———, ed. *Popular Literacy: Studies in Cultural Practices and Poetics.* Pittsburgh: University of Pittsburgh Press, 2001.

Tyler, Stephen. "Post-Modern Ethnography: From Document of the Occult to Occult Document." Clifford and Marcus 122–40.

Villanueva, Victor. "The Personal." *College English* 64.1 (2001): 50–52.

Watson-Grego, Karen Ann. "Ethnography in ESL: Defining the Essentials." *TESOL Quarterly* 22.4 (1988): 575–92.

West, James T. "Ethnography and Ideology: The Politics of Cultural Representation." *Western Journal of Communication* 57 (1993): 209–20.

Yager, Kristi. "Composition's Appropriation of Ethnographic Authority." Kirklighter, Vincent, and Moxley 37–44.

Zebroski, James, and Nancy Mack. "Ethnographic Writing for Critical Consciousness." *Social Issues in the English Classroom.* Ed. C. Mark Hurlbert and Samuel Totten. Urbana, IL: NCTE, 1992. 196–205.

5

Shifting Figures

Rhetorical Ethnography

GWEN GORZELSKY

INTRODUCTION

IN THE PAST TWENTY YEARS, critical ethnographers committed to under-standing the cultural and political ramifications of their research method and its texts have provoked a transformation of ethnographic fieldwork and, espe-cially, ethnographic writing. They have done so in significant part by demon-strating the inherently figurative, literary nature of their texts' depictions. In the process, they have argued persuasively that ethnography must actively intervene in the interests of research subjects when those subjects face unjust, exploitative, or repressive circumstances.

I contend that critical ethnographers' attention to figurative language—especially metaphor—can contribute to social change in a way that produc-tively revises the interventionist model they propose. Specifically, by craft-ing a rhetorical form that puts competing figurative systems in dialogue, ethnographers can shift our own metaphorics. As a result, we can change our participation in the social situations we research—that is, in the social situations where we are participants as much as we are observers, given the nature of our research method. Although such changes by no means equal (or guarantee) systemic transformation, changing the microdynamics within larger systems in fact generates a ripple effect. Although we cannot predict or control such ripples, encouraging them provides one of our most effective and ready means of cultivating systemic change.

I begin this argument by examining how experimental and critical ethnographers have used attention to the literary, reflexive dimensions of their texts to produce more ethical representations and to further social change. Next, I draw on the work of anthropologist Gregory Bateson to show that metaphor grounds our unconscious primary process thinking and thus our foundational premises and relational habits. By integrating metaphoric and linear thinking, experimental ethnographies can work to revise such premises and habits, to convey the systemic shape of social relations, and to promote social balance, equity, and justice. Using Gestalt theorists' work, the next section demonstrates methods for recognizing and analyzing our underlying metaphors in order to see—and perhaps revise—our foundational assumptions and relational habits. The following section extends composition studies' work with metaphor to illustrate how critical ethnographers can draw on Bateson's and Gestalt theorists' formulations to compose texts whose rhetorical form recognizes both researchers' and subjects' underlying metaphors; puts those metaphors into dialogue; analyzes them; and fosters changes in researchers' metaphorics. The final section demonstrates this rhetorical ethnography to show how it can help researchers shift our perceptual and relational habits and thus cultivate systemic change.

CRITICAL EXPERIMENTAL ETHNOGRAPHY

In recent years, critical ethnography has confronted the potentially exploitative, damaging effects of ethnographic research on its subjects. For instance, historically, ethnographic texts Westerners wrote about other cultures have sometimes furthered political, economic, and cultural colonization of those cultures by Western powers. Similarly, ethnographic texts written about an ethnographer's own culture can exploit the power differences between researchers and subjects (for instance between university researcher and public-school teacher) to diminish the social or political status of subjects' self-representations when those conflict with the ethnographer's supposedly objective depiction. Because they recognize that language formulates lived experience in a limited, subjective way, critics such as George Marcus, Paul Rabinow, and Barbara Meyerhoff and Jay Ruby worry about the way ethnographic representations inevitably swallow subjects' voices in the researcher's textually enacted agenda. To address these problems, critical ethnographers such as Faye Harrison and Min-Zhan Lu and Bruce Horner emphasize the importance of using their research to foster social change when subjects experience conditions that appear manifestly unjust. They hold that such intervention is one of the researcher's ethical obligations.[1]

To address these issues, critical ethnographers have begun to work substantively with writing as the medium ethnography uses to produce knowledge. They argue that ethnography's literary nature fundamentally shapes the knowledge it generates. This literary character has contributed to the dangers ethnography can pose to its subjects. For instance, by depicting his subjects in *Tristes Tropiques* as Rousseauesque noble savages, Levi-Strauss simultaneously infantilizes them with respect to industrialized Western cultures. Similarly, Edward Said's *Orientalism* shows how many Western depictions of Easterners figure them as intellectually, morally, and politically inferior to Occidental peoples. By analyzing such depictions in published ethnographies, theorists such as Meyerhoff and Ruby argue, researchers can better understand the inevitably figurative nature of languaged representations. Such analysis provides the basis for ethnographers to take a reflexive approach toward the literary, figurative aspects of their own depictions of others (and themselves, as participant observers). Furthermore, it can prepare researchers to experiment with ways to produce and textually enact dialogue between themselves and subjects. Such work, theorists argue, can help ethnographers to deal productively with the ethical challenges the research method poses. By consciously using literary structure and devices in composing their own texts, they conclude, ethnographers can put the genre's literary nature in the service of the kind of social change critical ethnography encourages.

Various ethnographers have produced self-consciously literary, reflexive ethnographies. They undertake experimental forms of writing that work to put multiple subjects' voices in tension with the ethnographer's perspective. For instance, Karen Fox's "Silent Voices" uses a series of columns on each page to present three separate voices (a victim's, an abuser's, and her own), and although Fox theorizes her depiction, she never ultimately resolves the differences among the three representations of child sexual abuse. Similarly, Fischer and Abedi's *Debating Muslims* impressively counterpoints the representations of an American Jewish ethnographer with those of his Iranian Muslim informant/research assistant/coauthor. Furthermore, the book explicitly examines the way metaphor shapes Judeo-Christian and Muslim cultural perceptions. Like many other experimental ethnographies, it includes explicitly reflexive sections on how the researchers' backgrounds and investments shaped their perceptions and, ultimately, their text's representations. Of course, such experimental texts still take shape through the textual choices—the agenda—of the writing ethnographer. Nonetheless, they explicitly try to show the limits of the researcher's perspective and to evoke some of the possible alternative perspectives, especially those of various research subjects.[2] Thus an emphasis on the literary and reflexive aspects of ethnographic texts—especially the figurative aspects—has grounded critical ethnography's efforts to produce more ethical depictions that contribute positively to social change.

METAPHOR IN ETHNOGRAPHY

In this section, I draw on Gregory Bateson's work to show how one form of figurative language—metaphor—grounds our foundational premises, perceptual structures, and relational habits. Extending Bateson's theory, I suggest that critical ethnographers integrate metaphoric and linear thinking in our texts. In doing so, we can more effectively revise our own foundational premises and habits; depict the systemic shape of our ethnographic sites and our participation in them; and cultivate social change.

Critical ethnography's effort to encourage such change by attending to figurative and reflexive language use dovetails with Bateson's work on metaphor. A cultural anthropologist who also conducted research in biology and psychology, Bateson pursued a career that spanned roughly fifty years and included anthropological fieldwork in Bali; research on alcoholism and schizophrenia at the Palo Alto Veterans' Administration Hospital; studies of porpoises to investigate prelinguistic mammalian communication; and work with larger ecological systems. Across these contexts, Bateson explored metaphor as a crucial basis of human perception and interaction.

He contrasts the functions of metaphoric thinking with those of purposive, rational thinking. He argues that metaphor forms the basis of primary process thinking, which is black and white, is unable to differentiate among quantities, and is without a symbol for the negative. Based on studies of animal communication, Bateson demonstrates that communication among preverbal mammals focuses on the contingencies of relationship (366–67). He concludes that play—the basis of abstraction and metaphor—enables mammals to use context cues to establish the status of particular interactions (for example, as real or mock fights) and thus the relationship between actors (177–93). In contrast, the evolution of language allowed communication to focus specifically on subjects other than relationship, such as objects (367).

Thus although we can, of course, communicate about relationships through language, Bateson argues that the vast majority of human communication about relationship is rooted in our prelinguistic mammalian origins. Thus that communication is primarily nonlinguistic. We convey it through kinesic and paralinguistic signals such as facial expression, involuntary tensions of voluntary muscles, tone, pitch, tempo shifts, hesitations, respiratory irregularities, and so forth (367–70). These signals are metaphors that stand for fuller responses, as a playful nip symbolizes a real bite. Whereas metaphoric nonverbal communication (or analogic communication) focuses on relationships, verbal language (or digital communication) supports conscious reasoning, which is inherently purposive and focuses more on objects than on relationships.

As language has developed, kinesics and paralanguage have evolved as well, growing richer and more complex, Bateson claims. Analogic, or iconic, communication fulfills needs verbal language is unsuited to meet. As the basis of unconscious primary process thinking, it generates myth, dream, and art. In contrast, he suggests, language and consciousness evolved to enable us to pursue purpose by the shortest logical or causal path. For instance, digital language helps us to categorize and to distinguish proportions. Because it is organized to do such work, consciousness uses linear thinking and heavily screens out information irrelevant to its purposes. Thus it comprises a fraction of the events in the total mind. As a result, Bateson argues, conscious views of the nature of self and world differ systematically from more holistic views.

In contrast, unconscious processes focus on relationship, which involves circuits and systems. Therefore, iconic thinking uses holistic circuits rather than linear patterns. Perception of and communication about relationships takes place mainly through such primary process thinking. Thus metaphor (as the basis of that thinking) characterizes all human communication and plays an indispensable role in it (205). As a result, metaphors reveal our unconscious premises about specific relationships. But perhaps more importantly, metaphors reveal our unconscious premises about relationships and relationality in general. That is, they indicate our assumptions about how to form and conduct relationships, as well as about position, interaction, and the rules of communication. Thus to understand human relationships—and different conceptions of relationships—we must examine our metaphoric thinking.

According to Bateson, relationship as such "*is* the exchange of messages."[3] States such as "'dependency,' 'hostility,' 'love,'" are actually "patterns immanent in the combination of exchanged messages" (275). As humans establish such patterns unconsciously in infancy, we form habits that operate below the level of consciousness. Bateson argues that habit economizes time and energy. As he explains, human communication relies on circuits that carry neurophysiological messages to produce perception. Those circuits generate feedback loops that carry messages initiated both within and outside the body, and these messages prompt adaptive change. Through such feedback loops, we form abstractions based on our relevant experiences. We learn to perceive and respond to particular *kinds* of signals from our environment. These abstractions produce habits that free learning energy to deal with new problems (257–58).

By shaping our processes of interacting with others, habit produces character traits that arise from our unconscious relational patterns. Thus for Bateson, character traits emerge from the relational habits we develop in early childhood. These habits produce a perspective that is neither true nor false but, as Bateson says, "a way of *punctuating events*" (300). Because they form in primary process thinking, Bateson concludes that the unconscious contains "not only repressed material but also the *habits* of gestalt perception" (301). Thus metaphoric primary process thinking generates the message patterns that constitute both our relationships and our relational habits.

Yet this thinking remains largely ignored by our conscious, purposive rationality. Because metaphoric thinking emerges from our systemic nature, linear purposive thinking has difficulty grasping it. Bateson emphasizes the systemic nature of our internal biological and communicational systems, arguing that they are actually subsystems within larger systems that include both our physical and social environments. Using examples of the blind person's cane and the scientist's microscope, he shows that the communication circuits that shape us extend beyond the physical body. Ultimately, we are subsystems within the world ecosystem. Accordingly, our communication circuits exist at the level of the brain, the brain-body combination, and the individual-environment combination.

But the limits of consciousness tend to make the systemic nature of self and world imperceptible to consciousness (Bateson 450). Because consciousness by nature screens out the majority of available information to focus on that which furthers its purpose, it encourages us to see the world as a chain of causal events rather than as a network of circuits. Thus it tends to blind us to our systemic nature (internal and external). Of course, such purposive, linear thinking plays a crucial role in humans' survival. Nonetheless, it poses a crucial danger, namely that conscious purpose can override the balance of bodily, social, and ecological levels of system. Therefore it can generate pathologies because we often try to change certain variables without understanding the systemic consequences (451).

Bateson argues that because we tend to modify our environment rather than our behaviors, we risk maximizing particular variables at the expense of systemic balance. Western epistemology, he holds, particularly encourages this tendency and therefore fosters pathologies. Citing the alcoholic's mind-over-body thinking as an extreme example, he contends that a competitive epistemology undergirds the Western worldview. As a result, we attempt to outdo one another and our own bodies in competitive symmetrical relationships rather than establishing complementary relationships where appropriate. By encouraging mutually destructive behaviors such as addiction, arms races, and efforts to control rather than complement our natural environment, this worldview poses serious risks to human (and world) survival. Bateson declares, "If we deeply and even unconsciously believe that our relation to the largest system which concerns us—the 'Power greater than self'—is symmetrical and emulative, then we are in error" (336). In his view, the price for such error is high: "It is doubtful whether a species having *both* an advanced technology *and* this strange way of looking at its world can endure" (337).

Because linear, purposive rationality filters our pictures of the world through narrow causal lenses, it often prompts us to respond to systemic crises with blame and projection. That is, we fail to see ourselves as part of the system containing the problem, and we blame either the system or ourselves, rather than modifying our role within the system. Because our systemic world precludes the possibility of "simple lineal control," the only remedy is for us to learn how to think systemically (443–44).

To do so, we need to integrate our metaphoric primary process thinking with our purposive rationality. In Bateson's terms, this means integrating the categorizing communication of linear rationality with the metaphoric, relationship-focused language of primary process thinking. In other words, we need to revise our "*habits* of gestalt perception" and communication.

Bateson's work with various psychological disorders illustrates the need for a systemic balance between the two kinds of thinking. As his research illustrates, maximizing metaphor produces schizophrenia, while maximizing purposive rationality produces neurosis. Schizophrenics fail to recognize the metaphoric—rather than literal—nature of fantasy. In contrast, neurotics fail to recognize the truth within fantasy's metaphors (which they usually repress or discount). To survive at both the individual and species levels, Bateson contends, we must learn to operate more holistically by integrating levels of mind (conscious, unconscious, and external). That is, to understand ourselves as parts of a system, we must understand ourselves relationally, as parts of the whole, rather than trying to maximize our own good as individuals or as a species. We can develop this understanding by working to integrate metaphoric and linear thinking.

Such change is difficult. Our character traits or habits of gestalt perception form self-validating worldviews. Nonetheless, Bateson notes that such fundamental changes do occur as a result of "psychotherapy, religious conversion, and in other sequences in which there is profound reorganization of character" (301). Such changes call into question the basic abstractions of worldviews such as competitive or complementary relating. Because they revise the habits that form our relationships (and thus our identities), these changes "denote a profound redefinition of the self" (304).

Such change involves a fundamental shift in epistemology, like that of the recovering alcoholic. An epistemological shift by nature changes one's rules for perceiving and understanding experiences (as does, for instance, a shift from competitive to complementary thinking). In other words, it changes our established habits of primary process (or metaphoric) thinking. Psychotherapy can facilitate such changes, Bateson argues, by acting like play. That is, it can enable patients and therapists to experiment with the unconscious rules that shape the patient's communications and thus his relationships. Such changes can emerge through experimentation with these rules within a safe context

(191–92). Bateson's descriptions of therapeutic methods emphasize that in this play, therapists try to bring patients to recognize the contradictions inherent within their foundational rules or assumptions. Through this process, these typically unconscious presumptions enter awareness at least partially. Such awareness opens them to question and change. When it succeeds, this process can allow people to form new foundational presumptions more readily (as adults); close the loopholes we use to escape our worldviews' contradictions; help people change the habits resulting from our foundational premises; promote recognition of unconscious learning's role in shaping us; help us to direct such learning; and encourage us to recognize how particular contexts foster particular kinds of learning (302–3).

Bateson proposes two ways of cultivating such changes, particularly the change from individualist to systemic thinking. Although acknowledging that such change is extremely difficult, he contends that it is possible. First, he explains that changing the rules of communication within an established system in itself promotes systemic revision. Because communication involves the flow of messages through circuits, "to act or be one end of a pattern of interaction is to propose the other end. A context is set for a certain class of response" (275). Thus, a change in the expected pattern on one end of the circuit prompts a change on the other end. Based on studies of porpoise-trainer interaction, Bateson concludes that whereas such changes can cause "severe pain and maladjustment," if met generatively, "the total experience may promote creativity" in the form of new behaviors (278). Thus developing awareness of our unconscious relational rules and experimenting with them can promote revisions of identity.

Second, Bateson argues that holistic experiences make us more aware of our systemic selves by broadening the view purposive rationality offers. Such experiences include love, art, poetry, dreams, music, the humanities, and religion. They integrate levels of mind (unconscious, conscious, and external) and so encourage change in our unconscious premises. By learning to adopt the view they cultivate, we can better optimize systems' balance rather than maximizing particular variables. In doing so, we move away from fostering pathology and toward cultivating systemic health.

This systemic approach directly addresses the concerns and goals of critical ethnographers. First, it fundamentally revises the researcher's relation to the other (her subjects). Specifically, it suggests ethnographers integrate our concerns with the literary and reflexive dimensions of our texts. By calling us to attend both to our subjects' metaphors and to our own as a way of understanding foundational premises and interactional rules, Bateson's work puts a literary approach in the service of the reflexivity critical ethnographers advocate. At the same time, his work also uses this literary approach to promote the social change many critical ethnographers desire. It does so by encouraging researchers to scrutinize and revise our own roles within the system. In Bateson's view, such change is perhaps the most viable way to pursue social transformation. He holds that control in a nonlinear world is a question "more akin to art than to science, not only because we tend to think of the difficult and the unpredictable as contexts for art but also because the results of error are likely to be ugliness" (268). He suggests that social scientists replace our desire to control the world with "a more ancient, but today less honored, motive: a curiosity about the world of which we are part. The rewards of such work are not power but beauty" (269). Critical ethnography, with its focus on reflexivity and the literary dimensions of representation, seems well positioned to undertake such work.

As ethnographers, we can draw on Bateson's work in two ways. First, we can try to craft our ethnographies as works of art that integrate levels of mind (unconscious, conscious, and external). Second, we can use the analytic sections of our texts to engage in the serious play Bateson describes. That is, we can analyze our own metaphors to bring our unconscious relational rules into awareness and to experiment rhetorically with alternative sets of rules. In doing so, we can change our roles within the systems we study (and inhabit, given Bateson's understanding of the global social system).

GESTALT: ACCESSING METAPHORS

In this section, I show how Gestalt theory's emphasis on play with metaphors can help us extend Bateson's work to produce research studies that effectively pursue critical ethnography's goals. Based in early twentieth-century experiments with visual perception, Gestalt postulates that humans perceive both material and psychological phenomena in wholes or patterns, rather than in fragmented units. Bateson draws on early Gestalt research in his work. Some of the school's later branches have focused on clinical and organizational psychology applications to extend Gestalt theory. One of these branches has developed from a 1951 text still considered foundational in the field, namely Perls, Hefferline, and Goodman's *Gestalt Therapy: Excitement and Growth in the Human Personality.*

Like Bateson, Perls et al. emphasize the role of metaphor and of kinesic and paralinguistic signals in communication, relational habits, and—ultimately—personality. In the first half of the book, they offer experiments for the reader to undertake in charting how she embodies tensions and what those particular embodiments accomplish (and mean).[4] One such experiment urges readers to correlate such tensions with "appropriate expressions of popular speech" to understand them:

> I am stiff-necked; am I stubborn? I have a pain in the neck; what gives me a pain in the neck? I stretch my head high; am I haughty? I stick my chin out;

am I leading with it? My brows arch; am I supercilious? I have a catch in my throat; do I want to cry? I am whistling in the dark; am I afraid of something? My flesh creeps; am I horrified? My brows beetle; am I full of rage? I feel swollen; am I ready to burst with anger? My throat is tight; is there something I can't swallow? My middle feels queasy; what can't I stomach? (165)

The accessibility of such common figures of speech makes them a useful heuristic for understanding one's responses and relational patterns. For Perls et al. our kinesics and paralinguistics embody metaphors that denote fuller responses an individual is curbing. If such restraint becomes chronic, they argue, it produces long-term bodily tensions that generate problems from bad backs to headaches to stomach ailments. From their perspective, one can develop awareness, first of the tension, next of what it restrains, and finally of alternative ways of coping with the underlying response other than by repressing it. Like Bateson's research on mammalian communication, schizophrenia, and neurosis, Perls et al.'s work with metaphor holds that it reveals fundamental attitudes, assumptions, and stances that, taken together, form our identities. Further, the Gestalt theorists suggest analyzing kinesics and paralinguistics to identify our underlying metaphors. They build on that work by then advising readers to analyze such metaphors as a basis for recognizing and revising their foundational assumptions.

Like Bateson, Gestalt theorist Joseph Zinker holds that the primary process thinking that forms our perceptions is fundamentally figurative.[5] Like Perls et al. he uses kinesics and paralinguistics to bring unconscious metaphorics and their attendant foundational assumptions into awareness. Zinker believes the experienced world (or the phenomenological world) is inherently personal and private because our individual psychophysiological processes shape it. Thus he advocates what he calls *phenomenological listening*. In this approach, one hears an other's experience in that person's terms instead of trying to interpret it. Rather than accessing an other's unmediated experience in doing so, "we allow this experience of the system to evoke figures, images, and metaphors in ourselves" (*In Search* 34). In Bateson's terms, the phenomenological listener uses systemic primary process thinking rather than linear purposive, rational thinking in attending to another person. As a result, his perception can "organize itself around another's wholeness" by focusing on the process, rather than content, of interactions (*Body Process* xiv).

This approach involves attending to interlocutors' figurative language and embodied metaphorics. Describing an example interlocutor, Zinker says, "If we construct a 'process picture' of him, made of his words, his voice, his physical choreography, his way of gazing sadly, then that picture, that idea, that metaphor will 'pull for' seeing a part of his wholeness" (*Body Process* xiv). Although Zinker emphasizes that this picture is neither objective nor complete, he contends that it can offer insights "where awareness has not yet traveled" (*Body Process* xiv). By using metaphor to foster a systemic rather than linear perception, phenomenological listening can increase awareness of interlocutors' basic assumptions, worldviews, and phenomenological experiences of reality (*Body Process* xiv). Zinker holds that developing such awareness is essential to insight and real self-revision. Thus his work extends Perls et al.'s approach to analyzing metaphor as a means of recognizing and revising unconscious foundational assumptions.

Perls et al.'s work stresses the importance of metaphors in speech as well. It does so by emphasizing the role of rhetorical habits in shaping perception and identity:

> From one angle, it is useful to define "personality" as a structure of speech habits and consider it as a creative act of the second and third years; most thinking is subvocal speaking; basic beliefs are importantly habits of syntax and style; and almost all evaluation that does not spring directly from organic appetites is likely to be a set of rhetorical attitudes. . . . A child forming his personality by learning to speak is making a spectacular achievement. . . . We may think of the sequence (a) pre-verbal social relations of the organism, (b) the formation of a verbal personality in the organism/environment field, (c) the subsequent relations of this personality with the others. Clearly the right cultivation of speech is one that keeps this sequence flexibly open and creative throughout: habits that allow what is pre-verbal to flow freely and that can learn from the others and be altered. (321)

As in Zinker's phenomenological listening, here the emphasis shifts from the content of what is said to the process used to say it. That is, Perls et al. emphasize that perception (as shaped by "basic beliefs") is structured by "*habits* of syntax and style." Similarly, evaluation is structured by "a set of rhetorical attitudes." Thus by attending to such rhetorical habits as processes that shape perception, we can bring foundational assumptions into awareness and open them to question and change, as we do in phenomenological listening.

Perls et al.'s description of identity formation implicitly recalls Bateson's characterization of the relationship between primary process thinking and language-based purposive thinking. The Gestalt theorists' "pre-verbal social relations" parallel primary process thinking, whereas "the formation of a verbal personality in the organism/environment field" and "the subsequent relations of this personality with the others" evoke the sublimation of that thinking into relational habits and conscious purposive rationality. Their speech ideal, which would "allow what is pre-verbal to flow freely," suggests the importance of thawing relational habits and integrating metaphoric primary process thinking with linear thinking. By emphasizing rhetorical habits (such as language-based metaphors), they extend Bateson's and Zinker's work with the embodied metaphors enacted through kinesic and paralinguistic cues. By advising readers to examine such metaphors for the foundational premises they reveal, these theorists provide a method to pursue the work Bateson's research suggests is necessary. They do so by extending Zinker's phenomeno-logical—or systemic—listening more explicitly to speech, as well as to kinesics and paralinguistics.

More recent work by Gestalt theorist Gordon Wheeler has developed this method further. Like Bateson's work, Wheeler's advocates accessing foun-dational assumptions by examining people's relational habits. By insisting that such examination requires participation in an interactional exchange, Wheeler implicitly invokes Bateson's circuit-based model of communication. Such work, he explains, makes possible the recognition of foundational premises, a recognition that opens those premises to question and change:

> . . . therapeutic change flows from *going to the contact that is possible[,]* and . . .
> the complex interpersonal intervention of joining-and-analyzing that contact
> process, thereby destructuring it, unblocks the rich and spontaneous possibil-
> ity of a new and more satisfying creative adjustment, a new organization of
> self in the field . . . gestalt formation means a resolution of figure and ground,
> in terms of each other . . . ground resolution is itself highly structured and
> enduring over time[,] and . . . our understanding of contact and of our clients
> is enhanced by direct attention to these ground structures. (145–46)

For Wheeler, *ground* is much like the habits of primary process thinking Bate-son characterizes as established in early life and thereafter stored in the uncon-scious as the internalized perceptual practices that shape our understandings of the world.[6] *Figure* here denotes the focus of a person's awareness at a given time. To form a new gestalt, or perceptual whole, one must integrate the inter-nalized habits of ground with the focus of a current awareness. This integra-tion involves partial revisions of both the structures of ground (or habits of pri-mary process thinking) and the initial perception of whatever person, interaction, or object is figural. Thus to evoke change, the figure must connect with existing structures of ground. Wheeler describes this process as best facil-itated by explicit engagement in and examination of an interaction. Such examination of course includes both embodied and language-based metaphors. The combination of engagement and analysis enables the interlocutors to rec-ognize the foundational assumptions structuring their responses.

Thus "destructuring" the contact process involves developing awareness of relational patterns and the presumptions grounding them. The resulting "rich and spontaneous possibility of a new and more satisfying creative adjust-ment" in and of itself opens the newly recognized presumptions to scrutiny and change. That is, Wheeler's approach provides a method for pursuing Bateson's view of therapy as a way of changing people's relational habits or rules of communication. The resulting "new organization of self in the field" entails a revision of one's way of relating to her environment. This kind of revision is necessary to accomplish Bateson's goal of preparing people to think systemically as well as in linear mode. Thus Wheeler's method elaborates those Perls et al. and Zinker provide. As a result, it enables us to work productively with the insights Bateson's work offers.

Perls et al.'s theory of organism-environment contact and change clarifies how the awareness offered by Wheeler's method fosters such change in people's relational habits:

> The process of creative adjustment to new material circumstances always involves a phase of aggression and destruction, for it is by approaching, laying hold of, and altering old structures that the unlike is made like. When a new configuration comes into being, both the old achieved habit of the contacting organism and the previous state of what is approached and contacted are destroyed in the interest of the new contact. Such destruction of the status quo may arouse fear, interruption and anxiety . . . but the process is accompanied by the security of the new invention experimentally coming into being. Here as everywhere the only solution of a human problem is experimental invention. The anxiety is "tolerated" not by Spartan fortitude . . . but because the disturbing energy flows into the new figure. (232–33)

In Perls et al.'s view, change in one part of a system (or communicational circuit) precipitates change throughout the system because of its inherently relational nature. That is, "both the old achieved habit of the contacting organism and the previous state of what is approached and contacted are destroyed in the interest of the new contact." For instance, when one begins to think in complementary rather than competitive terms, the status of others in one's environment shifts. First, one perceives those others as potential partners rather than as potential competitors. Second, one's kinesic and paralinguistic signals to those others change as a result of one's revised perceptions. Therefore others receive very different messages about specific interactions and their overall relationships with the changed individual. In Bateson's terms, the pattern of interaction proposed is now very different. The new pattern provides a transformed context for others' responses. By altering one's initiatory communication, one implicitly proposes a different response. Others' reactions are likely to change accordingly. In short, Perls et al.'s understanding of organism-environment contact fleshes out Bateson's broad view of how changes in individuals' thinking can promote systemic change.

In doing so, their model provides tools for using Bateson's work to produce critical ethnographies more effectively. To begin, we can recognize that one of the most productive ways for us to encourage social change is to use our ethnographies to revise our selves and our relations with the systems in which we live and work. First, by learning to understand our texts as artistic undertakings, we can expand our capacities to think systemically. That re-orientation will fundamentally enlarge—and shift—the kinds of insights we generate through our research. It will revise our choices and uses of theoretical frameworks and our uses and interpretations of our data. Second, by including analyses of our own and subjects' metaphors in those interpretations, we can recognize and potentially alter relational habits that perpetuate inequity, social conflict, misunderstanding, and disrespect. By examining our subjects' metaphors, we can increase our understanding of their foundational assumptions and perceptual habits. Thus we can use such analyses to promote critical ethnography's goals of social harmony and change.

RHETORICAL ETHNOGRAPHY: USING METAPHORS

This section draws on composition studies work with metaphor to show how ethnographers can use Bateson's and Gestalt theorists' work to enact a dialogue between researcher and subjects. We can do so by crafting a rhetorical form that juxtaposes metaphors from different—even incommensurable—discourses and uses analysis to put those metaphors into dialogue.

Compositionist Kristie Fleckenstein draws on Bateson's work to flesh out her notion of "somatic writing," an embodied practice that integrates metaphoric and linear thinking. By associating metaphoric thinking with embodied experience (and primary process thinking), Fleckenstein links it to immersion in one's phenomenological experience. In contrast, she associates linear thinking with simile (and discourse) and thus links it to emergence from one's experience. "Immersion, reflecting the metaphoric *is* logic of corporeal coding, and emergence, reflecting the *as if* logic of discursive coding, are dialectically related in nonlinear, undulating movements" (295). Because embodied experience makes us more aware of our physical, social, and other contexts, it inherently promotes the systemic thinking Bateson advocates. Because discursive thinking prompts us to categorize, consider causality, and recognize gradations, it promotes analysis.

Fleckenstein argues that somatic writing must include both kinds of mental processes to integrate systemic thinking into conscious linear thinking. Through immersion, we can experience and respond to our various contexts; mentally evoke our readers; and write from our subjectivities. Through emergence, we can examine "the abstract *as if* logic of politics, of ideology, of hegemony." As a result, we return to "the responsibility of and for boundaries" (297–98). For Fleckenstein, this combination brings the systemic awareness of primary process thinking and embodied experience into conscious, discursive thought:

The crucial qualities of writing somatically are not formal but (dis)positional, and . . . require a commitment "to partiality, irony, intimacy, and perversity" (Haraway, *Simians* 151). To embody writing, writers must make a contradictory but complementary commitment to immersion and emergence. Immersion is characterized by the moments in writing (and living) when the boundaries between self and reality dissolve, when we experience that slippage between the *is* and the *as if.* It is not a transcendence of or an ascent beyond the transacting levels of context, but a burrowing into . . . identity and . . . place. As writers and as knowers, we come to be *only* by our engagement with(in) a multilayered corporeal scene. . . . Essential to immersion is the sense that individual (and rhetorical) subjectivity is an amalgam of actor, action, and environment. . . . Knowledge of the world and the self, [Morris] Berman explains, results when a "not self" and a "self" permeate each other. Selfother (somatic mind) exists because the mutual blurring of boundaries between inside and outside create the being-in-a-material-place. Self is not lost in the process; awareness of self as a discrete organism separate (and separable) from one's environment is lost.[7] (295–96)

As Fleckenstein demonstrates, the integration of embodied, positioned awareness with linear thinking promotes a revised sense of self—one that recognizes self as part of its environment and structured by that environment. This revised self-awareness is precisely the systemic thinking Bateson advocates. Fleckenstein's work is useful because she offers a method for encouraging that thinking through a particular writing practice. Specifically, she suggests that in writing we should cultivate and draw on our embodied awarenesses while developing discursive thinking as well. Because fostering that embodied awareness amplifies metaphoric, primary process thinking, it brings such thinking into our written texts. In doing so, it teases this unconscious thinking into our conscious awareness. Not only does that process open such unconscious thinking to scrutiny and analysis, it fundamentally revises our prior patterns of linear, purposive thinking. That is, in Perls et al.'s terms, it changes "the old achieved habit of the contacting organism." Thus Fleckenstein's somatic writing provides a compositional approach to pursuing the work advocated by Bateson and undertaken by Gestalt theorists.

I build on Fleckenstein's approach in "Writing Awareness," an essay on the way ethnographic writing can foster a dialogue among metaphoric systems to revise instructors' understandings of teacher-student dynamics. Specifically, I use a case from my own teaching to explore how an instructor can access and analyze her own embodied metaphorics. Examining my metaphors prompted me to attend more closely to students'. In the process, I realized that my embodied metaphorics in fact conflicted with my consciously held pedagogical beliefs and values. As the article shows, I used this recognition to begin training myself to attend to the metaphorics I embody in the classroom. As a result, this work allows me to expand my awareness of the communication patterns I am initiating with students and, in Bateson's terms, inviting them to complete.

This kind of analysis is equally fruitful in ethnographic encounters. To apply it in ethnographic research, I propose several steps. First, as ethnographer, I attend to the embodied metaphors enacted by people in the field—both by subjects and researcher. Second, I also attend to language-based metaphors used in the field. Third, I attend to the figurative language that emerges as I draft the ethnographic text generated out of such field research. In this approach to ethnography, part of that text's work involves emphasizing and analyzing all three sets of metaphors. This ethnographic composing process extends Fleckenstein's somatic writing by explicitly incorporating embodied awareness into the text both as representation (in the depiction of subjects' and researchers' figures) and as topic of analysis. In the spirit of literary ethnography, I propose crafting the text to foreground the various sets of metaphors encountered, not only by analyzing them but also by weaving them substantively into the narrative.

This combination of literary emphasis and analytic examination can help researchers develop a more reflexive, more dialogic form of ethnographic writing. Just as "Writing Awareness" examines the metaphorics I embodied while teaching, we as ethnographers can examine the metaphors we embody in the field and in our texts' depictions. In doing so, we can increase awareness of our foundational assumptions and how they shape our perception and representation of our research subjects and sites. In the process, we can also explore subjects' metaphors and take stock of how researcher's and subjects' figures harmonize, conflict, or remain disconnected. In pursuing this process in "Writing Awareness," I learned that I wanted to shift some of the embodied metaphorics I was enacting in my teaching. Thus the composing process made my teaching more reflexive by fostering a dialogue between my metaphorics and my students' metaphorics. Using this process in ethnographic research can prompt similar recognitions. The next section demonstrates how I have undertaken a comparable path in my ethnographic work as I compose the representation of a community literacy project I studied.

Rhetorical Ethnography: An Example

Using the rhetorical ethnography just described, I conclude by depicting an impasse that arose between my and my research subjects' figurative systems. Through this depiction, I show how ethnographers can use a rhetorical form that crafts a dialogue between such conflicting figures to promote personal and systemic change.

This particular conflict arose during my research on "Struggle," a community literacy program designed to support urban teens and parents in examining and pursuing their life goals. In the process of that work, they strengthen key relationships and support systems. As one of "Struggle's" four planner-facilitators, I played a role that combined participation with observation. Currently, I am writing a book that includes two ethnographic chapters on the program. Of the various stories I tell, one focuses on how those of us in the planning group negotiated our differences in designing "Struggle" and building coalition among ourselves.

I chart how my own metaphorics intersected—and conflicted—with those of the other planners.[8] By analyzing the foundational assumptions my own metaphors reveal, I examine how my perceptual habits shaped my understanding of subjects' (my colleagues') worldviews. Because this analysis enables me to grasp the conflict between my metaphorics and my subjects', it helps me to recognize how my stance as a researcher initiated a particular relational pattern or, in Bateson's terms, a particular communicational circuit. In the process of composing ethnographic depictions of "Struggle," I realized that through this stance, I set the stage for a narrow range of possible responses from research subjects. This realization brought me new awareness of my discomfort with the research stance I was using, a discomfort I had not previously recognized. As a result, it prompted me to initiate what Wheeler calls the "rich and spontaneous possibility of a new and more satisfying creative adjustment" or what Perls et al. call a revision of "the old, achieved habit of the contacting organism." These steps have involved, in large part, the quest for a revised metaphorics and practices for internalizing that metaphorics. Although the figures I found did not spring directly from my subjects' metaphors, the process of crafting a rhetorical ethnography that put those metaphoric systems into dialogue helped to initiate my search. In addition, this composing process has furthered both the search and the project of internalizing a new set of figures.

The conflict between my metaphors and those of my "Struggle" colleagues emerged periodically, although not always explicitly, in our interactions. Rooted in our divergent visions of social change, this conflict often arose in our planning discussions of how to produce program materials that would inspire participants. Because "Struggle" is grounded in a Presbyterian church and often engages participants precisely through that grounding, we intermittently discussed the possibility of using Judeo-Christian symbols and language in program materials.

On one occasion, Wayne, "Struggle"'s leading architect and the church's pastor, expressed his frustration at needing to use such symbols implicitly rather than explicitly. Joyce, another "Struggle" planner and an elder of the church, had just asked Wayne whether the path depicted in "Struggle"'s logo was inspired by the path imagery linked to a "personal exodus" of life work, a motif church members often associated with the Old Testament's exodus story. Confirming her guess, Wayne explained his frustration at the sense that he could not articulate the religious ends implied by "Struggle"'s Christian roots. "Do you notice the problem we're having in suggesting what is the 'end'?" he asked. "This coming kingdom of God is this place where there is equity and peace and justice."

Wanting to suggest an alternative conception of that end, I mentioned a book I had recently read that argued that the progressivist *telos* amounted to a reworking of the Judeo-Christian millennialist narrative.[9] Wayne replied that progressivists had reinvented that tradition's mythology, "the dream of the human race, that there is a promise that you'll be in a right relationship with others." He continued, "The difference is that with kids in the community, I am constrained from saying that there is such a thing as redemption." After further conversation, he concluded, "I think that one of the problems that we are having with 'Struggle,' and it's a real intellectual weakness, is that we haven't suggested what the *telos* of life is, or suggested that life has promise."

Reflecting later on the conversation, I realized that I had not managed to articulate why I saw the progressivist reworking of Judeo-Christian mythology as so significant. During other conversations with my "Struggle" colleagues, I tried to explain that my particular experience of a Roman Catholic childhood had led me to understand that version of the myth as a story of self-negation, an ethics of guilt and the renunciation of all worldly joy. In contrast, my graduate school encounters with critical theory had offered another kind of redemption narrative in (post-)Marxist theory. That story similarly emphasizes peace, equity, and justice, as well as wholesale social change.

Its critiques of social, economic, and cultural inequities as systemically produced problems strongly imply the need for sweeping change that would replace all existing institutions and practices with new versions. Such theory tends to critique small-scale or gradual change as a form of accommodation or, worse yet, complicity. In short, it takes root in a metaphorics of revolution. For instance, in an argument for the importance of theory, Louis Althusser quotes Lenin: "'Without revolutionary theory, no revolutionary practice'" (166). To produce such theory, Althusser argues, one must engage in critique:

> But . . . theoretical *expression* of a solution that exists in the practical state cannot be taken for granted: it requires a real theoretical labour, not only to work out the specific *concept* or *knowledge* of this practical resolution—but also for the real destruction of the ideological confusions, illusions, or inaccuracies that may exist, by a radical critique (a critique which takes them out by the root). So this . . . theoretical "expression" implies both the *production* of a knowledge and the *critique* of an illusion, in one movement. (165–66, emphasis is in original text)

Taking out illusions by the root suggests removal of a weed, just as the destruction of illusions or inaccuracies implies that clearing such obstructions enables us to access the truth. (Althusser argues that we can reach truth through a materialist dialectic that pushes inherent contradictions in our knowledges and practices through various stages to resolution). Coupled with his quotation of Lenin, this theorist's figures of speech imply that wholesale social change is necessary and requires the annihilation of incorrect views.

Based on my responses to critical theory, I think such figures must have intersected with the metaphors of my primary process thinking. The same may be true of figurative language from Michel Foucault's work. Unlike Althusser, Foucault downplays the significance of ideology and does not hold that we can reach fundamental truth. In contrast, he emphasizes the institutional and discursive aspects of power, claiming that political theory wrongly tries to understand power by theorizing sovereignty. "What we need, however," he concludes, "is a political philosophy that isn't erected around the problem of sovereignty, nor therefore around the problems of law and prohibition. We need to cut off the King's head: in political theory that still has to be done" (121). To do so, we must re-invent disciplinary and institutional practices: "The problem is not changing people's consciousnesses—or what's in their heads—but the political, economic, institutional régime of the production of truth" (133).

Despite their clear differences on the questions of ideology and truth, I admired both theorists, and as I reflected on my fieldwork, I realized that their figures had merged with the metaphors grounding my own primary process thinking. Like Althusser's imagery, Foucault's symbolic decapitation invokes revolutionary change. To the extent that I enacted that metaphor in my relations with research subjects, I initiated what Bateson would call one side of a relational circuit. That is, I implicitly played the role of a social agitator, suggesting that people make wholesale changes in their thinking, their lives, and their social world.

My reading of Althusser had prompted me to see ideology as a kind of mystification. That view implies the need for *de*mystification, which, in Althusser's argument, emerges as the responsibility of the intellectual. Without conscious awareness (and despite my reservations about Catholicism), I brought into the field a figure of the academic as part of a quasi-priestly class that mediates between people and truth by demystifying the ideologies people presumably cannot understand for themselves. That is, I implicitly invited people to respond as laypersons to a religious authority, whether they reacted as adherents or apostates.

On recognizing and analyzing these metaphors and the foundational assumptions they reveal, I encountered an irony. My own relational stance mirrored the implicitly proselytizing approach I associated with the Christian narrative. Both stances implicitly (and sometimes explicitly) asked others to change themselves and their world, as well as to renounce their existing views, habits, and investments. Although I was uncomfortable with the Christian narrative and concomitant stance my colleagues held, I was in fact enacting a comparable stance with a slightly different content (critical theory). In some moments, we interacted like missionaries from rival churches attempting to convert one another.

I began to recognize this head-to-head relational pattern only toward the end of my fieldwork and afterward as I composed my ethnographic representation of "Struggle" and its evolution as a collective project. In the text, I try to foreground both sets of metaphors, such as my colleagues' path to redemption and my images of social revolution. Through the composing process, I have pursued a version of Wheeler's method of "joining-and-analyzing" the contact between my colleagues and me. Although only part of this joining-and-analyzing took place during the interaction, transcribing tapes of our conversations and examining the dynamics they contained enabled me to pursue the analysis after contact had concluded. In transcribing the tapes and reading (and rereading) the transcripts, I partially relived the initial interactions. While doing so, I allowed the experience to "evoke figures, images, and metaphors" and thus undertook a distanced version of Zinker's phenomenological listening. That evocation encouraged Bateson's systemic primary process thinking. Through a Wheeler-style analysis of the figures evoked, I worked toward a holistic understanding that integrates such primary process thinking with linear thinking.

This work has increased not only my awareness regarding the relational patterns I was initiating but also my understanding of the implications of those patterns. This growing awareness has prompted me to feel distaste for the approach I was unreflectively taking. Although the recognition has been uncomfortable, it has spurred me to begin experimenting textually with metaphors that can help me adopt a revised stance. That is, this awareness has encouraged Wheeler's "new organization of self in the field." It has prompted a new gestalt, or holistic understanding, which entails a "resolution of figure and ground, in terms of each other." In other words, it has prompted me to seek to reconstruct the relational patterns I establish with others, to shift my habits of perception and communication.

I have begun this work in part through the process of composing my ethnography. Rooted in the initial depiction of both sets of metaphors and the analysis of the conflict between them, the work continues in my textual experiments with metaphors that attempt to work toward dialogue. For instance, interaction with "Struggle"'s participants and my colleagues helped me to understand the importance of community members' aesthetics. Thus my ethnography argues that to build coalition with such groups I, as an academic with different aesthetic sensibilities, must learn to respect and incorporate community members' aesthetics into any representations of a community-academy project. I conclude that a dialogic ethnography might undertake such work by weaving critiques of historical determinism into stories highlighting human agency and hope (two key aspects of the community-based aesthetics I encountered). To represent such efforts metaphorically in my text, I suggest that critical theory isolated from community endeavors resembles a spring rill likely to evaporate in summer's heat. By merging with the larger stream of popular discourse and aesthetics, I argue, this rill could help shift the currents of individual and social life. Thus my text's simile proposes a significantly revised stance, a markedly different relational circuit between my subjects/colleagues and me.

Of course, the question is whether and how this simile might shift to metaphor, that is, how it might move from my purposive, linear thinking into the primary process thinking that shapes my kinesic and paralinguistic signals—and thus my relational stance. In Perls et al.'s understanding, this shift takes place as part of the process of encountering and creatively adjusting to "new material circumstances." Such circumstances include new awareness—like my new contact with the form and implications of my relational stance. In adjusting to such new circumstances, I inevitably grasp and alter the old structure (or in Bateson's terms the primary process thinking) that underlies my communicational habits. As a result, I perceive others and interactional situations in a new way because, as Perls et al. explain, "both the old achieved habit of the contacting organism and the previous state of what is approached and contacted are destroyed in the interest of the new contact."

I can chart this gradual change by briefly documenting my search for new metaphors, a search partly initiated by my fieldwork and the process of composing my ethnographic depiction of that fieldwork. The recognition of my stance in relation to others prompted me to seek new figures for change and for my relationship with the larger world. Finding myself drawn toward Zen and Taoist imagery, I read translations of various classic texts from those traditions. Images of water as change agent permeate these works. For instance, the opening lines of chapter 43 of "Te" ("Virtue") in the *Te-Tao Ching* declare, "The softest, most pliable thing in the world runs roughshod over the firmest thing in the world. / That which has no substance gets into that which has no spaces or cracks" (1–2).[10] As in many of the text's verses, softness overcomes hardness, and weakness overcomes strength.[11]

Here change results not from imposition or insistence but from aligning oneself with what is, learning to work with or around existing forces. The text holds up "the Way" as the rules of the universe, rules the wise person strives to recognize (usually in the laws of the natural world) and to practice in personal and social affairs. According to the *Te-Tao Ching*, the Way is the source of both lasting change and personal and social stability. In contrast, the text depicts changes brought about by force as inevitably generating a backlash. Thus chapter 32 of "Tao" concludes, "The Way's presence in the world / Is like the relationship of small valley streams to rivers and seas" (11–12). In contrast with the revolutionary metaphorics of critical theory, the _Te-Tao Ching_'s figures emphasize changes that begin as small initiatory moves and grow in size and strength as they merge with comparable energies. Eventually, such changes join to form the resources—literally, the water resources, metaphorically the social and cultural resources—of an entire world.

By incorporating such imagery into my thinking, as well as my ethnographic text, I have begun the slow process of revising my perceptual habits. This revision involves seeing myself not as an acolyte (a source of demystification) or revolutionary vanguardist (a kind of missionary) but as a small spring. Working in terms of that figure, I ask myself how I can flow around obstacles, and I seek the downhill path toward other streams, that is similar approaches. This effort entails working to change myself rather than others. As the concluding lines of chapter 32 suggest, taking this attitude toward change involves seeing myself as part of a larger system, merging with others moving toward the same ends, and flowing with—rather than against—the terrain. Perhaps even more significantly, it means attempting to recognize and work within a larger systemic balance, seeing myself as a subsystem within a larger whole. In Bateson's terms, it requires optimizing balance rather than pursuing my own goals (even goals like my vision of social justice).

This approach enacts Bateson's holistic thinking in two ways. First, it fundamentally shifts the focus from individualist to systemic perception by prompting me to look at my claims and actions in terms other than the binaries of "true or false," "ethical or unethical," and "just or unjust." Instead, it highlights the kinds of relational circuits my words and actions initiate with others in my environment because it asks whether I am flowing with or around them, rather than against them. Second, because it works through imagery, this approach is inherently artistic. Therefore it forms one of Bateson's means of integrating purposive rationality with primary process thinking. Thus this work is slowly revising the foundational premises that ground my perceptual and relational habits. As a result, it is revising those habits as well.

This revision sprang partly from the composing process I used to depict my ethnographic fieldwork. That is, by crafting a rhetorical ethnography whose form puts my subjects' metaphors and my own in dialogue with one another, I developed awareness that prompted me to pursue these changes. By representing both sets of figures and analyzing their implications, I recognized some of my formerly unaware foundational premises. The resulting discomfort spurred me to seek holistic means of changing those premises.

Thus I argue that the process of composing such a rhetorical ethnography can prompt personal change. Juxtaposing and analyzing researcher and subject metaphorics can increase the researcher's awareness not only of her own foundational premises but also of her relational stance toward subjects and *their* foundational premises. When she encounters tensions between her unaware premises and her conscious values, or when she experiences discomfort or dissatisfaction with those premises, the researcher is spurred to change by her own internal response. Thus such a rhetorical ethnography can promote the researcher's self-revision.

Bateson's work, like that of Perls et al., shows that such individual changes transform relational circuits. As a result, they initiate revisions in the larger systems in which the researcher lives. Because this approach fosters systemic change through efforts to revise self rather than others, it is both more feasible and more ethical for ethnographers. It obviates the problems of paternalism and colonialism by focusing the researcher's impetus toward social change on revising self rather than attempting to persuade or push others into changing. It addresses the problems of ideology and disciplinary discourses by dealing with their effects at the level of the researcher's own practices, namely her relational habits. Thus it revises Harrison's and others' interventionist approach to critical ethnography, enabling us to cultivate systemic change by using our work with others to better see—and change—our selves.

NOTES

1. Marcus and Fischer describe the critical ethnography movement and some of its formative texts in *Anthropology as Cultural Critique*. Mortensen and Kirsch discuss the critical ethnography movement's concerns specifically in relation to composition studies in *Ethics & Representation in Qualitative Studies of Literacy*.

2. For examples of experimental ethnographies, see Austin; McCarthy and Fishman; Mienczakowski; and Schaafsma. Marcus and Fischer, like Mortensen and Kirsch, describe further examples.

3. Emphasis is in the original text unless otherwise noted.

4. A more recent edition of the work places the experiment descriptions after the theoretical section, as the authors originally intended. They reversed the order of the two sections in the 1951 edition to suit their publisher's wishes. Because I cite the 1951 edition, I describe its structure rather than that intended by the authors.

5. Notably, Zinker, with Bateson, also sees schizophrenic delusions as metaphors that reveal some element of truth about key relationships.

6. However, for Wheeler the term *ground* also includes the content of events, relationships, and so forth, that have shaped one's present perceptions and identity.

7. Fleckenstein quotes Donna Haraway's *Simians, Cyborgs, and Women,* and Morris Berman's *Coming to Our Senses.*

8. If space permitted, I would also document and analyze key tensions between community participants' metaphors and my own.

9. See Tuveson.

10. For background on the *Te-Tao Ching* as an earlier version of the *Tao-Te Ching,* see the introductory sections of Hendricks's translation. My interest in these materials developed from my work with Gestalt theory, which was significantly influenced by Zen Buddhism and Taoism.

11. See also chapters 30, 32, and 36 of "Tao," or "The Way."

WORKS CITED

Althusser, Louis. "On the Materialist Dialectic." *For Marx.* Trans. Ben Brewster. New York: Pantheon, 1969, 163–218.

Austin, Deborah A. "Kaleidoscope: The Same and Different." Ellis and Bochner. 206–30.

Bateson, Gregory. *Steps to an Ecology of Mind.* Chicago: U of Chicago P, 2000.

Berman, Morris. *Coming to Our Senses: Body and Spirit in the Hidden History of the West.* New York: Simon & Schuster, 1989.

Ellis, Carolyn, and Arthur P. Bochner, eds. *Composing Ethnography: Alternative Forms of Qualitative Writing.* Ethnographic Alternatives Series. Vol. 1. Walnut Creek, CA: AltaMira, 1996.

Fischer, Michael M. J., and Mehdi Abedi. *Debating Muslims: Cultural Dialogues in Postmodernity and Tradition.* Madison: U of Wisconsin P, 1990.

Fleckenstein, Kristie S. "Writing Bodies: Somatic Mind in Composition Studies." *College Composition and Communication* 61.3 (1999): 281–306.

Fox, Karen V. "Silent Voices: A Subversive Reading of Child Sexual Abuse." Ellis and Bochner. 330–56.

Foucault, Michel. "Truth and Power." *Power/Knowledge: Selected Interviews & Other Writings, 1972–1977.* Ed. Colin Gordon. Trans. Colin Gordon et al. New York: Pantheon, 1980. 109–33.

Gorzelsky, Gwen. "Writing Awareness." *Journal of the Assembly for Expanded Perspectives on Learning.* 6 (2000–01): 29–39.

Haraway, Donna. *Simians, Cyborgs, and Women.* New York: Routledge, 1991.

Harrison, Faye V., ed. *Decolonizing Anthropology: Moving Further toward an Anthropology for Liberation.* Washington, DC: American Anthropological Association, 1991.

Hendricks, Robert G., ed. and trans. *Lao-Tzu Te-Tao Ching.* New York: Ballantine, 1989.

Levi-Strauss, Claude. *Tristes Tropiques.* New York: Random, 1997.

Lu, Min-Zhan and Bruce Horner. "The Problematic of Experience: Redefining Critical Work in Ethnography and Pedagogy." *College English* 60.3 (1998): 257–77.

Marcus, George E. "Rhetoric and the Ethnographic Genre in Anthropological Research." Ruby. 163–71.

Marcus, George E., and Michael M. J. Fischer. *Anthropology as Cultural Critique: An Experimental Moment in the Human Sciences.* Chicago: U of Chicago P, 1986.

McCarthy, Lucille Parkinson, and Stephen M. Fishman. "A Text for Many Voices: Representing Diversity in Reports of Naturalistic Research." Mortensen and Kirsch. 155–76.

Meyerhoff, Barbara, and Jay Ruby. Introduction. Ruby. 1–35.

Mienczakowski, Jim. "An Ethnographic Act: The Construction of Consensual Theatre." Ellis and Bochner. 244–64.

Mortensen, Peter, and Gesa E. Kirsch, eds. *Ethics & Representation in Qualitative Studies of Literacy.* Urbana: NCTE, 1996.

Perls, Frederick, Ralph E. Hefferline, and Paul Goodman. *Gestalt Therapy: Excitement and Growth in the Human Personality.* New York: Dell, 1951.

Rabinow, Paul. "Masked I Go Forward: Reflections on the Modern Subject." Ruby. 173–85.

Ruby, Jay, ed. *A Crack in the Mirror: Reflexive Perspectives in Anthropology.* Philadelphia: U of Pennsylvania P, 1982.

Said, Edward. *Orientalism.* Chicago: Kazi, 1996.

Schaafsma, David. *Eating on the Street: Teaching Literacy in a Multicultural Society.* Pittsburgh Series in Composition, Literacy, and Culture. Pittsburgh: U of Pittsburgh P, 1993.

Tuveson, Ernest Lee. *Millennium and Utopia: A Study in the Background of the Idea of Progress.* New York: Harper, 1964.

Wheeler, Gordon. *Gestalt Reconsidered: A New Approach to Contact and Resistance.* New York: Gardner, 1991.

Zinker, Joseph C. Foreword. *Body Process: A Gestalt Approach to Working with the Body in Psychotherapy.* By James I. Kepner. New York: Gestalt Institute of Cleveland P, 1987. xi–xvii.

———. *In Search of Good Form: Gestalt Therapy with Couples and Families.* Jossey-Bass Social and Behavioral Science Series. San Francisco: Jossey-Bass, 1994.

6

Writing Program Redesign

Learning from Ethnographic Inquiry, Civic Rhetoric,
and the History of Rhetorical Education

LYNÉE LEWIS GAILLET

> In two of the most dynamic eras of its historical development, rhetoric was dialectically involved with accounting for cultural differences, formalizing social conventions, and translating shared beliefs into practical action. This ethnographic dimension is vital if the civic tradition in rhetoric and moral philosophy is to be more than a source of nostalgia for lost republican virtue.
>
> —Thomas Miller, "Rhetoric Within and Without Composition"

IN A RECENT ISSUE OF *Rhetoric Society Quarterly* devoted to feminist historiography, Rich Enos asks, "How can we bring rhetorical events back to life and make them as vivid and meaningful as our colleagues in composition?" He goes on to explain, "gains in composition studies that have been achieved by using ethnographic research methods can serve as an illustration for historians of rhetoric who can hope for similar achievements . . ." (68). As both a historian of rhetoric and a writing program administrator (WPA) at a large urban campus, I find it interesting that both Miller (himself a WPA and a fine historian) and Enos evoke the "ethnographic dimension" in their calls to "bring rhetorical events back to life." Connections between culture and rhetoric have been the focus of scholarship in rhetoric-composition for over two decades. In his opening statement for the Conference on College Composition and Communication (CCCC) 1988 Octolog Panel, Bob Connors (another WPA and fine historian) asked how "culture created rhetoric, and how [has] rhetoric then recreated the culture?" (7). He concluded with the following edict: "Meaningful historical writing must teach us what people in the past have wanted from literacy so that we may come to understand what we want" (7). Connors's 1988 words were prophetic, evidenced in his field by the recent proliferation of published nineteenth-century studies that redefine archival research, methodology, and rhetorical history in terms of social exigencies. Additionally, most of these recent histories concerning nineteenth-century developments in rhetoric-composition adopt the idea or practice of civic rhetoric as a cornerstone for their research and often culminates in a plea to restore instruction in civic rhetoric to the composition classroom. This "plea" for a reexamination of civic rhetoric in nineteenth-century scholarship is echoed in the current scholarship of other rhetorical periods as well. Recently, however, the rhetoric-culture strand of scholarship in the field has increasingly embraced civic rhetoric's connections to and implications for adopting ethnographic pedagogy—herein lies the hope for breathing life into rhetorical events and moving beyond nostalgic considerations of an education based on civic tradition and moral philosophy.

Consider the impact of civic rhetoric (along with accompanying pedagogical strategies) on textbook production, a sometimes-useful way of gauging a theory's chances for survival. The last two decades of composition studies witnessed the publication of classical rhetoric texts that adopted traditional-classical pedagogical exercises designed for first-year writing classes—works that naturally include discussions and exercises in civic rhetoric (see Horner, Crowley and Hawhee; D'Angelo). These texts are gaining popularity, but unfortunately are not yet (and perhaps never will be) widely adopted, in part because teachers are often uncomfortable or resistant to teaching the classical tradition or maybe because teachers and students alike do not make the necessary leap required to translate the study of historical rhetoric into an active skill. However, other recent composition texts— fueled by composition theories and practices such as service learning, ethnographic methodologies, and social process approaches to composition instruction—are reviving theories and practices of civic rhetoric in writing classes in visible ways. These popular texts indirectly offer contemporary applications of ancient rhetorical principles tangibly connected to both students' self-interests and community-based research. For both rhetoric and composition, ethnographic inquiry and community-based research and rhetorical engagement promises to expand notions of civic rhetoric beyond traditional agonistic conceptions of "the good man speaking well," intensify in both subfields an interest in conducting primary research, and to give vitality and immediacy to two courses of study often considered arcane on the one hand and simply utilitarian on the other. This chapter discusses the recent role this revival can play in transforming composition instruction, filtering my discussion of civic rhetoric in curriculum design through the lens of eighteenth- and nineteenth-century classes in moral philosophy, the contemporary concept of the metropolitan university philosophy of education, and the vital role WPAs must adopt if this revival is to go beyond current fashion and impact curriculum across the disciplines.

Linda Flower discusses university and community issues when she writes that "town and gown" relationships have always been strained, have always been marked by asymmetries of power. She also notes that the current enthusiasm for community-based work is at least to some degree a function of cyclical interests, and that this enthusiasm will wane unless community-based work is "rooted in the intellectual agenda of the university" (96). Flower calls for community-based work that is animated by a spirit of inquiry and rooted in the intellectual work of the academy, which means that community-based work must be connected to research.

Community-based work requires research. Any serious interrogation of "community" requires inquiries into the nature and meaning of communities themselves. And any serious, sustained community-based work that avoids the cyclical attentions of academic fashion requires the sustained activities that community-based research can provide. One way, then, of working through the problems of cyclical interests in community-based work and the relatively narrow views of community is to focus on the research functions of writing programs and to pick up on much older rhetorical traditions in the form of a renewed focus on civic rhetoric in our writing programs. Tom Miller tells us that "a civic philosophy of rhetoric can enable us to bring our work with service learning, new technologies, and political controversies into a unified project that challenges the hierarchy of research, teaching, and service that limits the social implications of academic work and devalues the work of the humanities" ("Rhetoric Within" 34). If we adopt Miller's stance, then civic rhetoric becomes the catalyst not only for what we do in the English department and the university but also a powerful catalyst for refiguring our work outside the university as well. These ideas are not novel but rather call for a return to the ideal of the eighteenth-century public intellectual.

EIGHTEENTH-CENTURY CLASSES IN MORAL PHILOSOPHY

During the late eighteenth century, professors of moral philosophy in the British cultural provinces included the study of English literature, composition, and rhetoric in their course curriculum—all students were required to take these courses. Working in the margins of the British realm, moral philosophy professors such as Adam Smith and John Witherspoon were training their students to compete with Oxford- and Cambridge-educated students for jobs and social position. These first professors to teach English studies could be defined as "civic rhetoricians," professors "concerned with the political art of negotiating received beliefs against changing situations to advance shared purposes" (Miller, *The Formation of College English* 34). In many cases, these professors delivered public lectures in English to citizens interested in social, political, and economic advancement, and later the curriculum of the public lectures found its way into the university courses. Of note, the universities of Edinburgh and Glasgow were also urban and governed in part by town councils comprising local citizens and merchants who encouraged changes in university curriculum to reflect concerns of business and local industry. Core courses in moral philosophy addressed these interests and concerns.

Moral philosophy classes, particularly in the late-eighteenth-century universities in Scotland, concerned rhetoric, economics, and ethics while promoting "a conception of language that emphasized the moral value of the study of aesthetics" (Court 14). Paving the way for later courses in moral philosophy, Adam Smith, chairman of the Moral Philosophy and Logic Department at Glasgow University from 1751 to 1764, modified his novel Edinburgh University course (1748–1751) to merge his thoughts on literary criticism with his interests in ethics and economics. Franklin Court explains, "The philosophical rationale behind his case for the formal study of English literature was closely connected to his thoughts on 'sympathy' and his argument for the education of the 'good man' (the 'good bourgeois') and 'studious observer'" (12). Smith's civic humanism, traced to Cicero's thoughts on civic duty, prompted him to devise a course of study that would eventually link the self-interest of his students with public concerns. Smith believed that the formal study of literary characters' ethical and unethical behavior—based on "close textual examination and interpretation"—would lead students "to share experiences and feelings over time through a process of associative, imitative identification that naturally approved good acts and deplored evil ones" (Court 12). Smith was enormously influential, and subsequent classes in logic and moral philosophy reflect his influence. Like moral philosophy classes of the eighteenth century, composition courses remain our core requirement for all students and provide unique teaching moments for blending students' self-interests with civic participation. Obviously, the Scottish democratic ideal of education is not the same "democratic ideal" we hold today, but the moral philosophy classes still have much to teach us as we revise the aims of writing instruction to include civic concerns. "If we truly feel that we writing teachers are the heirs of the rhetorical tradition," explains Bruce Herzberg, "we may take great comfort in making this connection the basis of a civic discourse pedagogy." Viewing the aims of communication in terms of civic rhetoric has the potential for changing the face of contemporary English departments (and institutions of higher learning) as well. Indeed, numerous composition teachers have already refigured writing courses along these lines (see course designs in Shamoon et al.). Deeper curricular changes, however, begin with changes in writing program (re)design. Civic rhetoric and service learning provide frameworks for education—and "good" writing and writing instruction—in terms of preparing our students to enter local communities in hopes of advancing the common good in the face of changing political needs. As Elizabeth Ervin tells us, "because it immerses us in the discourses and behaviors of civic participation, service learning provides us with a case study of what it means to write with a civic tongue—that is, to write truthfully and responsibly in ways that are consistent with the democratic processes our profession purportedly values" ("Learning to Write" 145).

The question that comes to mind for many educators, however, is whether civic discourse should be the focus of modern rhetorical education, particularly in light of narrow cultural or institutional expectations that insist students simply need to learn conventions of academic discourse in entry-level writing courses. Educators who question whether composition teachers are now dictating morality rather than teaching writing skills pose a larger philosophical objection to writing classes with a civic bent. I am not apologetic in advocating that students should take moral responsibility for their own actions and a moral interest in local communities. However, I do not advocate dictating moral beliefs or actions. In the courses I envision at my institution, students pick which communities they wish to enter (usually based on their own religious or personal beliefs, prior experiences or interests, or responses to local issues), and teachers and administrators help provide access to the sites while teaching skills necessary for meaningful rhetorical engagement. I think the answer to the question of whether we should include the realm of civic rhetoric in our writing classes is a resounding yes, supported by recent critical pedagogy scholarship, the New American College movement sponsored by the Carnegie Foundation, and the metropolitan university philosophy of education (defined in the following section) adopted by many urban universities across the country.

Defining Metropolitan Universities

Hathaway, Mulhollan, and White define the *metropolitan university* as an institution that embraces an "interactive philosophy" leading to the establishment of a "symbiotic relationship" with its metropolitan area (9). Universities adopting this "interactive philosophy" have formed the Coalition of Urban and Metropolitan Universities, which provides a network of annual conferences, publications, and grants for its members to unite "universities that share the mission of striving for national excellence while contributing to the economic development, social health, and cultural vitality" of urban and metropolitan areas *(Information on the Coalition)*. The coalition publishes a quarterly journal, *Metropolitan Universities Journal: An International Forum*, targeted primarily to departments of sociology, higher education, and policy development. However, as the WPA in an urban university that is a member of the Coalition of Urban and Metropolitan Universities, I find these articles invaluable in understanding both the university's broader commitment to and symbiotic relationship with the metropolitan Atlanta area, as well as the role the composition program might play in this interactive philosophy.

⊙✿⊙

Brownell's description of the role of the "true" metropolitan university (as opposed to a university simply located in an urban environment) summarizes both various definitions of the *metropolitan university* found in the scholarship and my conception of a writing program informed by civic rhetoric:

> The opportunity and burden of the metropolitan university—if it is to be a metropolitan university—is to serve the entire urban region and all its diverse populations, interests, and elements. It cannot deal only with the inner city underprepared or the suburban professionals; it must be concerned with the needs of both. It cannot identify its interests solely with the largest city in its region or with its suburbs, but rather help them to recognize mutual interests and work together. The most important role of the metropolitan university is to be a facilitator, communicator, convener, and bridge. What other institution, except perhaps the government itself, has the capacity to interpret one group to another, serve as a neutral site and forum where problems can be discussed and resolved, bring the latest knowledge and technologies to bear on the dispossessed, join the vigor and capacity of business with the compelling needs of the public at large, and, perhaps most importantly, help restore a sense of *civitas* [civic responsibility], of belonging to one polity and community? (23)

This synthesis of the mission of the metropolitan university leads to a broader conception of the traditional "responsibilities" of university faculty: teaching, research, and professional service. In the metropolitan university model, faculty members (while meeting the highest scholarly standards of the academic community) are encouraged to reconsider and more fully merge these duties, which are never mutually exclusive. For example, metropolitan university faculty must seek research opportunities linking basic investigation with practical applications appropriate for the classroom. Faculty must adopt responsibility for educating students to be informed and effective citizens, as well as preparing them for their chosen professions and occupations. Additionally, faculty must contribute to the metropolitan area's quality of life while developing close partnerships with area enterprises in mutually beneficial ways (not just serving as experts disseminating information). Interestingly, the metropolitan university definition of *faculty responsibilities* correlates with the revised Carnegie Classification 2000 ranking, which now adopts the term *Doctoral/Research Universities-Extensive* for the highest ranking category. In addition to a commitment to graduate education, institutions receiving the highest Carnegie ranking must now demonstrate commitment to teaching and service. A senior scholar at the Carnegie Foundation who supervised the new classification system, Alexander McCormick, explains that the categories were revised because foundation leaders were concerned that "the categories had come to weigh institutions' research activities too heavily, at the expense of other aspects of their missions, such as teaching and service" (Basinger A31). This reconfiguration of the Carnegie Classification categories is certainly beneficial for institutions aligned with the philosophy of urban and metropolitan universities.

THE COURSE

The primary teaching premise of a metropolitan university philosophy of education states students must be "informed and effective citizens, as well as capable practitioners of professions and occupations" *(Information on the Coalition)*. This mandate echoes traditional aims of a rhetorical education and provides fertile ground for revising our current curriculum based on our discipline's rich history of civic interaction.

Inspired by metropolitan university philosophies, I recently piloted an ethnographic writing course in civic rhetoric and writing based on principles of service learning and public literacy instruction at my institution, Georgia State University. The ethnographic approach in this course takes advantage of the local exigencies and encourages students to take advantage of the unique research opportunities available in Atlanta and surrounding communities. Higher education task forces advocating a metropolitan university philosophy of education indicate that the quality of student learning is directly related to the quality of students' involvement in their education. It is not enough, in other words, to say that a writing curriculum will involve public issues or demand that students venture out into their communities. Charles Ruch and Eugene Trani explain:

boundaries between the classroom and the community can be made perme-
able, and the extent to which the flow of ideas and people is accelerated is
the mutual benefit of both. However, the full impact on the curriculum will
not be met by including only community activities. Inductive pedagogy, case
methodology, and cooperative learning strategies will need to be introduced
into the classroom. Only by restructuring the instructional process so classroom content is tied with community experience will the full potential of
these boundary-spanning strategies be achieved. (233–34)

Based on a rhetorical philosophy of composition instruction and founded on
the pedagogical approach advocated by Elizabeth Chiseri-Strater and Bonnie
Stone Sunstein, authors of the class text *Fieldworking: Reading and Writing
Research,* the ethnographic-based writing class answers the call for incorporating community experience in the academic classroom. Those involved in
this project are "inventing" a new curriculum and pedagogy—adopting an
interdisciplinary approach to writing instruction that is new and exciting for
teachers and engaging for students; moreover, we are creating scenarios for
conducting primary research and producing writing assignments tied to community experiences.

Specifically, students pick a site to investigate. Most of the course assignments concern or occur at the students' sites. Projects include mapping exercises, observations in the field, interviews, oral histories, artifact gathering and
analysis, and videotaping—along with "traditional" research and documentation exercises. The students submit a well-organized portfolio the final week
of the course including all of the course assignments, a complete narrative
(research paper with traditional bibliography), and reflection essay. Each component of the final portfolio has been peer-edited or presented to the class, in
some cases graded, and revised over the course of the term. Students' projects
cover a range of topics and communities. The students choose their research
sites based on their own interests and experiences in a particular local community, institution, or organization.

I am attempting to move the course and the larger curriculum more
clearly in the direction of studying and practicing "civic rhetoric," encouraging students to move from the role of observers to participants in community
affairs, while still allowing students to pick their own sites—one of the
course's greatest strengths. *Fieldworking,* which offers a comprehensive course
of study including excellent assignments and sample portfolios, was the ideal
text for our first attempt at ethnography in the first-year writing course. However, I find myself now departing a bit from the *Fieldworking* approach in the
reconfigured course, directing students to both historical and contemporary
readings that address civic rhetoric and more forcefully moving students
toward active communicative participation at their sites. I want students to
grasp fully the concept of the potentialities within civic rhetoric, to under-

stand the term's historical implications (and mutations). As Miller explains, we need to "move beyond simple nostalgia for the civic virtues of 'a good man speaking well,'" an ideology serving to "distinguish citizens from women, the uneducated, and others who lacked public authority" ("Rhetoric Within" 34). The "civic tradition" addressed exercising power through discourse.

Works such as Elizabeth Ervin's *Public Literacy,* a slim text packed with clear explanations of public literacy and the public sphere, wonderfully insightful examples, case studies, and interesting and challenging heuristics; Shamoon et al.'s *Coming of Age,* which includes thoughtful explorations of the possibilities inherent in civic-based writing courses; and Paul Collin's *Community Writing: Researching Social Issues through Composition,* a student text encouraging students to define, understand, and ultimately "enter" communities as sites of research—are all ideally suited for this reconfigured first-year writing course; they bridge the chasm between disciplinary connotations of first-year writing courses and the desire to engage in the civic-minded metropolitan university philosophy of writing instruction.

I have likewise expanded the focus of our teacher mentoring sessions to include concerns of civic rhetoric and community. Those of us engaged in the ethnographic pedagogy lead training colloquia advocating a civic approach to teaching first-year writing. Bruce McComiskey's *Teaching Composition as a Social Process* and Shamoon et al.'s *Coming of Age* serve as excellent teacher resources for this course. In addition to offering teachers lucid analyses of social-process rhetorical inquiry and the postprocess movement in composition, these works provide detailed assignments and course designs that teachers might use to move students beyond observations of sites and artifacts toward rhetorical intervention. I am gradually "infusing" most of our teaching assistant (TA) mentoring meetings with discussions of civic rhetoric and community involvement. We are making grassroots progress. Those TAs who have taught the course encourage other TAs to adopt this methodology; these TAs also present their experiences at area conferences and colloquia.

This reconfiguration of the class addresses what Elizabeth Ervin has labeled composition teachers' "increasing dissatisfaction with teaching writing in ways that objectify 'society' rather than foster students' direct interaction with it" ("Course Design" 43). By training TAs to encourage students to enter the public sphere and engage in public writing, we are helping to. restore in both graduate and undergraduate students "a sense of *civitas,* of belonging to one polity and community" (Brownell 23). I also want to underscore the fact that curriculum development efforts such as this—long-term, ongoing, and collaborative—are essential for creating necessary broad-based program changes. If we do not engage both WPAs and teachers in curriculum development and teacher training, program changes run the risk of being top-down or unsupported (or both) and therefore doomed to fail. Perhaps more important,

if departmental support for ethnographic inquiry is not evident, this pedagogical approach loses its "bite"; students will neither value the classroom experience nor appropriate civic communicative action long term.

In his article, "What Are We Talking About? Re-Imagining Community
in Service Learning," Kevin Ball explains that as students participate in
Freirean inquiry concerning their "relationship with the world," they become
the "subjects of their own destiny, and they realize their roles as Subjects in the
World and with the World." Ball is concerned (as am I) that critical pedagogy
often neglects "individual and local issues, thereby silencing those students
meant to be empowered." As a result students are often unaware of and thus
unable to view diverse local cultures and communities as worthy sites of investigation and participation (130). Students view the occasional encounter with
classroom pedagogy that extends beyond classroom walls for what it is: an
anomaly—an experimental blip on the educational radar screen, not viewed as
authentic or even sanctioned by university practice. Perhaps as their teachers,
we do too. We have few examples of writing program design that match the
numerous course designs and individual faculty initiatives. WPAs (with support from college administrators) must back community partnerships, ethnographic inquiry, and a philosophy of civic rhetoric in sequenced writing
courses. Certainly, ethnographic writing projects and attempts to build them
into a coherent program design reflect attempts to bridge perceived gaps
between university education and the "real" world; however, do singular experiences heighten students' awareness of community or motivate students to
actively engage in civic activities long term? Just as important, we must ask
how limited "term projects" benefit local communities. The scholarship of our
field repeatedly raises these questions, but for me the answer lies in writing
program (re)design. Sustained community involvement and instruction in
civic rhetoric must be the focus of sequenced writing courses. The course I've
described is a start—a good start because virtually all of our students are
required to take first-year composition—but this course should serve only as
an introduction to the principles and practices of civic engagement.

A fully developed writing program based on community research and
writing promises to fulfill metropolitan principles of education and increase
the likelihood that classroom experiences will foster sustained involvement
when students return to their own communities. Ethnographic research and
writing projects conducted in the name of civic rhetoric answer the current
expectations of students and administrators alike while furthering aims of the
rhetorical tradition—making interdisciplinary knowledge useful in the public
sphere. We need to design programs of study that introduce students (and
their teachers) to primary community research and documentation, foster
relationships between students and communities that are mutually beneficial
and extend beyond one academic experience. Teachers need to understand the

department's commitment to writing instruction informed by civic practice and local exigencies. In addition, WPAs must be allowed to expand the scope of their job descriptions to actively build symbiotic relationships with the community; individual teachers (particularly TAs) do not have the resources or time necessary to forge community relationships.

The work of WPAs is often strangely defined and dual in nature. As Rita Malenczyk explains in a recent issue of *Writing Program Administrator*, we are not administrators "in the same sense deans and college presidents are administrators." She argues "that the difference between a WPA and a dean or a higher-level manager is that WPA work, like the work of more traditional academic disciplines, is grounded in research and scholarship and is ultimately intellectual and pedagogical rather than managerial" (18). I envision our writing program moving away from a primary identity as a coordinator of service courses and toward a new type of institutional system with multiple purposes, functions, and activities tied to student, teacher, and administrative research. Think of this institutional system in terms of the various relationships a writing program can have—with a department, with a college or university, and with communities outside the university. As research-based institutional systems that can coordinate meaningful and related work across and outside the university, writing programs are potentially powerful institutional systems that foreground the work of writing teachers, researchers, administrators, and students within the university.

The benefits of ethnographic inquiry based on the rhetorical tradition are made apparent in Enos's waxing metaphor calling for renewed research methodology in rhetorical study: "archaeology and rhetoric may have seemed to be far apart in the grooves of academia, but their cross-fertilization enriches both disciplines and offers fruits for analysis that yield a bountiful harvest" (78). If we take a longer view, then in the hands of composition studies the marriage of ethnography and civic rhetoric has the power to transform institutions and communities when ethnographic practice is determined by local exigencies and adopted not only by teachers and students but administrators as well.

WORKS CITED

Ball, Kevin. "What Are We Talking About? Re-Imagining Community in Service Learning." Ed. John Paul Tassoni and William H. Thelin. *Blundering for a Change: Errors and Expectations in Critical Pedagogy*. Portsmouth, NH: Boynton/Cook, 2000. 128–43.

Basinger, Julianne. "A New Way of Classifying Colleges Elates Some and Perturbs Others." *Chronicle of Higher Education* 11 August 2000: A31+.

110   *Lynée Lewis Gaillet*

Brownell, Blaine A. "Metropolitan Universities: Past, Present, and Future." *Metropolitan Universities: An Emerging Model in American Higher Education.* Ed. Daniel M. Johnson and David A. Bell. Denton: U of North Texas P, 1995. 17–26.

Chiseri-Strater, Elizabeth, and Bonnie Stone Sunstein. *Fieldworking: Reading and Writing Research.* Boston: Bedford St. Martins, 1997 (2nd ed. 2001).

Collins, Paul. *Community Writing: Researching Social Issues through Composition.* Mahwah, NJ: Erlbaum, 2001.

Connors, Robert. Octolog. "The Politics of Historiography." *Rhetoric Review* 7 (1988): 5–49.

Court, Franklin. *The Scottish Connection: The Rise of English Literary Study in Early America.* Syracuse, NY: Syracuse UP, 2001.

Crowley, Sharon, and Deborah Hawhee. *Ancient Rhetorics for Contemporary Students.* Needham Heights, MA: Allyn and Bacon, 1999.

D'Angelo, Frank J. *Composition in the Classical Tradition.* Needham Heights, MA: Allyn and Bacon, 2000.

Enos, Richard Leo. "The Archeology of Women in Rhetoric: Rhetorical Sequencing as a Research Method for Historical Scholarship." *Rhetoric Society Quarterly* 32.1 (2002): 65–79.

Ervin, Elizabeth. "Course Design, English 496: Senior Seminar in Writing." *Composition Studies* 26.1 (1998): 37–57.

———. "Learning to Write with a Civic Tongue." Ed. John Paul Tassoni and William H. Thelin. *Blundering for a Change: Errors and Expectations in Critical Pedagogy.* Portsmouth, NH: Boynton/Cook, 2000. 144–57.

———. *Public Literacy.* New York: Longman, 2000.

Flower, Linda. "Partners in Inquiry: A Logic for Community Outreach." *Writing the Community: Concepts and Models for Service Learning in Composition.* Ed. Linda Adler-Kassner, Robert Crooks, and Ann Watters. Urbana, IL: NCTE, 1997. 95–117.

Hathaway, Charles, Paige E. Mulhollan, and Karen A. White. "Metropolitan Universities; Models for the Twenty-First Century." *Metropolitan Universities: An Emerging Model in American Higher Education.* Ed. Daniel M. Johnson and David A. Bell. Denton: U of North Texas P, 1995. 5–16.

Herzberg, Bruce. "Civic Literacy and Service Learning." Ed. Linda K Shamoon, Rebecca Moore Howard, Sandra Jamieson, and Robert A. Schwegler. *Coming of Age: The Advanced Writing Curriculum.* Portsmouth, NH: Boynton/Cook, 2000. CD insert.

Horner, Winifred. *Rhetoric in the Classical Tradition.* New York: St. Martin's, 1988.

Information on the Coalition of Urban and Metropolitan Universities. Coalition of Urban and Metropolitan Universities. 24 August 2000. <http://www.ucf.edu/ metroplitan/coalition.html>.

Malenczyk, Rita. "Fighting across the Curriculum: The WPA Joins the AAUP." *Writing Program Administrator* 24 (2001): 11–23.

McComiskey, Bruce. *Teaching Composition as a Social Process.* Logan: Utah State UP, 2000.

Miller, Thomas P. *The Formation of College English: Rhetoric and Belles Lettres in the British Cultural Provinces.* Pittsburgh: U of Pittsburgh P, 1997.

———. "Rhetoric Within and Without Composition: Reimagining the Civic." *Coming of Age: The Advanced Writing Curriculum.* Ed. Linda K. Shamoon, Rebecca Moore Howard, Sandra Jamieson, and Robert A. Schwegler. Portsmouth, NH: Boynton/Cook, 2000.

Ruch, Charles P., and Eugene P. Trani. "Scope and Limitations of Community Interactions." *Metropolitan Universities: An Emerging Model in American Higher Education.* Ed. Daniel M. Johnson and David A. Bell. Denton: U of North Texas P, 1995. 231–43.

Shamoon, Linda K., Rebecca Moore Howard, Sandra Jamieson, and Robert A. Schwegler, eds. *Coming of Age: The Advanced Writing Curriculum.* Portsmouth, NH: Boynton/Cook, 2000.

PART II

Place-Conscious Ethnographies: Situating Praxis in the Field

7

Open to Change

Ethos, Identification, and Critical Ethnography in Composition Studies

ROBERT BROOKE and CHARLOTTE HOGG

ONE OF THE TRUISMS of ethnographic research is that the research itself will change you. In the research encounter with some Other culture, your understanding of your own culture—and your own self—will transform. As Clifford Geertz has shown *(Works and Lives)*, traditional ethnography is full of such descriptions of personal change, from Levi-Strauss's growing disillusionment with colonial culture in *Tristes Tropiques* to Margaret Mead's outright critique of American sexuality in *Coming of Age in Samoa*. More recently, ethnographic writing has become more explicitly autobiographical as a means of addressing real issues of representation and authority. For instance, Marjorie Shostak meditates on what it means for herself to be a woman in response to her dialogues with her Australian counterpart *(Nisa; Return to Nisa)*; Vincent Crapanzano questions the transformative power of friendship and projective identification in *Tuhami: Portrait of a Moroccan;* and Ruth Behar explores the personal wounding that comes from ethnographic practice in *The Vulnerable Observer*. In composition studies itself, the personal location of the literacy ethnographer has also become a subject of much conversation—witness the roundtable article "The Politics of the Personal" in September 2001 *College English,* featuring the remarks of Deborah Brandt, Victor Villanueva, Anne Ruggles Gere, and Ellen Cushman, among others. Compositionist Ralph

Cintron, in his recent *Angels' Town,* even suggests that ethnographic knowledge is outright dependent on the character, the "ethos," of the ethnographer. He writes, "the persuasiveness of the ethnographic knowledge claim is constituted through and through, both in the moments of fieldwork and the moments of the final text, by ethos" (4). In short, the "self" of the ethnographer—and the changeable nature of that self—has emerged as a major question in ethnographic practice.

This article probes this question of the changeable ethnographer's self. We are motivated to do so because we have each experienced such changes. We have not remained the composition researchers we were when we began studying elderly rural women in Paxton and successful rural schools in Henderson, Albion, or Cedar Bluffs. In the process of our research, we have come to call ourselves "regionalists." This new way of understanding ourselves is intriguing in how we discuss our work with other compositionists at national conferences, write our ethnographic research, and enact local community projects in Nebraska. From our experience, thus, we are convinced that changes in public self, in "ethos," are a direct consequence of our work. We suspect, with Cintron, that such changes are central to ethnography.

For this collection on critical ethnography, we want to extend Cintron's move toward an examination of "ethos" as it explicitly affects critical ethnography. What sort of changeable self is specifically implied when ethnographers see their work as critical?

Of course, what is and is not "critical ethnography" as opposed to just plain "ethnography" is an open question these days. In the recent *Critical Ethnography in Educational Research,* for instance, series editor Michael Apple writes that there are "more than a few differences within the multiple orientations that might be labeled 'critical'" (Carspecken x), and author Phil Carspecken begins with a request to "put away, as best you can, all your preconceptions of what 'critical' means. Wait to see what sense I give this term" (2). Given the shifting meanings of the term, every author who uses it probably means something a bit different by it.

As we understand the term *critical ethnography* from our position as composition scholars, the term applies primarily to two related sets of educational issues. First, *critical ethnography* emerges from an extensive body of work in critical pedagogy in which the goal of teaching is to engage students (or other groups of learners) in the dialogic work of understanding their social location and developing cultural action appropriate to that location. This body of work for us harkens back to Paulo Freire and moves through Ira Shor and Henry Giroux in contemporary U.S. education. Second, *critical ethnography* emerges equally from researchers interested in the ethics of representation or the question of how research on a cultural group can represent that group fairly as well as reciprocating in the economics of research itself. Ellen Cushman and

Michelle Fine seem to us clear representatives of this position. Drawing on these two bodies of work, we understand critical ethnography as a research practice, primarily related to education, whose purpose is to use a dialogue about a cultural context to develop critical action while remaining highly attuned to the ethics and politics of representation in the practice and reporting of that dialogue and resulting action.

Because we see critical ethnography as emerging from these two strands, we see the question of the "ethos" of the researcher as directly implicated by such work. If the practice of critical ethnography is truly dialogic, culturally active, and ethically representative, then that practice necessarily implies real change in the self-conception of the ethnographer. In this chapter, we work out these implications, initially by examining the question of ethos primarily through Kenneth Burke's thoughts on the subject, then exploring how we see our ethos as influenced by our own ethnographic encounters in rural Nebraska, and finally by considering how the concept can become useful for others working in composition.

ETHOS, BURKE'S IDENTIFICATION, AND CRITICAL ETHNOGRAPHY

For us, Ralph Cintron's theoretical speculation in *Angels' Town* poses the question of ethos in a way that, with extension, could become more useful for critical ethnography. As Cintron explains, he is drawn to an Aristotelian exploration of ethos as a textual performance of character intended to persuade. The way an ethnographic text creates the character of the researcher is one of the main ways that text justifies the claims about a studied culture. As Cintron puts it, "the central point is that ethos and logos—or character and a rational knowledge claim—are linked so that knowing something of a person's character helps us to judge that person's knowledge claims" (3). Cintron thus becomes fascinated by a "minor trope" in contemporary ethnographic writing, whereby the writer presents "a connection between the fieldsite and some deeper life-pattern of the ethnographer's" (7), so that the writing of an ethnography occurs through "negotiations that become explicit between observation and memory, between brand new experiences and very old experiences, and it is through processes like these that real fieldsites become understood both as objects of knowledge and as extensions of life-patterns or ethos" (8). In short, for Cintron, in written ethnographies, writers' constructions (from memory and life-pattern) of an "ethos" for themselves become a crucial filter through which the field site emerges as meaningful (the patterns of !Kung women's lives become meaningful partly because Marjorie Shostak presents herself as an aging American woman with cancer trying to make sense of her life as a woman—her textual char-acter influences the field site readers see).

How might an exploration of ethos inform critical ethnography, where the character of the researcher affects not just the written representation but the dialogic process, the collaborative cultural action, and the reciprocity that are now seen as imperatives in critical work?

Cintron poses this question directly in relation to an Aristotelian descrip-tion of *ethos,* where ethos is a textual feature created by the speaker or author as one means of persuading others to accept the text's knowledge claims. As we suggested, even in Aristotelian terms the question of ethos is intriguing for ethnographers because it points directly to the personal connection of ethno-grapher and cultural site. But we believe the question of ethos becomes even more central when posed in Burkean terms when explored through Burke's refinement of ethos as identification and consubstantiality.

Burke's refinement of Aristotle, especially in *A Rhetoric of Motives,* sug-gests that the relationship between writer and reader is more than just a tex-tual feature contributing to persuasion. It is formative of the entire rhetorical field itself. For Burke, identification between persons is the fundamental act in rhetoric, at both foundational and persuasive levels. Foundationally, we make the effort to listen or read, Burke says, only when we already believe the speaker or writer is engaged with us in a common project of some sort (no matter how far apart their approach to that project may be). We are persuaded when we come to believe that the speaker or writer speaks for us in some way. Hence, identification, or the means by which two dissimilar persons come to be identified as "with" each other in some significant sense, is the fundamen-tal rhetorical act. Some sort of identification must be in place at a mostly unconscious social level for communication to occur at all. And implied in this foundational level of identification is the equally foundational fact of human division. Burke writes:

> Identification is affirmed with earnestness precisely because there is divi-sion. Identification is compensatory to division. If men *[sic]* were not apart from one another, there would be no need for the rhetorician to proclaim their unity. (22)

Given the reality of division, the processes of identification can lead at their best to "consubstantiality," Burke's fancy word for "actingtogether" *[sic]* where separate individuals or groups undertake common projects or form common ways of living. At their worst, the processes of identification can be manipu-lated by unscrupulous rhetors to create false or misleading identifications linked less to the common good and more to the personal advancement of the rhetor. In either case, the rhetorical act exists through a project of identification, whereby separate persons are—however momentarily or symbolically—moved from their distinct difference to a common shared space. Overall, in Burke's rhetoric the "ethos" or "ethical" relationship of writer to audience becomes less an ancillary means of persuasion of knowledge claims, and more a fundamental problematic shaping human culture. Rhetoric "is rooted in an essential function of language," he writes, "the use of language as a symbolic means of inducing cooperation in beings that by nature respond to symbols" (43). This "cooperation" exists at the moment of ethos, as the speaker's project and person is identified with the listener's project and person at a level far deeper than any Aristotelian *logos*. Hence, says Burke, "the rhetorician and the moralist become one at that point where the attempt is made to reveal the undetected presence of such an identification" (26).

We believe that Burke's reformulation of the concept of ethos via identification matches more closely the questions of social action being posed by critical pedagogues. For example, the ethic of consubstantiality seems implied in Freire's constant emphasis on dialogue with the people so that the social programs developed are directly relevant to local people and conditions (and even in his demand that the vocabulary used come from the people). Similarly, Giroux's and MacLaren's macroanalysis of the hidden curriculum, of the ways educational policies and programs actually work against the improvement of the lives of people, seems from this point of view an analysis of manipulative identification, the analysis of rhetoricians and moralists revealing "undetected identifications" in public policy.

Burke's terms, thus, provide us a way of looking at the critical ethnographer's relation to the studied contexts, through at least two guiding questions:

1. What are the identifications established in this project between ethnographer and study participants on the one hand, between ethnographer and implied reading audience on the other, as well as among all three peoples (ethnographer, participants, reading audience)?

2. What are the "consubstantial" common projects developed here, and how have they come into being? To what degree are these projects an "actingtogether" *[sic]* on the part of the (necessarily?) divided people, and to what degree are these projects the product of manipulative identifications that serve the writer but not necessarily those represented by the writing?

These questions help us to sharpen our understanding of what it means to say ethnography is a process that leaves the researcher "open to change." When seen from such a perspective, the necessary unsettling reality of ethnography becomes clear. At the very least, even traditional "objective" ethnographers cannot help but be reidentified at a fundamental level, regardless how clear a distinction they try to preserve in written work between "research subjects" and "professional audience." For the critical ethnographer who attempts to develop programs and representations in dialogue and reciprocity with participants, this unsettling may go much farther. In Burke's terms, any critical ethnographic project should require a fairly complete reformation of the field of foundational identifications, the coming-to-articulation of emergent consubstantial identifications, and a constant worry about and awareness of the manipulative identifications that lurk in this particular rhetorical context.

Furthermore, in the process of critical ethnography, we cannot help but form new identifications (on what Burke would call the fundamental level), developing with participants new understandings of "actingtogether" *[sic]* that give shape to our social worlds. In both the conduct of ethnography and the writing of the ethnographic report, we can neither help but draw on those identifications, nor can we avoid the self-work involved in negotiating between consubstantial and manipulative identification.

Or at least this is how it seems to us. When we examine our own engagement with rural communities on the Great Plains in the past few years, we believe we see our "ethical fields" open to exactly these sorts of change.

ETHOS ON THE GREAT PLAINS

Identification and Reidentification: How We became Regionalists

If Burke is right, and "identification" is really a foundational act in every rhetorical encounter between disparate peoples, then in principle we ought to be able to trace the ways ethnographers—especially critical ethnographers—develop identifications with those they study. In our ethnographic engagement with rural Nebraskans, we have each found this to be so. Those engagements have changed our identifications, both at the foundational level of who we feel ourselves to be and at the more public level of the construction of our academic work.

Some background facts: In 1994, while a master's degree student at Oregon State, Charlotte began writing about her home in Paxton, Nebraska, in creative nonfiction classes, and her dissertation project, starting in 1997 after her return to the University of Nebraska-Lincoln, became an ethnographic study of women's literacies in Paxton. About the same time in 1997, Robert began working with an extensive teacher research program through the National Writing Project, called Rural Voices, Country Schools, and charged in part to document what is good in kindergarten-through-twelfth-grade rural education. In both cases, we began our work from a specific and fixed self-identification—Charlotte the creative writer and compositionist, returning as researcher and feminist to what had once been home; Robert the composition theorist and National Writing Project director, serving as advisor to a local team of teacher researchers.

But ethnographic work leaves us open to change, to reidentification. At a foundational level, both of us have forged new "identifications" with the regions we researched. At the strategic level of our conscious rhetoric, both of us are writing increasingly as self-identified regionalists. Charlotte's papers for the last two Conference on College Composition and Communication (CCCC) (and a nonfiction essay) have emphasized in part her own rural woman's literacy; Robert has just completed a book with the local Rural Voices, Country Schools research team, *Place-Conscious Education: Writing Instruction for Community Involvement*. For us, our research has resulted in a change in identification, a restitching of the fabric of ethos.

Both of us have been involved in separate ethnographic studies in which the participants identified themselves regionally as rural Nebraskans. Our thinking about regionalism emerged through opening ourselves up to the ways in which the participants in our studies defined their work and lives and the ways they understood the world. In short, the regional lens we use for reading our ethnographic studies was largely generated by identification with participants.

We illustrate this process with Charlotte's ethnographic research project involving older women from her hometown in western Nebraska (population approximately 500). The study was to elicit a greater understanding of the ways in which older women in the village use literacies in their lives and in the community. In the course of her research, Charlotte moved from an "ethos" of feminist academic interpreter of her research to an "ethos" of regionalist, needing to represent the continuity between her experience and that of the older women she studied.

First, Charlotte found she needed to negotiate her identification with her study participants. As is too often a common move, she first approached her study as merely interpreter of her research. Although she had moved away ten years prior, Charlotte still had many ties to the community and naïvely assumed in early stages of research that she had a strong sense of what she would find in her ethnographic inquiry. In the beginning stages of research, Charlotte made the assumption that she would not need to create an ethos as researcher because most in town knew her or at the very least knew of her or her relatives from the area. And although her familiarity allowed participants to trust Charlotte sooner than they perhaps would an outsider, she soon realized that a new kind of identification process occurred in which she was seen not only as a former resident but also as a scholar. Her involvement with this project led to a negotiation of her identification with her hometown.

The older women in Paxton seemed to envision her as both grand-daughter figure and doctoral student—and because they revered education, her pursuit of her doctoral degree was a highly respected endeavor to them. Wrote one woman in her study, "It's astounding to those of us who knew a little tow-headed youngster only a few short years ago. 'A few short years ago' to us only, not to you who have climbed over a thousand hurdles in the pursuit of your dream. We, too, will share in your pride when you earn that cherished sheepskin." What Charlotte began to realize as she interviewed women from her hometown was that for them her identity as a scholar was deeply linked with her connection to Paxton. One woman described the ways in which the town laid claim to her and her accomplishments, explaining, "I think of Hillary [Clinton]'s little village raising a child. You are what you are because you came from Paxton." She went on to make connections to Charlotte's education and the influence of the older women in town who deeply value education:

> "I don't know if [these women] are the sole source, but one thing [my husband and I have] talked about many times is the desire for education in Nebraska is so much greater than it was in Kansas and so much greater than it was in Missouri for higher education, past high school. And while not all of these [older] women went on to get an education, neither did they stop studying. It wasn't just one or two, there's a whole bunch of them."

It seemed correlated that Charlotte was motivated to receive her Ph.D. and came from this specific regional context. She herself was an example of the ways in which literacy was conjoined with place and noticed that many other descriptions of literacy practices were also bound in place. And because of this relation between learning and place, the women Charlotte spoke with simultaneously appeared to assume not only that she was the expert but also a kind of teacherly tone as if to remind her that they, too, were experts. Thus, the ethos Charlotte found herself conveying with these women was largely in response to her perception of their sense of her. More significantly, Charlotte began to make connections between their descriptions and rendering of literacy lives in Paxton and her own experiences; this resonance led her not only to reidentify with the women in her study by way of regionalism but also to reconsider her own literacy experiences.

Creating and sustaining ethos for the ethnographic research through interaction with participants was only the beginning of situating her ethnographic self and identity in new terms. For Charlotte, making a space for her memories and identification with her hometown allowed her to step back from the "rational" role of ethnographer and interpreter and become a part of the ongoing conversations among participants in her study. She listened more for the ways the women defined and described their literacy and did less worrying about a suitable framework for her dissertation that would illustrate her theory prowess. In the process of her own reidentification, she was also led to a way of thinking about the women in her study in ways she had not thought about before.

Local place and region was at the core of the literacy work done by the women in Charlotte's study. Older women in her hometown used literacy in various ways: to evoke and sustain a sense of place and heritage for members of the community, to educate citizens of the town to keep (literally) the town alive, and to sustain themselves as learners, readers, and writers. The women read local and regional texts (Bess Streeter Aldrich, a Nebraska author, was a common favorite) and wrote local and regional histories. In the processes of creating, shaping, and conducting these literate activities, these women— writing for the county newspaper, working at the library, writing memoirs, participating in community groups such as extension clubs, the Garden Club, and United Methodist Women, among many others—were generating and recording a regional identity and culture. This identity, steeped in region, allowed them to negotiate the patriarchal agrarian culture surrounding them while performing literate acts that empowered them.

As Charlotte wrote about these women for her study, she increasingly found she needed to join with them in articulating a regionalist ethos. Rather than interpreting the local culture solely within the framework of academic feminism, which allowed for limited ways of understanding the rural women's lives in this culture and context, Charlotte sought to make sense of the women's literacy through their regional understanding. Simply put: the women taught her how to read the culture by sharing how region serves as a meaning-making concept in their lives. In the final draft of her dissertation, she wrote of the older community women as sponsors of literacy for the whole community. She described how these women's work preserved the history and practices of their region, taught those values to succeeding genera- tions, and sought to foster regional self-sufficiency. Charlotte positioned her- self as the direct recipient and even inheritor of these women's sponsorship, now crafting a new text that would articulate the value of their work to a new compositionist audience. In short, through the practice of her research, Charlotte reidentified the nature of her professional ethos, shifting from an ethos of somewhat detached literacy interpreter to an ethos of a regional woman academic extending the values and shaped by the sponsorship of the women she studied.

In many ways, Charlotte's ethos was meant to serve as a bridge between the implied audience and the women in her study. She made an effort to con- struct a text that negotiated between these elements through a regionalist lens while still allowing for inclusion of feminist theory. Furthermore, she strove for a tone in her writing that sought to model the older women with whom she had worked because through reidentification her imagined audience expanded beyond compositionists to include rural Nebraska women. She began chapters by striving to ground readers in story—in discussions of sponsorship, for instance, she wrote a collage of scenes that described different moments of sponsorship between the older women and her family, meant to demonstrate the reciprocity of sponsorship acts in Paxton. Although Charlotte alone produced the text, in Burkean terms this way of writing was an effort to encourage identification among the implied audience, participants, and researcher. And through the process of reidentification undergone with research participants, Charlotte was able to convey an ethos for her implied audience that sought to negotiate the identification of the regionalist lens with the scholarly identification with the composition audience.

DIALOGIC ACTIVISM

Consubstantiality and Manipulation

Charlotte's research shows the shaping power of Burke's idea of ethos as identification. But Burke's notion of "identification" goes beyond the simple act of self-identification, of—in our example—now calling ourselves *regionalists* where before we might not have used that term. For Burke, the force of identification speaks to the very heart of the rhetorical enterprise. In identifying yourself with another, you open yourself to the twin possibilities of "consubstantiality" or acting together on a common project versus "manipulation" or using a more-or-less false identification for nefarious self-advancement.

These aspects of Burkean identification strike us as most related to critical ethnography. One might say that *consubstantiality* is the goal critical ethnography strives for, whereby the research leads to a common project defined with the participants for the mutual benefit of all. And one might say that *manipulation* is a term for critical ethnography's critical impetus—the naming of the false identifications whereby policy makers and even ethnographers have spoken "for" but not "in the best interests of" those they supposedly represent. If, in the research moment, we reidentify ourselves as "with" our participants, then as writers we have to take on a different project. We have to imagine a new project, a new role, out of which we speak together with our participants as more or less equals, even if we are the ones doing the actual writing. And this is a very different project than that of traditional ethnography, where at the moment of writing the researcher really is "representing" those that were studied.

In Robert's teacher research project for Rural Voices, Country Schools, for instance, what happened is that together the team of nine researchers plus a wider circle of colleagues, parents, and students at the eight schools developed new projects for themselves.

At the outset, the research project felt like a traditional representation task. Following a nationwide competition, the National Writing Project had invited teams of teacher researchers in Arizona, Louisiana, Michigan, Pennsylvania, Washington, and Nebraska to describe "what is good in rural teaching." Initially, the Nebraska team began focusing on what the participating teachers were already doing in their schools. They found they were drawn to teaching that connected especially to local communities, controversies, regional understanding, and history. They got most excited about projects such as a cross-curricular secondary English and biology unit where students examined the ecology of the local Platte River in the historical contexts of the bird and human migrations and in the legal and scientific contexts of water rights controversies between cities and farms, farms and wildlife, and states' rights and national government. Equally exciting were elementary-school projects where children adopted buildings in their small towns and, with the help of adult newspaper archivists and town old-timers, learned the stories of those buildings, their transformations, and the historical forces shaping those changes. Initially, just representing these good teaching practices seemed enough.

But as the team heard these teachers' stories of developing such projects, they found themselves becoming increasingly "critical." Regularly, the teachers on the team described systematic impediments to such projects, including administration's unwillingness to let teachers collaborate across subject areas, prescribed literary and social studies readings that focused on national or international history and left no room for local heritage, and state policies that wanted to consolidate almost all small rural schools into larger units under a rhetoric of efficiency. The team found, in short, that the prevailing concepts of education worked against the kinds of learning they valued. In response, the team decided their work needed to do more than represent teachers' best practices. Increasingly the work thus shifted to three new sets of projects that (1) critiqued these prevailing concepts, (2) celebrated the alternatives in local teachers' practice, and (3) sought to enact programs that might help change the general nature of rural education.

The team began jointly crafting several projects that flowed from this new understanding of their work: (1) the Rural Institute program, in which they added to general Nebraska Writing Project practice some direct investigation of teaching that linked to local resources and knowledge; (2) a series of public presentations for national and local audiences demonstrating the value of "place-based" education (and celebrating Nebraska in the process); and (3) creating public engagement or public advocacy moments. Here are three examples of such moments: the teacher who took her students to testify before the state legislature on the issue of school consolidation, the teachers who developed in-service workshops in Great Plains schools, and the team's collaboration with nine school districts in designing locally appropriate writing assessment as an alternative to national tests. In short, through the ongoing research program new projects were collectively developed from new understandings of themselves as regionalists.

This work has radically altered the writing Robert does as a university professor. Although he has begun using some of the regionalist ideas developed in this wide cluster of relationships in his literary nonfiction and teaching, he has not, as researcher or writer, published a representation of these good people's work and lives outside of these joint projects. This research has generated enough "consubstantial" work that a more pressing collaborative writing task to choose is almost always available. Since 1997 when the team began this work, Robert has been lead writer on several grant applications "with" the people on the team to create funding to allow them to lead rural institutes. He guided the team through the process of developing a book prospectus for the forthcoming *Place-Conscious Education* collection and managed the negotiations with the press editor to secure a contract. But these are very different projects, say, from writing a book on his own "about" these eight teachers. And each of the teachers' own projects also has something of this consubstantial flavor. One instance was a community night in Henderson, Nebraska, where the auditorium filled with townspeople to hear high school juniors read their homages to characters in the community and family past. In another instance, the Waverly, Nebraska, sophomore writing workshop took over a weekly column in their local newspaper to showcase to the community their celebrations and critiques of rural life. And for the National Public Radio program the team developed, teachers, students, and community adults all read their own writing about rural place. In all these cases, the research effort created "common" projects out of a defined set of new roles for the participants, formed from the identification that exists when the research happens.

In Burke's terms, Robert wants to see these projects as emerging from consubstantiality. They are projects "formed with" the research participants, aimed not at representing them in any traditional narrow sense, but instead at various minor activisms in the world the participants jointly inhabit. To imagine such projects, Robert has gone through rather far-reaching reidentification in Burke's sense, coming to see these people as colleagues and to view some of their problems and obstacles as his own. These emerging common projects have caused him to advocate for regional and rural education and to intervene in public policy in new ways.

Frankly, part of this work is scary. Although he "identifies with" his many colleagues in Henderson, Aurora, Albion, and Waverly, he is quite aware that these towns are not his home communities. He grew up in Denver and sometimes gets things wrong. In a workshop last summer, for instance, an Aurora teacher took him to task for a poem he wrote that had the wrong farm machinery in the field for the time of year he described. He did not know a tractor from a skidloader. The danger certainly exists for manipulation in the Burkean sense. In writing about the "we" of these common regional projects, Robert may well be eliding real differences between himself and them, and co-opting their lives for his own ends. But, if we rightly understand Burke, only the unscrupulous rhetorician knowingly manipulated identification for his own advancements. For the rest of us, consubstantiality is an open question. A researcher and a community come together; out of their dialogue new, joint projects are formed and articulated; and perhaps all these people begin artic-ulating themselves as part of a new and different "we." If the process is truly dialogic, then the new projects and the new "we" are truly consubstantial. But inequities of power and inabilities of self-knowledge may also be there, lead-ing to manipulation either willful or unconscious. We're not sure from inside the process that differentiating would be easy.

BURKE'S ETHICAL CHALLENGE

We want to leave you with an insight and a challenge. If our interpretation of Burke and our analysis of our own experience are at all accurate, then we have shown how Burke's concept of ethos as identification may have explanatory power for the conduct of critical ethnography. Ethos is certainly at stake in ethnography. But the nature of that stake is significantly deeper than an Aris-totelian approach can show. For Aristotle, "ethos" is simply a textual feature, one of several "available means of persuasion" open to writers as they attempt to sway their audiences. Burke's insight, by contrast, is that ethos may also be foundational. Who we are, how we identify ourselves with others, and the very scope of the projects we undertake are all a product of the identification power of ethos. To complicate ethos in this way means that ethnographers have the potential of coming to a project with the assumption that they are not alone in the research endeavor but are part of a complex process that allows for the boundaries of researcher and the researched to blur as identifications emerge and play out in the text and in action beyond the text.

The challenge, of course, comes from the double-sided possibility of con-substantiation and manipulation. If, as our title suggests, ethnographic research leaves us, as researchers, open to change, then being challenged by the nature of the change may be right. For Aristotle's rhetorician, "ethos" is a mostly conscious process, a construction of self that is aimed at persuasion. But for Burke, ethical identification is foundational, and therefore in that odd human space significantly beyond consciousness. We are who we are because we identify, and hence the projects we imagine may be truly consubstantial but may perhaps be as easily one of several varieties of manipulation, of which conscious manipulation is only the simplest to discern. Our hope is that this Burkean language and contextualization applied to ethos as it relates to critical ethnography can provide a more thorough marker by which to define and grapple with the moments and occasions where manipulation takes place.

As emerging regionalists because of our critical ethnography in Great Plains communities, we see ourselves implicated in these processes. They challenged us. We urge you to be also challented in your own ethnographic encounters.

WORKS CITED

Behar, Ruth. *The Vulnerable Observer: Anthropology that Breaks Your Heart.* Boston: Beacon, 1996.

Brandt, Deborah, Ellen Cushman, Anne Ruggles Gere, Anne Herrington, Richard E. Miller, Victor Villanueva, Min-Zhan Lu, and Gesa Kirsch. "The Politics of the Personal: Storying Our Lives against the Grain." *College English* 64.1 (September 2001): 41–62.

Brooke, Robert, ed. *Place-Conscious Education: Writing Instruction for Community Involvement.* New York: Teachers College Press/National Writing Project, 2003.

Burke, Kenneth. *A Rhetoric of Motives.* Berkeley: California UP, 1969.

Carspecken, Phil. *Critical Ethnography in Educational Research: A Theoretical and Practical Guide.* New York: Longman, 1996.

Cintron, Ralph. *Angel's Town: Chero Ways, Gang Life, and the Rhetorics of the Everyday.* Boston: Beacon, 1997.

Crapanzano, Vincent. *Tuhami: Portrait of a Moroccan.* Chicago: U of Chicago P, 1980.

Cushman, Ellen. *The Struggle and the Tools: Oral and Literate Strategies in an Inner City Community.* Albany: State U of New York P, 1998.

Fine, Michelle. *Disruptive Voices: The Possibilities of Feminist Research.* Ann Arbor: Michigan UP, 1992.

Freire, Paulo. *Education for Critical Consciousness.* New York: Continuum, 1987.

———. *Pedagogy of the Oppressed.* New York: Continuum, 1985.

Geertz, Clifford. *Works and Lives: The Anthropologist as Author.* Stanford, CA: Stanford UP, 1988.

Giroux, Henry. *Pedagogy and the Politics of Hope: Theory, Culture, and Schooling: A Critical Reader.* Boulder: Westview, 1997.

———. *Teachers as Intellectuals: Toward a Critical Pedagogy of Learning.* Boston: Bergin & Garvey, 1988.

Hogg, Charlotte. "From the Garden Club: Women Cultivating Identity and Culture through Literacy." Diss. U. of Nebraska-Lincoln, 2001.

Levi-Strauss, Claude. *Tristes Tropiques.* 1955. New York: Atheneum, 1974.

McLaren, Peter. *Life in Schools: An Introduction to Critical Pedagogy in the Foundations of Education.* 3rd ed. New York: Longman, 1998.

Mead, Margaret. *Coming of Age in Samoa.* 1922. New York: Mentor, 1949.

Shor, Ira, ed. *Freire for the Classroom: A Sourcebook for Liberatory Teaching.* Portsmouth, NH: Boynton/Cook/Heinemann, 1987.

———. *Empowering Education: Critical Teaching for Social Change.* Chicago: U of Chicago P, 1992.

Shostak, Marjorie. *Nisa: The Life and Words of a !Kung Woman.* New York: Vintage, 1981.

———. *Return to Nisa.* Cambridge, MA: Harvard UP, 2000.

8

State Standards in the United States and the National Curriculum in the United Kingdom

Political Siege Engines against Teacher Professionalism?

JOHN SYLVESTER LOFTY

THE ENGLISH LIKE TO OPINE that an Englishman's home is his castle; similarly, many teachers in the United States until recently have claimed that once their classroom doors are closed they can teach what and how they like. If independence from surveillance and censor ever was the case, then it is fast changing as the teaching profession comes under a perceived "attack" by those seeking to raise educational standards. The challenge, though, comes not only from state legislation and central government but also from a siege mentality within the ranks of teachers themselves; some have resisted pedagogical changes that might well have enhanced the success of their work in generative ways.

The sturm-und-drang quality of educational reforms in the United States and the United Kingdom has prompted educators to ask how curriculum changes will affect the short-and long-term character of teaching and learning. State agencies in the United States and central government in the United Kingdom increasingly control curriculum development by writing the standards, monitoring how teachers incorporate them into their teaching, and by assessing standards' impact on raising students' achievements. But how is teachers' professionalism affected by increasing government regulation of education? The concept of *professionalism* is itself undergoing a complex set of sea changes that I will argue is problematic for both teaching and learning. Darling-Hammond, policy analyst, writes:

> The very definition of "professionalism" in teaching has been turned on its head in public schools. Rather than connoting a high level of training and knowledge applied to practice that must, above all else, serve the needs of clients in intellectually honest ways, many policy makers and administrators use the term to mean unquestioning compliance with agency directives. . . . The "professional" teacher in common parlance is one who *does things right* rather than one who *does the right things.* (61)

Patricia Wasley, researcher for change, observes:

> Teachers' work has become less professional, more bureaucratic. Teachers are no longer able to make decisions in the best interests of their students because they are confronted by more external control, more paperwork, less time for planning and teaching, less involvement in curriculum decisions, and little control over student assessment issues. Teachers perceive that their status has changed, and they no longer command the respect the profession once had. (11)

John White, philosopher of education in the United Kingdom, argues that government's responsibility to ensure that the aims and content of education represent the people:

> does not rule out some elements of professional control. Teachers may have no privileged status in setting the wider, political goals, but they do have a special expertise when it comes to applying general prescriptions to the complexities of actual schools and actual classrooms. Where the line should be drawn between political and professional responsibility is a further question. (17)

This chapter looks at some of the effects on teachers and teaching of where that serpentine line is drawn, how it is drawn, and by whom. I refer to English teaching in two high schools where I conducted ethnographic studies, the first in Derbyshire, England, and the second in the state of Maine. The first portrait from interviews with Mary, a department head, presents secondary-level teaching in the inner-city school that I attended myself. In 1989 England and Wales sought to raise students' achievements (ages five through sixteen) by instituting a national curriculum (NC) to make explicit the structure, scope, and sequence of instructional goals. As Mary works to meet NC requirements for oracy (oral language), writing, and reading and to meet the personal needs of students with low academic aspirations, we see the ongoing challenge of designing effective instruction.

In sharp contrast, the second portrait profiles the work of a Maine department head teaching English to college-bound, senior-high students in a community with many more professional homes and doing so with far more autonomy than was available to her U.K. counterpart. In 1997 the state implemented the *State of Maine Learning Results* that sought to establish content standards although not a curriculum. This department chair has faced successfully the challenge of leading her colleagues in developing their own district-level *Results* that met, if not exceeded, the state's own guidelines.

From the perspective of critical ethnography, these portraits of teachers' work will explore key themes of power, resistance, identity politics, and liberation. The portraits illustrate a significant tension between two contrastive representations of what being a teacher means. We can plot these on a continuum between a totalizing bureaucratic regulation on the one hand and full teacher autonomy on the other. Toward the extreme of absolute government control, teachers become technicians, functionaries, or deliverers of a curriculum that a government agency designed. School inspections, teacher accountability, and national testing exert panoptic regulation over teachers' ability to design their own curriculum. Toward the other extreme, autonomy can be a problematic license to teach what and how a teacher chooses with minimal, if any, accountability to all stakeholders in education.

COMING HOME TO A NATIONAL CURRICULUM

To begin answering the question of how the standards that shaped their work affected these teachers' professionalism, I returned to the industrial midlands of Derbyshire to learn how English teaching had changed under the NC. I had read politicians' and government officials' claims about its impact on raising academic standards. But what did teachers themselves have to say? Without their perspectives and the situated knowledge that they enable us to develop, school reforms potentially will promise more than they ever can fulfill for students and at largely invisible costs to teachers' morale.

The success or failure of any curriculum will depend in large part on how well teachers can relate its requirements to the needs and interests of particular students, to their social backgrounds, and to the educational aspirations of themselves and their families. I walk from my home to school through a neighbourhood of redbrick council houses with gray slate roofs built in the 1930s. The estate was home to factory workers, labourers, and road haulage drivers. Until the pit closures of the 1970s and 1980s, it was home also to the families of coal miners. Despite industrial protests, the government closed down the area coalfields, and men had to look for other kinds of work. Women worked as nurses, as cleaners, and at other essential, underpaid services work. With hair in scarves or nets, many worked in the local paper mill and raised a generation of latchkey children.

Four hundred students from age eleven to sixteen now attend a school that with the exception of a few new classrooms is largely unchanged from the 1960s. Patchwork squares of new tiles punctuate the original roof—an approach to maintaining school buildings indicative of a local economy where unemployment is high. (From 1991 to 1997, in the sixteen to nineteen year age group, unemployment rose in the United Kingdom from 16.4% to 18.2% for men and from 12.7% to 14% for women.) Millbrook is now emerging from the most difficult period of its history. In the fall of 1998, teachers learned that the local education authority (LEA) had proposed to close their school, dismiss the staff, and move students to Daleview, a well-resourced school in a middle-class area. Millbrook had falling enrollments and was judged to provide an "inadequate educational experience." Parents hotly protested the proposal to close their own local community school; in turn, Daleview parents equally protested the proposal to merge Millbrook into Daleview, a plan that would have dramatically increased the number of students from working-class families at Daleview.

The LEA responded to reactions against the merger by asking Her Majesty's Inspectorate of Schools (HMI) to evaluate Millbrook's program. After a two-day visit by HMI, staff learned that Millbrook had been designated a failing school in need of "special measures," a severe judgment that places all aspects of a school's program of studies under extremely close and frequent scrutiny by inspectors. Resignation further deepened the already low morale of teachers in the aftermath of the HMI inspections.

My first visit to Millbrook in 1998 was prior to the HMI inspections. Teachers were under pressure to raise students' scores on national tests, yet staff spoke very positively about their school and were enthusiastic about all that their students could accomplish. As a veteran teacher and head of the English department since 1995, Mary knew clearly the kind of program she wanted for her students and believed deeply in their abilities. Her heartfelt commitment to best serve Millbrook students is expressed through her long-term efforts to motive them and to raise their academic aspirations. When she first came to the school, she asked, "Why wouldn't we teach Shakespeare to basic [lower level] students?" Then she explained to me the difficulties of selling her curriculum to students and also to fellow teachers. She pushes hard for what she believes students need and for the best way to do things.

Readers will need introducing to the NC that all schools must "deliver." As problematic as a delivery concept of curriculum and instruction is for many U.S. teachers, the term is widely used in the United Kingdom. Ironically, *to deliver* denotes both "to liberate" from constraints and "to transfer or transmit." The first meaning conveys well, then, an educational climate in which teachers are challenged through their teaching to find freedom from curricular constraints while obliged to implement a curriculum that they have not developed themselves.

ᘒᛜᘒ

The widespread but questionable public belief that academic standards had fallen led the then Conservative government to pass the 1988 Reform Act that established the NC, which features core subjects (English, math, science) and foundation subjects (design and technology, information technology, foreign language, history, geography, music, art and physical education). In 1989 the mandated NC was phased in. No curriculum change ever had been implemented so swiftly. It fulfilled a campaign promise to raise standards in the government-maintained schools in England and Wales (about 19,000 elementary and 4,000 secondary) by ensuring that all students would receive a broad, balanced curriculum.

The NC for English prescribes in detail the range of work, key skills, standard English and language study to be taught during each of four key stages, ages five through seven, seven through eleven, eleven through fourteen, and fourteen through sixteen. At the end of each key stage, students' progress through the NC is assessed by national tests that set achievement standards on an eight-level scale. Standards at level two should challenge seven-year-olds; level four, eleven-year-olds; and levels five and six, fourteen-year-olds. By Key-stage four, students are preparing to take the General Certificate of Secondary Education (GCSE) exams in up to seven subjects. Students then leave school or take advanced-level exams at eighteen required by higher education.

After rapidly implementing the NC, the need for revisions was soon apparent. In 1995 government assured schools that this version would be in place for five years to provide much-needed stability. Yet when the New Labour Party came into office it immediately inscribed the educational system by instituting in 1998 a Literacy Strategy for elementary-age students. (Now also mandated for the first years of secondary education.) Judging that too many pupils were underachieving, government sought to raise standards by requiring one hour of highly structured literacy and numeracy instruction every day. The latest initiative is the most restrictive and represents unprecedented government intervention into teachers' work; it prescribes what is to be taught, the means, and sets rigid time allocations. By contrast, the Conservative government never prescribed teaching approaches.

In both the United Kingdom and the United States, the politics of who develops the curriculum and how it is implemented has strongly shaped teachers' attitudes to working with standards. Teachers' responses depend on and over time change in reaction to evolving policies and initiatives for their own grade levels. Although U.K. teachers now broadly accept the NC, when first introduced teachers reacted strongly to its extreme level of detail and implementation by government mandate. Prior to 1989, few teachers imagined the extent to which any government could arrogate responsibility for curriculum standards. Teachers regarded consultations between the former National Curriculum Council and themselves as scant, token, and accelerated; teacher ownership was virtually nonexistent. To its credit, the Qualifications and Curriculum Authority (QCA) worked hard to elicit more input from teachers, and the 1995 and the 1999 versions more fully reflected their perspectives.

TEACHING AND ASSESSING ORACY: IN TEACHERS WE TRUST?

Before the NC teachers were free to give more or less attention to developing students' competence in speaking and listening; many teachers gave less, assuming that over time different kinds of talk would occur in the context of other English work. Oracy now is integrated fully into the English curriculum along with reading and writing. By ensuring that all teachers provide all students with structured opportunities to practice a range of different kinds of talk, teaching according to the NC effectively prevents teachers from neglecting oracy.

The range requirement prescribes the different purposes for talk that students must practice, for example, explanation, description, narration, argument, persuasion and analysis. Requirements specify that "pupils should be given opportunities to talk in a range of contexts, including those that are more formal. They should be encouraged to adapt their presentation to different audiences and to reflect on how their talk varies" (Department for Education 17).

This section describes how a computer simulation designed to provide practice opportunities for fourteen-year-old students to practice oracy influences teachers' freedom to design their own instruction and to assess learning. The simulation involved students in collaboratively solving a murder mystery. Every fifteen minutes, a printout provided each group with the next clue to find the murderer. In structuring talk, teachers must promote different kinds of group work so that, "In taking different roles in group discussions, pupils should be introduced to ways of negotiating consensus or agreeing to differ" (DFE 17).

Most students' motivation was very high for much of the exercise. They were engaged by quickly piecing together the jigsaw puzzle of clues that the printouts provided. Students talked animatedly as they tried to figure out what had happened by guessing, reasoning, and building one set of inferences on another. Driven by a complex game of critical thinking, the collaborative activity fostered valuable problem-solving skills. The session ended with each group presenting its interpretation of who committed the crime.

Students' learning appeared significant and meaningful to teacher and students alike. As the session progressed, Mary moved from group to group to observe her students at work, to answer questions, and to make criterion-referenced assessments of their speaking and listening skills for the mandated oracy assessments. The NC prompts teachers to think continually about their need to demonstrate and document how and where they meet its various requirements. Her planning always attends, then, to the ways in which each oral activity can satisfy the criteria to practice over time different kinds of talk.

> Most assessments would hit two boxes [kinds of talk]. I think you cannot let the tail [assessment] wag the dog, too much. You say, "this is what we are going to do." And you can look at it [an activity], and think, right, it will hit one box whatever you do. You have to keep your eye on the fact that you have to keep your eye on all of the boxes at some point. . . . The directive is that you must provide the students with the situations which will get them the best grade. You have to. That is your job.

Mary's concern with "hitting the boxes," however, shows the danger of assessment reductively driving (in contrast to being meaningfully integrated into) instructional and curricular goals. Oracy assessments are given the same weight as are the external tests for reading and writing, but teachers themselves assess oracy. Some teachers rightly fear that its curricular importance will diminish if the public regards oracy assessments as subjectively based on teacher observations of their own students. In contrast, Standard Achievement Tasks are set for reading and writing. The scores that parents read in the newspaper form the basis for public judgments about the effectiveness of each school's instruction.

The Office for Standards in Education (OFSTED) monitors and regulates the quality of education in the United Kingdom, specifically the standards that schools and teachers must reach. OFSTED inspections require a one-week visit every four years. (The cycle can be longer or shorter relative to students' national test results and to previous inspection findings.) An inspection team comprehensively reviews all aspects of school curricula, directly observes teachers at work, and targets areas to improve. Unfortunately, but with good reasons, many teachers regard OFSTED as a Big Brother government agent, an attitude antithetical to a professional development model that promotes teacher-driven program change. Furthermore, preparing the exhaustive paper trail of evidence to document teachers' oral assessments proved time-consuming for teachers to compile and for OFSTED inspectors to read.

To return to the question of what teaching and assessing oracy reveal about the effects of the NC on teachers' professionalism: the condition for being a professional that teachers have substantial autonomy to initiate thoughtful instructional practices that meet students' needs is satisfied here. Although the NC specifies teaching a wide range of talk, the provision does not determine the means by which teachers meet the requirement. Teachers are free, then, to design instruction attuned to students' learning needs and local interests.

The condition, though, for being a professional that national-level regulatory bodies place trust in teachers' accurate and responsible evaluations of students' work is violated in this example. Because teachers' own judgments, individually, collectively, or both, in interschool groups are minimally trusted, external moderators surveil all teacher evaluations. Mary must document and justify her assessments in a time-consuming and painstakingly detailed process that promotes unreasonably high levels of anxiety.

When OFSTED officials inspect a school, they will ask for assessment evidence. If teachers' morale is shaped in part by how OFSTED officials recognize their professional expertise, then we would not expect to see teachers placed in such a defensive position. The issue is not that teachers are asked to provide adequate, appropriate evidence for their assessments, but that they are asked for ever-increasing amounts. Documenting takes much-needed time from other work. Although OFSTED's intent is to ensure quality, one harmful effect has been to undermine teachers' credibility. Monitoring needs to be understood in the context of increasing politicization of education over assessment and teaching. Lori Poulson argues:

> [A] number of aspects of English and its teaching have been highly politicized, and curriculum policy has been shaped by the beliefs and prejudices of an influential minority of right-wing campaigners. In particular, agencies such as OFSTED have been particularly vocal in making claims about the benefits of whole-class teaching and the relative benefits of different teaching methods. . . . There has [sic] been concerted attacks on assessment through coursework, and on teachers' emphasizing individual and group work at the expense of whole-class teaching. (112)

A One-Size Reading Curriculum for All Students

When assessing the value of curriculum standards and the kinds of English programs that they promote, teachers will ask how a program serves not only the need to demonstrate understanding of a subject but also to discover and pursue students' own intellectual, emotional, and social needs and interests. Whether in the United Kingdom or in the United States, subject English increasingly is defined in terms that encompass the personal, social, and cultural realms of language use. Increasingly, we hear our students asking, "beyond a grade, what is in this for me?" From kindergarten to college English, students value opportunities to explore these domains as readers, writers, and speakers as well as to shape their own emerging identities.

Given the different kinds of students who attend Millbrook and their varied career aspirations, Mary faces a double challenge: to design English programs that will provide the kinds of talking, reading, and writing the NC requires; second, to meet her students' needs for literacy activities attuned to their own interests and to the work world they soon will enter. In terms of curriculum design, however, how well can one size fit all students? Mary is caught in the tension between her professional responsibility to develop a curriculum that best serves particular students' needs and her nonnegotiable duty to ensure that her program meets NC requirements for reading.

For students ages fourteen to sixteen years, "Pupils should be introduced to major works of literature from the English literary heritage in previous centuries. They should also read literature by major writers from earlier in the twentieth century and works of high quality by contemporary writers" (DFE 20). Although the range encompasses American and multicultural literature, the primary emphasis is ensuring that students are conversant with canonical British literature. The NC offers a list of canonical texts that pupils should read: two plays by Shakespeare, drama by major playwrights, two high-quality works of fiction by major writers published before 1900 and two post-1900 works, a section of poems by major poets again published both before and after 1900. Mary comments:

> This was the contentious section. How did this fit in with what staff were doing anyway? You looked at it and thought, "my goodness! We have got all that to include. It looks like a tremendous list." Teachers' response was, "how are we supposed to do all of that?" At the back of your mind all the time, you have to keep the orders [for English] in your head and juggle those around with any examination criteria that might occur.

Many teachers were overwhelmed by the scope of what the NC now required them to cover. Although initially daunted, teachers such as Mary and her colleagues were able to manage the task by determining what they already were covering, a valuable strategy to prompt teachers to review the adequacy of the existing range of literature taught. The NC for eleven- to thirteen-year-old students allows for much wider latitude of instructional approaches than does the NC for those who are age fourteen to sixteen years. As students prepare for the GCSE exams, much more formal writing and teaching replace personal responses to text and project work.

In terms of respecting teachers' professional abilities to select their own texts for students, the issue is twofold: the means by which periodic curriculum reviews are set in motion and the reviews' complete authority over teachers. Mary's professionalism is compromised as she considers how to meet government imposed curriculum requirements.

> You walk about with all this baggage in your head. You know you have got to do autobiographies, biographies, journals, diaries, letters, travel writing, leaflets. We carry this baggage around with us. We are very careful to include in our planning that all these things are there. It's the proving bit, the actual documentation.

Her words, "You know you have got to do . . ." conveys again the coerced response to the imperative language of the NC. When Mary describes her own instructional goals, her agency and language of ownership is so different, "I want my pupils to be able to. . . ."

Mary has taught for more than twenty years, continued graduate-level education, read widely, and successfully led her department. She knows well the kinds of texts that will motivate and be worthwhile for her students to read. Yet the high degree of prescriptiveness in statements about the range of literature and nonfiction that students must read conveys a limited trust in the judgments that teachers would make regarding what is appropriate reading. Government officials would reply that it must prescribe readings because many U.K. students previously have not been exposed to an adequate range. Although this situation most likely is true in some schools, a profession-based solution is for teachers to become much more informed about what readings are available and then to argue for their value. The profession at large, however, has been remiss to its own grave detriment in taking this initiative.

STUDENT ASPIRATIONS: "YOUNG PEOPLE DON'T THINK THEY ARE GOING TO GET JOBS"

To understand how well the NC meets the language needs of those students who were not college bound, I talked with a group about their research into the lives of parents and grandparents who worked the coalmines. This project, though, was done not in school but by a local church leader who gathered the teenagers who "hung out" in the churchyard. My conversations offered a window on students' responses to uses of literacy the NC did not immediately address, for example, to use language to discover and express self, to build community among students, and to explore one's own culture and history.

In a conversation that echoed Paul Willis's discussions of why working-class boys get working-class jobs, Becky, then in her last year of school, described for me the kinds of work that women of her mother's and grand-parent's generation had done:

> They didn't have any choices *either.* They had to stay at home and clean the house. They couldn't get jobs down pit. I don't know [what other work was available]. I don't think that women did work that much in them *[sic]* days. I think they just stayed at home and looked after kids. If the women had kids, they didn't have any choices but to stay at home. They couldn't have worked anyway. (emphasis added)

If the previous generations of women had few options to work outside of their homes, then what about Becky's own generation?

> Young people don't think they are going to get jobs. They think they don't have to bother [in school] because they aren't going to get jobs anyway. I don't think they think there are any decent jobs that young people could have 'cause of all unemployment. They are just going to end up on dole. That's what happens most of time. No decent jobs, stay at home watching TV. Not doing much. I wouldn't like it.

Many women will work in low-paid services industries. A few will go into careers that require college diplomas such as nursing or business. Careers for men are limited to various forms of unskilled or skilled manual labour. Sadly, many young people will start their work lives unemployed with no faith in credentials to enhance their work options beyond those of their parents. Although encouraged to seek further qualifications, few students will do so.

The process of portraying the lives of people that students knew and cared about connected them to their neigbourhood's history, and enabled them to find their own voices as writers. But a minister did this English outside of school; his goal was to empower disaffected youngsters by enabling them to vividly encounter their own identities in language, culture, and history. Empowered students, however, do not necessarily possess the kinds of literacy the NC values and measures. If students do not gain certain language skills, then their work options are diminished, no matter how motivated to write about their lives and community.

Such projects embody a social-construct conception of English that is strategically different from that of the NC. In conversation, students and teachers design their own learning. Building on Maxine Greene's concept of "curriculum as possibility," Patricia Stock explains that, "Teachers in a dialogic curriculum ask students to pose curricular invitations for themselves and one another and to use the resources available to them to learn what they need and want to know. That is, teachers in a dialogic curriculum teach students to become self-directed learners" (34).

To use language for personal and social purposes is consistent with the kinds of talk and writing that the NC requires, for example, to encourage students to write "for aesthetic and imaginative purposes" (DFE 23). These purposes, however, are much less likely to receive direct attention by teachers as they plan instruction because the formal language of the NC does not itself evoke interpersonal and creative uses of language.

After hearing Mary talk about the difficulty of motivating students not only to achieve high enough grades for college but also to aspire to further schooling, I question how well any English program designed to serve NC requirements can also address older students' focus on their future lives. By fifteen, many students feel the need to leave school, find work, and often to start families. How reasonable is it, then, to expect one curriculum to serve equally well those who are willing and able to prepare for exams and those who by age fourteen already are disaffected but cannot yet leave school until age sixteen?

For those students who leave after high school, English programs at least must address the acid test of meeting their perceived needs. Opportunities to explore the life worlds of language can have more appeal, relevance, and utility than do academic and school uses for literacy. Mary strongly encourages and provides opportunities for her students to talk and write about their own lives in meaningful ways. For example, they write and publish their own poetry. But her first nonnegotiable duty is to prepare students to take rigorous GCSE exams that require detailed knowledge of set, canonical texts and to demonstrate that knowledge, for example, by analytic and argumentative writing. This priority constrains Mary's ethical commitment and her ability to design programs that also can offer students the kind of English that so engaged Becky and her friends by meeting their sociolinguistic needs.

Patricia Wasley observes, "Definitions of professional practice commonly agree that professionals develop a specialized knowledge base from which appropriate decisions can be made on behalf of clients; that professionals have the ability to apply that knowledge in individual, non-routine circumstances; and that they have a strong ethical commitment to do what is best for the client" (16). As a professional, Mary should be free to design a literacy program attuned to local students' needs and interests and that supports national standards.

I began this chapter by asking how the NC has reshaped teachers' work and has affected their professional identity. We have seen, for example, that although required to teach and assess oracy, Mary is free to design her own creative approaches. We also have seen how the NC and preparing students for the GCSE exam limits her choice of readings and the kinds of English that she can offer to those students who are not college bound.

One curriculum for all schools, given inevitable variations in how it is taught, potentially can unify instruction and ensure that all students receive the highest quality of education. Teachers expending energy thinking about how to meet curriculum goals in which they have had insufficient professional investment, however, undercut the intent. For Mary, the amount and detail of documenting required to support her assessments has promoted defensiveness and low morale among her staff and has taken critical time away from preparing and working with students and from teachers' own professional development.

Government officials would counter that the close monitoring needed to ensure the quality of assessments and, in turn, of instruction are essential so that all teachers in all schools meet all of the various NC requirements. School inspections do have value in monitoring schooling to ensure that students receive the quality of education to which they are entitled under the 1988 Reform Act. But the authoritarian way that OFSTED has done this prompts us to argue that our profession needs to be trusted more broadly than it is to enable it to regulate its own practices.

Teachers report that OFSTED inspected schools less aggressively in 2002 than in 1997 and shares more information directly with teachers. Principals talk now about schools being encouraged to monitor their own standards. Internal surveillance, however, equally undermines teachers' professionalism. By asking teachers to self-regulate, government's apparently hands-off approach is panoptic because the standards are still government-developed ones and is potentially divisive as teachers monitor and evaluate each other's work.

TEACHER PROFESSIONALISM IN THE UNITED STATES

The school district in the state of Maine that I describe next offers a very different picture of how teachers' professionalism is affected by government regulation from that of Mary's school in Derbyshire. Relative to her school at the bureaucratic end of the continuum of control, this Maine high school is closer to the end of teacher autonomy. Before Maine implemented its *Learning Results* in 1997, the school already had developed its own *Results* that on a standard-by-standard comparison met, if not exceeded, those of the state.

As the English committee developed its *Results,* Kate, the English department chair, consulted the standards for English language arts the International Reading Association (IRA) and National Council of Teachers of English (NCTE) developed, her own professional organization whose work she strongly supports. As we shall see, however, many of her teachers, beginning and experienced alike, strongly resisted change and what they saw as a threat to their autonomy to teach both what and how they saw fit.

A program of well-resourced professional development committed to raising standards by meaningful, planned change from behavioral-to out-comes-based education has facilitated the high level of curricular initiatives evident in Kate's school. The resources for regular professional development in a modern, well-equipped school district owe much to a diverse local economy. Although many families work in fishing and marine-related services in this coastal community, a number of professional-class parents work in various businesses, light industry, commerce, and other white-collar jobs. Many high school students (60% to 65%), both young men and women, will attend college in and out of state. The local economy also has benefited from retiree investments in real estate and from a heavy influx of tourists. Schools have gained tax dollars sufficient to provide well-resourced facilities and to ensure adequate staff and programs for a very high-quality education.

STATE OF MAINE LEARNING RESULTS

When I spoke with Maine teachers in 1997, their work was not framed as yet by the state's *Results* as was U.K. teachers' by the 1989 NC. Throughout our conversations, however, the *Results* offered one set of standards against which aspects of Kate's practices could be compared and as a discussion document for what she believed her students needed. The Maine *Results* are based on six guiding principles that describe the competences and dispositions that students must achieve by the time they graduate. A student must be, "a clear and effective communicator, a self-directed and life-long learner, a creative and practical problem solver, a responsible and involved citizen, a collaborative and quality worker and an integrative and informed thinker" (Maine Department of Education 3). The *Results* are conceived not as discrete subjects, but as "areas of learning that will embrace a number of discrete courses or disciplines" (Maine iii). The areas are: career preparation, English language arts, health and physical education, mathematics, modern and classical languages, science and technology, social studies, visual and performing arts.

Compared with the 50-page specific descriptions of what students must receive under the NC for English in the United Kingdom, the ten pages of *State of Maine Learning Results* for English are succinctly and more generally organized around eight standards. For example:

A. Process of reading: Students will use the skills and strategies of the reading process to comprehend, interpret, evaluate, and appreciate what they have read.

B. Literature and culture: Students will use reading, listening, and viewing strategies to experience, understand, and appreciate literature and culture.

. . .

G. Stylistic and rhetorical aspects of writing and speaking: Students will use stylistic and rhetorical aspects of writing and speaking to explore ideas, to present lines of thought, to represent and reflect on human experience, and to communicate feelings, knowledge, and opinions. (Maine 11)

The *Results* present up to twelve performance indicators for each standard at grade levels pre-K–2; 3–4; 5–8; and secondary. For example, under reading, at pre-K–2 students will "2. Demonstrate an understanding that reading is a way to gain information about the world" (13) and by secondary grades, students will "1. Demonstrate an understanding that reading is a gradual process of constructing meaning and revising initial understandings." (13) My own interest, however, is not in the content of the standards themselves but in how teachers assess their value relative to their own curriculum goals and to their relative autonomy to determine what they will teach. The Maine Department of Education has been careful to state that the *Results* are to be read neither as a curriculum nor as an attempt to determine pedagogy.

PRIVATE AND PUBLIC DOMAINS OF CURRICULUM: WHAT IS A TEACHER'S OWN BUSINESS?

Although Kate was frustrated in the 1980s by her school district not having written curriculum guidelines to suggest educational goals, that situation changed when she became department chair. She asked teachers to develop *Learning Results* for their district. If we contrast this participatory approach to developing district-level *Results* with the top-down model of the NC that excluded anything but token input, then the process that Kate describes was exemplary. The process incorporated the professional input of all stakeholders of education from teachers and curriculum consultants to parents and students.

Yet Kate's department strongly resisted a task that proactively positioned teachers with their own *Results* in place by the time the state issued its *Learning Results.* The reasons for that resistance reveal a key feature of teachers' own perceptions of their professionalism.

> In this department it was painful on many days when we had to work on *Learning Results* because people were so resistant to them. They didn't see any application to the classroom. . . . Teachers were not on task. They were difficult to work with. They didn't want to do it. They saw the work as stupid. "Why are we doing all this stuff? This isn't our job!" People don't see

thinking about what you are doing, really being reflective about your practice, as valuable. . . . They wanted to be left to do what they wanted to do.
Everyone in the department felt that the curriculum was their business. They
felt they should be the ones to determine the curriculum.

Previously Kate had asked her teachers to submit written curricula to document the scope of their work. Her request, however, struck several teachers as
an attempt to standardize their work and to deprive them of their perceived
right to teach what and how they chose. The two most recalcitrant yet successful teachers were recent graduates in their late twenties.

Although Kate was critical of and puzzled by her teachers' nonreflective
attitude toward their work, she quickly pointed out that "they were not
unusual teachers. That is typical of teachers. I have taught in other schools. I
think that the teachers in the other schools felt the same way." Kate otherwise
respected and enjoyed her colleagues. "These were my friends." As we consider these teachers' belief that her request to develop *Results* challenged their
autonomy, we need to recognize that their resistance affected Kate's morale.
Her membership in a professional community was undercut by several colleagues' refusal to participate in anything but token ways.

On an individual level, developing *Results* for all teachers infringed on
what many saw as their right to complete autonomy. The process for Kate,
although personally hard for two years, was a professionally enriching one. "I
enjoy thinking about those kinds of things, and many of these *Results* are
things that are near and dear to my heart anyway. Near and dear to most English teachers' hearts. Who wouldn't feel that understanding the power of the
spoken and written word was important for students?"

A further measure of Kate's independence from state regulation is that as a
department chair she and her faculty felt able to reject those state *Results* that
did not complement and hence support their own conceptions of teaching. "I
feel that as far as the state of Maine *Results* and the NCTE standards, we already
have meshed them into our own, or have rejected them for whatever reason we
felt we wanted to reject them. So that is why those documents are important,
but I feel ours can stand on their own right now." The school also adopted one
standard from the NCTE that the state did *not* require. For teachers to address
an extra standard on students' participation in different literacy communities
takes teaching time and it could have led teachers to question the need for their
students to participate in literacy communities beyond those of the school. That
Kate and her teachers accepted the standard's importance indicates their independence from the need for state approval and a conviction about the value of
standards the NCTE, their own professional organization developed.

Teachers might have seen the absence of a local standard from the state's
standards as an implied lack of its immediate value and utility. But teaching

to minimal compliance, in contrast to taking initiative, limits severely the scope of teachers' own professional growth. We have seen this major issue already in the United Kingdom. Most important, when teachers do not reach for what they believe in, when they do not engage in what Hannah Arendt describes as "enlarged thinking" (Robinson 14), then the curricular richness of what they might offer to students is severely limited. Over time, Kate's development initiatives did lead to hard-earned transformations of teachers' attitudes. Teachers moved from holding private, territorial attitudes toward curriculum as their own business, to holding attitudes of curriculum as a publicly shared, professional collaboration.

In considering the question of what is a teacher's own business, we need to distinguish between teachers resisting the request to make their individual curricula public, and teachers resisting the standardization of their work by the imposition of *Results* that all teachers then must meet. If we accept that a teacher's freedom is circumscribed by the ethical imperative to make decisions that best serve students' academic needs and to document where and how teachers do this, then resisting public accountability is unreasonable. Peers, parents, and administrators gain much by fully understanding teachers' work.

On the other hand, if we believe that for teachers to be professionals they must participate in developing the standards that shape their work, then resistance to state mandates in the United States and to government mandates in the United Kingdom, is understandable and essential to building a professional culture. The teachers I spoke with also had resisted the *State of Maine Learning Results* because the consultations between the Department of Education and teacher groups had appeared more token than real, the same scenario as in the United Kingdom. For teachers not to resist would have forfeited the measure of autonomy that they possessed. But in the situation of Kate's department, teachers initially were resisting collaborative work through which as a group they did achieve professional voice and recognition in their own district.

STUDENTS AT RISK: "YOU NEED TO START WITH SOMETHING UP THERE FOR ALL STUDENTS"

Teachers in Maine and in the United Kingdom, too, commonly ask whether the standards are intended and can apply to all students. To their credit, the *State of Maine Learning Results* state from the outset that without regard for specific career and academic plans, "These standards establish goals for what all students *should know and be able to do,* including students with unique learning needs and/or identified disabilities. . . . A comprehensive, personalized planning approach will be helpful in this effort to identify and meet the unique needs of individual students" (Maine V).

As much as Kate enjoys working with her most able students, many of whom will go on to college, she is equally committed to teaching students with "unique learning needs":

> I would really hate to see poverty of curriculum for some students. I have seen that, and I don't like it. That is one of the things that as department head I have been working hard to eradicate. I don't want to see courses called "three strikes and you are out." If I were a parent, I would be enraged if my kid had reading or aspiration problems and was put in a course written all over it "terminal English student." No chance of ever surviving.

From her earliest teaching, Kate has worked hard to develop strategies that will enable all students to succeed, however limited their abilities, motivation, or aspirations might appear initially:

> I think there are different strategies to achieve the *Results*. I think it is unrealistic to think that all kids are going to be able to do these in the same way or at the same age. But we need to have the expectation that standards are for all kids. That is one thing that we have made some progress on in this school. Teachers are encouraged to treat *all* students the same, to put them in the least restrictive environment, to give them lots of help and to give them as much help as they need. I have had kids in my college prep class who were learning disabled. You could barely read what they had written. But their minds were just as sharp as could be.

Given that much teaching often has been a one-size-fits-all approach, adapting approaches is critical if standards are to serve alike the most and least able students. Kate describes how her teaching of reading supports that end by building literacy communities:

> About three years ago we started an independent reading program, and we encouraged kids to read a lot and read more. The teacher checked in with the student to see if he or she was reading a book [by] having a book talk. The program fosters independent reading and creates a culture of literacy communities because it gets kids talking about books. They can join a book group or read books and go home and talk to their parents. I see the least able kid function very well with those book talks.

From the perspective of promoting literacy communities, these reading practices illustrate well the potential for literacy to promote conversation for all students within the classroom and between home and school. The independent reading program offers one kind of literacy community and thereby works toward meeting that standard. Because the school reading program preceded teachers writing their own standard, it clearly reflects what they regarded as an important reading practice to represent in their own district's *Results*.

Recall now the students in England who built a literacy community through an oral history project; this work, though, was done not in school but through a church group. Teaching under the NC with written exam assessments, Mary was unable to design the same kind of individualized literacy program than Kate's teachers can. Consequently, Mary is less able than Kate to motivate at-risk students to remain in school. When teachers write standards, then they gain public affirmation of their own professional knowledge and they are able to fulfill their ethical commitment to serve all students' needs and interests.

"Snapshot" versus "Whole-Reel" Assessments

Teachers' reliance on different ways to assess students' learning offers a key point of comparison between the effects of standards on teacher professionalism in the United Kingdom and in the United States. The Maine Educational Assessment tests (MEAs) predate the *Results* by a decade but only recently have been used to assess students' and teachers' progress toward achieving them. Although Kate notes her students' performances on the MEAs, she has little to say about them; her students take the MEAs in grade 11 and typically do well. Kate's focus is not on external testing but on developing assessments that measure adequately her students' progress toward reaching her own district's *Results*. For Kate, the snapshot MEAs provide much less information for formative assessment purposes than is available through reading students' portfolios and watching students present their learning before a peer audience. She devotes little time to prepare students to take summative tests and much more time to develop continuous, "whole-reel" assessments.

Over time, Kate's attitude about the value of large-scale assessments has changed:

> Ten years ago I would have been more enthusiastic about racing ahead and trying to think up some assessment tools. I feel now that we really need to get down with this and take our time and work our way through it. I think the assessment will reveal itself through the work that we are doing. I think it's going to take a lot more time than I ever thought it would. At this point in my career, I feel like I need to learn to be more patient, to hurry up and wait.

Given that we tend to think of assessment as deliberately applying objective criteria to the features of a piece of work, Kate's belief that "the assessment will reveal itself through the work that we are doing" might appear overly subjective. In the past, she would have "raced ahead" to develop "assessment tools." Now, however, recognizing a more complexly integrated relationship between assessment and learning, she closely observes teaching and learning until the means of assessment become visible in the work itself. In that one dense statement, Kate reveals the depth and complexity of her professional judgments.

By comparison, the assessments available in the United Kingdom to Mary and her students are much less intuitive, rely much less on the judgments of individual teachers about students' growth over time and rely more on paper-and-pencil tests. The Qualifications and Curriculum Authority (QCA) developed these tests, and they are administered at the end of each key stage. The issue here is not the utility of criteria, which feature strongly in rubric assessments now popular across the United States, but in the heavier reliance in the United Kingdom on snapshot rather than on wholereel evidence. The 100% teacher assessment of the GCSE exams in the 1980s was very popular with teachers even though it involved extra work. To ensure reliability, teachers discussed their assessments with colleagues from a consortium of area schools.

Teachers' sharing of their understanding of curriculum standards became community-building conversations that represented real occasions for professional development. That teachers were entrusted to assess the writing of their own students, and of other teachers' students' writing, too, signaled government's respect for teachers' competence and trustworthiness. This respect has been undercut, however, by the pervasive use of the tests and by much heavier weighting of the GCSE exam in relation to teachers' own assessment of their students' course work.

Government officials, school administrators, and parents all too often view school scores as an accurate measure of teacher and school effectiveness. But the gross misuse of high-stakes test scores has been problematic in the United Kingdom and across the United States, as Alfie Kohn argues in *The Case against Standardized Testing*. Interpreting scores is a complex process. In both countries, the public naïvely have equated low scores with poor schools and teaching without factoring in, for example, the socioeconomic resources of one district in relation to another, the "value" that teachers have added to students' entry-level abilities, or even the validity and reliability of the tests themselves.

The problem has been compounded with media reporting scores in descending order, an issue in the United Kingdom with "league tables" of schools. Government stigmatizes failing schools by imposing special measures on them. In a democracy, government must ensure that professions do serve the public good by being responsible for the quality of services that they provide. But the means of assessing and reporting on the quality of education must address the complexity of learning and reflect teachers' knowledge and expertise with assessment.

TOWARD BUILDING A PROFESSIONAL CULTURE

This chapter provides an overview of the work of Mary, one U.K. teacher whose professional autonomy and attendant ability to meet the academic and interpersonal needs of all students, particularly those about to leave school, is heavily constrained by an NC, school inspections, and national assessments. In contrast is the work of Kate in Maine who enjoys a degree of autonomy that allows her to design instruction that meets and exceeds state-mandated *Learning Results*. Her students perform well on state tests, but the tests do not take time away from her teaching.

At the time of this research in 1997–1998, relative to each other, these teachers occupied positions at the opposite ends of a continuum between totalizing bureaucratic regulation and full teacher autonomy, between deterministic control and liberatory decision-making. At the time of publication, however, these teachers' positions most likely will have shifted. U.K. teachers conceivably could have more participation in curriculum design and assessment and Maine teachers could have less. Teachers and administrators, for example, in Massachusetts, California, and Ohio already encounter state standards and testing beyond their control. And now on the national level, president George Bush's "No Child Left Behind Act" of 2001 challenges each state to develop an action plan to provide greater accountability by testing students in grades 3–8. My purpose here is to prompt readers to recognize the positions that circulate among all stakeholders in education and to consider why professionalism is increasingly important to improve the quality of public education.

The issue is not simply that teachers strongly resent unprecedented government intervention in the curriculum where previously they had much more autonomy. Sergiovanni and Starratt argue that control is critical for teacher motivation:

> Teachers and students have expressed a demand for control over their work environment and, indeed, over their destiny. The need for autonomy that many educational participants express is based on the principle of self-government, self-control and determination. Teachers, in particular, display formidable credentials in terms of professional expertness as justification for expression of this need. (139)

The kind of autonomy for which I am arguing is not for an extreme independence free from accountability, but rather for empowered teachers who are able to explore and exploit the possibilities for a curriculum that liberates both teachers and students alike. Teachers are not under surveillance but are fully trusted professionals. Extreme regulation brings what Wise referred to in 1979 as "legislated learning" with the attendant problem of a "tell-me-what-to-do" mentality. When imposed standards legislate new practices, as valuable as the practices may or may not be, an external locus of control is much less likely to elicit teachers' support than when professional development prompts teachers themselves to make informed curriculum and instructional choices. Unless and until teachers actively support standards, the extent to which they ever can transform teaching and learning is much diminished.

The discourse of literacy, power, and resistance come into play here as teachers and policy makers contest how and by whom *literacy* is to be defined. Public debate about standards is itself ideologically freighted with references, for example, to canonical works, to standard English, and to what Brian Street describes as the "objectifying [of] language at school." He writes, "In the classroom we observed, teachers appeared to treat language as though it were something outside both the students and themselves, as though it had autonomous, non-social qualities that imposed themselves upon its users" (116). He further observes, "Indeed, much of the debate about literacy 'standards,' currently highlighted in the work of Hirsch (1987, 1988) and Bloome, Puro and Theodorou (1989) in the USA, does make explicit as well as implicit reference to nationalism" (126).

With the expressed purpose of raising the national standards, government has become increasingly involved in the business of schooling, and teachers have become less involved in making professional decisions essential to meeting students' needs. How might we begin to resolve the tension between teacher autonomy and what Darling-Hammond refers to as 'accountability' and what Shulman presents as "obligation" to the public and to the policy makers that they serve? In terms of critical ethnography and advocacy, what might teachers do to build and to sustain a professional culture that would satisfy both the public and the profession?

The challenge that teachers now face in building a professional culture is part of the larger problem of a profession without clearly defined structures to resolve the tension between teachers' individual autonomy and their public accountability. As Darling-Hammond observes, "The structure of the profession is critical here, for it defines the groups' boundaries and its reach. Teaching has suffered from the lack of such a professional structure—a community within the community—by the balkanization of the occupation and by its failure to seek resolution of competing claims for accountability and autonomy from within and without" (68).

In Maine, Kate has argued that one of several obstacles to getting teachers to develop learning *Results* and performance indicators collaboratively was teachers' belief that they were autonomous agents; teachers were suspicious of any attempts to hold them accountable to what they viewed as a standardization of their work. Although Kate's principal, Isaac, valued standardizing "what you would hope would be the outcomes for students," Isaac was keen for teachers to create their own curricular pathways to reach these goals:

As an instructor, the teacher is adding his or her own person to the material, their own interpretations, their own variations on presentations, their own ways to engage students. I certainly don't see it as a lock-step approach. Historically, teachers have been the queens and kings of their own classrooms. They have ruled, more or less, in terms of the instruction that is taking place in that classroom. And anything from the outside is perceived as threatening to some extent. That is part of what makes fundamental change in school so difficult to achieve. If teachers feel that there is flexibility in the instructional process on a day in and day out basis while working toward the same generalized goal across classrooms, then change will be more palatable. One proof [of successful change] would be at the end of that process are students achieving the same goals regardless of how you have got there?

As a principal actively involved in developing new models of school leadership, Isaac understands well the need for change. But he recognizes that lasting changes in how teachers approach their work are unlikely to occur by state mandate alone:

For change to take place in a school, or as a whole in individual classroom, those people being affected need to see what the benefit is not only for the students that they work with but also for themselves as a teacher. I don't mean that in a self-serving way but how will it enable them to do their work better, more constructively. You need to be able to show and demonstrate what those benefits are while at the same time not demeaning what that individual has done in the past.

Creating a professional culture within school minimally requires three conditions. First, teachers need to revision and effect fundamental changes in their practice that in Isaac's words represent not simply "a veneer of change" but are "really taking place at a gut level." My point here is not to propose particular changes, but to enable teachers to see the challenge to enhance student learning as generative, transforming, and evolving in response to new knowledge about teaching and learning. Most teachers will need professional development support to do that effectively over time, for example, by the innovative and powerful approaches to leadership developed by the Maine School Leadership Network and described in *Becoming Better Leaders* by Donaldson and Marnik.

A second condition is that teachers share with peers more than their own practices and textbook lore about usage, what North refers to as the "articles of faith that purportedly underlie a literate community to which the students aspire" (30). For example:

The grammars' drills on subject/verb agreement, then; the rhetoric's injunctions to be clear, unified or concise; the readers' modeling of modes and styles. . . . Hence, it isn't that these formulations are untrue, exactly. Rather, they offer, under cover of pedagogical necessity, a selective, simplified, inevitably distorted version of a far more complex body of knowledge about what it is to learn or do writing. (30–31)

Unless and until teachers are better able to articulate that "complex body of knowledge," teachers will remain at the level of practitioners, of technicians, and hence vulnerable to the reform proposals from those who assume the role of "experts." In contrast, for teachers to be members of a professional community, they will need the practitioner knowledge that my own new teachers hungrily and rightly demand, but they also must have the knowledge of the theories that inform and render their classroom practices fully intelligible both to themselves and to other stakeholders in education.

A third condition is that teachers need extended periods of time both to reflect on their individual work and to collaborate if by default teachers are not simply to continue working alone. The cost of teachers continuing to go in their own directions most likely will be very high. When school districts do not provide adequate time for teachers to share their goals, best practices, and questions, teachers' growth and that of a professional culture to sustain it is severely limited; the norm of three professional days a year is wholly inadequate.

In political terms, by working in isolation teachers maintain a profession of individuals divided by the lack of a common vision, shared practices, and group cohesion. Conversely, unity potentially will empower teachers to limit the extent to which a government, a state, or a school committee otherwise can impose, without real consultation, its own agenda for curriculum, instruction, and assessment. Professional unity can empower teachers to move toward self-determination and to enter on an equal footing into dialogue and public debate with policy makers and all who invest in improving the quality of our schools.

WORKS CITED

Bush, G. W. *No Child Left Behind.* http://www.rethinkingschools.org/bushplan.htm.

Darling-Hammond, Linda. "Policy and Professionalism" in *Building a Professional Culture in Schools.* Ed. Ann Lieberman. New York: Teachers College P, 1988.

Department for Education and the Welsh Office. *English in the National Curriculum.* London: Her Majesty's Stationary Office, 1995.

Donaldson, Gordon A., and George F. Marnik. *Becoming Better Leaders: The Challenge of Improving Student Learning.* Thousand Oaks, CA: Corwin, 1995.

Kohn, Alfie. *The Case against Standardized Testing: Raising the Scores, Ruining the Schools.* Portsmouth, NH: Heinemann, 2000.

Maine Department of Education. *State of Maine Learning Results.* Augusta, ME: Maine Department of Education, 1997.

North, Stephen M. *The Making of Knowledge in Composition: Portrait of an Emerging Field.* Portsmouth, NH: Boynton/Cook, 1987.

Poulson, Louise. *The English Curriculum in Schools.* London: Cassell, 1998.

Robinson, Jay. "Literacy and Lived Lives." *Literacy and Democracy: Teacher Research and Composition Studies in Pursuit of Habitable Spaces.* Ed. Cathy Fleischer and David Schaafsma. Urbana, IL: NCTE, 1998.

Sergiovanni, J. Thomas, and Robert J. Starratt. *Supervision: Human Perspectives.* New York: McGraw-Hill, 1988.

Shulman, L. S. "Autonomy and Obligation: The Remote Control of Teaching." *Handbook of Teaching and Policy.* Ed. L. S. Shulman and G. Sykes. New York: Longman, 1983.

Stock, Patricia L. *The Dialogic Curriculum: Teaching and Learning in a Multicultural Society.* Portsmouth: Boynton/Cook, 1995.

Street, Brian V. *Social Literacies: Critical Approaches to Literacy in Development, Ethnography and Education.* London: Longman, 1995.

Wasley, Patricia. *Teachers Who Lead: The Rhetoric of Reform and the Realities of Practice.* New York and London: Teachers College P, 1991.

White, John. *Education and the Good Life: Beyond the National Curriculum.* London: London Educational Studies, Kogan Page with the Institute of Education, University of London, 1990.

Willis, Paul. *Learning to Labour: How Working Class Kids Get Working Class Jobs.* New York: Columbia UP, 1981.

Wise, A. E. *Legislated Learning.* Berkeley: U of California P, 1979.

9

Debating Ecology

Ethnographic Writing that "Makes a Difference"

SHARON McKENZIE STEVENS

WHAT IS THE BASIS FOR ethnographic authority? This question draws increasing attention in response to critiques of positivist claims to objectivity. According to Carl Herndl, traditional ethnographers textually construct their authority by declaring their presence at a field site, then by suppressing that presence. This device erroneously suggests that texts can transparently represent cultures and that observers do not impact what they observe. In contrast, recent self-reflexive ethnographies have highlighted that how ethnographers choose to claim authority is contingent and rhetorically constructed. For example, in *Translated Woman*, Ruth Behar crafts her ethos around a recognition that she has herself changed in consequence of her research, reversing the postcolonial critique that ethnographies assist in transformations of the cultures they represent. Ralph Cintron, in *Angels' Town*, also writes self-reflexively, but in his case he reaffirms the distance between himself and the field site he has so assiduously attempted to order in his writing. What these contrastive examples suggest is that questions of authority no longer center only on whether to write self-reflexively, but also on what form of reflexivity to adopt and to what purpose.

My thanks to Tilly Warnock, Tom Miller, and the students of Tom Miller's Community Literacy Practicum for helpful comments on early drafts of this chapter.

Questions of authority and representation are central in my own research because I focus on an issue that has been culturally relegated to the jurisdiction of ecologists or experienced land managers. For the past year I have conducted interviews and observed discussions about whether and how to graze cattle in Arizona. As a rhetorical critic, I consider my field site to be the system of claims that define this public debate. Those interested in the outcome of this debate approach it through several topics—such as by questioning the economic value of ranching or by contrasting ranching with pressures for other land use such as development and recreation. One especially dominant way of debating the value of livestock is through science-based argument. I am consequently confronted by the perceived incongruity of commenting on this conflict from an ethnographic, rather than a scientific, perspective. To the ranchers, activists, and government agents who are key to this debate, the role of a rhetorical critic is anything but self-evident. In this context, self-reflexivity is not just a fashionable way to write, but also a response to the discomfort I routinely feel in my fieldwork as many of my informants challenge the authority of nonscientists to write about a "scientific" issue. For me to write with authority in this context requires that I construct a relationship to the debate that reconfigures its boundaries to include the work of an ethnographic observer trained in rhetorical analysis.

My choice of field site is in many ways a form of "studying up." Measures such as funding allocations and media coverage suggest that both career academics and the public typically grant greater cultural power to scientific rather than to ethnographic knowledge. However, the questions my site raises about authority and knowledge are also pertinent to other contexts. For many in the field of rhetoric and composition, a particularly salient form of ethnography is teacher research, which can be thought of as "studying down." However, the challenge many teachers experience when adapting theory to practice still raises questions about the nature of knowledge ethnographic study generates. What type of validity does our knowledge have? Is knowledge only knowledge if it provides a complete and practical explanation of the problem it addresses? Questions about the validity of ethnographic knowledge are crucial to ethnographic writers. How writers understand their knowledge impacts how they write. The opposite is also true. How we craft our accounts impacts the validity of our knowledge and the way our work will be useful in practice.

Feminist technoscience scholar Donna Haraway, through her concept of "diffraction," provides one thoughtful response to questions of knowledge and authority. Although Haraway does not use diffraction to describe explicitly ethnographic writing, her juxtaposition of diffraction with reflexivity invites its application by all writers concerned with how to understand and represent their relationship to their area of study. Haraway focuses on the optical metaphors underlying these two terms and voices concern that reflexivity suggests the replication of what already exists, as if our knowledge was the mirror image of what we study. She prefers to think of knowledge and writing as having the potential to "make a difference in the world," just as the patterns light creates are changed when that light is diffracted by passing from one medium to the next (16). The goal of making new, different knowledge is epistemically radical within an ethnographic tradition that has historically attempted to somehow capture the essence of a field site. Along with this radical epistemic comes an implied ethical imperative to choose carefully what type of difference that we, as ethnographic writers, choose to make.

This chapter reviews a history of ethnographic writing and discusses how a postmodern crisis of representation has led to increased reflexivity. Because of its extensive ethnographic tradition, I draw heavily from anthropology, addressing its applicability to the discipline of rhetoric and composition. Finally, I demonstrate how Haraway's concept of diffraction can fit within this tradition and I further develop its usefulness as a heuristic for ethnographic writers, demonstrating one possible application of that heuristic by reference to my own research.

Before explicitly addressing these topics, however, I wish to share a field account that demonstrates their significance. This is an account of the first public meeting I attended as part of my fieldwork. I have added some basic interpretations to signal the account's relevance to this article. Although the following account describes a typical scene that I have encountered in my study of public discourse, I mean for it not only to introduce my field site but also to tell a story about the role ethnographers have in knowledge production. This is a story about how I both physically and rhetorically position myself as I enter a new situation. It is a story about marginal observers who suddenly find themselves observed, yet still marginal—and it is about their discomfort and consequent decisions to reposition themselves. It is a story about a reflexivity initiated when those who are studied choose to look back at observers. It is a story that raises questions about ethnographic research and writing and about the significance of the meanings recorded in field notes and, by extension, ethnographic write-ups. Finally, most important, it is also a story about claiming the authority to speak and about the conflict created when different discursive traditions intersect. I intend for this story to provide more questions than answers, questions about how positioning and reflexivity affect the type of authority ethnographers construct and the type of knowledge they produce. I understand this story's significance to be not in the individual characters, but rather in the relationships between them.

FROM OBSERVATION TO PARTICIPATION IN DEBATE

After a moment's hesitation, I entered the conference room, wondering why there was no sign to announce the location of the public meeting I had come to observe.

Once inside, however, I did not need anyone to tell me that I should take a seat in one of the chairs lining the walls, rather than at the oblong table in the center of the room—a table that I correctly inferred was intended for members of the Science and Technical Advisory Team (STAT). I chose a corner seat near a woman who sat without interacting with the others present. A few other attendees were also quiet, but many stood in groups of two or three, talking together, or helping themselves to the ample refreshments provided for the meeting.

I had come today because STAT's recommendations would influence the outcome of the Sonoran Desert Conservation Plan (SDCP)—a countywide effort to identify key areas for conservation. The SDCP's mandate is to develop a management plan that preserves biodiversity while simultaneously accommodating economic stakeholders in the region, such as developers and ranchers. I was interested in learning more about the public process behind the SDCP because it incorporated many of the same concerns that, for years, had been part of a controversial debate over whether, and how, to graze cattle in southern Arizona's desert grasslands. Until now I had primarily studied this debate through private interviews with ranchers, environmental activists and conservationists, government agents, and scientists. I thought it probable that some of those I had interviewed would be at the STAT meeting, but none were, which heightened my disappointment when the STAT chair skipped the first item on the agenda, "Introductions." Throughout the meeting everyone at the table addressed each other almost exclusively by first names. This frustrated me. As with the combination of ample refreshments, on one hand, and the absence of a sign identifying the meeting location, on the other, the skipped introductions seemed to mark a tension generated by including the public in a meeting of an already-formed committee. Nonmembers of STAT were clearly welcome, but the committee's assumed knowledge was not translated in a way that was meaningful to outsiders such as myself.

As the conversation bounced from one person seated at the table to the next, I took notes on the business of the day: new funding sources had been verified; a plan the committee developed had received buy-in from the relevant agencies and governments; the "board," whomever that was, had been able to purchase a ranch in response to a completed scientific study. I had a rough idea of what people were talking about and wrote down key words, names of places, and titles of ordinances. However, I wondered if I understood enough to be able to examine my notes and write a coherent field account. It was as if the conversation I was recording was in a shorthand I did not know and my own notes were an even more reduced version of the meanings being communicated. What sort of knowledge was I generating given all these reductions? I found myself wondering how others seated along the walls, who I was now privately referring to as "wallflowers," perceived this public meeting. Were they also having trouble following the conversation? Did they also feel as marginal as I? Or had they been a part of the process long enough that the committee's discussion made sense to them?

The meeting continued. "Andrea," who I guessed was an ecologist, briefly explained a series of maps posted on one wall of the conference room. As she gave her presentation, the "wallflowers" beneath her maps became oddly near the center of attention. A couple fidgeted. As Andrea moved down the line, one man bobbed up from his seat and ducked past the oblong table, displaced to a standing position near the door. When a few more wallflowers rose as a group, the room broke into laughter, acknowledging the simultaneous invisibility and visibility of those seated where Andrea was standing. Andrea continued her monologue. She ended at a map near where I remained seated, a map that represented her team's near-final recommendations on how to classify the county's land according to biologically more or less sensitive habitat areas.

After the presentation, another STAT member elaborated on how the decisions the maps represented had been arrived at. He pointed out that STAT did not have PVAs (population vulnerability analyses) available for most species that the fieldwork had been based on. This lack of species data had prompted the committee's choice to focus on habitat. The STAT member openly discussed the disconnect between ideal knowledge—the PVAs—and the knowledge readily available for management decisions. Thinking to myself about the cultural model of science as something that can arrive at sure knowledge—knowledge that can then be confidently used to compel a clear decision—I was pleased that this man openly accepted a model that fit better with most rhetorical accounts of science. That is, he seemed at home with a science that generated partial and contingent knowledge that was nonetheless informative to management decisions. This model of knowledge mitigates against tendencies to displace the responsibility for decisions from human agency onto objectivist truth-claims. As I was nodding in approval, however, a man seated along the wall opposite to me spoke. Apparently the discussion had evoked for him also a comparison with a model that expected certainty from science. His reaction to the comparison, however, was not as positive as mine.

This man asked the committee why its members did not just go out and collect the missing data. He said that he was concerned that recommendations were being made without a scientific basis. A STAT member discussed more fully the fieldwork and science that had been used when creating the maps, explaining that STAT had created a list of fifty-six key species to use as environmental indicators. Rather than use these to create a "species-by-species management plan," STAT had opted for a habitat management plan, which many perceive as a more holistic approach.

The man questioning STAT was not appeased. He asked what the committee would do to make the indicator species "invulnerable."

Now the speaker from STAT was confused. "Invulnerable?," he queried.

The man patiently explained: If you have vulnerable species, you need to make them invulnerable. Was this not the purpose of the SDCP? I noted to myself that the man must have extrapolated from the term population vulnerability analysis. *He was using the term* vulnerable, *however, in a way that the confused STAT member would not have, taking language out of its original context and giving it meanings that were incommensurate with its original use. To support his concerns, the man cited lectures he had attended and textbooks he had read. He had clearly studied the issues he was discussing, but I thought that his manner of speaking—such as citing a textbook using the same form an academic would use to cite a journal article—suggested incomplete inclusion within the scientific discourse community STAT represented. Confident, however, in his ability to speak as a peer, the man made his final point: STAT needed to know how each indicator species responded to fire and termites and other stressors. He asked if the committee had that information.*

This type of information is difficult to obtain, explained a STAT member.

No, countered the speaker at the wall, to the laughter of many in the room. The man did not acknowledge the negative response. He cited a textbook that included a simple process for conducting PVAs. To this, a STAT member simply repeated that the process was not as simple as it appeared, adding that getting PVAs on all the species in the study could take years. In the meantime, decisions needed to be made. In evidently growing frustration at his rebuffed attempts to participate in the deliberations, the man asked: What if natural disasters occur? What about earthquakes? Certainly biotic communities are vulnerable to earthquakes?

Up to this point those who had been addressing the man had been speaking patiently with him and seriously trying to discuss his concerns. At this point, however, one young scientist exclaimed: "Earthquakes?! I disagree." The chair of the committee began actively to keep the questioner out of the conversation, calling on other raised hands in the room and naming people at the oblong table. But the discursive boundary between those at the table and those seated along the wall had been bridged. More people joined the debate. Some comments were welcome: announcements of meetings, requests for simple clarifications. Many, however, created conflict. At one point, the scientist who had scoffed at the mention of earthquakes called a question "naïve" that to me sounded competent. At another point, a latecomer responded to a mention of the need for "management buy-in" to the scientific studies by asking: "What about the property owner? You're forgetting the property owner." To this interruption, another person along the wall exclaimed in an incredulous tone: "But we're talking about biology!"

Those at the table started responding in ways that reminded me of a lesson on neo-Aristotelian rhetoric. A few times they answered interjections and questions by saying that "you"—those along the wall—had the wrong audience for their concerns, or that the meeting's purpose did not include anything but science. To the woman with the "naïve" and critical question, two STAT members pointed out that she had not attended all the committee's meetings, suggesting that her questions had once been relevant but were no longer at issue within the community of fuller participants. After all, as a STAT member emphasized, the SDCP process had been going on for years. Whatever knowledge this woman brought with her, it did not fit within the parameters of the ongoing conversation. Finally, one STAT member who had been quiet throughout the debates summarized her colleague's comments by reiterating the scientific purpose of STAT, pointing out that the meeting was not an appropriate forum for debate, and suggesting that all dissent be deferred until when the SDCP Steering Committee, to which STAT reported, would hold its next public meeting. The chair of STAT then adjourned the meeting.

I left wondering how people like me were supposed to make comments in this context. What authority did the public have when even those members willing— and able—to devote their afternoons to meetings, those who had clearly studied to develop their scientific expertise, could still not speak in a way adequate to affect the decision-making process? For a short time, the STAT scientist who had contrasted a PVA approach with the habitat analysis that STAT had instead adopted had been able, without anxiety, to make vulnerable the contingencies of the scientific process, accepting responsibility for its outcome. But the woman who spoke near the end of the meeting re-created the rhetorical boundaries between science and choice, deferring debate to a management meeting. This rhetorical construction of boundaries, this separation of science from decision-making, has implications for me in my position as an ethnographer and a rhetorical critic. I am seeking to comment on a debate whose outcome is deeply impacted by the creation and deployment of scientific knowledge. Although I consider myself to be science-literate, I am not a scientist, and I am not prepared to construct knowledge that addresses a scientific community according to its own conventions. Does this mean that my authority as an ethnographer ends where science begins?

Reconceiving Authority as Authorship: The Invention of Reflexive Ethnographic Writing

As a rhetorical critic, I consider my field site to be the type of place the Aristotelian term *topoi* references, a metaphoric site of argumentation rather than a clear geographic space. This emphasis holds even though the debate I am studying is localized in the desert grasslands of southern Arizona. The debate about whether cattle should be grazed in these areas relies heavily on ecology-based claims about the positive, neutral, or negative effects of cattle on desert grassland habitat. To focus my study, I have chosen to analyze the epistemic grounds of a set of contrasting claims about a cluster of related ecological interactions. I have classed these claims according to three major positions. (1) The grazing habits of cattle break up crusted-over topsoil and transform decaying vegetation to fertilizing manure. Therefore, when managed correctly, cattle can help in the restoration of grasslands. (2) The grazing habits of cattle promote topsoil erosion and destroy vegetation. Therefore, cattle do nothing but harm to the desert grasslands of southern Arizona. (3) Although cattle are not a wholesale direct benefit to desert grasslands and may cause harm if allowed to graze incorrectly, they can nonetheless be managed in a manner that sustains ecosystem health and productivity.

Following the tradition of cultural anthropology, especially as George Marcus has articulated and reconfigured it, I understand my function as an ethnographer to be an analysis of "cultural logics" ("Ethnography" 81). In my case, a cultural logic is an interconnected system of knowledge-claims and associated actions that cohere around a typical position that is taken within my chosen debate. Accordingly, I consider the previous three scientific-managerial claims—that is, science-based claims that support specific management actions—to be indicators of three contrasting cultural logics. Yet identifying these logics is only the first step of analysis, a "thin" description at best. As I seek to develop my understanding of these logics, I let techniques of rhetorical analysis be my guide. In particular, I am working from an approach to "social-epistemic rhetoric" James Berlin articulates in "Rhetoric and Ideology in the Writing Class." According to Berlin, social-epistemic rhetoric contends that "the real is located in a relationship that involves the dialectical interaction of the observer, the discourse community (social group) in which the observer is functioning, and the material conditions of existence" (488). Although Berlin clarifies that he is not arguing that nothing exists outside of language, Berlin does intend to claim that everything we know is thoroughly constituted by meanings shared and negotiated in our relationships with others. Knowledge, then, is a relationship, not a bounded object. Therefore, as I seek to understand a particular cultural logic, I need to account for the relationships that constitute it.

Ecological knowledge about cow-plant interactions, for example, is not lying around in the desert grasslands of southern Arizona waiting to be discovered. It is communicated among scientists in journals and textbooks, among ranchers seeking to optimize grass production, and between scientists and the interested public in workshops on the way, for example, to conduct one's own vegetation transect—a highly valued scientific method for determining changes over time in species composition. However, soil, cows, and plants are also a constitutive part of these relationships. Indeed, they are such key participants that an influential science studies theorist, Bruno Latour, assigns agency to the "nonhumans" (such as bacteria or soil) that impact the social construction of knowledge. Consequently, if my role as a rhetorical analyst requires that I position myself within the complex of relationships that constitute the cultural logics I wish to understand, I must also somehow position myself in a relationship with the nonhuman contributors to those logics. I run into difficulty here, however. As a routine interview question, I ask my informants what they read. The sources they have named to me—*The Journal of Range Science, Conservation Biology, Western Livestock Rancher*—are sources that I can interpret with easy competence. But I have not "gone native" to the point of becoming a producer, rather than just a consumer, of these claims, despite my increasing ability to understand how ecological factors such as fires, soil types, rainfall patterns, and the propagation of introduced plants vitally impact the types of knowledge that can be produced about cow-grass interactions. Like the man who interrupted the STAT proceedings with his versions of science, my attempts to move from observation to participation, attempts that fall far short of seeking full scientific initiation through standard academic and career channels, would be laughable within the conventions of the institutionalized scientific community.

This recognition, however, is in some ways a gift, one that keeps me reflexively questioning how I wish to be responsible to my field site. Some of my informants have themselves indirectly reminded me of the limits of my knowledge, as in the case of a biologist working for the U.S. Fish and Wildlife Service who criticized an anthropology student who, I am told, had a similar topic to mine. This student concluded that some of my interviewee's management decisions were ecologically harmful. The biologist questioned the anthropologist's authority to make that argument, exclaiming: "He's never even done a land [vegetation] transect!" Like this prior student, I, also, will not participate in the specific type of human-plant relationship that is structured by a vegetation transect. I need to account for the way the absence of this relationship impacts my own knowledge claims.

However, despite its limitations, the knowledge I create does have a certain type of validity and a clear relationship to ecology. Ethnographers always will have limited access to the relationships they study insofar as they must become a constitutive part of any relationship they seek to know, shaping those relationships in the process. In my case, the cultural power accorded to scientific authority, and the consequent exclusions of outsiders from gaining easy access to that authority, simply highlights what leaders in the field of anthropology and qualitative sociology are belatedly recognizing pertains to all ethnographic work. In the wake of what George Marcus and Michael Fischer call a "crisis of representation in the human sciences," postmodern critiques of classic, objectivist styles of ethnographic representation have become ubiquitous (Marcus "On Ideologies"; Clifford and Marcus; Denzin; Denzin and Lincoln). Many of these critiques hinge on the recognition that a culture is not an entity that can be isolated from a contingent set of relationships with its observer, even when that observer is an ethnographer who spends his legendary three years in a foreign culture. This indenture may fully initiate the ethnographer into the anthropological community, but most likely not into the community he observes. Whether the field of meanings and relationships that an ethnographer chooses to study is culturally powerful, as in the case of science-based management, or culturally less powerful, as in the case, for example, of the assigned writing of college freshmen, the old anthropological ideal of definitively describing and fully explaining a studied culture is now considered unobtainable.

As an illustration of this shift in anthropological expectations, Renato Rosaldo provides a whimsical but, as he suggests in another context, accurate and imprecise history of classic ethnographic norms (32). Rosaldo narrates the story of a Lone Ethnographer who travels to "a distant land" to do fieldwork, undergoing heroic trials before finally returning home to write a "definitive work" under a "mask of innocence," never recognizing his complicity with imperialism (30–31). In other words, the Lone Ethnographer never acknowledges the full system of relationships and connections that his work establishes between him, his audience back home, and the "natives" he writes about, let alone the power differentials inherent in those relationships. This mythology points to an ethnographic authority derived, on one hand, from an emphasis on the ethnographer's distance from "his native" (31), and, on the other, the ethnographer's personal prowess in overcoming that distance, only to reestablish it in the process of writing. According to Rosaldo, this classic mythos is integrated with a theoretical perspective that prompts the analyst to understand culture as a static system—a system that can unproblematically be objectified. Hence, any change in cultural logics occasioned by the new relationships established with the ethnographer can be ignored. However, Rosaldo argues, since the late 1960s this classic approach to society as a static system has given way to "an alternative project that attempts to understand human conduct as it unfolds through time and in relation to its meanings for the actors" (37). This developing anthropological perspective fits better with the relationship-conscious social epistemic of Berlin. The positioning of the ethnographer with respect to the culture she seeks to describe and understand is now seen as an interpretive act, one of many interpretations that constitute a cultural field shaped by meaning in action.

One place that this shift in ethnographic approach appears is in styles of writing. On the most basic level, the explicit presence of the ethnographer within her writing is itself a major change in representational practice. According to Herndl, a classic form for locating the ethnographer worked through a confessional declaration of firsthand experience, or an "arrival story," followed by the subsequent textual absence of the ethnographer:

> Ethnographies establish the uniqueness of the writer's experience by introducing what one critic calls the "I was there" element. They subsequently suppress the sense of the writer's genuine participation throughout the remainder of the text in order to establish the "scientific" authority of the "observation." This is often manifested by what has become known as the "arrival story," the poetic description of the ethnographer entering the native scene. This trope establishes the fieldworker's presence, authorizes her account, and then allows her to recede from the following description. (325)

In this 1991 article, Herndl continues by pointing out the continuing ubiquity of this trope within ethnographies of composition, questioning why new anthropological strategies for writing self-reflexively have not become more of the norm within his own discipline of rhetoric and composition. Within some branches of anthropology, such as the critical anthropology associated with George Marcus, James Clifford, and Michael Fischer, reflexivity is now an assumed writing practice, a necessary means of acknowledging the instability of any attempted conceptual splitting of subject and object. In reflexive practices, the ethnographer-author locates herself textually relative to the culture studied, thereby acknowledging that position affects perspective. For example, in my opening field account I identify most closely with those others who, like me, chose seats along the wall, even though all those in the meeting were equally unknown to me. Although in this example I interpret position literally, the same holds for figurative positioning as is done when a writer represents her politics or her social identity, perhaps in terms of class or gender.

Some writers take this reflexivity even further than a simple self-location, explicitly addressing the intersubjective relationships established between the researcher and those she studies. For example, Charlotte Davies analyzes how both her interpretations and those of her informants change during the course of an interview (96–104). Yet this type of relational interaction is not limited to either interviews or contemporary studies. As Michael Taussig shows repeatedly in his rereadings of classic ethnographies, the relationships colonial ethnographers established with the cultures they contacted altered the understanding and desires of both colonized and colonizer, in spite of ethnographic representations to the contrary. Many contemporary ethnographers now reflexively eschew the old pattern of textually suppressing their presence as an observer. Instead, they write in ways that acknowledge the relationships they create with informants and they discuss how those relationships shape the cultural logics they represent in their writing (for example, Behar, Rosaldo).

Not all forms of self-reflexivity, however, have the same effect or constitute the same type of textual authority. In his article "On Ideologies of Reflexivity in Contemporary Efforts to Remake the Human Sciences," Marcus describes several forms of reflexivity and analyzes how different strategies of reflexive writing serve different "theoretical and intellectual purposes" (190). He identifies four forms, which he labels "the null form of reflexivity . . . self-critique," "sociological reflexivity," "anthropological reflexivity," and "feminist reflexivity" (192–201). He is critical of the first two. He acknowledges that the subjective self-questioning of the null form accomplishes a critique of objectivist ethnographic accounts, thereby opening up space for new forms of writing. However, he claims that the null form's emphasis on subjectivity does little else of value and makes itself vulnerable to claims of narcissism (192–94). In this form of reflexivity, the ethnographer effectively negates his own authority, claiming the impossibility of knowing anything beyond himself. If I were to end with the self-questioning that closed the field account at the beginning of this chapter, I would be producing a null form of reflexivity. The second form of reflexivity Marcus discusses, the sociological form, commits the opposite crime, affirming the ethnographer's ability to know without acknowledging the partiality and limits of her knowledge. As this writing style, which Marcus claims the ground-breaking sociologist Pierre Bourdieu exemplifies, either locates reflexivity at the margins of the text or turns reflexivity itself into an object. This type of reflexivity reproduces conventional ethnographic practices (194–96). For Marcus, neither of these two forms effectively address the crisis of representation and the consequent attempts to craft a more ethical and self-aware ethnographic authority.

However, these forms do have their attractions, as is evident in Kathleen Dixon's "Gendering the 'Personal.'" This highly reflexive article in part addresses Dixon's difficulty in understanding a female student she establishes a relationship with as part of a multiyear ethnographic project. Published in *College Composition and Communication* four years after Herndl's *College English* publication, I interpret this essay as a response to calls such as Herndl's to adapt to the needs of composition researchers the reflexive writing practices current in the ethnographies of other disciplines. Dixon's essay oscillates between a self-conscious, self-critical subjectivity and a desire to reach beyond that subjectivity to understand the "other," the student "Elizabeth," on her own terms. On one hand, Dixon is reflexively aware that, as a teacher, she is most comfortable establishing what she considers to be a masculine gendered homosocial relationship. On the other hand, as she concludes her article, she articulates her desire to be able to say, in response to Elizabeth's writing: "It was your story, your perspective, and when I read it I understood it" (274). Dixon's desire to understand the other reproduces the traditional anthropological urge for definitive knowledge, with the difference that her fidelity to the limits of her subjectivity refuses to allow her to represent herself as obtaining that knowledge. Her essay hints that her difficulty understanding Elizabeth's writing stems from the same source as her difficulty establishing a satisfying teacher-student relationship with Elizabeth. The "other" remains distant. In this respect, Dixon reverses the trope of the Lone Ethnographer by claiming that distance was not crossed.

However, Dixon's approach is only one form of reflexive writing. According to Marcus, other extant reflexive forms have the potential to alter the possibilities of representation and knowledge production within ethnographic writing even more significantly. "On Ideologies of Reflexivity" continues by delineating two additional forms of reflexivity, anthropological and feminist, that better suit Marcus's desires. Marcus connects anthropological reflexivity to Fred Myers's "politics of location," a form of writing that acknowledges how any culture studied is already implicated in a precon-structed set of historical connections, meanings, and representations. The ethnographer-author then attempts to negotiate critically these received meanings in a power-sensitive manner. This is a context-constrained reflex-ivity, one exemplified by the attempts of Myers and his colleague Bette Clark, to support Australian aboriginals' desires to control the meaning of an encounter that was being given widespread political and media attention (Myers, "Locating Ethnographic Practice"). The representational practices Myers and Clark ultimately chose are highly conditioned by the relationship of mutual support that they establish with the aboriginals. Marcus claims that Myers's reflexivity in this case effectively changes anthropology's under-standing of its purpose. That is, Myers's approach eschews the received tra-dition of attempting to create neutral, transparent representations. Instead, recognizing that representational practices are embedded in relationships charged by power differentials, Myers calls on disciplinary practitioners to become more self-conscious of the effect that adding their representations will have on the politics of meaning. In this type of reflexivity, the ethnogra-pher's authority is configured as the agency to symbolically act within the constraints of a preconstituted system of meanings.

Marcus saves his greatest praise for the feminist reflexivity Haraway's "positioning" represents, which produces highly situated knowledge that "con-stitutes an invitation to critically respond to its partiality . . . [assuming] that all work is incomplete and requires response (and thus engagement) from those in other positions" ("On Ideologies" 198). In *Modest_Witness*, a text published subsequent to Marcus's article, Haraway further develops her understanding of the knowledge she constructs, referring to her ideal method of inquiry as "dif-fraction"—writing that can "make a difference in the world" (16). By using an optical metaphor that, unlike reflection, highlights how images change in response to mediation, Haraway argues that attempts to achieve authentic rep-resentation fail to recognize that a writer's representations themselves consti-tute a partial aspect of reality. Writers are not mirrors, not reflectors, but cre-ators. This creativity does not invalidate the knowledge that writers produce, as if the presence of a writer somehow made knowledge less authentic. Instead, writers' creativity gives their knowledge the ability to be a new invention, something different, but nonetheless connected to other meanings through a complex web of relationships. This web, like the Internet, highlights the limi-tations of any single person's access to its field of material-semiotic meanings, as well as the contingency of the meanings that person then makes while fol-lowing the links of the web (6, 246). This web, like a game of cat's cradle, allows a skillful participant to take a preexisting pattern of relationships and tem-porarily reconfigure it into something new (268–71). The potential of posi-tioned authors to enter into relationships and make something different out of them is what gives knowledge-production its power to create change—and what makes authors responsible to their creative acts.

Haraway's concept of *diffraction* develops the concept of positioning that Marcus praises as a particularly valuable form of reflexivity. It is important to note, therefore, that Haraway explicitly distances her writing from reflexive forms: "My suspicion is that reflexivity, like reflection, only displaces the same elsewhere, setting up the worries about copy and original and the search for the authentic and the really real" (16). However, Haraway's use of the term *reflexivity* is more limited and specific than is Marcus's. Because of her sensitivity to the optical metaphor underlying the term *reflexivity*, Haraway refers to reflexivity in the singular rather than acknowledging multiple possible forms of reflexivity, forms with multiple possible rhetorical impacts. For the sake of consistency, I continue to use Marcus's looser definition of *reflexivity*, including diffraction as a particularly powerful form of it.[1]

Although Haraway's explicit focus is feminist technoscience studies, her method also provides a valuable way to think through the ethics of representation in other forms of culture studies, including more explicitly ethnographic approaches. Haraway's epistemology effectively addresses the felt sense of loss occasioned by the crisis of representation in anthropology and subsequent challenges to the truth-value of ethnography. By embracing diffraction, writers can productively respond to this loss of one type of authority by instead acknowledging to themselves, as well as to their readers, that they are involved in the creation of what Haraway refers to as partial, situated knowledge. This acknowledgment opens up new possibilities for writing. Writers who are aware of the contingency—and the politics—of their representations may choose not to fall back on received ethnographic forms. Instead, as they establish relationships within the system of meanings they study, and as they invite readers also to enter into that system of meanings, writers bear the full responsibility of their agency as the knowledge they produce becomes, as Marcus claims in "Ethnography in/of the World System," part of the system they are studying.

If Haraway's concept of *diffraction* presents a compelling epistemology, it does not decisively answer the question of how to produce knowledge or how to write. Instead, by clustering around the term a set of ethical concerns, Haraway points to questions that can act as guides for writing. What are the relationships that a writer wishes to establish with the system she studies? In an ethnography, what relationship does she want with her informants? With the meanings they communicate? What meanings and representations are already current in the system studied, and what are their political impacts? What relationships already exist among informants? How do differences in power shape those relationships? What sort of institutionally and discursively conditioned power differences are informants likely to see between themselves and the researcher?

These questions focus on the relationship between ethnographer and informant in the field. But the relationship between ethnographers and readers is also a necessary focus. What meanings about the field site are already available to readers? How will those meanings shape how they interpret what the ethnographer writes? What genres do readers expect from an ethnographic writer? What possibilities are available to the writer to alter those genres—as, for example, Carolyn Ellis and Arthur Bochner do with the genre of the handbook chapter, turning it into an autoethnographic dialogue? What does the writer hope will be the impact of the knowledge she produces? How can she work within the social constraints that will condition the reception of her work? How can she shape meanings into purposive rhetorical acts? And, if she explicitly chooses to adopt a diffractive reflexivity modeled after Haraway's, how does she make the contingencies of her knowledge productions vulnerable to scrutiny? How does she recognize the politics of her representations and the partiality of her perspective even as she commits publicly to the aspect of reality that her own knowledge creates?

ANALYSIS IN THE CONTEXT OF RELATIONSHIPS

The previous questions are all phrased as if the writer will answer them alone. Certainly, the ethnographer-author ultimately has a large degree of responsibility for his representations, mitigated by his inability to control fully reader response. However, each question also focuses on the relational qualities of meanings. What readers of a text already know will shape their interpretation of it, as will genre knowledge shared between readers and writers. Similarly, informants influence the relationship that is established between them and ethnographers and the knowledge that is created out of those relationships. It is in the context of these specific relationships, consequently, that the questions that closed the previous section are best answered.

Certainly, my preformed ideas about how I would answer those questions were embedded in the way I approached my informants. For example, they influenced how I first introduced myself to informants. Similarly, the sample interview questions I submitted to the Human Subjects Committee reflected my theoretical concerns. Conscious that my study would be only one representation among many that impacted Arizona's grazing debates, I determined to ask my informants what reading sources they would most recommend to the interested public. By this question, I hoped to map a system of representations that followed my readers' inclinations and not just my own, and I imagined ways I would write to point readers to those texts my informants valued, some of which might contradict my own in purpose, at least, if not also in meaning. However, I could not make the majority of my decisions until after building relationships with my informants.

One impact of the relationships I established with informants was that my understanding of my own identity relative to the debate changed. As I first asked people for contacts, I often declared my personal connections to antigrazing arguments so that people would know my prior understanding was fairly one-sided. However, in an early interview with a father-son ranching team, a story reminded me of an uncle who I had not thought of recently—an uncle who happened to be a rancher in another state. Over the next months I found myself recalling half-forgotten knowledge of my uncle's experiences—his economic frustrations, for example, or his discomfort when, for the sake of family, he allowed my father to hunt his land in spite of the compassion he felt toward wildlife. At the same time, I tried to relive my experiences as a child playing on my uncle's ranch in the summer, and I thought of my older brother's continuing devotion to the land he had visited and revisited as he grew from childhood to adolescence. To my brother in particular, that land had become an idealized—even sacred— space. These memories shaped the background knowledge I subsequently brought to my research. I found myself wondering to what extent my experiences were similar to those of ranchers who claimed, for example, the deep importance to them of a cultural identity formed from living and working all their lives on a particular parcel of land. In addition to maintaining my environmentalist affiliations, I increasingly identified myself as the niece of a rancher. Whereas this new way of connecting myself to the debate does not somehow give me a more transparent view of my informants' perspectives, it does demonstrate the influence informants may have over ethnographers' identities, self-representations, and general relationship to the site they study.

My relationships with my informants have also had a deep impact on the knowledge I have created, although they have not determined it. The remainder of this section is an extended example based on my analysis of the three ecology-based cultural logics identified in the first paragraph of the section "Reconceiving Authority as Authorship." My form of analysis is deeply impacted by the ethical claims the relationships my informants and I have established made on me. However, the knowledge I have ultimately produced is diffracted in the sense that it does not try to replicate, describe, or explicate the knowledge-claims made by those informants. Instead, it diffracts them through the lens of rhetorical criticism, altering their relationship to grazing debates in politically nonneutral ways. The following story, taken from one of my final interviews, introduces one of the key relationships that influenced my analytical choices. It also demonstrates how, in my experience, informants themselves call on me to be reflexive about the way I respond to their knowledge-claims. What is an ethical way to respond to what informants share with me? How can I respect them and their ways of knowing while simultaneously writing from my own perspective as a rhetorical critic?

I was interviewing a rancher in his home's expansive great room. The room's focal point was the rear entryway, two large sliding glass doors that provided a view of many square miles of the ranch's grasslands. This had once been my informant's home, but, retired, he now lives down the road. His successor, who I had interviewed previously, was hosting us, at times joining in our recorded conversation.

At my request, the retired rancher had just finished explaining the combination of social and ecological processes that had led to the degradation of some of the land I had driven by on my way to the interview. The land had been partially developed with dirt roads dividing it into real estate parcels, but then the developers had abandoned it. The rancher explained that the erosion caused by these roads, together with weed encroachment, gave the land its currently abused appearance. Without prompting, the rancher then added his view of what needed to be done to improve this land, a prescription that intersected with the ecological processes that, by then, had become a primary focus for me. The rancher said that if a salt block was put on this degraded land for a week or two, the cattle would break up the soil, eat off the "decadent grass" and eradicate brush, thereby making new grass seedlings establish more easily.

Perhaps I looked skeptical or maybe the rancher was simply aware how heavily contested his management claims were. To his explanation, the rancher appended the caveat: "Now, you don't have to believe all this, you know."

The rancher laughed loudly. I joined in his laughter, but I did not feel sure of myself. I liked him. In addition to the debt of gratitude I routinely feel during an interview, I saw this man as welcoming and personable, an engaging and honest storyteller, and an experienced, responsive informant. I wanted to believe him. But I responded honestly: "Well, I'll tell you. I can't believe everything that everyone's told me, because it doesn't add up. I don't know."

The rancher paused, then responded in a quieter tone. "Well. Anyhow. I hope that what I tell you is believable."

"I'm not the person to judge." This response must have won some approval because the elderly man spoke more energetically again, interjecting his agreement: "Oh yeah!" I continued: "Everyone I talk to I know knows more about it [grassland ecology and management] than I do."

The rancher did not let the subject drop with my disavowal. "I know that," he said. "But there's a common sense evaluation of a statement." The younger rancher, our host, noted his agreement: "Yeah."

Were these ranchers asking me to validate their knowledge? To not judge it, but at the same time look favorably on it? I do not know, but I felt pressure to declare my position on the issue as openly as they had—and I did not know what my position was. I did not even want to have a position. I responded: "Yeah. You're obviously speaking from experience." I believed that, and I still do. But I also consider well informed the antigrazing activist who, when taking me on a driving tour of the state, pointed to this same piece of land as an example of overgrazing. These contradictions prevent me from validating the knowledge of all my informants, at least in a way that approvingly reflects exactly what they say.

The younger rancher took lead of the conversation, ultimately changing the subject. But I found myself consciously and unconsciously returning to mull over this interchange about knowledge and credibility. What was my position relative to the ecological knowledge-claims I would be discussing as a key topic of debate? What position could I take that would respect my informants, their knowledge, and their experience? Committed to my statement "I'm not the person to judge," I found myself seeking a way to discuss the epistemic basis of blatantly conflicting knowledge claims without locating myself in a position that took one as more true or false than the other.

It was in this context, one fully shaped by a relationship dialogically established between me and my informants, that I decided to model my analysis partially on the "symmetrical" method Wiebe Bijker and David Bloor before him describe, a method they use to produce a social analysis of, respectively, technology and mathematical knowledge. Because this method is committed to using the same analytical framework to account for true and false beliefs (for Bloor) and historically successful and unsuccessful technologies (for Bijker), questions of truth and falsity can be elided. Although this works well to reexamine the historically settled cases Bloor and Bijker analyze, it is even more useful in a case such as mine where the claims being studied have not yet achieved consensus. The approach of Bloor and Bijker is also valuable because it can be reconciled with the relation-based social epistemic of Berlin, thereby acknowledging my disciplinary relationships as well as those I have with my informants. Bloor, for example, demonstrates how education shapes what children consider to be true and thereby ultimately conditions both the premises and patterns of inference mathematicians make. Bijker, in a series of three cases, considers how disciplinary training, advertising, public discourse, and socioeconomic relationships together shape the meanings given to technological artifacts. These approaches together provide me with a set of tools for accounting for ecological arguments that do not rely on scientific judgments of truth or falsity, but that instead stress how meaning is communicated and negotiated in relationships.

By briefly mentioning a specific method of analysis, I do not mean to recommend it universally. Rather, I recommend explicitly situating analytical choices within the context of relationships to address concerns raised during the research process. Creating situated knowledge, however, is only one goal derived from Haraway. Diffraction also involves explicit partiality. How ethnographers position themselves in their writing strongly conditions what form their partiality takes and whether that partiality is visible to readers. Partiality has two components. Bloor addresses the first, realizing that a teleological realism can account for the mathematical knowledge he prefers to account for sociologically. In my case, just because I can do a symmetrical analysis of ecological knowledge-claims does not mean that no other ways of accounting for those claims exist that might be equally or more persuasive in other contexts. The theory I produce will be partial in the sense that it will not displace all other theories. For example, I have chosen not to build on relationships with my informants in a way that reproduces the claims of some antigrazing activists that ranchers deliberately lie in economic self-interest, or the claims of some ranchers that antigrazing activists care more about personal power than about the environment. Neither of these analyses serve a concern that I have increasingly developed throughout my study, which is to respond to the debate in a way that does not attempt to resolve contradictions, but that does point to ways to move beyond the political sticking points that have clustered around ecological accounts of truth and accusations of falsity. Yet I acknowledge that these polarizing analyses of motivations are persuasive to many. This aspect of partiality recognizes that multiple approaches toward the same issue may have validity.

The other component of partiality makes reflexive writing even more important. Partial knowledge is interested, not neutral. This is the type of partiality that originally guided my choice to eschew an analysis of scientific truth and falsity in favor of a symmetrical analysis. However, even though an apparent neutrality attracted me to a symmetrical analysis, shortly after claiming it I began to recognize that its results are not, in fact, neutral. There is a deconstructivist logic to it, one that undermines epistemic claims that are understood by those who make them to be neutral reflections of noncontingent ecological processes. Consider the following paragraphs taken from a draft of the conclusion of a four-chapter analysis of the three cultural logics I have identified.

What my analysis suggests is that the debate over whether "cows plant grass" can be fruitfully reconfigured as a debate over possible futures, rather than over reified scientific truths about the present. The National Academy of Science mining site designations of rehabilitation, restoration, and reclamation, which I have chosen to apply to rangeland science, are merely a convenient way of considering the ecosystems that might result from basing management actions on one set of truth-claims rather than the other. In this designation, those who value cows as an effective management tool for grassland (re)construction and who also value the grass cover provided by introduced African grasses such as Lehmann's, a colonizer of disturbed soils,

*are following a route to rehabilitation. That is, by stressing the importance of cattle
grazing they are advocating what they consider to be a viable habitat that accommodates the human activity of ranching while nonetheless seeking a renewable grass
resource. Those who completely oppose cattle grazing on southern Arizona's grasslands and who promote grassland fires and native plant revegetation are instead
trying to (re)construct a full restoration of a past habitat known primarily through
the accounts of early European explorers. Finally, those who follow a last set of
claims that do not consider cows essential to habitat (re)construction but think that
cattle can nonetheless be made to fit with ecosystem goals, perhaps as a partial sub-
stitute for fire, are more in line with a route to reclamation, an attempt to (re)con-
struct a habitat similar to a disappeared past, but one that accommodates change,
substitution, and human activity.*

*Each of these scientific-managerial positions is more complex than its represen-
tation within my analysis, and each contains variation within it. Additionally, the
categories of rehabilitation, restoration, and reclamation, are, within this context,
my own applications, creating artificial boundaries that do not fully contain the
arguments debaters make. However, what my reconfiguration points to is that the
debate over grazing southern Arizona's grasslands, which primarily occurs as contradictory statements over what is true scientifically, depends heavily on a static
conception of the environment that is in fact dynamically changing. Certainly, most
of those involved in this debate recognize change, but typically place that change
somewhere on a linear continuum moving either toward the improvement or the
disappearance of a taken-for-granted valued habitat. Instead, multiple possible
futures are at stake, as all those in the debate are attempting, differently, to alter the
habitat to create a future that is different than what the ecosystem is today. Which
future habitat is most valuable cannot be taken for granted, but will only be decided
within a power-laden political arena. Consequently, any scientific truth-claim
about what helps or hinders ecosystem health can only be verified and enacted
within a particular set of managerial desires, aimed at a particular set of goals.
These goals, then, together with the desires underpinning them and the human
activities included within them, are deeply implicated in the debate and will not be
resolved solely through an appeal to a version of science that does not address these
other divisions.*

These paragraphs demonstrate how I have chosen to resolve my relationship to scientific claims. First, I noticed that the contradictory indicators of
cultural logics that I had identified were typically accompanied by a set of differentiated beliefs about the value of fire and introduced African grasses. Several of my informants pointed out to me that the argument that cows were
vital to grasslands is also an African import, an idea Allan Savory, who began
his career in what was then the Northern Rhodesian Game Department,
developed (xix). Scientific journals, especially the *Journal of Range Science*,

taught me how different grasses responded to different ecological conditions. A reference in one of these articles to other types of landscape and habitat (re)construction projects, specifically postfire and postmining (re)construction, provided me with a comparative framework to think about the goals of grassland (re)construction (Richards, Chambers, and Ross 626). Following these links, I developed a method of thinking about the epistemic basis of ecological claims that was goal-oriented rather than truth-oriented, one that created space in my writing to acknowledge each cultural logic without needing to dismiss any as scientifically ungrounded. This allows me to establish a relationship with scientific claims from my position as a rhetorical critic and ethnographer. However, although my approach connects me and my arguments to ecological claims, I am not following academic rules for ecological discourse. Instead, I am reshaping the possibilities for participation within the debate to include an approach and set of concerns that are suppressed within an exclusively scientific way of thinking about ecological processes.

The space I have created has extant analogues within the debate. For example, the Arizona Common Ground Roundtable—a collaboration between the Morris K. Udall Center for Public Policy, the Nature Conservancy, and area ranchers—has tried to develop a sense of shared goals (such as to preserve open space) before examining how to reach those goals. Yet my analysis is different from this in the sense that it does not assume shared values or goals, but rather seeks to highlight differences to make them vulnerable to discussion. This is a diffraction of the debate I am studying, one that reconfigures the grounds of argumentation away from a historically deadlocked conflict to one that may be more vulnerable to change through dialogue.

This reconfiguration of the debate, like all diffraction, is not neutral, a recognition I wish to make explicit in my writing. By connecting each set of claims to contingent futures, I simultaneously highlight both human values and human agency to impact the outcome of ecological processes. Ecology becomes socioecology, with contingency, human choice, and human responsibility taking the place of a world determined by science. To the extent that readers accept this diffraction, it alters the power of the cultural logics I am studying. For example, my approach rejects a cultural model, which Bronislaw Szerszynski identifies, claiming that science has the moral power to tell us what to do to save the environment. My interviews with antigrazing activists suggested the importance of that model to their discourse because their discussions relied heavily on scientific knowledge to justify their position while morally delegitimating contrary viewpoints. Other types of claims are also potentially undermined by diffraction. By pointing to the future rather than the past, for example, I make contingent the value of the cultural tradition of ranching.

An analogue exists between my approach to scientific knowledge claims and my approach to ethnographic forms of authority. Both types of knowledge are partial and shaped by the contingent relationships knowledge-producers enter into within an extant system of meanings. The production of both types of knowledge involves human agency, not a passive reception of truth or meaning. Consequently, humans also have responsibility for the knowledge they produce. The value of different claims can be at least partially measured by the consequences of these claims, by their impacts, by the futures they create.

To say that knowledge is partial, situated, and contingent is not the same as claiming that the producers of knowledge have no authority. Old forms of authority have certainly been undermined, whether by the crisis of representation in the human sciences or by its scientific parallel occasioned by constructivist accounts of science in the tradition of historian Thomas Kuhn or sociologist Robert Merton. However, challenges to objectivist forms of authority have made way for the development of new forms, such as Haraway's diffraction. Although these forms are reflexive about their limitations and their partiality, they are nonetheless effective ways to know and to act in the world, valid ways to participate in the cultures they reciprocally constitute.

NOTE

1. Haraway continues her critique of reflexivity by writing, "Reflexivity is a bad trope for escaping the false choice between realism and relativism in thinking about strong objectivity and situated knowledges in technoscientific knowledge" (16). This critique is analogous to Marcus's commentary on the null form of reflexivity and its "sociological" opposite as represented by the objectivist impulses of Bourdieu.

WORKS CITED

Aristotle. *Aristotle on Rhetoric: A Theory of Civic Discourse.* Trans. George A. Kennedy. New York: Oxford UP, 1991.

Behar, Ruth. *Translated Woman: Crossing the Border with Esperanza's Story.* Boston: Beacon, 1993.

Berlin, James A. "Rhetoric and Ideology in the Writing Class." *College English* 50 (1988): 477–94.

Bijker, Wiebe E. *Of Bicycles, Bakelites, and Bulbs: Toward a Theory of Sociotechnical Change.* Cambridge, MA: MIT P, 1995.

Bloor, David. "Wittgenstein and Mannheim on the Sociology of Mathematics." *Studies in History and Philosophy of Science* 4 (1973): 173–91.

Cintron, Ralph. *Angels' Town: Chero Ways, Gang Life, and Rhetorics of the Everyday.* Boston: Beacon, 1997.

Clifford, James, and George E. Marcus, eds. *Writing Culture: The Poetics and Politics of Ethnography*. Berkeley: U of California P, 1986.

Davies, Charlotte Aull. *Reflexive Ethnography: A Guide to Researching Selves and Others*. London: Routledge, 1999.

Denzin, Norman K. *Interpretive Ethnography: Ethnographic Practices for the 21st Century*. Thousand Oaks, CA: Sage, 1997.

Denzin, Norman K., and Yvonna S. Lincoln. "Introduction: The Discipline and Practice of Qualitative Research." *Handbook of Qualitative Research*. Ed. Norman K. Denzin and Yvonna S. Lincoln. 2nd ed. Thousand Oaks, CA: Sage, 2000. 1–28.

Dixon, Kathleen. "Gendering the 'Personal.'" *College Composition and Communication* 46 (1995): 255–75.

Ellis, Carolyn, and Arthur P. Bochner. "Authoethnography, Personal Narrative, Reflexivity: Researcher as Subject." *Handbook of Qualitative Research*. Ed. Norman K. Denzin and Yvonna S. Lincoln. 2nd ed. Thousand Oaks, CA: Sage, 2000. 733–68.

Haraway, Donna J. *Modest—Witness@Second—Millennium.FemaleMan©—Meets—OncoMouse™. Feminism and Technoscience*. New York: Routledge, 1997.

Herndl, Carl G. "Writing Ethnography: Representation, Rhetoric, and Institutional Practices." *College English* 53 (1991): 320–32.

Kuhn, Thomas. *The Structure of Scientific Revolutions*. 3rd ed. Chicago: U of Chicago P, 1996.

Latour, Bruno. *Pandora's Hope: Essays on the Reality of Science Studies*. Cambridge, MA: Harvard UP, 1999.

Marcus, George E. "Ethnography in/of the World System: The Emergence of Multi-Sited Ethnography." *Annual Review of Anthropology* 24 (1995): 95–117. Rpt. in *Ethnography through Thick and Thin*. Ed. George E. Marcus. Princeton: Princeton UP, 1998. 79–104.

———. "On Ideologies of Reflexivity in Contemporary Efforts to Remake the Human Sciences." *Poetics Today* 15 (1994): 383–404. Rpt. in *Ethnography through Thick and Thin*. Ed. George E. Marcus. Princeton: Princeton UP, 1998. 181–202.

Marcus, George E., and Michael M. J. Fischer. *Anthropology as Cultural Critique*. Chicago: U of Chicago P, 1986.

Merton, Robert K. *The Sociology of Science: Theoretical and Empirical Investigations*. Ed. Norman W. Storer. Chicago: U of Chicago P, 1973.

Myers, Fred R. "Locating Ethnographic Practice: Romance, Reality, and Politics in the Outback." *American Ethnologist* 15 (1988): 609–24.

Richards, Rebecca T., Jeanne C. Chambers, and Christopher Ross. "Use of Native Plants on Federal Lands: Policy and Practice." *Journal of Range Management* 51 (1998): 625–32.

Rosaldo, Renato. *Culture and Truth: The Remaking of Social Analysis*. 2nd ed. Boston: Beacon, 1993.

Savory, Allan. *Holistic Resource Management.* Covelo, CA: Island, 1988.

Szerszynski, Bronislaw. "On Knowing What to Do: Environmentalism and the Modern Problematic." *Risk, Environment and Modernity: Toward a New Ecology.* Ed. Scott Lash, Bronislaw Szerszynski, and Brian Wynne. London: Sage, 1996. 104–37.

Taussig, Michael. *Mimesis and Alterity: A Particular History of the Senses.* New York: Routledge, 1993.

PART III

The Nomadic Self:
Reorganizing the
Self in the Field

10

Critical Auto/Ethnography

A Constructive Approach to Research in the Composition Classroom

SUSAN S. HANSON

Personal narrative mediates [the] contradiction between the engagement called for in fieldwork and the self-effacement called for in formal ethnographic description, or at least it mitigates some of its anguish, by inserting into the text the authority of the personal experience out of which ethnography is made.
   —Mary Louise Pratt, "Fieldwork in Common Places"

The only way to fight a hegemonic discourse is to teach ourselves and others alternative ways of seeing the world and discussing what it is we have come to understand as theory, research, and practice.
   —Linda Brodkey, *Writing Permitted in Designated Areas Only*

MARY WAS THE FIRST STUDENT to voice a connection.[1] It was the last class meeting of a general curriculum composition course, and the students were ready to make a run for it. I had organized the order of the reading and writing assignments to demonstrate that autobiography and ethnography operate on a continuum and to suggest that the two forms of narrative are inextricably connected. The first writing assignment was an autobiographical essay and the last, an ethnographic essay based on the student's own field research. I was reviewing the path the students had taken from the autobiographical *Here* to the ethnographic *There*, from writing about the Self to writing about the Other, hopeful that the students would reflect on what they learned about points of view and voice, when Mary interjected, "It's like we're back where we started."

"Exactly."

Autobiography is a self-oriented narrative based on personal experience whereas ethnography is an other-oriented one based on systematic participant observation.[2] As a composition pedagogy, critical auto/ethnography enables subjugated others (read students) to do systematic fieldwork and data production about subjects other than themselves, but without concealing what they learn about themselves in the process. As Françoise Lionnet suggests, writers and readers must resist subscribing to the dominant conventions, resist assimilating, and resist reinforcing the practices and assumptions that relegate nonconforming texts to the margin (326). Critical auto/ethnography is a nonconforming text.

When I first encountered the term *autoethnography* while doing research in connection with a graduate course on fieldwork methods, I automatically presumed that it was intended to suggest that there is space within ethnography to locate the Self as a subject; a space to narrate, perhaps in some detail, aspects of the ethnographer's own experiences; a space other than the introduction to situate my story. Exhilarated by the possibilities, I consulted my committee members, fully expecting that they would share my enthusiasm.

"Do you mean reflexive ethnography?"

"No, I'm talking about *auto*ethnography—ethnography that is part autobiography."

"You don't want to write about yourself, do you?"

I thought to myself, "That's precisely what I want to do. How better to explain how I learned what I learned?" The idea that an ethnographer learns by and through systematic participant observation, and then suppresses (or disguises) the Self in the telling struck me then and strikes me still as problematic. But I was persuaded by the reactions, one after another, to accept that my "I-story" should not, would not figure in my thesis because, "No one wants to read about the ethnographer."

> The primary message is that, while we should be aware of our identities and how these may affect our field research, we should continue to work toward scientific observations of people and their cultures. The objective of ethnography should not be to learn more about ourselves as individuals (although that will happen), but to learn more about others. (Dewalt and Dewalt 291)

Therein lies the dilemma. Is producing a text that is both Self- and Other-oriented possible? And in what contexts is it appropriate, effective—even necessary, perhaps—to combine both points of view within a single narrative? The goal of this chapter is to explore that ground.

To be sure, the reflexive turn cleared the way within ethnography for the ethnographer to reflect on her own subjectivity. Yet, of those ethnographers who have risked slipping more of the Self into the body of their ethnography than is customary, few anthropologists, folklorists, sociologists, or sociolinguists have dared to describe either their methods or their texts as *autoethnographic* because the term is largely pejorative. Unlike the "auto" of autobiography, which is understood to connote the Self, the "auto" of autoethnography is short for *autochthon*, the primitive or native Other. The underlying assumption is that the autochthonous ethnographer, even one who is trained in "scientific" methods, is too close to (or inside) her data to analyze it critically.

You can imagine my disappointment.

The second time I encountered *autoethnography* was in connection with feminist autobiography, where the term was adopted to describe unconventional autobiographies. As an example, Lionnet suggests that autoethnography is "the process of defining one's subjective ethnicity as mediated through language, history and ethnographical analysis" (242). In other words, autoethnography is a personal experience narrative that distinguishes itself from traditional autobiography (and ethnography, for that matter) because the author does not conceal the practices that she seeks to counter or disrupt. As readers, such texts call on us to approach them through a lens that takes methods of resistance into account.

My aim in this chapter is to propose that *critical auto/ethnography* emerges at the interstices of autobiography and ethnography. I incorporate the slash (/) as a way to emphasize that critical auto/ethnography is committed, as is ethnography, to studying other people, but as an account of that process, it bridges the chasm between the autobiographical *Here* and the ethnographic *There* and lays bare the dynamics of self-other engagement. In the first section, I review briefly how the term *autoethnography* is defined and applied across disciplinary boundaries with the goal of mapping what *critical auto/ethnography* resists and enables. The second section focuses on critical auto/ethnography as composition pedagogy. Following Deborah Mutnick in *Writing in an Alien World*, I advocate developing a pedagogical practice that emphasizes what students bring to the classroom by encouraging them to contribute to the production of ethnographic knowledge by becoming participant-observers in discourse communities engendering communicative practices that reproduce or resist dominant notions of race, class, gender, and literacy. Critical auto/ethnography meets this need, as I argue in the concluding section.

WHAT IS CRITICAL AUTO/ETHNOGRAPHY?

> If ethnographic texts are a means by which Europeans represent to themselves their (usually subjugated) others, autoethnographic texts are those the others construct in response to or in dialogue with those metropolitan representations.
>
> —Mary Louise Pratt, *Imperial Eyes*

Anthropologists were the first to apply the term autoethnography to indigenous texts, much in the same vein as does Pratt in the epigraph. For example, Karl Heider used "auto-ethnography" to describe a "simple" method of soliciting oral explanations of everyday activities from autochthonous, or native, members of a community, so simple in fact as to seem automatic (Reed-Danahay 4). Deborah Reed-Danahay cites David Hayano as another early scholar of autoethnography, noting that "For Hayano, it is 'insider' status which marks autoethnography"—status "that a researcher may acquire, through socialization." But Hayano "is dismissive of what he calls 'self-ethnographic' texts" (5), the argument being that the story of the self is not the aim of ethnography. John Dorst adds another delineation to the mix, suggesting that "visually coded texts can be profitably thought of as 'auto-ethnographies'" (4). The important point to recognize here is because autoethnographic texts are often the *object* of ethnographic analysis, ethnographers generally avoid describing their own texts as such even when their research focuses on communities where they have "insider" or "native" status.

But there are exceptions. As an example, Lorraine Kenny describes *Daughters of Suburbia: Growing Up White, Middle-Class and Female* as "auto-ethnographic" because she returned to the place where she grew up to do her field research: "In studying my hometown," she says, "I became a native anthropologist of sorts," in part to confront and disrupt "the self-other dynamics that have typically left their imprint on ethnographic knowledge" (113). Nevertheless, the underlying concern within the disciplines that practice ethnography is two-pronged: first and certainly foremost, the tradition has been to study other peoples and cultures rather than one's own culture; second, because the so-called Others are now studying themselves, the concern (fear) exists that legitimating autoethnography may by extension render professional ethnography superfluous.[3]

Similar concerns pervade literary studies only with respect to the sanctity of autobiography. The concept of autoethnography is also one of many that feminists have proposed as a way to discuss and legitimate texts that challenge conventions of autobiography. Citing Zora Neale Hurston's autobiography, *Dust Tracks on the Road*, as form of autoethnography, "a kind of 'figural anthropology' of the self" ("Autoethnography" 242), Lionnet says, "In *Dust Tracks*, we have a clear example of the braiding or *métissage* of cultural forms" (262).

> *Métissage* is a form of *bricolage*, in the sense used by Claude Levi-Strauss, but as an aesthetic concept it encompasses far more: it brings together biology and history, anthropology and philosophy, linguistics and literature. ("Politics" 326; emphasis in original)

The idea of "figural" or figurative self-writing suggests that autoethnography is a method and mode of self-formation that aims, as does ethnography, to represent the culture of a collective by and through multiple forms of discourse. Mary Louise Pratt uses "autoethnography" similarly to describe "instances in which colonized subjects undertake to represent themselves in ways that *engage with* the colonizer's own terms" (*Imperial Eyes* 7). To Pratt, autoethnographic texts are produced by native-born subjects who appropriate dominant forms of representation to participate in Western forms of discourse as well as to "address literate sectors of the speaker's own social group."

Following Lionnet and Pratt, and building on the idea that "auto" can be understood as referring to the autobiographical Self, the ethnographic Other, and the visually coded Site, auto/ethnography might be more usefully thought of as a heteroglossic performance. The term heteroglossic emphasizes the dialogic engagement or intersubjective encounter. Historically, the field was out There, somewhere unfamiliar to the researcher. But increasingly the field is Here, on our own stage or "contact zone," to use Pratt's term. [4] Pratt's notion of "contact zone" is an especially useful concept in the context of this discussion because it emphasizes what is at stake when the research, writing, and reading all occur in the same space, on the same stage, as is clearly the situation with composition research and the teaching of writing. The term *performance* is intended to draw attention to culturally specific structures and codes of communication, such as those that enable readers to distinguish, for example, between genres. Every performance is marked by a combination of codes that designate it as either "authentic" or "inauthentic" depending on the audience, as Pratt suggests. In other words, something is going on in every performance, or speech event, be it in writing or otherwise, that suggests its appropriateness (or inappropriateness). Self-conscious cues are those that the actor-writer performs with a certain purpose or audience in mind, whereas the term *self-evident* suggests that we do what we do because we are not aware of or are not familiar with alternative ways, means, styles, methods, or customs of performing membership within a community, as would be the case when a writer enters a new writing community. As an example, when a student places her name in the top right corner of the first page of an essay, which seems to be the practice with virtually all new college students, her reason for doing so is usually self-evident: "That is how we always did it in high school." The practice marks her as an outsider in the academic community that follows a different convention. By comparison, when a student places her name in the top left of the page, followed by her instructor's name, the course name and number, and the date, the act is clearly self-conscious. The form is shorthand for "I know how to do this, and I want my reader to respond to my text accordingly." Academic discourse is a self-conscious performance.

The preceding example is not intended to suggest that the differences between self-evident and self-conscious cues are easy to distinguish or that communicative competence is simply a matter of learning the appropriate form. Indeed, acts of writing are exceedingly complex. And that is my point. I take the position, as does Lisa Delpit, that students need to learn the cues that are practiced within the academic community with respect to performances in writing if only so that they can resist them knowingly: "In this country, students will be judged by their product regardless of the process they utilized to achieve it. And that product, based as it is on the specific codes of a particular culture, is more readily produced when the directives of how to produce it are made explicit" (31).

What then is critical auto/ethnography?

Like its ethnographic counterpart, critical auto/ethnography is both a method and a text based on systematic participant observation and critical analysis. But unlike traditional ethnography, the narrator establishes her authority by representing herself autobiographically and foregrounding the discourse that she seeks to disrupt. The term *critical* is intended to deflect criticism that aims to discredit auto/ethnography on the assumption that it is not ethnography. In other words, critical auto/ethnography is both a method and a text that challenges and critiques autobiographical and ethnographic conventions and that can be understood as relying, at least in part, on the ethnographer's status as a subjugated Other to makes its case.

CRITICAL AUTO/ETHNOGRAPHY AS COMPOSITION PEDAGOGY

> This space is not a territory staked out by exclusionary practices. Rather, it functions as a sheltering site, one that can nurture our differences. . . . We can be united against hegemonic power only by refusing to engage that power on its own terms, since to do so would mean becoming ourselves a term within that system of power.
>
> —Françoise Lionnet, "The Politics and Aesthetics of Métissage"

Critical auto/ethnography emerges at the interstice of autobiography and ethnography, but as a research, writing, and reading strategy it encompasses literature, folklore, anthropology, sociology, linguistics, social history, and cultural geography. Additionally, because ethnographic research is central to much of the work that goes on within the humanities and social sciences as well as across the arts, business, education, law, and agriculture, showing students how the kinds of texts that form the basis of much of the scholarship that we assign as reading are produced makes good sense. It is a premise of this approach, however, that while reading surely improves writing, it is not necessarily the best place to begin in college composition classes, because to read well, which is to say critically, one needs to understand how language works in writing, how texts are constructed, what the choices are, how the pieces fit together, and to what end. And to understand writing, one needs to write extensively.

The critical auto/ethnography curriculum I discuss in the following section is designed to meet the demands and constraints of a ten-week quarter comprising eight writing assignments. Each of the first seven assignments represents a "stand alone" text and teaching opportunity, but together these auto/ethnographic fragments form the basis of the eighth assignment, the critical auto/ethnographic essay (see Figure 10.1). The research and writing process is unavoidably a linear one, with each assignment building on the one preceding it, but the approach is such that students come in contact with a far-reaching range of rhetorical styles, purposes, and practices. This in turn prepares them to decide for themselves which conventions they want to embrace and which they choose to challenge or resist when they construct their final assignment. As Pratt emphasizes, even though "subjugated peoples cannot

Autobiographical Narrative

                                                    Introduction

Field Research: First Impressions

Field Research: In-Depth Description

Annotated Bibliography

                                                    Body

Interview Transcription

Emerging Themes

                                                    Conclusion

Reflections

Critical Auto/Ethnography

FIGURE 10.1
The Critical Auto/Ethnographic Process (and Products)

readily control what emanates from the dominant culture," or what norms are prescribed, they should be able to "determine to varying extents what they absorb into their own" (*Imperial Eyes* 6).

The work begins in earnest on Day 1 when, midway through the class meeting, after all questions are asked and answered, I ask the students to "Describe in detail the past hour." Their responses to this prompt form the basis of our discussion on Day 2 when we focus on the differences and similarities between description and interpretation, and why description is inherently an interpretative process. "Writing does basically two things," I tell the students at the start of the next class. "It either describes or it interprets. Description and interpretation." I write the two terms on the board and draw a line between them:

Description _____ Interpretation

FIGURE 10.2
A False Binary?

"What is description?" I ask.

After the students settle on a definition, one that usually emphasizes something akin to "facts" and the absence of feelings or judgments, I remind the students that the prompt asked them to "Describe in detail." "Let's start from the beginning. What happened during that first hour? What caught your attention when you first walked in?"

> We constructed a list of details on the board, starting with the moment when the first student entered in the classroom. The discussion was lively, as the students tried to remember what happened when, and who said what to whom.
>
> "You said that this class was going to 'difficult.'"
>
> "Is that what I said?" I asked the rest of the class.
>
> "No, you said 'brutal.'"
>
> "But not like you meant it."
>
> "Describe what you saw or heard that made you think that I didn't mean it."
>
> "You were smiling."
>
> The list grew, but I didn't let up. "What about all of you? What did you notice about the people around you? Their gender, appearance, clothing, body language? Their names, even? What did they say when I asked them to introduce themselves?"
>
> The list grew longer still.
>
> "You took your chair from behind the desk, and sat up near us."
>
> I pressed the students to consider the space. "What might a reader need to know about this room to be able to understand what you meant or why it mattered that I moved my chair from behind the desk?"

Once the blackboard was full enough to make the point that description is potentially limitless if you take all of the data available through observation and participation into account, I asked: "Did everyone include all of these details in their response to the prompt?"

Sheepishly, they nodded "No."

"Why not?"

It wasn't more than a matter of minutes before they theorized that, even though they had participated in the same event, in the same space, at the same time, their written descriptions varied because they participated from different vantage points, took note of different events, imagined different readers, and made choices about what to write based on different experiences, expectations, and perspectives.[5]

Using their insights as a springboard, I add the terms *objectivity* and *subjectivity* to the writing equation. As the students articulate the issues that connect and separate the concepts, I add lines to the diagram:

Description —————— Interpretation

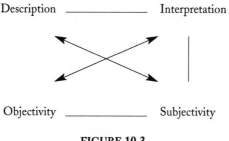

Objectivity —————— Subjectivity

FIGURE 10.3
The Metaphorical X

We discuss the metaphorical X that forms at the center of the diagram and the difficulties this space represents if, as subjective writers, our intent is to describe an event, place, or activity objectively—that is, to represent reality.

"It can't be done," I tell them. "You could spend the rest of your life writing about that one hour, and still not have said everything that could be said. You have to make choices, decide what matters. Interpretation figures in the process right from the start."

So begins the coursework.

Writing Assignment 1: Autobiographical Narrative

The student's autobiographical narrative marks the starting point of their research project. The prompt asks the student to "recreate an experience." Although many writing teachers "support some form of narrative or autobiographical writing as the most 'natural' place for the inexperienced writer to begin" (Shaughnessy 151), I am not convinced that there is anything "natural" about it. Indeed, students often say in their course evaluations that the autobiographical narrative was the most difficult of the writing assignments. I assign a personal experience narrative anyway, but for slightly different reasons: first, it helps me get acquainted with the students and the students with each other; second, it helps me help the students select a research topic that intersects with their own experiences, concerns, and interests.

As I read the students' responses to this first assignment (through an auto/ethnographic lens), I note what I recognize as the "seedlings" of research topics as a way to demonstrate to the students that they already know or have access to the kinds of knowledge that are the focus of research across the humanities and social sciences. We generally spend an entire class period uncovering the connections between their personal experiences and areas of academic interest.

> Because Bill had written about living in his car, a situation that prompted him to enlist in the army, I suggested among other things that he might want to research homelessness, but he protested. Vehemently. Because he worked at the university hospital, Bob had contact with and disdain for the homeless and disadvantaged who "take advantage" of the emergency room. Beyond that, there was nothing more he wanted to know about socioeconomic plight, little he could imagine learning that he didn't already know firsthand. So far as he was concerned, the homeless are responsible for their own situation, and like him, could do something to "change their life" if they wanted. I left it at that and moved on to the next student.

Several days later, Bill announced that he had decided to study one of the homeless shelters on the edge of downtown, I suspect in part to prove his point. He toured the mission, volunteered in the kitchen, and did an in-depth interview with one of the "clients." As his research progressed, Bob revealed one insight after another during class discussions, enlightening all of us. By the end of the term, he thought of himself as an advocate for the homeless rather than an adversary.

Writing Assignment 2: Initial Impressions

The next two writing assignments are field research assignments based on systematic participant observation. For the first assignment, I ask students to introduce their project, "map" the space, describe their initial impressions, and reflect on any preconceived notions they may have at the outset of their research as well as any questions that arise during their initial observations. In preparation, we discuss what to expect and how to handle the unexpected, the importance of securing permission, note-taking strategies, and writing while the experience is "fresh." The class discussion and readings focus on the connection between method and "findings," and the idea that "*what* the ethnographer finds out is inherently connected with *how* she finds it out" (Emerson 11).

Writing Assignment 3: In-Depth Description

For the second field research assignment, I expect something akin to a "thick description" to demonstrate to the reader "that you were there, *then*." During the time leading up to this assignment's due date, the discussion and readings center on writing options: the relationship between style and purpose; using and integrating first- and third-person points of view; how to describe people and processes; the mechanics of quoting; and issues related to narrating a scene as it unfolds, or "in-process," as opposed to reflexively. As with the first field research assignment, I resist setting a page requirement, but when pressed, I have told students to "write until you run out of time or out of things to say, whichever comes first." The responses to this assignment generally run from three to five single-spaced pages, although students have written as many as ten pages. Once their fieldwork is underway, frequently they will ask if they can do more, if they can keep writing even though they have already turned in the required assignments. "Absolutely." But I caution them as well, to use their best judgment, and not to overestimate how much they can accomplish by the end of the term. "This is a project you can come back to."

Ericka went behind the scenes at a gay nightclub as a "dresser" for a friend who performs in a drag show. "I knew that he was gay, because he 'came out' while we were still in high school, but I had never been to a place like that or seen John dressed as a woman." In her second set of field notes, Ericka described in exquisite, compelling detail every step in John's transformation, from foundation to prosthetics. During her oral presentation at the end of the term, Ericka said, "I couldn't believe it. He, she, I never know what to say. She, he, *she-eee* was *so-ooo* beautiful." Ericka showed us photographs as proof.

Writing Assignment 4: Annotated Bibliography

For this assignment, the students are expected to annotate a minimum of five resources, four of which must be "scholarly" texts. This leaves room for the students to annotate a Web site or brochure related to the subject of their research. The prompt asks the students to go beyond what is apparent from the title of the text and describe the purpose or thesis as well as the author's research methods. Students are also expected to describe briefly the contents, note what if anything captured their attention about the author's approach or ideology, and explain how the work might prove useful to their own project, as a theoretical framework or as a "model" for organizing their final ethnography. I ask them to limit their annotations to one full paragraph. The prompt also calls for an introductory paragraph explaining the overall theme and purpose of the sources cited. The responses to this assignment are generally two to three single-spaced pages.

This assignment is important on several levels. First, it introduces students to the basics of library research, including learning how to use the university's online or electronic library catalogue system, navigate the stacks, and reserve texts; evaluate the author's authority; quickly locate the thesis or purpose; judge the text's worthiness with respect to their own projects; find other links to their research project through published bibliographies; and write in the historical present: quote, paraphrase, cite, and document sources according to MLA (Modern Language Association) style.

The second reason this assignment is important is that the students, who are by now committed to their projects, either discover that their topic is "academic" and that other scholars recognize the subject as meaningful, or they realize that there is a "need" for the research they have undertaken:

> Jessie sent me an e-mail: "I am finding this enthralling and see how people could spend years working on these things! The [field research] is just a starting point! I am in the process of analyzing texts and trying to pick out just 5." While Jessie was trying to narrow the possibilities, Janet was panicking because she "could not find any books" on her topic. Martha is struggling also, but for an altogether different reason: "I couldn't find anything [about interdenominational wedding practices] that wasn't old and most of [those sources] were etiquette books." On the day that the annotated bibliographies were due Carl was quick to tell us, "I found a lot of sources, but no one did it [their research] the way that I'm doing it."

Writing Assignment 5: Interview Transcription

Because one of the goals of ethnography is to uncover the "member's meanings," I expect the students to interview a subject, record the interview on tape, and then transcribe the conversation. By this point, the students usually think that they understand the situation or event. Either that, or they do not have a clue. Regardless, the interview marks a turning point; it is a form of socialization—a move across the boundary that typically separates insiders from outsiders. I discourage the students from taking a preplanned list of questions and suggest instead that they approach the interview with only a question or two in mind to get the conversation going. "The important thing is to let the interviewee decide what you need to know." In advance, we talk about the importance of listening closely, even though the recorder is running, and "not filling the silence." "When the interviewee stops talking, don't assume that they're finished. Just wait, or count slowly to five in your head, because odds are that the interviewee will 'think' of something else to say. And that 'something else' may be just what you need to know." The students often discover from the interview that their own notions of the event or situation differ, sometimes dramatically, from that of their interviewees.

> Bill returned to class after interviewing one of the clients at the homeless shelter, eager to talk about what John had told him. "I don't know if what he said is true. I don't know if I should believe him. His story was like something out of a movie." I explained to class that truth is not necessarily the issue. "Maybe it was a pack of lies and maybe it wasn't. But whatever it was he told you, that is what he wanted you to know; you have to take it at face value."

I explain to the students that they need to ask themselves: "Why *this* story? What did the interviewee want me to learn?" I also make sure that they know just how long transcribing an interview can take (up to eight hours for every hour of tape, not counting time to describe the context of the interview or the nuances expressed) and suggest that they bear that in mind. Based on the transcriptions I estimate that their interviews run from fifteen to twenty minutes, which is enough to meet the needs of the assignment, although students are often motivated to do more than one interview.

Writing Assignment 6: Emerging Themes

Predictably, this is the most difficult part of process for the students because it demands that they approach all the texts they have produced thus far as critical readers rather than as writers—not an easy task. "Lay it all out, *everything* that you have written up to now plus whatever documents you've collected, and read through all of the texts as though you have never laid eyes on any of them before, as though it is someone else's project, someone else's writing."

- What do the texts suggest about the subjects? The author?
- What materials, processes, and practices are foregrounded?
- What does one have to know to participate in the situation or event?
- When and how do issues of race, class, gender arise?
- What are the sociocultural norms? Who sets the standards?
- What are the underlying assumptions? What is at stake?
- Do the interviewee's remarks reinforce the norms or challenge them?
- What is missing from the story? What does the omission suggest?

I meet with the students one-on-one to discuss their response to the prompt. They generally arrive at the conference feeling good about their projects, but overwhelmed by the mountain of "data." So, we talk.

"What did you learn? What came as the biggest surprise?"

"How do things work? What is the process or procedure?"

"Who is in charge? Who is the authority? Who stands to gain? What? And why?"

"What are the 'unwritten rules' of participation?"

"What would you want to tell someone who was going to pick up where you leave off?"

"What are you still curious about? If you could ask the people you worked with one more question, what would it be?"

I emphasize that the goal is not to establish a grand or universal truth. "Just stick to what you learned about the people and practices in that one situation." The responses to the emerging themes assignment generally run one to two single-spaced pages.

Writing Assignment 7: Ethnography: The First Draft

Here, the student draws from the previous six assignments, each a finished product, to create a larger work. This part of the curriculum is rich with learning opportunities such as: paragraph cohesion and variety; topic sentences and transitions; sentence and vocabulary variety; and the importance of defining methods and key terms. During the classes leading up to the first draft due date, I stress the writing and editing options, and recommend starting with the field notes and interview. "You can integrate the two into one continuous narrative by letting your interviewee help tell your story. Or you can excerpt your interview. Or, you can do both." By now, the students have read five to six professionally written ethnographic essays, case studies, or chapters from longer texts, and they have a fairly good idea of their options in terms of style and organization. We spend the better of part of one class period analyzing several of the assigned readings to get a sense of how much rhetorical "space" is devoted to the introduction, body, and conclusion, as well as what sorts of information ethnographers foreground in their introductions and what they "save" for their conclusions. I also encourage them to "mine" their annotated bibliographies for ideas.

The final paper is expected to be twelve to fifteen double-spaced pages. Because so much of what the students have written up to now is meaning-full, it is often a struggle for them to set aside some of "important stuff" and concentrate instead on recurring themes, analytical categories, and patterns of discourse. This is where peer editing comes into play. "Tell your readers as much as you think they need to know, but don't go over the page limit. If we have questions, we'll let you know." After I meet with the peer groups to discuss our responses, the students write a short, self-reflexive narrative, describing their project, expectations, findings, theories, unanswered questions, and epiphanies.

Writing Assignment 8: Self-Reflection

The self-reflexive essay is a dual-purpose assignment. When the students and I read and respond to the first drafts, questions and comments arise that are often best addressed reflexively in the conclusion. The self-reflexive essays also form the basis of the students' oral presentations. They are not required to read the reflections aloud, although it is always an option "because scholars do exactly that at conferences."

"They *read* instead of talk?"

"Yep, that's the 'convention.'"

"Why? It sounds so boring."

"Believe me, it can be. The key is to write in your own voice. Just tell your story." The oral presentations are expected run five to seven minutes and may include audiovisual support, photographs, excerpts from their taped interviews, and handouts.

And so ends the course.

HERE, THERE, BACK, AND BEYOND

When I started teaching composition I slipped a few field research writing assignments into the syllabus in place of the routine journal entries, mostly because the thought of journal writing leaves me cold, and I presumed that at least some of students felt similarly. Their response to the field note assignments, the quality and length of their writing compared to the rest of their work, and their level of curiosity about ethnographic methods confirmed my suspicions: students like writing when they "get" the point. The next year I based the writing and reading assignments on autobiographic and ethnographic methods, texts, and theory, believing that undergraduates might actually "take" to academic writing given the opportunity to approach it auto/ethnographically. They do. In "The Tidy House," David Bartholomae invokes Pratt's notion of the *contact zone* together with *autoethnography* and *transculturation* as a way to reimagine the writing classroom and the teaching of writing in general. But if we are going to change the curriculum, as Bartholomae suggests that we should, we need to change the way we talk about students and student writing. According to Bruce Horner, "For this to happen will involve giving voice to different, and suppressed stories, finding and sharing in our specific experiences and those of our students as yet untold tales of struggle, defeats, victories, and resistance, thereby teaching and learning from strategies of resistance and outright opposition" (28).

Now, as I look over all of the texts the students have produced since I first began teaching this approach and recall the near misses and successes, one thing is certain: every student is a good, even accomplished, writer in some respect. Contrary to my initial expectations, it is often the so-called basic writers who produce the most fluid field notes, in part I suspect because of the immediacy of the assignment, but also because (for once) they perceive of themselves as having authority. Similarly, the students who are marginalized in our culture because of their race, class, or gender, generally nail the emerging themes assignment because they know firsthand how hegemony works. But they are usually reluctant at first to "tell it like they see it," which should come as no surprise; they know the risks of voicing opposition all too well. As a rule, the honors students write strong autobiographical narratives, probably because they have had more practice performing competency as writers and readers, but they tend to resist working inductively, I suspect because they have already internalized other report-oriented approaches to research and writing. The "middle" students are most apt to embrace the overall process of critical auto/ethnography because, as many have claimed, "I feel like I am finally learning something." Their writing tends to demonstrate their enthusiasm, but they often attempt to support positions that fly in the face of their data. "Ethnography's argument is emergent," I tell them. "The thesis is where you end up, not where you start."

My analysis of several hundred research projects from students across disciplinary boundaries suggests that, as a text, critical auto/ethnography operates on a continuum between Self-oriented ethnography and Other-oriented autobiography. Even though the order of the writing assignments implies that the resulting narrative will follow a path from the autobiographical Here to the ethnographic There and back, the final drafts demonstrate a remarkable range of possibilities. In the final analysis, "prepared" students as well as those who have yet to discover or recover their *authority* as writers (and readers) benefit from doing substantive field and library research, writing, and critical analysis. In the process they learn firsthand how texts are constructed, theses emerge, authority is communicated, and to what end.

NOTES

I am deeply indebted to Brenda Brueggemann for her encouragement and comments as I wrote, rewrote, and revised this chapter. I would also like to thank Julia Watson for gently pushing me to think through the gaps in an earlier version. I am grateful to Patrick B. Mullen and Dorothy Noyes for their insightful questions, suggestions, and support. I am similarly grateful to the students who granted me permission to (re)present their views, voices, and experiences.

1. All of the student names are pseudonyms.

2. According to Sandra Stahl, "Other-oriented narrators underplay their personal role," whereas self-oriented narrators "emphasize their own actions" (qtd in Bauman 34).

3. Dean MacCannell suggests that "the role of the ethnographer is . . . effaced" (qtd in Dorst 7n).

4. According to Mary Louise Pratt, "'contact zone' is an attempt to invoke the spatial and temporal copresence of subjects previously separated by geographic and historical disjunctures, and whose trajectories now intersect" (*Imperial Eyes* 6)

5. This excerpt and others that follow are from my field notes

WORKS CITED

Bartholomae, David. "The Tidy House: Basic Writing in the American Curriculum." *Landmark Essays on Basic Writing*. Ed. Kay Halasek and Nels P. Highberg. Mahwah, NJ: Hermagoras, 2001: 171–84.

Bauman, Richard. *Story, Performance, and Event*. New York (and Cambridge): Cambridge UP, 1986.

Brodkey, Linda. *Writing Permitted in Designated Areas Only*. Minneapolis: U of Minnesota P, 1996.

Delpit, Lisa. "The Silenced Dialogue." *Landmark Essays on Basic Writing*. Ed. Kay Halasek and Nels P. Highberg. Mahwah, NJ: Hermagoras, 2001: 83–102.

Dewalt, Kathleen, and Billie Dewalt, with Coral Wayland. "Chapter Eight: Participant Observation." *Handbook of Methods in Cultural Anthropology*. Ed. H. Russell Bernard. Walnut Creek (London, and New Delhi): AltaMira, 1998.

Dorst, John. *The Written Suburb*. Philadelphia: U of Pennsylvania P, 1989.

Emerson, Robert M., Rachel 1. Fretz, and Linda L. Shaw. *Writing Ethnogrgphic Fieldnotes*. Chicago (and London): U of Chicago P, 1995.

Horner, Bruce and Min-Zhan Lu. *Representing the Other*. Urbana, IL: NCTE, 1999.

Kenny, Lorraine Delia. "Doing My Homework: The Autoethnography of a White Teenage Girl." *Racing Research, Researching Race: Methodological Dilemmas in Critical Race Studies*. Ed. France Winddance Twine and Jonathan W. Warren. New York: New York UP, 2000: 111–33.

Lionnet, Françoise. "The Politics and Aesthetics of Métissage." (1989) *Women, Autobiography, Theory*. Ed. Sidonie Smith and Julia Watson. Madison: U of Wisconsin P, 1998: 325–36.

Lionnet-McCumber, Françoise. "Autoethnography: The An-Archic Style of Dust
    Tracks on a Road." *Zora Neale Hurston: Critical Perspectives Past and Present*. Ed.
    Henry Louis Gates, Jr. and K. A. Appiah. New York: Amistad, 1993.

Mutnick, Deborah. *Writing in an Alien World*. Postmouth, NH: Boyton/Cook, 1996.

Pratt, Mary Louise. *Imperial Eyes* (1992). New York: Routledge, 1997.

———. Fieldwork in Common Places." *Writing Culture*. Berkeley: U of California P,
    1986: 27–50.

Reed-Danahay, Deborah E., ed. "Introduction." *Auto/Ethnography: Rewriting the Self
    and the Social*. New York (and Oxford): Berg, 1997.

11

Unsituating the Subject

"Locating" Composition and Ethnography in Mobile Worlds

CHRISTOPHER KELLER

Rather than tracing back the roots . . . to their source, I've tried to show how the roots themselves are in a state of constant flux and change. The roots don't stay in one place. They change shape. They change colour. And they grow. There is no such thing as a pure point of origin.

—Dick Hebdige, *Cut'n'Mix:*
Culture, Identity, and Caribbean Music

It becomes ever more urgent to develop a framework of thinking that makes the migrant central, not ancillary, to historical process. An authentically migrant perspective . . . might begin by regarding movement, not as an awkward interval between fixed points of departure and arrival, but as a mode of being in the world.

—Paul Carter, *Living in a New Country:*
History, Travelling, and Language

ASKING "WHEN?" AND "WHERE?"

PAST CONVERSATIONS ABOUT ethnographic research methodologies in composition studies have generally proceeded on a similar course with those in anthropology.[1] Questions about the authority of the ethnographic writer, the "fictional qualities" of ethnographic texts, the problematic complicity of ethnographic research and imperialist or oppressive institutions and nations, and the problematic construction and representation of "others" into texts have all come to the fore in both composition studies and anthropology, especially since the 1980s. This is certainly not a coincidence. That is, I do not mean to suggest that composition studies and anthropology have been moving on two similar, yet completely discrete, disciplinary tracks. Certainly a large degree of interdisciplinary feeding has taken place between the two: compositionists have often looked toward anthropology for knowledge about "culture," cultural formations, cultural studies in general, and ethnography, whereas several anthropologists have mined composition and literary studies for ways to examine the "rhetorical and discursive construction" of knowledge in anthropological and ethnographic texts.[2]

Cristina Kirklighter, Cloe Vincent, and Joseph Moxley, editors of *Voices & Visions,* for instance, ask important questions about the roles and status of ethnography for the field:

> What is unique about how compositionists conduct ethnography? Should positivism or postpositivism inform the authority of ethnography? To what extent should ethnographies be about the ethnographer, the research community, or the surrounding community? To what extent should an ethnographer act as a cultural worker or as an objective scientist? How can ethnographers "tell the truth" when doing so reflects negatively on the communities or when they cannot get respondents' written permission to be published? (viii)

These questions are important ones that compositionists must ask and seek answers to, yet these questions, perhaps, tend to look for large, generalized answers that can be applied to some imagined totality of composition studies and need, rather, to be phrased a bit differently: first, all of these questions need to be considered in light of the first one. That is, all of these inquiries need to be looked at closely in terms of how they are contextualized within composition studies. As is, the latter four seem to drift into the realm of larger, more universal questions about ethnographic practices. And second, rather than couch these questions in terms of "shoulds" and "cans," composition studies might better be served by asking "when?" and "where?" In other words, rather than ask "should" positivism or postpositivism inform the authority of ethnography; "should" ethnographies be about the ethnographer, the research community, or the surrounding community; "should" an ethnographer act as a cultural worker or objective scientist; and "how can" ethnographers tell the truth when doing so reflects negatively on the communities they study, compositionists might ask instead "when" and "where" each of these ethnographic priorities is feasible, necessary, and needed.

The previous questions as they are stated tend to posit composition studies (and the "fieldwork" within) as a homogenous entity, as a discipline that needs to decide (for good) on the right or wrong way of doing ethnography, and they do so without recognizing explicitly that certain contexts and research agendas call for certain forms of ethnography and ethnographic practices. George Marcus argues in "Anthropology on the Move" that ethnographic theories are too often derived outside of the contexts of ethnographic fieldwork: "My problem with much . . . ethnography is that its arguments and significance are not produced or given within the frame of ethnographic work itself but by the contextualizing discourses and narratives in which the ethnography comes to be embedded" (13). He continues by suggesting that those engaged in ethnographic research are "more actively selecting framing contexts, theoretical associations, and narratives for their ethnography, but they still mostly are not creating them within the heart of the ethnographic process of fieldwork and writing itself" (13). Therefore, instead of conversing about the ways in which ethnography "should" be conducted in composition studies, compositionists instead might engage in looking at the numerous social, institutional, political, and cultural contexts in which the various kinds of ethnographies will be relevant and needed to produce diverse knowledges. We tend to recognize that ethnographic texts focus on individuals, particularly individual students, but we need to remember that each of these students exists and is observed within specific contexts, contexts that first need to be examined closely to figure out the best forms of ethnographic inquiry for the situation at hand. In some cases, for instance, empirical studies might best suit the context and research study, whereas in other cases, the emphasis on the compositionist as a "cultural worker" is more important than attempts at objectivity and vice versa. By attempting to answer such large questions about ethnography for composition studies, those posed by the *Voices & Visions* editors, for instance, we end up making homogenous the various distinct contexts in which ethnographic research takes place.

On Getting Rid of Ethnography in Composition Studies

Considering so many contexts for and versions of ethnography in composition studies will no doubt open the proverbial can of worms. Like similar questions scholars and fieldworkers in anthropology pose, our questions seem to amass more quickly than our answers. And perhaps not surprisingly, then, many of our answers lead to conclusions that ethnography just cannot function in composition studies, that we cannot import such a methodology wholly into an academic discipline that does not have the means to support and contain it. In "Ethnography or Psychography?" Keith Rhodes argues that:

> Examining even an exemplary composition "ethnography" reveals that what composition "ethnographers" do, even at best, does not preserve much meaning for the term. "Ethnography" in composition does not explore cultures so much as it explores individual experience within closely defined cultural institutions. (31)

Drawing from Carrie Shively Leverenz's "Peer Response in the Multicultural Composition Classroom," Rhodes argues aptly that many composition ethnographers have not really used ethnographic methodologies practically or correctly, that "composition 'ethnography' simply is not thickly described writing that explores whole cultures, or even whole subcultures" (32). Rhodes, however, does not entirely blame the problematic situation of ethnography in composition on compositionists themselves but on how the genre has been imported into composition studies and how, consequently, the genre is not well suited for composition.

Such problems, for Rhodes, derive from ethnography itself as a genre that, perhaps, cannot function in composition because it tries to do too much. Rhodes believes that our ethnographic dilemmas occur when we in composition studies try to bring specific, large theories to bear on only limited observations, and consequently, "observers mainly see patterns already suggested by their own theories" (27). Conversely, another problem arises when composition scholars try to formulate new theories and general hypotheses based on only the limited data that classrooms can provide. Rhodes, then, suggests that composition studies should turn away from ethnography as a genre and toward a new one: "psychography." Psychography, Rhodes writes, is a distinct genre, a "thickly described writing exploring the connections of individual psyches with specific cultural conditions" that should be based on "reasonably extended study, moderate thickness of description, small focus groups, collaborative separation of teacher and researcher roles, self-conscious personalizing of all participants, and genuine concern for the dignity of the students and teachers being observed" (32).[3] Psychography as a distinct genre and research methodology in composition helps remove the tendency to homogenize our ethnographic approaches in the discipline. That is, psychography reminds us that we no longer need to worry about whether (all) compositionists "should" or "can" practice ethnography in certain ways because one now uses a genre that tailors to the specific researcher, research subjects, research site, institutional location, and other various individuals existing within it. Psychography allows teacher-researcher-observers to limit their methodological practices and generalizations by articulating clearly the specificities of each study, studies that do not necessarily need to be linked to all other psychographic studies in composition. These studies, then, are "reasonably" limited in what they attempt to convey.

Rhodes's notion of psychography certainly has great potential in its ability to narrow composition's research sites. It helps compositionists escape some of the problems of ethnographic practices: in particular, it allows composition ethnographers to worry less about their inabilities to "observe" student writers in great detail. Traditionally, ethnographers spend at least a year or two "in the field" watching their "subjects" closely. Certainly compositionists cannot really get "into the field" in this sense. Most compositionists interested in ethnographic research methodologies are not going to follow "student subjects" around campus and sleep in tents on dorm room floors to "observe" these individuals. Limited observations, those using psychography would argue, are acceptable for composition studies. Rhodes's psychography, furthermore, focuses on specific individuals, rather than an on entire "culture." Because codifying any "culture," let alone a "student culture," is difficult and problematic psychography "personalizes" its approach to only a few students, therein avoiding the problems of homogenizing and stereotyping student populations. Its methodology, this is to say, is cautious not to make large assumptions about individuals based on limited observations.

Rhodes's psychography adroitly replaces problematic versions of ethnography in composition studies, but I have reservations about adopting it wholly and giving up on ethnography altogether. My first concern is that Rhodes argues here against ethnography as it has been "traditionally" or "classically" conceived, as a practice that involves a representative from one "culture" who studies those of another "culture," the ethnographic textual product therein supposing some sort of Archimedian viewpoint of the ethnographic observer. This legacy of ethnography, George Marcus and Michael Fischer write in *Anthropology as Cultural Critique,* is a research practice in which the ethnographer "closely observes, records, and engages in the daily life of another culture—an experience labeled as the fieldwork method—and then writes accounts of this culture, emphasizing descriptive detail" (18). In this process, an ethnographer's task is to make a "strange" culture somehow more familiar to an audience by showing a holistic, total picture of "culture" and the subjects existing and behaving within. Working primarily against this "traditional" conception of ethnography, Rhodes and others in composition studies overlook the fact that this type of ethnography is perhaps an outdated one, that many anthropologists in particular have come to see the world not as a place where discrete cultures have specific and recognizable boundaries but instead as a place where diverse cultural groups interact and where cultural processes flow together and interact, therein erasing many strict boundaries and categories that used to make ethnographic practices possible.[4] Akhil Gupta and James Ferguson suggest, "Ethnographically, much of the best work today no longer fits within the model of a study of 'a culture,' while the most challenging contemporary fieldwork cannot be contained within the stereotypical 'among the so-and-so' mold" (2). Thus, for composition studies and other disciplines, the basis of judging ethnography can longer be whether one truly observes and studies a "culture" through and through.

My second concern about Rhodes's psychography is that it too greatly minimalizes compositionists' research agendas, narrowing their studies to only a few students in singular research sites to see how these few "connect," for instance, with a larger institutional framework of the academy. In this sense, composition's research sites—its locations for fieldwork—are limited to, essentially, a "manageable" classroom space only, thereby overlooking all other spaces and places that students dwell in, exist within, inhabit, and move between—important locations that compositionists might look toward to acknowledge and understand students and students' identities, their discursive practices, and their frames for making meaning better. Rather than exploring more locations, Rhodes wants to collapse the "research field" into small local sites for investigation. My argument here begins with the assumption that ethnography in composition must open up more spaces rather than close them. In doing so, we must then be satisfied with "partial knowledges" about those people, places, and things we study because no kind of ethnographic research can ever trace the whole picture—regardless how small the site of fieldwork. Thus, in rethinking ethnography for composition studies, I begin primarily by advocating ethnographic practices and theories that pry open other sites—both physical and non-physical—for ethnographic investigation, those that allow us to recognize and emphasize the constant movement and mobility of subjects, identities, and contexts. I agree with James Clifford when he notes that the ethnographer's "field-site opens onto complex histories of dwelling and traveling. . . . Fieldwork is less a matter of localized dwelling and more a series of travel encounters. Everyone's on the move, and has been for centuries: dwelling-in-travel" (*Routes* 2). Ethnography, in composition and elsewhere, must begin to trace paths of circulation and travel rather than assume the fixity and rootedness of its subjects.

Using Rhodes's "psychography" as a springboard into issues about ethnography in composition studies, this chapter, furthermore, recognizes that the use of ethnographic practices and theories in composition studies are difficult, problematic, and complex, but it argues that many of these problems and difficulties stem not so much from ethnography as a genre—or research methodology—that just does not fit very well in composition but instead that these problems derive from the ways in which we in composition tend to imagine, minimalize, and construct our conceptions of spaces and places, the ways we have defined the (limited) locations in which ethnographic research might take place. I argue here that first debunking the traditional "mise-en-scene" of composition's classroom "field research" and looking more closely instead at the ways composition studies research might engage in multisited ethnographic practices is necessary.

ETHNOGRAPHY AND THE "SITUATION" OF THE SUBJECT

In many cases ethnographic practices in composition studies have been used to more effectively uncover and grasp various student "identities" and "subject positions," those functioning within numerous cultural and social frameworks of race, class, gender, and sexuality, for instance.[5] This section examines some of composition's recent thought about the relationships between "student identities" and ethnographic practices to show how such thinking tends to be grounded in concepts and theoretical paradigms that "fix" or "stabilize" student subjects in time and place. I hope to offer a way to start unsituating the subject in composition, not in the hopes that we'll stop looking at subject positions entirely, but instead so that we might better understand and use ethnographic practices and other research methodologies that recognize student subjectivities as always on the move, always changing, and always shifting within, among, and between various locations and spaces. In doing this, I argue for multisited ethnographies in composition studies, something I discuss in the final section of this chapter. First, however, considering these "subjects" in composition studies and the research agendas structured in a bit more detail is necessary to understand them better.

In her book *Composition in the University*, Sharon Crowley argues that both current-traditionalism and process pedagogies treat the "student subject" similarly:

> Process and product have more in common than is generally acknowledged in professional literature about composition, where the habit of contrasting them conceals the fact of their epistemological consistency. A truly paradigmatic alternative to current-traditionalism would question the modernism in which it is immersed and the institutional structure by means of which it is administered. Process pedagogy does neither. It retains the modernist composing subject of current-traditionalism—the subject who is sufficiently discrete from the composing context to stand apart from it, observing it from above and commenting on it. (212–13)

Crowley's critique here is important on two accounts. First, she see as problematic the way that student subjectivity is often theorized in composition studies as entirely separate from writing contexts. Second, this critique extends to the ways that student identities and subjectivities have become the center of composition's theoretical and pedagogical debates. Numerous composition scholars, no doubt, spend a great deal of time complicating student identities and subjectivities with theoretical rigor by locating (and asking students to locate) such identities in networks of history, class, gender, race, and sexuality—to understand and recognize the plurality of subject positions from which one speaks, writes, and lives. Crowley, however, questions the ways that such conversations have directed the field by commenting, somewhat suspiciously, that "student identities are the subject of composition" (227).

Similarly, in her article "Finitude's Clamor," D. Diane Davis also contests the modernist notion of the writing subject, what she calls the "myth of immanence" or the "figure of the self-present *composing* subject" (121). Building from Crowley's arguments, Davis recognizes that:

> Of course, this notion of the composing subject has been massively critiqued by feminists and critical composition pedagogues, who aim to help the self-directed student come to terms with the ways in which her thoughts are already shaped by her own historical and cultural situatedness. From here, though, the challenge is typically to help the student writer become conscious of and then speak from her own radical positioning—that is, to embrace an identity founded on that positioning and disclose it in writing as the basis for her own arguments and ideas. (121)

Even radical and critical writing pedagogies, however, "which presume that identity is constituted and plural," Davis contends, "have a tendency to reproduce the myth of immanence by encouraging students to consider themselves *presentable*" (121). Thus, writers are prone not only "to fits of self assertion but more importantly: writers very sure of who they are and what they know," and such an understanding of writers, Davis continues, intimates that writers exist apart from writing contexts, the world, and others (121–22).

This notion of the "self-present composing subject" has also been critiqued in composition studies' versions of ethnography. Student subjects have been examined and studied not as individuals standing "immanently" in the world but instead as individuals who are culturally and socially "situated" in larger groups, larger cultural and social formations that provide knowledge about writing contexts. I do not mean to suggest that one can conflate all ethnographic practices in composition studies. Yet, many theories and practices of ethnography in composition studies look first and foremost at students as individuals grouped and bound within various cultural, social, political, and institutional communities, and then argue that if ethnographers in composition can better observe and understand these groups, their behaviors, values, beliefs, and daily practices, then one might better understand their situations as students and as writers and readers. Beverly Moss demonstrates this point by suggesting, "finding out what students did outside class was the key to helping them succeed in school" (154). To look at the situations of discourse production and interpretation by students, in other words, our ethnographies, according to Moss, must look at "situations" of students in specific "extracurricular" cultural, social, gender, and economic settings and positions.

Whether through ethnographic methodologies or not, such beliefs have been prominent in facilitating composition's social and cultural "turn." However, many ethnographic theories and practices in composition studies tend to falter on two accounts when they study these cultural and social "situations" of student writers: first, when they view students as members of "fixed" groups wherein all members' identities are identical, thus positing some type of pure cultural difference between these groups. And second, problems arise when ethnographers view the classroom as a simple microcosm of the larger social and cultural formations, as reflections or shadows of what's going on in the "outside" world, therein erasing the classroom's status as a place where meanings, conflicts, and discourses are made rather than as a mere reflection of things going on elsewhere. I would like to examine two essays about ethnography in composition studies that will help pinpoint the problematic and complex nature of the genre in the discipline and will help establish the need for multisited ethnography.

In "Ethnography and Composition," Beverly Moss writes that:

> the goal of an ethnographer is to study, explore, and describe a group's culture. . . . It is through examining such ordinary, daily routines of a community that ethnographers are able to accomplish their ultimate goal: to describe a particular community so that an outsider would see it as a native would and so that the community studied can be compared to other communities. (155)

This type of ethnography problematically relies on a conception of cultures as discrete and isolated entities that exist in pure difference from one another, thus neglecting to see how and where cultural blurring and sharing exist. Moss's version of ethnography also posits the culture under study as homogenous and fixed, rooted in time and place to offer up a strict basis of comparison to another fixed culture. For Moss, the purpose of ethnography is to make the strange more recognizable, and "only through such careful comparisons can researchers start to develop a global picture of cultural groups" (155). This kind of ethnographic practice binds the subjects under study to certain "naturalized" categories and groups before the study even begins. In this sense, too, the ethnographer posits an unproblematic "we" the "outsiders" against a distinct and unproblematic "native insider." Ethnography becomes a simple "link" between an uncomplicated spatialized "here" and "there," as well as other simplified binaries such as "us" and "them." Moss's "cultural comparisons," in addition, assume a form of original separation, which is bridged when the ethnographer comes in contact with the "natives" and produces an ethnographic text not within a shared world but a text that reaches across cultures and between societies.[6]

Kay Losey, in "Describing the Cultures of the Classroom," details the difficulties of providing "multiple perspectives" in classroom ethnographies, the complexities of allowing ethnographic practices to articulate the "polyphony" of voices and viewpoints of both students and instructors. Losey also fears that classroom ethnographers will represent the class as a "single community" sharing a "single culture." She contends instead that classrooms comprise a "number of smaller communities, each with its own culture," and in one class in particular that she observed, "There were Mexican-Americans, Anglo-Americans, Portuguese-Americans, Asian-Americans. Some people spoke English as their first language. For others, English was their second language or third language. The classroom I studied had a number of different communities with a number of different perspectives" (86). Losey here and in the rest of her essay problematically conflates terms such as *communities, groups,* and *cultures* and then uses each of these three terms nearly synonymously with the various ethnic groups being discussed.

These loose and problematic uses of such terms aside, Losey's ethnographic vision imagines classrooms as simple shadows of the outside world:

> With regard to identifying groups in the classroom, remember that the school and the classroom do the bidding of the *larger society.* Issues of power, status, and dominant ideologies that are negotiated and circulated in the community and larger society are likely to be *reflected* in the classroom. The same groups in struggle in the *larger society* may well be in conflict on a smaller scale in the classroom. (89; emphasis added)

Losey views the classroom as a microcosm of the world. If racial problems exist, for instance, *out there,* then teachers might expect the same racial problems to be "reflected" in the classroom. I do not mean to suggest as an alternative that the classroom is a space isolated from "larger society," but I think it more feasible to see how discourses from the "larger society" circulate and move through the classroom, therein viewing the classroom as a place where these discourses may be dealt with, discussed, and manipulated in certain ways. Rather than imagine the classroom as a mirror that reproduces on a smaller scale what stands in front of it, it is important that we not erase the power of classroom spaces to allow students to create their own positions to the larger society rather than replicate what already exists elsewhere. In short, to rethink some of our ethnographic practices and theories in composition, we must view the classroom as a place that is a "piece" of this larger society, one that connects to and helps construct other pieces. If not, we deny the validity of the classroom as a place where student "subjects" can negotiate, make, and remake knowledges and discourses.

Ethnographic practices, in short, need to consider how the classroom is a location that connects to other locations, locations that subjects constantly inhabit, dwell in, and move between. Both Moss and Losey perceive the ethnographic student subject as fixed in certain ways. For Moss, the student subject is bound to his or her cultural identity as defined by its rootedness in a distinct "culture" and "home." Similarly, Losey argues for ethnographic practices that view students as part of "communities" or "groups" based almost entirely on their ethnic backgrounds, which again fixes student identity and subjectivity by elevating the category of race as most crucial to one's group status and "identity." Losey, in addition, sees only the need to observe the student subjects in the classroom. Because the classroom "reflects" accurately what is going on in the "larger society," there appears then to be no need to examine other locations and their influences on students' subject formations, other places and spaces that ethnographers might trace and study to recognize important connections to classrooms.

MULTISITED ETHNOGRAPHY FOR COMPOSITION STUDIES

I have discussed several ways ethnographic practices in composition and elsewhere are difficult and problematic because they often "fix" subjects naturally in their "proper" cultural spaces and identities. I also have suggested that much of the difficulty of incorporating ethnographic practices in composition studies derives from how we in composition have constructed, viewed, and imagined places, spaces, and locations—often regarding only singular classroom spaces as manageable and important for sites of ethnographic fieldwork.

Julie Drew writes in "The Politics of Place" that "we fix students in classrooms, imagining through such pedagogical norms as race, class, and gender writing topics that we've placed academic writing within a cultural context that will both attract and challenge students to think and write critically" (63). Drew, furthermore, suggests that we have fixed and localized students in classrooms spaces because, first, "naming the writers in our classrooms 'students' is a way of confining them, reducing them to knowable objects, by intimating that one aspect of their discursive and intellectual lives is accurately representative of the whole" (62).

Despite the ways that composition research and scholarship have tended to fix the student in classroom spaces, Drew argues that "students-as-travelers, however, are *already* engaged in various forms of critical thinking and would best be served by an increased understanding of theories and practices of discourse that will help them move more successfully between and among the various spaces they inhabit" (63–64).[7] Drew adeptly asks us to consider not only what sorts of connections and insights we miss when we do not adequately theorize the trope of "student writers," but also she asks that we consider how viewing the classroom as the only location in which student writers produce and use discourse limits our theoretical and pedagogical possibilities.

I agree with Drew that we need to see student writers as people who constantly move, forge attachments to various locations, and remain unfixed in cultural groups and identities. However, I would like to complicate Drew's argument by questioning her use of the word *traveler* and by looking more closely at relationships between location and ethnography in composition studies. First, *traveler* in Drew's argument is meant to serve as a general metaphor for movement—no doubt a necessary one. The words *travel* and *traveler*, however, often carry connotations of movement that people choose and often enjoy. The numerous forms of movement that people engage in, however, do not always reflect such conditions. Thus, in theorizing students as people who are "always on the move," we must remember that *traveler* might not accurately convey other experiences of movement such as exile, displacement, immigration, migrancy, diaspora, and tourism, for instance. The word *traveler* in some ways may serve as an umbrella term for these others, but we must be careful not to conflate the experiences of movement of all students.[8]

Drew's notion of traveling, moreover, fits in with other cultural theories that question Western assumptions that spaces are easily categorized and marked off with boundaries. Akhil Gupta writes, "Our concepts of space have always fundamentally rested on . . . images of break, rupture, and disjunction. The recognition of cultures, societies, nations, all in the plural, is unproblematic exactly because there appears an unquestionable division, an intrinsic discontinuity, between cultures, between societies, etc." (1–2). We in composition studies should start to complicate our understanding of place and location with greater terminological scrupulousness and theoretical rigor and complicate the relationships, juxtapositions, and boundaries of composition's places and locations—the ethnographic practices and theories that composition studies use are a good context in which to begin thinking about how to ask and answer such questions.[9]

George Marcus's idea of a multisited ethnographic practice provides some groundwork in which to theorize concepts of place, movement, and subjectivity in composition studies ethnography. Multisited ethnography begins with the assumption that any cultural identity or activity is constructed "by multiple agents in varying contexts, or places, and that ethnography must be strategically conceived to represent this sort of multiplicity, and to specify both intended and unintended consequences in the network of complex connections within a system of places" ("Imagining" 52). Therefore, any multisited ethnography follows connections among places; tracing and describing the various relationships "among sites previously thought incommensurate *is* ethnography's way of making arguments and providing its own contexts of significance" ("Anthropology" 14). And finally, one might understand the basis of multisited ethnography by recognizing another of its precepts: "If there is anything left to discover by ethnography it is relationships, connections, and indeed cultures of connection, association, and circulation that are completely missed through the use and naming of the object of study in terms of categories 'natural' to subjects' preexisting discourses about them" ("Anthropology" 16). Multisited ethnographic practices ask that ethnographers recognize how various (shifting) contexts and places construct identities, as opposed to ethnographic methods that locate subjects in fixed spaces where identities are made static. Furthermore, multisited ethnographers trace connections among multiple places and locations previously believed incommensurate, and they recognize the potential of multisited ethnography to raze naturalized categories that fasten subjects to fixed identities positions. Multisited ethnographies in composition might begin work on "unsituating" the student subject from its often rigid positioning—whether these are categories of race, class, gender, or "the student" in general—because multisited ethnography attempts to juxtapose student subjects among and within various sites and locations to counteract the often unbending categories that naturalize students in particular groups and communities. In other words, we might begin to start pulling up the roots that have been planted.

This chapter is meant to construct a broad understanding of multisited ethnography for composition studies by outlining its principles and potential for the field. In doing so, I have tried to lay the foundations for this type of ethnography by showing the problems and complexities of other versions of ethnography in composition as well as some of the larger problems in the field regarding the way identities and subject positions are often fixed and bound within certain cultural, social, and political categories. However, what this chapter cannot do is lay out every possible way in which multisited ethnography can be used, when it can be used, or where it can be used. I've really only begun to answer "why" it can be used. I would like to close, however, by sketching a few possible directions for making the types of connections among places and locations that multisited ethnography advocates. First, I see great potential in multisited ethnographic practices in composition studies that begin to trace carefully connections among the locations of youth, the ways in which students as "young" people inhabit and move between various locations and positions of youth. This certainly has links to studies in popular culture but also might lead to a larger investigation and understanding of the "locations" of youth.[10] In "Youth, Culture and Modernity," Johan Fornas suggests that in addition to being a physiological phase of life, youth is also:

> a social category, framed by particular social institutions—especially school, but certain rituals as well such as confirmation or marriage, legislation directed toward age limits and coming of age, and social acts such as leaving home, forming a family, getting educated and finding a profession. And . . . youth is something which is culturally determined in a discursive interplay with musical, visual, and verbal signs that denote what is young in relation to that which is interpreted as respectively childish or adult. (3)

Although this is not the place to develop a theory of youth spaces for composition and ethnography, Fornas offers evidence of the fruitfulness of such studies.

Second, a multisited ethnography for composition studies might delve into nonphysical locations such as cyberenvironments and explore the ways that student identities are always in a state of constant flux because of their "travels" and "movements" through these cyberplaces where they are always interpreting and producing various forms of discourse from a variety of social, cultural, and political positions.[11] And finally, multisited ethnography in composition could look more closely not just at the places in which student move among—those places previously "incommensurate" with composition studies—but could also look at the numerous ways in which students move. This means more ethnographic methods that examine how students move—how we can begin to theorize and use more specific and scrupulous terms such as displacement, exile, and migrancy in addition to other forms of movement such as tourism, pilgrimage, and travel. Applying these more rigorous and meticulous accounts of diverse forms of movement will no doubt benefit the entire project of multisited ethnography for composition studies.

What I have laid out here is no doubt a broad and quite different version of ethnography for composition studies—one that breaks sharply with traditional versions of ethnography that rely on close observation and empirical evidence, although these are not entirely out of the realm of possibility for multisited ethnography. Multisited ethnography, we must remember, assumes in large part that ethnographers are never going to be able to get the "whole picture." Thus, we need no longer worry about limiting the scope of ethnographic investigations because the complete story is always out of the realm of textual possibility. Holism is beside the point because multisited ethnography is not really about completeness or accuracy of representation. Rather, it is about mapping new locations of study, adding what's in the picture, and tracing those connections therein, with the realization that many of these connections are fleeting. When we begin to construct ethnographies:

> whose objects are no longer conceived as automatically and naturally anchored in space [we] will need to pay particular attention to the way spaces and places are made, imagined, contested, and enforced. In this sense, it is no paradox to say that questions of space and place are, in this deterritorialized age, more central to anthropological representation than ever. (Gupta and Ferguson 47)

The chasm between what ethnographers can know face-to-face and what they can know through the big picture is no doubt riddled with practical, political, and epistemological difficulties. Certainly some will suggest that multisited ethnography spreads the research field too thin, not allowing for "thick description." And others certainly are right to fear that this focus on "mobility . . . and multiplicity of options makes our culture invisible" (Peters 87). When culture becomes "invisible" then ethnographic practices will appear useless to those who understand ethnography's purpose to be solely the observation and study of "cultures"—"cultures" with clear boundaries and locations. Multisited ethnography in composition studies, however, is not concerned with "culture" per se—as a codifiable and mappable entity—but instead it is concerned with our status and our students' status as culturally transparent and spatially mobile people whose frames for the construction of meaning and contexts for the production of discourse constantly metamorphose in the wake of movements to, from, and between local and global, physical and nonphysical, terrains.

NOTES

I want to thank both Sid Dobrin and Susan Hegeman for their numerous comments and criticisms of this chapter as it has gone through numerous versions and revisions.

1. I use the designation *anthropology* somewhat loosely in this chapter as a matter of convenience to discuss similarities and differences generally among academic disciplines. However, in using the term *anthropology* I in no way mean to suggest that I am covering all perspectives or lines of thought in that discipline but instead only a relatively small contingent of thinkers and their ideas that might be considered "anthropological."

2. Although several anthropological books and articles focus specifically on the "rhetoric" of anthropological knowledges, this trend in anthropology is often marked by the publication of James Clifford and George Marcus, eds., *Writing Culture: The Poetics and Politics of Ethnography* (Cambridge: Harvard UP, 1986). For more recent writings on this topic, see George Marcus, *Ethnography through Thick & Thin*.

3. *Thick description*, a term borrowed from Gilbert Ryle, is Clifford Geertz's description of ethnographic writing whereby large conclusions are drawn from small and densely textured facts. Thick description places great emphasis on the way cultures function through symbols. Culture, that is, should be understood as an accumulated totality of symbol-systems in which individuals make senses of themselves and their world. For Geertz, then, the anthropological analysis of culture is not "an experimental science in search of law but an interpretive one in search of meaning" (*Interpretation* 5). See Clifford Geertz, *The Interpretation of Cultures* (New York: Basic, 1973). See especially Geertz's "Deep Play: Notes on a Balinese Cockfight," which appears in *The Interpretation of Cultures*, as a central ethnographic text employing thick description, and what has become known more largely as "interpretive anthropology."

4. For more critiques of "traditional" or "classical" ethnography, see James Clifford's *The Predicament of Culture*, Stephen Nugent and Cris Shore, *Anthropology and*

Cultural Studies (London: Pluto P, 1998) and Roger Sanjek, *Fieldnotes: The Making of Anthropology* (Ithaca, NY: Cornell UP, 1990).

5. Other relevant texts in composition studies that look closely at the ways the field has dealt with student subjects and identities are Susan Miller, *Textual Carnivals*, John Clifford, "The Subject of Discourse," *Contending with Words: Composition and Rhetoric in a Postmodern Age*, ed. Patricia Harkin and John Schilb (New York: MLA, 1991) 38–51, Joseph Harris, *A Teaching Subject: Composition Since 1966* (Upper Saddle River, NJ: Prentice Hall, 1997), and Michelle Baliff, "Seducing Composition: A Challenge to Identity-Disclosing Pedagogies," *Rhetoric Review* 16 (1997): 76–91.

6. For more critiques of "cultural comparison" approaches in ethnography, see Arjun Appadurai, "Putting Hierarchy in Its Place," *Cultural Anthropology* 3.1 (1988): 36–49.

7. The notion of students as travelers who produce and interpret various sorts of texts both inside and outside the academic classroom echoes some of the distinctions Anne Ruggles Gere makes between curriculum writings and "extra-curriculum" writings in "Kitchen Tables and Rented Rooms."

8. James Clifford's *Routes*, especially chap. 1, looks closely at the various ways we might define and use these problematic terms about movement in ethnographic and anthropological discourses.

9. In composition studies, those who have begun theorizing *ecocomposition* have started looking closely at the relationships between places and discourse. See Christian Weisser and Sidney I. Dobrin, eds., *Ecocomposition: Theoretical and Pedagogical Approaches* (Albany: State U of New York P, 2001), especially Dobrin's chapter "Writing Takes Place."

10. Other productive and rich studies of the locations and spaces of youth are Henry Giroux's following works: *Fugitive Cultures: Race, Violence, & Youth* (New York: Routledge, 1996); "Where Have All the Public Intellectuals Gone? Racial Politics, Pedagogy, and Disposable Youth," *JAC* 17.2 (1997): 191–205; "Public Pedagogy and the Responsibility of Intellectuals: Youth, Littleton, and the Loss of Innocence," *JAC* 20.1 (2000): 9–42; and *Stealing Innocence: Youth, Corporate Power, and the Politics of Culture* (New York: St. Martin's, 2000).

11. See also Nedra Reynolds, "Composition's Imagined Geographies: The Politics of Space in the Frontier, City, and Cyberspace," *CCC* 50.1 (1998): 12–35; Todd Taylor and Irene Ward, *Literacy Theory in the Age of the Internet* (New York: Columbia UP, 1998), and Marc Auge, *Non-Places: Introduction to an Anthropology of Supermodernity* (London: Verso, 1995).

WORKS CITED

Carter, Paul. *Living in a New Country: History, Travelling, and Language*. London: Faber, 1992.

Clifford, James. *The Predicament of Culture: Twentieth-Century Ethnography, Literature, and Art*. Cambridge: Harvard UP, 1988.

———. *Routes: Travel and Translation in the Late Twentieth Century.* Cambridge, MA: Harvard UP, 1997.

Crowley, Sharon. *Composition in the University: Historical and Polemical Essays.* Pittsburgh: U of Pittsburgh P, 1998.

Davis, D. Diane. "Finitude's Clamor: Or, Notes toward a Communitarian Literacy." *College Composition and Communication* 53.1 (2001): 119–45.

Dobrin, Sidney I. "Writing Takes Place." *Ecocomposition: Theoretical and Pedagogical Approaches.* Ed. Christian R. Weisser and Sidney I. Dobrin. Albany: State U of New York P, 2001. 11–25.

Drew, Julie. "The Politics of Place: Student Travelers and Pedagogical Maps." *Ecocomposition: Theoretical and Pedagogical Approaches.* Ed. Christian R. Weisser and Sidney I. Dobrin. Albany: State U of New York P, 2001. 57–68.

Fornas, Johan. "Youth, Culture, and Modernity." *Youth Culture in Late Modernity.* Ed. Goran Bolin and Johan Fornas. London: Sage, 1995. 1–11.

Gere, Anne Ruggles. "Kitchen Tables and Rented Rooms: The Extra-Curriculum of Composition." *College Composition and Communication* 45.1 (1994): 75–92.

Gupta, Akhil. "Space and Time in the Politics of Culture." Paper presented at the 87th Annual Meeting of the American Anthropological Association, Phoenix, Arizona, November 16–20, 1988.

Gupta, Akhil, and James Ferguson. "Culture, Power, Place: Ethnography at the End of an Era." *Culture, Power, Place: Explorations in Critical Anthropology.* Ed. Akhil Gupta and James Ferguson. Durham, NC: Duke UP, 1997. 1–29.

Hebdige, Dick. *Cut'n'Mix: Culture, Identity, and Caribbean Music.* London: Methuen, 1987.

Kirklighter, Cristina, Cloe Vincent, and Joseph Moxley. "Introduction." *Voices & Visions: Refiguring Ethnography in Composition.* Portsmouth, NH: Boynton/Cook, 1997. vii–xiii.

Leverenz, Carrie Shively. "Peer Response in the Multicultural Composition Classroom: Dissensus—A Dream Deferred." *Composition Theory for the Postmodern Classroom.* Ed. Gary A. Olson and Sidney I. Dobrin. Albany: State U of New York P, 1994. 254–73.

Losey, Kay. "Describing the Cultures of the Classroom: Problems in Classroom Ethnography." *Voices & Visions: Refiguring Ethnography in Composition.* Portsmouth, NH: Boynton/Cook, 1997. 86–94.

Marcus, George E. "Anthropology on the Move." *Ethnography through Thick & Thin.* Princeton, NJ: Princeton UP, 1998. 3–29.

———. "Imagining the Whole: Ethnography's Contemporary Efforts to Situate Itself." *Ethnography through Thick & Thin.* Princeton, NJ: Princeton UP, 1998. 33–56.

Marcus, George E., and Michael M. J. Fischer. *Anthropology as Cultural Critique: An Experimental Moment in the Human Sciences.* Chicago: U of Chicago P, 1986.

Miller, Susan. *Textual Carnivals: The Politics of Composition*. Carbondale: Southern Illinois UP, 1991.

Moss, Beverly J. "Ethnography and Composition: Studying Language at Home." *Methods and Methodology in Composition Research*. Ed. Gesa Kirsch and Patricia A. Sullivan. Carbondale: Southern Illinois UP, 1992. 153–171.

Peters, John Durham. "Seeing Bifocally: Media, Place, Culture." *Culture, Power, Place: Explorations in Critical Anthropology*. Ed. Akhil Gupta and James Ferguson. Durham, NC: Duke UP, 1997. 75–92.

Rhodes, Keith. "Ethnography or Psychography? The Evolution and Ethics of a New Genre in Composition." *Voices & Visions: Refiguring Ethnography in Composition*. Portsmouth, NH: Boynton/Cook, 1997. 24–36.

12

Protean Subjectivities

Qualitative Research and the Inclusion of the Personal

JANET ALSUP

SINCE THE EARLY 1980s, qualitative research has become increasingly valued in the humanities and education as a viable mode of inquiry and scholarship. Responding to researchers such as Shirley Brice Heath, Linda Brodkey, and Mina Shaughnessy, those working in the disciplines of education and composition studies began to recognize what social anthropologist Clifford Geertz and sociologists of the Chicago School of the 1920s and 1930s had recognized long before: qualitative, empirical research offers advantages over more quantitative, experimental, and quasiexperimental studies when the research subjects are people and the research foci are primarily human behaviors and interactions. An emphasis on individual experience, cultural and social issues, identities, inequities, and researcher self-reflexivity are some the characteristics of qualitative research that make it attractive to humanists and educators.

To clarify, I use the phrase *qualitative research* to denote a type of research that, as Denzin and Lincoln explain, "is multi-method in focus, involving an interpretive, naturalistic approach to its subject matter . . . [and] that describe[s] routine and problematic moments and meanings in individuals' lives" (3). I am also referring here to qualitative research that is empirical; that is, that is based on observations of people, events, and phenomenon in natural or slightly modified settings. Critical ethnography, the focus of this book, is a culturally and socially active brand of qualitative research that explores the effects of race, class, and gender on the social contexts and material lives of research participants and primary investigators.

But qualitative research has not been accepted in the humanities and social sciences without question. The very characteristics that make researchers value qualitative research are, paradoxically, sometimes the same reasons that make others leery of it: its acceptance of multiple interpretations of a singular data set, its tendency to vary widely in form and focus (from interview-based studies and case studies to more naturalistic studies emphasizing the researcher as cultural participant rather than outside researcher), and the wide variety of methods of data analysis that are acceptable to qualitative or ethnographic researchers. To some this variety in design and method of analysis is evidence of the versatility and usability of qualitative paradigms; to others, it is evidence of a lack of standards, rigor, and validity.

Researchers coming out of the so-called positivistic (that is, based on the epistemological belief in the existence of external validity) tradition have resisted qualitative research because of its denial that "truth" can transcend the personal or, in other words, that research results can be understood as separable from the researcher and research context. Although modern "hard" scientists do not often make such simplistic assertions about research, qualitative research has been called "soft scholarship" by those associated with the these so-called hard sciences (for example, chemistry, physics, economics, psychology), and the positive sciences are often seen as the "crowning achievements of Western civilization, and in their practices it is assumed that 'truth' can transcend opinion and personal bias" (Carey 99, qtd. in Denzin and Lincoln 7).

Therefore, a history of epistemological conflict exists between those devoted to the quantitative and qualitative paradigms, and this actual historical conflict has grown into an almost mythic one. The conflicts between those who are qualitative researchers and those who are quantitative researchers have often been oversimplified and turned into binary oppositions that put scholars into niches—usually either a postmodern, relativistic, and even politically correct niche (qualitative) or a traditional, serious, naïve, and positivistic one (quantitative). I do not want to engage in such reductive binaries here. However, I think recognizing the existence of this lore of opposition is important in understanding why qualitative research (and by association the use of the personal) has often had to justify its scholarly existence. Therefore, later in this essay I discuss one possible reason for such binaries in hopes that such a discussion will help us understand recent debates over the use of the personal.

Undoubtedly, one of the most recent and hotly debated issues to surface about qualitative or ethnographic research concerns the use of personal narrative or anecdote as a form of self-reflexivity. Researcher self-disclosure has become almost a generic convention in qualitative text, but some researchers question whether this use of autobiographical narrative is a valuable practice in constructing and reporting qualitative or ethnographic research. Such author-saturated research, as Clifford Geertz (himself often accused of such self indulgence) calls it, has become the target of criticism. Author-saturated research texts can make the researcher as much of the story as the researched and narrate engaging stories about research participants, researchers, and research contexts. Gesa Kirsch, who has often argued for the necessity of self-reflexivity in research texts, also expresses concern over the tendency toward extreme author saturation. She writes: "I am concerned about two tendencies in author-saturated texts: on the one hand, they can become shallow and per-functory; on the other, they can become self-indulgent and narcissistic" (Kirsch and Mortensen 77). Jane Gallop has likewise argued that the cause for worry is not "scholarship that seems narrowly personal but rather scholarship where the personal does not recognize itself as such and thus passes for the universal" (1150). The combination of such a researcher-centered approach and unexamined confidence in a single interpretation is the result of self-disclosure in its self-indulgent extreme. But concerns over the misuse of the personal do not constitute denial that the personal has a place in academic or scholarly work.

This chapter attempts to problematize the postmodern tendency for ethnographic or qualitative research writing to be framed by details of the researcher's personal life, primarily represented through narrative. When I use the term *personal* I am here referring to life stories, anecdotes, or narratives placed within or framing research texts. It has become commonplace and even expected for the qualitative researcher to share something of her expectations, personal history, reasons for initiating the study, or personal interactions with participants for the text and analyses that result to be valued and found credible by those within the qualitative paradigm. Some qualitative researchers who have done this successfully are anthropologist Ruth Behar and sociolinguist Deborah Tannen. Throughout the 1980s and 1990s this generic convention was praised and accepted by qualitative scholars such as Yvonna Lincoln and Egon Guba, Margaret LeCompte and Judith Preissle, Joseph Maxwell, and Gesa Kirsch, who all wrote texts describing the practice of qualitative or ethnographic research and included discussion of the benefits of self-disclosure and self-reflexivity as a way to increase the trustworthiness of research results.

Although the discussion of the pros and cons of inclusion of the personal have been going on sporadically for more than fifteen years, recently the discussion has gained increased attention and notoriety (see "Special Focus: Personal Writing" in *College English*, and "Against Subjectivity," *PMLA*). Scholars and researchers have begun to ask hard questions about the inclusion of the personal narrative in the ethnographic or qualitative report. They wonder whether self-disclosure is essential to establishing the ethos or trustworthiness of the researcher and if such personal admissions really do increase the credibility and value of the research by informing readers of the researcher's assumptions and subjectivities. These scholars and researchers also wonder if such personal revelations may distract the researcher (and the reader) from the true goals and foci of the research and even potentially encourage unfair bias against the researcher, her research, and her now exposed positionality. These scholars (for example, Berube, Gallop, Brandt, and Herrington, among others) posit that perhaps the pendulum has swung too far and that extreme researcher self-reflexivity might backfire and paradoxically distance the researcher from her participants and marginalize researchers whose subjectivities may not be valued in academic cultures. In short, they worry that perhaps qualitative researchers have indulged in too much of a good thing.

In this chapter, I (1) revisit and reiterate some of the benefits that researchers have stated for including the personal; (2) review some of the risks that others have identified in recent years about the use of the personal that are possible (and even likely) when a researcher engages in personal revelations within a research text; (3) explore one possible reason why qualitative research has a historically lower position in academia as a knowledge-making enterprise, and (4) analyze examples from my qualitative dissertation study as a way of rethinking the use of the personal in qualitative research so that researchers and readers can have the benefits of self-reflexivity while minimizing some of the stated risks. I also describe an issue closely related to the use of the personal—the issue of disciplinary authority and how the amount of self-disclosure a researcher engages in may be dependent on the professional context in which she works.

I do not argue that personal reflexivity and narrative accounts or researcher experiences, expectations, assumptions, and biases should not be a part of qualitative texts—quite the opposite. Self-reflexivity adds to the trustworthiness of qualitative research by making known the researcher's social and cultural position in relationship to the participants and contexts under study. In this way, the researcher can demonstrate metacognitive awareness that heightens the intellectual rigor of the project. I am not arguing for the exclusion of the personal, but for a more thoughtful, purposeful, and reasoned inclusion of it. I am also calling for the continued reexamination and questioning of the practice among qualitative researchers. In a postmodern world where the Cartesian conception of truth has been dismissed and intellectuals now believe in a multidimensional or contextual truth, a self-reflexive researcher stance seems to be a necessity when seeking or creating new knowledge. However, as qualitative researchers we must be careful about how we make such revelations and be aware of the possible effects (positive and negative) they may have on readers, research participants, and the bodies of knowledge we are creating. We do not want to fall into the distinct yet equally dangerous traps of relativism, voyeurism, narcissism, or extreme self-criticism that can lead to a decrease of researcher ethos in the eyes of readers and critics.

REVIEWING THE BENEFITS OF THE PERSONAL

As most readers will surely know, many qualitative researchers, ethnographers, and humanists have argued for self-reflexivity and admission of personal subjectivities when conducting research or analyzing research texts. Gesa Kirsch writes that one of the first criticisms of objective research was made by Ann Oakley who engaged in feminist, collaborative, nonhierarchal, interactive interview-based research with her participants, working class, pregnant women (*Women* 2). She decided that she could not remain neutral and detached but had an ethical obligation to inform the women about medical and community resources. Many researchers who followed also took a critical or social activist approach to research design, an approach that required researcher disclosure and personal interaction with participants—they were doing research not only to learn about participants, but also to help them as well. Such revisions or critical analyses often include the historical, cultural, and social locations of positionalities of researchers and research participants to best represent and analyze the research texts identified during the study. Although such inclusion of the personal does not reach the level primarily addressed in this chapter (the personal narrative or anecdote), it does begin to help us see why critical qualitative researchers were valuing reflexivity more than ever before in the late 1980s and 1990s. Other non-feminist theorists of qualitative research, such as Joseph Maxwell, also sing the praises of self-disclosure. He writes, "recognizing your personal ties to the study you want to conduct can provide you with a valuable source of insight, theory, and data about the phenomena you are studying" (16). Additional qualitative theorists researchers agree, including Strauss and Corbin and LeCompte and Preissle.

Although none of these sources directly address the use of full-blown personal narratives, such stories seem one way of identifying the subjectivities and positionalities of researchers, something that most qualitative and ethnographic experts seem to agree is a worthwhile (and sometimes methodologically and ethically necessary) goal. The benefits of self-disclosure or the inclusion of the personal primarily concern trustworthiness of research findings and analyses. The assumption is that the more readers (and to some extent participants) know about the gender, social class, racial, ethnic, and cultural identities of researchers, the better they are able to situate the study and its results and understand what they mean in the context in which they were developed.

SOME RISKS OF THE PERSONAL

Aristotle described the concept of *ethos* as the establishment of the trustworthiness of the speaker (or the modern writer) in relationship to his audience. The speaker or writer can establish such trustworthiness in several ways— one of which (Aristotle tells us) is through the telling of narratives (personal *or* impersonal) that demonstrate the speaker's wide experience and knowledge of the issue about which he is speaking. Such narratives, or stories, can also serve as examples within an inductive argument. In other words, narrative offers one means of building ethos or justifying action. Although qualitative researchers have taken up a variation of this idea about the ethos of narrative, they have broadened its significance to be evidence not only of researcher ethos but also the ethos of the knowledge that a researcher claims to have discovered. When a researcher includes personal stories in a research text, this broadening makes the balanced and effective use of narrative even more important.

Social philosopher Michel Foucault also writes about the use of the personal. He describes the dangers of personal narrations or what he calls "confessionals." In *The History of Sexuality,* Foucault writes about the dangers of a societal compulsion for confession because it always exists within an unequal power relationship: the confessor is compelled to do so by a more powerful individual or entity who is planning to exploit the confessor's story. Contemporary embodiments of the confessional can be seen on talk shows that encourage individuals to tell their individual, sometimes embarrassingly or dangerously personal, stories for a wide audience. Such revelations supposedly allow both the confessor and the audience (or those compelling the confession) to, at best, learn about some important aspect of human life from the speaker's story and, at worst, to simply be entertained. However, as anyone who has ever watched or even heard about *The Jerry Springer Show* knows, personal revelations do not always increase audience learning or exaggerate the ethos of a speaker; paradoxically, they can backfire and lead to anger and distrust of him or her. The very person who is "bearing her soul" becomes the target of criticism. Why is this?

Foucault writes that the authority who is confessed to (that is, Jerry Springer, or one could say the television audience) "requires the confession, prescribes and appreciates it, and intervenes in order to judge, punish, forgive, console, and reconcile" (62). In other words, the authority does not necessarily react positively to the confessor. If we see the "confessions" or personal revelations of a researcher in this light, as "requirements" of a larger intellectual or academic society or even the ideologically constructed genre of qualitative research, the practice becomes problematic. If researchers are expected to reveal their positionalities, even expected to do so to be seen as ethical researchers, then the possibility for readers (that is, other academics, participants, the general public, the media) to "judge, punish, forgive, console, and reconcile" is opened up and the risk can be great for the researcher. That readers should judge a research study and evaluate its accuracy and credibility might be seen as a positive, and I would agree; however, such judgments should be based primarily on the research texts and their analyses, which are informed by the subjectivities of the researcher, not vice versa—just as Aristotle's use of narrative was in the service of argument, was in the service of intellectual endeavor, and was above all a rhetorical or persuasive act; Foucault's description of the confessional, although not directly related by him to any research or writing practice, views narrative ethos as in the service of voyeurism, and voyeurism rarely leads to increased ethos for those that are the subject of its gaze. Foucault's view could be seen as a warning to those of us invoking the personal in our research texts. There are additional risks, as well. For example, the researcher-writer, on revealing his subjectivities to an audience, may find that the audience passes judgment not only on his work, but also on his person, especially if he addresses social, gender, racial, or ethnic issues.

Of course, not all autoethnographers have found themselves at the center of such controversies (see, for example, the work of Mike Rose and how it has been widely accepted in composition studies). I assert that these risks are very real and should be of concern to qualitative researchers. All uses of the personal are not equally successful or effective, and surely the use of the personal can be overdone. However, the danger exists of labeling all self-revelation and reflexivity useless, and this extreme position is also dangerous. To explore the ways that the personal can be used effectively in qualitative research texts, understanding not only the reasons for its inclusion but also the arguments for its total exclusion from scholarly work is important. Only by examining the two extremes of the argument can a middle ground be identified. So let us take a look at one of the possible causes for the argument for the exclusion of the personal from scholarly inquiry. The next section posits that one reason for the condemnation of the personal in some circles is its allegiance with feminist theories and methodologies that have traditionally been marginalized in academia.

THE PERSONAL AS A FEMINIST CONSTRUCT

Feminists in many disciplines (many of them are cited in an earlier section) have called for the inclusion of the woman's story, of the female perspective in a predominately patriarchal world. This perspective often makes itself known in the form of narrative or anecdotal personal revelations. The reasons why feminists and the female have been long associated with the personal are complicated. Perhaps the reason is that such a representation of self is different from how men have normally constructed themselves and their knowledge and because women are seeking their own place. Perhaps it is also, as Sherry Ortner argues, that women have always been associated with "nature" and men with "culture," and because women are associated with all things earthly (for example, birth, blood) they are more associated with the body versus the mind and hence "naturally" talk about things in a more personal (and less esoterically intellectual) way. Perhaps the personal expressions women have engaged in proliferate because it is the only form of expression the patriarchal world will fully accept. These hypotheses are clearly reductive in their binarism and unfair to the intellectual potentialities and accomplishments of women. However, there is historical truth within the literary and academic world to the commonplace that women have traditionally been associated with emotion, not intellect, and hence that feminism has been associated more with the personal than with the intellectual.

The association of the woman with the personal has lingered, and with the connection of feminist theory and methodology to qualitative research, its connection to personal revelation, storytelling, interaction with human participants, and political motives has endured and must be addressed by researchers. Diane Wolf writes in *Feminist Dilemmas in Fieldwork* that, "Feminists (and others) have argued that being objective and value-free is not only impossible, since we all carry experiences and values that shape our vision and interpretations and since, by virtue of our presence as outsiders, we intervene in the normal flow of life, but it is also undesirable (see Cancian, 1992)" (4). Such descriptions of the feminist researcher are common, and others have argued similar needs for including the personal in qualitative texts. Ann Oakley in *Experiments in Knowing* makes the argument that feminist (and other sociopolitical methodologies) have in part created the binary between qualitative and quantitative research that now is a commonplace in academia. She argues that this binary was created out of a long history of gender politics that positioned men as "hard" scientists, as well as the truth and knowledge-makers in a positivistic world, and women as those who consumed this knowledge. Therefore, feminist intellectuals, and by association many social and humanistic disciplines toward which women gravitated professionally and that associated themselves with human research and social and political issues, began to believe that qualitative research was the only type of research that was ethical and trustworthy when studying human beings. One further implication in Oakley's argument is that because of the identification of qualitative research with marginalized groups, it inherently is open to attack by those who see it as less rigorous and "true."

Perhaps this identification of qualitative research with women and other marginalized populations is part of the reason why some scholars may view personal revelations, even when they avoid the narcissistic, the relativistic, or the voyeuristic, as less intellectually valuable. Although we might reject this characterization of self-reflexivity and anti-intellectual, it may explain why qualitative research has sometimes come under attack, and it certainly gives qualitative researchers even more cause to reevaluate how we use the personal in our research.

THE PERSONAL AS NARRATIVE

Before I discuss specific suggestions for alternative ways that we can use the personal in our research texts (and research processes) to claim the benefits of reflexivity and minimize the risks, I need to talk about one more characteristic of the personal as I conceive of it: often the personal admissions and revelations that occur in research writings take the form of narratives or stories. They are the telling of personal anecdotes that situate the researcher into the context of the study and among the lives of the participants. These anecdotes or stories are often parallel to case study methodology: a common type of qualitative research that involves the narration (and description) of the experience of individual research participants.

Many of the early understandings about narrativity (see Bruner and Labov) emphasized linearity in form and singularity of purpose as important to a well-formed narrative. In their understandings and analyses of narrative a clear beginning, middle, and end is found, as well as a stated theme of the story that can be easily identified. Conversely, Leslie Bloom argues that women's lives (and Stanton Wortham argues men's lives) can be understood only if one dismisses traditional notions of coherence and linearity as essential to narrating experience. Bloom asserts that women's narrative will not follow a "traditional" structure moving from exposition, through climax, and to a more or less neat resolution that usually puts the narrator in the role of hero or victor. Instead, she claims that women's narratives generally contain many subplots, complexities, twists, turns, and often contain no clear climax or neat resolution summing them up. At times in a narrative, a narrator might present herself as the hero; at other times she may describe herself as the victim of circumstances—all in the same story. Bloom hypothesizes that such narratives represent what she calls the "non-unitary" subjectivities of women (in contrast to a single, "unitary" subjectivity), or the various and often competing roles such subjectivities (or identities) play in the lives of women who must regularly balance the competing demands of family and career and must often make difficult negotiations between competing demands on their time.

If we accept the notion that personal narratives could be included in qualitative research texts as well as recognized and considered by researchers during the research process, then we need to ask ourselves how to integrate them most effectively. In other words, if we agree that the personal should be a part of our research, then the question becomes *how* should it become a part. I think the concept of nonunitary subjectivity offers one possible solution to this problem. If the researcher recognizes that her subjectivity, her positionality, is not unitary, but is often conflicting and multiple and contextual, then it becomes less likely that the researcher will be read by others as being rigid in her relationship with participants or in her analysis of research participants or situations, self-obsessed, or only seeking some sort of voyeuristic exposure. The multiplicity of the representation of nonunitary subjectivity erases the ease with which a researcher can indulge in these behaviors (or be perceived to be indulging in them) because the representation of a unitary, singular self is required for such oversimplified intellectual approaches or readings.

Let me give an example. Imagine that a researcher was engaging in a study of the literacy practices of ninth graders in an English class in an inner-city high school. The researcher is a white, middle- to upper-class academic woman and the classroom teacher and many of the students are African Americans from working-class backgrounds. The researcher includes a story in her final research text that describes how when she was in the ninth grade she too experienced many of the same problems the student participants in her study experienced: not having enough money to buy things she desired, arguments with parents, and difficulty succeeding in school, for example. In this way, the researcher tries to "connect" herself to her participants as well as explain why she was interested in conducting research with this particular group of individuals: for example, she could relate to them, she could understand their problems. Her intentions are good; however, I assert that she has left out a large part of her story. She has told of a singular subjectivity, one part of her identity that is significant to the study and left out others. By doing so she has left herself open to critique and accusations of bias and narcissism. One can imagine participants and readers reacting with statements and questions such as, "How can she compare her privileged experiences with those of the students in the study?" and "She has no right to equate her relatively pedestrian experiences with the very difficult ones experienced by her participants."

This researcher might have avoided such criticisms by representing her subjectivity instead as nonunitary, as multiple, and as contradictory. She could have told stores about herself as a white girl in a predominately white public school and how she and her classmates reacted to issues of racism and poverty in the world that seemed so far from their own. She could have written about felt similarities with the students and teacher in her study, but she could have also written about how she felt like an outsider in the school so unlike the one she attended and therefore had to work hard to establish trust in her participants. Such admissions could feel like a risk to the researcher; there is the possibility of being called racist and of engaging in "othering" or exoticising of her participants. However, by representing and retelling multiple expressions of self, the researcher would have a better chance of establishing and maintaining researcher ethos while adding to the credibility, usability, and trustworthiness of her study.

This example brings me to a discussion of what I call "reciprocal" nonunitary subjectivity. The reciprocity is realized when the researcher discloses or narrates personal experiences for the purpose of increasing mutual understanding with research participants instead of simply in an attempt to establish an often-simplistic (and sometimes insulting) "connection" with them. Therefore, not only should the researcher recognize her own nonunitary or multiplicity of subject positions, but she should also disclose these positions for the purpose of improved communication with participants (and hence increased mutual understanding). Additionally, and to take the concept of reciprocal nonunitary subjectivity one step further, the researcher should expect the subjectivities of her participants to be as varied and contradictory as her own. Michael Bérubé writes that the "worst form of subjectivism" comes in the form of scholars' "projecting their own interpretive idiosyncrasies onto their research while blithely believing that they've finally grasped the object as in itself it really is" (1066). "Finally grasping the object as in itself it really is" would be an act of ignoring the multiple subjectivities of research participants and asserting that full understanding of these participants has been reached as a result of the researcher's hard work, intelligence, or keen insight into the research context. Such as assertion is an oversimplification, and, as such, surely incorrect. The researcher sees merely one slice of the lives, personalities, and subjectivities of her participants, and she should not pretend to have deeper knowledge. Reciprocal, nonunitary subjectivity works in two directions: from the researcher toward the researched, and vice versa (see Figure 12.1). The researcher narratively presents her subjectivities as multiple and multifaceted, and she recognizes that her participants' subjectivities are similarly complex.

But the researcher must be aware of and must address another brand of reciprocity when conducting and reporting on qualitative research in which she discloses the personal through narrative: reciprocity in understanding the nonunitary subjectivities of readers and the expectations readers have that a

FIGURE 12.1
Simple Reciprocal Nonunitary Subjectivity

researcher will recognize at least some of the variability in potential readership and express an intent to further communicate with such an audience.

This understanding complicates the practice of reciprocal nonunitary subjectivity as well as the researcher's practice (see Figure 12.2). Not only does the researcher need to recognize the multiple subjectivities of herself and her participants, she must be mindful of a real or ideal audience and the multiple positionalities this audience might represent. Again, such recognitions usually take place through or within narratives because of the opportunity narrative provides to explore subjectivities at length through the detailed retelling of a series of significant life events or research experiences.

However, this readership, similar to the previously described hypothetical audience of *The Jerry Springer Show,* will have the power (and the right) to react to (or even judge) the research text and the ethos of the researcher. Whereas understandings of audience are always to some extent an act of guesswork or projection by the researcher-writer and dependent on the researcher's reasons for conducting the research (for example, doctoral dissertation, tenure book project, or pursuit of personal interest) as well as the context in which this research is conducted (for example, a graduate program, a postsecondary institution, or production of a manuscript for public consumption), the researcher has an obligation to recognize the potential for a range of nonunitary positionalities of her audience and how such positionalities may intersect with her own. Without such an attempt at recognition, these intersections can occur in several ways and may lead to unpredicted consequences for the researcher-writer if her work is interpreted in ways she never imagined or in ways that undermine (or even attack outright) her researcher ethos.

Certain authorities are connected with certain subjective positions in academia. As a graduate student, the authority I inherently possessed was different than for a professor, and my authority as an assistant professor is different from what it will be when I become an associate professor. Within the university a clear hierarchy exists that correlates with degrees of authority individuals possess. Within this hierarchy, graduate students are close to the

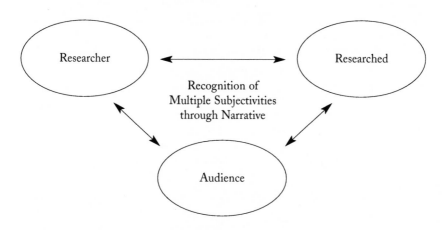

FIGURE 12.2
Complex Reciprocal Nonunitary Subjectivity

bottom. They are they protégées, the professor wanna-bes, who are currently being educated in a professional body of knowledge, while also being inducted into a professional discourse community that exhibits certain hierarchal qualities. Of course, I was a graduate student when I wrote my dissertation. The personal disclosures I made were more likely to be judged as bias than as statements of positionality. I had to earn the right to speak from my own position, and as a graduate student I had not yet done so.

Consequently, the concept (and actual use of) reciprocal nonunitary subjectivity by a qualitative researcher has at least two dimensions—the dimension of interaction and recognition of the complexity of subjectivities of the researcher and the researched and the dimension of an awareness of the multiple possible positionalities of an audience often representative of a professional discourse community (in our case primarily academia) in which a researcher works. The hierarchal arrangements of universities cannot be ignored, and a graduate student researcher conducting dissertation research must be aware of the dangers inherent in putting her ethos at risk. She is working with a tenuous ethos anyway—she is still developing a name and a right to speak in the profession. Taking risks by revealing a great deal of personal information, especially personal information that is not nonunitary or reciprocal in nature, leaves the student researcher at risk of being accused of bias, untrustworthiness in analysis, and even sloppy research design. So what are the implications of such audience awareness? Do graduate students (and even untenured faculty members) necessarily labor under different standards than the rest of researching academics? I stop short of admitting that this is the case; perhaps I am simply idealistic, but I prefer to see the difference not as an acceptance of the basic inequity of the academic world, but as an issue of level of awareness of nonunitary subjectivity and by association an understanding of the expectations of an academic audience, and the dependence of these expectations on the positionality of the researcher-writer

I think often we have viewed ourselves as having singular subjectivities (that is, female, working class, academic, white) and as such in either a collaborative or oppositional relationship to the subjects under study. Including personal narratives or self-reflexive accounts in a research text can be more effective and useful if the researcher is aware of the concept of nonunitary subjectivity and tells her story with this in mind. In other words, I seek to expand Bloom's concept of nonunitary subjectivity by arguing that it should work reciprocally between the researcher and the researched and between the researcher and the audience for which her work is intended.

PROTEAN SUBJECTIVITIES: AN EXAMPLE

I would like to analyze two brief examples from my research to exemplify what I mean by reciprocal, nonunitary subjectivity. In this research, I included several autobiographical narratives to frame my study and to provide context about my subjective relationship with the data and the research process, and I analyze segments of these narratives. By including these narratives I was following the instructions that I had received in research classes and in many of the texts I had read that have been mentioned throughout this chapter. However, as you will see from my examples, I saw the inclusion of these narratives as essentially straightforward and unproblematic. In fact, I thought omitting them would be problematic.

This research included three case studies of first-year writers and their instructor at a major midwestern university with a particular focus on authority: how the authorities displayed and enacted by the students and the teacher in the class were often unpredictable, mutually powerful, and, most important ill-suited to encouraging effective teaching and learning. My point in sharing excerpts from these case studies is not to represent them as perfect examples of nonunitary subjectivity; in fact, almost two years after the fact, I think my use of multiple representations of self was inconsistent and could have been done much more effectively to establish my ethos as a researcher. However, I think the examples might demonstrate one early (although naïve and incomplete) attempt at expressing reciprocal nonunitary subjectivity as a researcher and may also help me develop my argument in this chapter.

I believe that if I had been aware of the value of expressing reciprocal nonunitary subjectivities I may have experienced fewer political complications after my research became public and the participants read what I had written. The teacher who was described in my study was unhappy with her portrayal in my research text and accused me of bias and inaccuracy. I deeply regret her response. I am hypothesizing that one way I may have avoided such unpleasant and even harmful repercussions is to have engaged in fewer assertions of a unitary researcher and participant subjectivity that I was supposedly in the process of "figuring out" throughout the project and more assertions of an awareness of the multiple subjectivities of myself and my research participants. My research indeed hints at such reciprocal awareness of nonunitary subjectivity, but I predominately present myself as a singular researcher with one subjectivity and one identity and the teacher-participant as a singular individual with a unitary set of pedagogical goals and personal motivations. This portrayal of unitary subjectivities is, of course, oversimplified and false and provided built-in ammunition for readers to take up and direct toward me as accusations of bias. So the use of the personal, at least in part, had the exact opposite effect as my intent: instead of standing as evidence of awareness of my subjectivity and prior assumptions and hence increasing my ethos as researcher and the trustworthiness of my results, it was instead viewed by the teacher-participant as evidence of misinterpretation. Instead of forming a more communal relationship with the teacher-participant, my narrative self-disclosures served only to separate and distance myself from her.

However, as previously stated, my self-disclosures were inconsistent in how effectively they reflected nonunitary subjectivities. The first example following is an example of quite unitary, nonreciprocal disclosure of personal subjectivity, a self-disclosure that I believe served to undermine my researcher ethos. This small anecdote shows my failure to use the personal to connect rather than sever, to express mutual respect rather than reductive analysis:

> *Excerpt 12.1: A Unitary Approach to Subjectivity.* In the middle of struggling with my own teacher biases (and my own guilt about feeling so judgmental of a colleague) something changed. I actually talked to the instructor in an informal setting. I read the teaching journals she kept during the semester for the purpose of this study, and I discovered that she was a lot like me. She was a young teacher, and she was struggling with many of the same issues I was. She worries about her authority in the classroom, if the students respected her knowledge, if her assignments were fair and clear. I finally understood what she did in the classroom. I began to see that not only is this study about the students and their growth as thinkers and writers, but it is also about the instructor, Claudia, and her growth as a teacher.

In this passage I assert a degree of "understanding" of Claudia and the class she is teaching that exaggerates the amount of insight I could possibly gain about her based on the research texts I had collected (interview transcripts, video tapes of her teaching, her teaching journal). In my attempt to "connect" with her and express how alike we are, I oversimplified her subjectivity (as well as my own). The sentence "I finally understood what she did in the classroom" is the obvious example of my articulation of this reductive "fixing" of her subjectivity in space and time. In my misguided (yet well-intentioned) attempt to disclose my thinking processes during the study and how they developed and changed as data was collected and analyzed, I succeeded in reducing Claudia's teacher subjectivity to a single, unitary, easily definable set of characteristics that I claim to finally "understand." By association, I also define my own subjectivity as singular—I am a researcher who finally is able to figure things out.

The next case study is an example of a more successful attempt at expressing my nonunitary subjectivities as a researcher and the conflicts and struggles that marked my research process. The admission of these conflicted feelings and how they affected my researcher stance serves to characterize me as a researcher who truly engaged in a process and who recognizes this process as central to the research project and understanding its implications. This passage is an example of self-disclosure that exhibits a sense of reciprocal nonunitary subjectivity. My narrative recognizes and admits to uncertainty, doubt, and confusion as I began the study and resists any attempt to oversimplify my understandings or the subjectivities and motivations of the teacher participant:

> *Excerpt 12.2: A Nonunitary Approach to Subjectivity.* When I started this project, I struggled with my biases. Throughout my researcher journal that I kept during the project, I made notes of times when I felt frustrated and even angry with Claudia and how she taught her class. I would write comments about my growing awareness of my biases and how I did not agree with Claudia's focus on structure and form or her lack of attention to the overwhelming silence and apathy evident in the class. Often, I did not like what I saw the teacher doing in the class because it was so different from what I did. This is unflattering to admit, but through my little window on her classroom, I found it easy to criticize and critique—easy to think of ways that I would do it differently. I was very judgmental.

Not only does this narrative provide an example of a specific research practice important to establishing researcher ethos (for example, keeping a researcher journal), but in it I also admit to conflicting thoughts and emotions during the project's early stages.

The concept of reciprocal nonunitary subjectivity as one way of using the personal in a more effective manner certainly highlights the protean or changeable nature of the qualitative research paradigm. Subjectivities are context specific and therefore inherently changeable depending on the research site, the nature of the interchange between participant and researcher, and the assumptions and expectations each brings to the project. A full understanding of researcher, researched, and audience subjectivities in no way makes the research process easier; on the contrary, it makes the qualitative researcher's job even more complex and challenging. However, a stance of nonunitary subjectivity as portrayed in personal narrative is perhaps one way qualitative or ethnographic researchers can use the personal as it was intended by those such as Kirsch without running the risks of voyeurism, narcissism, or oversimplification of research participants and texts.

The attempt to be reciprocal in one's understanding of multiple subjectivities is extremely difficult, and surely no researcher will be successful at it at all times. However, as a methodological and analytical theory, reciprocal, nonunitary subjectivity may be a way to use the personal anecdote or the narrative that is not simply an exercise in voyeurism or self-indulgence but is instead a purposeful researcher stance that may increase the perception of the intellectual rigor of qualitative research and researcher ethos. Stories cannot be included in a research text simply because they are a catchy way to begin a text or because of a reductive belief that telling a personal anecdote or sharing one's fears and worries as a researcher will inherently improve the quality of one's research. It has to go much deeper than that. It is much more complicated. The person doing the research must be evident in the research text, but not as a cardboard cutout who interacts with participants and readers as if they were similarly one-dimensional beings. Instead the researcher must see herself as a multifaceted being, interacting with participants in a particular intellectual context. If a researcher can engage in this type of reciprocity of nonunitary thought and attitude, she can heighten her researcher ethos and improve the quality of her research.

WORKS CITED

Behar, Ruth. *The Vulnerable Observer: Anthropology That Breaks Your Heart*. Boston, MA: Beacon, 1996.

Bérubé, Michael. "Against Subjectivity." *PMLA* 111 (October 1996): 1063–68.

Bloom, Leslie Rebecca. *Under the Sign of Hope: Feminist Methodology and Narrative Interpretation*. Albany: State U of New York P, 1998.

Brandt, Deborah. "Protecting the Personal." *College English* 64.1 (September 2001): 42–44.

Brodkey, Linda. "On the Subjects of Class and Gender in 'The Literacy Letters.'" *College English* 51.2 (February 1989): 125–41.

Bruner, Jerome. "Life as Narrative." *Social Research* 54 (1987): 11–32.

Carey, James W. *Communication as Culture: Essays on Media and Society*. Boston: Unwin Hyman, 1989.

College English 64.1 (September 2001).

Denzin, Norman K., and Yvonna S. Lincoln. *The Landscape of Qualitative Research: Theories and Issues.* Thousand Oaks, CA: Sage, 1998.

Foucault, Michel. *The History of Sexuality.* Vol. 1. London: Lane, 1979.

Gallop, Jane. "The Inevitability of the Personal." Forum. *PMLA* 111 (October 1996): 1150.

Geertz, Clifford. *The Interpretation of Cultures.* New York: Basic Books, 1973.

Heath, Shirley Brice. *Ways with Words.* Cambridge, England: Cambridge University Press, 1983.

Herrington, Anne. "When Is My Business Your Business?" *College English* 64.1 (September 2001): 47–49.

Kirsch, Gesa. *Ethical Dilemmas in Feminist Research: The Politics of Location, Interpretation, and Publication.* Albany: State U of New York P, 1999.

Kirsch, Gesa E., and Peter Mortensen, eds. *Ethics and Representation on Qualitative Studies of Literacy.* Urbana, IL: NCTE, 1996.

Labov, William, and J. Waletzky. "Narrative Analysis: Oral Versions of Personal Experience." *Essays on the Verbal and Visual Arts.* Ed. J. Helm. Seattle: U of Washington P, 1967. 12–44.

LeCompte, Margaret, and Judith Preissle. *Ethnography and Qualitative Design in Educational Research,* 2d ed. San Diego: Academic, 1984.

Lincoln, Yvonna S., and Egon G. Guba. *Naturalistic Inquiry.* Beverly Hills, CA: Sage, 1985.

Maxwell, Joseph A. *Qualitative Research Design: An Interactive Approach.* Thousand Oaks, CA: Sage, 1996.

Oakley, Ann. *Experiments in Knowing: Gender and Method in the Social Sciences.* New York: New, 2000.

———. *Women Confined: Towards a Sociology of Childbirth.* Oxford, England: Martin Robertson, 1980.

Ortner, Sherry. "Is Female to Male as Nature is to Culture?" *Woman, Culture, and Society.* Stanford, CA: Stanford UP, 1974. 67–87.

PMLA 111 (October 1996).

Rose, Mike. *Lives on the Boundary.* New York: Penguin, 1990.

———. *Possible Lives: The Promise of Public Education in America.* New York: Penguin, 1995.

Shaughnessy, Mina. *Errors and Expectations: A Guide for the Teacher of Basic Writing.* New York: Oxford UP, 1977.

Strauss, A. L., and J. Corbin. *Basics of Qualitative Research: Grounded Theory Procedures and Techniques.* Newbury Park, CA: Sage, 1990.

Tannen, Deborah. *You Just Don't Understand: Women and Men in Conversation.* New York: Ballantine, 1990.

Wolf, Diane L., ed. *Feminist Dilemmas in Fieldwork.* New York: Westview P, 1996.

Wortham, Stanton. *Narratives in Action: A Strategy for Research and Analysis.* New York: Teachers College P, 2001.

PART IV

Ethnographies of
Cultural Change

13

Changing Directions

Participatory-Action Research, Agency, and Representation

BRONWYN T. WILLIAMS and
MARY BRYDON-MILLER

IN THE CLASSROOM, literacy education is all about intervention. Students enter the classroom and we, as teachers, work with them to make them more critical and creative readers and writers. Regardless of our pedagogical approach, the age group, or the specific goals of a course, we interact with our students. We are active and engaged and see our larger purpose as teachers to enact some form of transformation by teaching the students what we know. However we do it, with whatever pedagogy, for whatever reasons, we act.

Literacy research, on the other hand, has often implicitly followed a model of the sciences and social sciences that is grounded in assumptions of detachment and positivism. There is an assumption, even among qualitative researchers and ethnographers, that we should maintain a necessary distance while observing the participants of a study. The goal of ethnographers is to stand back politely, observe, record, and not get involved in changing the lives of the people in the community they are watching. The preferred methodology is to be "regularly present, unobtrusive, quiet, and too 'busy' to help children with their work, but never too busy to smile, acknowledge their presence, and say 'hi'" (Dyson 25). To do otherwise would be to create responses and introduce biases that might interfere with the observations and analysis of the participants' culture, in the way that breathing on a petri dish would spoil the culture growing there. It is a point of view encapsulated in statements such as, "initiating change in people's behavior [is] an aim which is disputed or ideologically unacceptable to many ethnographers who wish to remain observers of change that is happening irrespective of their actions" (Robinson-Pant 168), and "The goal [of the ethnographer] in negotiating a role is to interfere as little as possible with the daily routines in the community" (Moss 158).

This approach to ethnography has been opened to critique in recent years. Some scholars have challenged the ethics of ethnographers' representations of "others" (Sullivan), others have interrogated the ability of the ethnographer to represent truth (Clifford), others the seductive power of the ethnographer (Newkirk), and some have questioned whether, as Heisenberg might remind us, we can assume that we can observe any phenomenon in an accurate, thorough manner and not, through our observations, alter the outcome in some way.

Even within these critiques of truth and bias, however, there remains a central understanding that the ethnographer observes and perhaps even participates, but does not intervene in an activist manner to change the material conditions of the people in the community. As Alan Rogers notes, many ethnographers "attempt to adopt an outsider stance towards the situation they are analyzing, even when challenging the dominant literacy community. They may see themselves as critics, but they are all still observers rather than actors" (218).

Rogers's criticism touches on key ethical questions for scholars engaging in ethnographic research, particularly in terms of literacy in the community: Is watching and recording enough? What responsibilities do researchers have to help change the material conditions of the participants of their research? What legitimacy do researchers have in representing the experiences of others? Although some have called for more "activist" methodologies that urge more dialogue and reciprocity with participants (Cushman, *Struggle*), researchers using ethnography in literacy studies have yet to focus systematically on questions of who defines the issues of research, generates and owns the information, and by doing so enacts social change for the participants. As Rogers argues, teachers and literacy researchers must ask themselves the question, "whose side are you on?" "If literacy is tied into the power structures of society, where do we stand? Where do we come from and where are we going?" (218).

In this chapter we will argue that, rather than observe, literacy ethnographers have the opportunity, and the responsibility, to work with members of a community in a way that is fundamentally more participatory and transformative. We draw on the theories and practice of participatory action research to illustrate how researchers seeking to study literacy and culture can also work with people in the community to identify important issues, generate knowledge that belongs to everyone involved, and work toward tangible social change.

We will also address how employing participatory action research in ethnographic studies helps mitigate against imposing a grand interpretive structure on the experiences of the participants by seeking the multiple interpretations of all involved in the project, foregrounding the interpretations of those who have experienced oppression and marginalization. In doing so, participatory action research emphasizes issues of power and representation that arise when using ethnographic methods. Specifically it addresses the tensions that exist when members of the dominant culture work to empower those outside of the culture to represent themselves or define their own agendas and needs. We demonstrate how those engaging in participatory action research can use such critiques from feminist, critical race, and postcolonial theories as catalysts for interrogations of their positions of privilege and power when working with members of the community.

LITERACY, COMMUNITY, AND ACTIVISM

In many ways, much of the groundwork for using approaches in community literacy research has been established by scholars in the New Literacy Studies such as Brian Street, and David Barton and Mary Hamilton. They have challenged the autonomous model of literacy as a set of stand-alone skills to be mastered and have instead emphasized recognition of multiple literacy practices that exist and overlap in communities. They argue that such literacy practices are always contextual, historically situated, and embedded in broader social goals and cultural practices. Consequently "literacy practices are patterned by social institutions and power relationships, and some literacies are more dominant, visible, and influential than others" (Barton and Hamilton 8).

The consequence of this approach to literacy studies has been to move beyond the classroom to consider how literacy develops and functions in different settings and domains of life. It has also encouraged researchers to reconsider accepted hierarchies of literacy and to explore how literacies that might have previously been dismissed as trivial or irrelevant in comparison with the "proper" literacies represented and reproduced in educational and governmental institutions in fact serve quite well the people who use, develop, and employ them. This has shifted the focus for researchers in New Literacy Studies from examining community members to discover why they were deficient in the acquisition of accepted literacy forms, to studying what literacy practices already exist in communities, how community members employ such literacy practices, and how those practices often conflict with and are marginalized by the institutional forms of literacy that represent the dominant culture. This has led to ethnographic studies of community literacy practices around the world such as a study of several generations of immigrants to an East London neighborhood (Gregory and Williams), research in multilingual communities in northern Ghana (Herbert and Robinson), Welsh farmers' literacy practices (Jones), and adult education programs (Pitt). Such research has done much to broaden our understandings of the multiple and fluid nature of literacy in any given culture.

At the same time, scholars such as David Bleich and Ellen Cushman have advocated the need for literacy teachers and scholars to get beyond the walls of the academy and act as agents for social change in the community. Bleich notes that the tradition of the detached observer actually can act to "conceal problematic social disparities between researcher and researched" (179). And Cushman argues for a "deeper consideration of the civic purpose of our *positions* in the academy, or what we do with our knowledge, for whom, and by what means" ("Rhetorician" 377; emphasis in original). For Cushman such a consideration should lead us out of the privileged institutionalized settings in the academy and into more activist work in our communities. Cushman's call is one that she supports through her actions. In her work with minority and working-class urban women Cushman not only describes their literacy practices, but also intervenes on a practical level to help them engage in practical actions such as writing letters to obtain better housing (*Struggle* 29). Cushman is not alone in engaging in literacy projects outside of the college classroom. Other scholars in chronicling their work, however, discuss their initial frustrations with the way in which community members may see the work and the goals of the researcher quite differently than the scholar. Ruth Ray and Ellen Barton, for example, in working with elders and with people with disabilities note that, "communities are mainly invested in meeting their own goals" (214) and that researchers need to be flexible in recognizing that the original conception of a project may change substantially when community members are engaged in the process and reshape the issues in terms of their own interests and values.

Ray and Barton exemplify, and recognize, the problematic nature of the literacy scholar going forth into the community in a paternalistic, positivist, and authoritarian manner. "We had to re-define our ethical commitments to these communities not in our terms but in theirs" (214). This kind of self-reflection, along with calls for more activism from literacy scholars and a rethinking of the nature of literacy practices in the community are all important steps toward a more participatory, activist, and egalitarian way of conceiving of the work of the literacy ethnographer. It is important for scholars to recognize the existing literacy practices in the community as valuable, to treat community members' knowledge and goals with respect, and to recognize the responsibility of scholars to engage in work that will result in substantive social change. Even these positions are an uphill battle in the academy. The traditions and ideology that support detached, elitist, and hierarchical approaches to ethnography remain deeply entrenched in the attitudes of scholars such as Susan Peck MacDonald who criticizes the idea of even making room in literacy research for the voices of community participants: "But if *our* 'subjects' happen to be wrong or confused or resistant in what they are thinking, then adding their voices to *our* research may contribute little of importance to the knowledge developing in the field" (114; emphasis added). We as scholars need to work toward an acceptance of the principles that people are not "subjects" who, along with their knowledge, somehow belong to us because we believe we are developing knowledge in a professional "field."

Instead what we need is a systematic approach to working with community members that addresses fundamental intellectual and ethical issues of social change, power, representation, and the purposes and ownership of knowledge. If we are to work with community members in a responsible and thoughtful manner to help them change their material conditions, then we need to work in partnership with people, understanding that both sides have knowledge to offer, goals to achieve, and concerns about how knowledge is used and represented.

PARTICIPATORY ACTION RESEARCH

Participatory action research provides a model for such practice. Inspired by the work of educators and social activists such as Paulo Freire and Myles Horton (Adams), participatory action research combines aspects of popular education, community-based research, and action for social change. Emphasizing collaboration within marginalized or oppressed communities, participatory action research works to address the underlying causes of inequality while at the same time focusing on finding solutions to specific community concerns. Participatory action research has its roots in the early 1970s as researchers such as Fals Borda in Colombia, Marja-Liisa Swantz in Tanzania, and Rajesh Tandon in India and others began to realize that community concerns, especially those faced by the people of the developing world, were not being addressed by the "technological fix" mentality of academics working within the traditions of positivism. In the United States as well researchers and community activists were beginning to come together to try to find ways to address issues of poverty (Horton), environmental health (Merrifield), and community development (Reardon et al.). (See Brydon-Miller "Education" and Fals Borda for fuller descriptions of the historical roots of participatory action research.) And Kate Ronald and Hephzibah Roskelly have noted that

Freire's conceptions of participatory and liberatory pedagogy can be connected to the work of educational pragmatists such as John Dewey (Ronald and Roskelly). Participatory action researchers have drawn on several theoretical sources including Marxism, feminism, and critical theory. Patricia Maguire *(Doing Participatory Research)* first established the links between feminist theory and the practice of participatory action research in her work with battered women and continues to expand the understanding of the ways in which feminist theory might inform practice. Critical theory as well has provided a framework for many participatory action researchers (Brydon-Miller "Breaking," and Comstock and Fox) to articulate their conviction that the process of conducting research can take many forms and need not rely on the tenets of positivism as the only means of establishing credibility.

Participatory action research challenges the assumption that to be valid, the research process must be objective and value-neutral, acknowledging instead that all knowledge generation is embedded in systems of power and that academics have traditionally been deeply implicated in maintaining existing structures of economic and political privilege. The participatory action researcher strives to make these processes more explicit and more accessible to members of the community through popular education and training. One of the values most central to the practice of participatory action research is a belief in truly democratic processes of community decision-making and action and a respect for the knowledge and efficacy of members of communities often thought incapable of acting in their own interests. This approach is different from the traditional sense of academic noblesse oblige that has led many well-intended researchers to attempt to solve critical social problems by studying communities from the outside, often resulting in incomplete understandings of issues and subsequent ineffectual and unwelcome interventions. John Gaventa tells the story of a friend, a former coal miner and local activist, who took a government engineer to a site where runoff from a strip mine was polluting a stream, a clear violation of local law.

> My friend showed him the silt oozing into the water. As also provided for the law, he exercised his right as a citizen by asking the inspector to file a complaint against the responsible mining company. The expert official studied the situation. He drew out this map and documents. And then he said, "I'm sorry, I cannot take action. According to my map, there is no stream there." (22)

Participatory action research, on the other hand, engages members of the community as equal partners in the research process and acknowledges their right to equal ownership and control of the knowledge that is generated as a result. From the identification of issues, to the development of research tools, through the gathering and analyzing of data, to the implementation of action based on this information, this is conceived of as an egalitarian, collaborative process. The researcher brings to the process his expertise and resources as a trained academic, at the same time members of the community bring their lived experiences, their keen understanding of the issues, and their commitment to change. Without their engagement and active participation, the process will inevitably fail.

Ethnography has always recognized the importance of drawing on the knowledge of community members, but has stopped short of truly valuing this expertise. Instead ethnographers have insisted that only with their interpretation, their intervention, that this raw material could be manufactured into some useful product. The problems of representation posed by the researchers' monovocal and unified interpretation and presentation of community practices, as commonly practiced and privileged in the academy, have been noted by scholars such as Lucille Parkinson McCarthy and Stephen Fishman, who argue that although "the impersonal voice of academic writing can describe various interpretations or opinions, it is not well designed to capture the diverse ways informants go at the world and their diverse discourses, exactly what naturalistic inquiry aims to construct" (156). Such criticisms of traditional ethnography are useful. What is needed in the field now is an approach to working in the community that will not only get the voices of community members included in the researcher's work, but also will genuinely collaborate with community members so that they become creators of knowledge and authorship, rather than only subjects who are written about. If we accept postmodern notions about the contingent and constructed nature of "truth" then we should be searching for meaningful methods for including the multiple perspectives of people in the community. This requires more than having a single researcher study or work in a community. Even if she includes the voices of the participants in her work, such voices are still chosen by the researcher for an article that is produced from the mind and perspective of the single author. If we truly want to engage multiple perspectives, we need to begin with the process of defining research questions and goals, and continue through the generation of knowledge, including gathering and interpreting the information as well as creating documents and texts about this information. Participatory action researchers believe that given the right tools and support, community members are quite capable of engaging in these processes of interpretation and implementation on their own. Such an approach is, in fact, the only way in which sustainable social change can ever take place.

One concept drawn specifically from Freire's work is the notion of cycles of action and reflection. Together the community engages in a process of reflection, of examining the conditions that have led to their oppression. Based on this shared understanding, they then plan and carry out action designed to address some specific concern, following which they again gather together to consider what effect their action has had, how it has or has not changed the circumstances of their lives, and how best to take the next step. One emphasis of participatory action research is on sustainability. Can the community continue the cycle of action and reflection after the researcher has gone? Marja-Liisa Swantz, one of the earliest pioneers of participatory action research, recently reported on her continuing research in southern Tanzania. Although still very much involved in the work herself, over the nearly thirty years that she has been engaged in these communities, many local activists have clearly become engaged in processes of knowledge generation and action, and their efforts have resulted in substantive change in areas such as access to credit for rural women and threats to local fishing communities. Describing her work with Tanzania women, Swantz observes:

> The whole process is first of all about equality, believing in the women and giving them their chance, treating them as adult mature people. . . . The right kind of communication guides women to use their knowledge and to acquire new skills, it empowers them and creates a new kind of awareness. (Swantz, Ndedya, and Masaiganah 391)

Similarly James Kelly, Lynne Mock, and Darius Tandon describe the impact of their work with leaders of the African-American community in Chicago, "The cumulative impact of this work is that combined efforts with shared decision-making can be an enriching, ennobling and grounding experience, an experience which integrates professional roles and personal beliefs with a concrete sense of justice with dignity" (354).

Participatory action research projects take many forms. In some cases the community is already well organized and has identified critical issues and brings in the researcher for her specific expertise in gathering and analyzing data. In other cases, the researcher's first role is as an organizer helping the community to develop a shared sense of identity and purpose around which the research can take place. Most cases fall somewhere between these two extremes with the researcher engaging with a community that has begun to identify common concerns but without a clear sense of how to go about addressing these issues in an effective manner. On rare occasions, the researcher might be a member of the community. Most often, however, the researcher comes to the process as an outsider, someone who cannot know the experiences that have shaped the lives of community members nor the circumstances that have created the problems she or he is there to address. Participatory action research projects can use quantitative as well as qualitative methods, although the emphasis is on developing methods that are easily adaptable to community settings and that do not rely on expensive technology or incomprehensible statistical analyses. Many participatory action researchers also incorporate more creative means of engaging participants in the process of knowledge generation. Art, music, and theater can all be used as ways of giving community members an opportunity to explore their experiences and to identify shared concerns (see for example, Lykes, Brydon-Miller "Glimpse").

Although not widespread, examples of participatory action research in community literacy projects exist that offer important perspectives on what can be accomplished through such approaches. One project with women in Bombay began with the women identifying a concrete, short-term literacy goal, in this case creating a petition to the police to protest illegal alcohol sales. Such a short-term goal gradually grew into a larger list the women generated, including using petitions for political purposes, reading legal documents, reading bus schedules, and reading religious books. The ensuing work with the women involved collaborating with them to create a literacy education program, which continued to function in the community. Along with the literacy education, the project also resulted in changes in some of the women's sense of power in regard to issues such as the socialization and education of their children (Samant).

Another example involved work through the Highlander Center with the community of Bumpass Cove, Tennessee. Community members were concerned about potential toxic wastes being illegally dumped in a local landfill. To raise grievances with state health officials, community members needed to understand more about the nature of the chemicals they suspected were being dumped and the possible health effects of those chemicals. Researchers worked with community members to find, read, and summarize work from chemical and medical dictionaries. Community members were able to compile a list of the chemicals and the health effects to bolster their positions in interactions with state inspectors. As Merrifield asserts, "But its impact was much more than a list. For the first time people began to feel that they had some control over the information, some beginnings of a feeling of power vis-à-vis the experts" (80).

Adopting a participatory action research approach requires not only a change in direction for the researcher, from observer to actor, but also changes the one-way direction in which much ethnography expects knowledge and expertise to flow—from the researcher to the participants—to a more complex and truly dialogic process in which all are involved in research, reflection, and education. Many ethnographers, including several cited in this chapter, have recognized the problematic nature and limited utility of top-down models of literacy education and community development. Literacy is "always embedded in socially constructed epistemological principles. It is about knowledge: the ways in which people address reading and writing are themselves rooted in conceptions of knowledge, identity, being" (Street 7). If we are going to work for literacy in the community in a way that is genuinely transformative and sustainable, we must recognize the necessity to work with community members both to draw on their existing knowledge and to create together new ways of generating knowledge and action that are more responsible, empowering, and ethical.

QUESTIONS OF POWER AND REPRESENTATION

Lest we paint too rosy a picture, however, we must acknowledge that, like any other process of collaboration, participatory action research is plagued by personal misunderstandings, constraints of time and resources, and the pressures of both internal and external systems of power and authority. For the participatory action researcher the task is to impose equality within a setting that is inherently unequal. The researcher carries with him all of the power and privilege associated with being a member of the academic elite. He has a title, business cards, access to a language of theory, and esoteric knowledge that, even when he chooses not to display it, is available to him and recognized by others. Privilege does not disappear; you cannot make it go away or pretend it does not exist. At the same time it is important to realize that authority in the community does not automatically come with academic credentials (Cushman and Monberg 167). Instead, it is important to acknowledge your power and your place within the political and social hierarchies and to find ways to put this to use in supporting the efforts of community groups to achieve social change. What Cushman and Monberg call *social reflexivity* is a process of earning the authority to represent community members through:

> the careful interaction and knowledge making with the individuals in the study, where we negotiate, through reciprocity, the power and status related to our positions. Social reflexivity demands that the researcher and participants openly negotiate their interdependent relations using dialogic interaction. (171–72)

Participatory action research certainly does not erase inequitable power relations and, in fact, raises new sets of questions about power and representation. How does a researcher encourage, but not coerce, participation? How, in a more dialogic and collaborative relationship with community members, can a researcher be aware of issues of misunderstanding and exploitation? Who possesses the agency to represent the work of the researcher and community members in the end? Who gets to speak, to what audience, and for what ends? Feminist, critical race, and postcolonial theories all provide perspectives on issues of power and privilege that help to frame the work of the participatory action researcher.

As Maguire ("Uneven") points out, in addition to its focus on the importance of including considerations of the role of gender in social research, feminist theory has highlighted several other important considerations for those engaged in transformative practice including an examination of multiple identities and interlocking systems of oppression; an acknowledgement of issues of voice, power, and representation within our work; and an appreciation for the relevance of everyday experiences. Feminist theory has also challenged traditional approaches to research by rejecting neutrality and emphasizing relationships, commitment to community, and engagement in social action.

Gesa Kirsch notes that collaboration is a common thread that runs through much feminist-influenced research and offers both the researcher and the community members several potential benefits including a sense of mutual benefit and empowerment and the development of meaningful relationships (158). At the same time, Kirsch reminds us that power dynamics shape all human relations and that the relationships between a researcher and community members "embody the potential for misunderstandings, disappointments, and power inequities" (161). As researchers and teachers then we have to recognize that not only will not all community members appreciate or benefit from our work, but also that instead of meaningful relationships, our work may cause others "discomfort, confusion, or even emotional pain" (161).

Critical race theory, in addition to highlighting the continuing presence of racial inequality and its pernicious effect on all aspects of our society, emphasizes the importance of what Delgado has called *counterstorytelling*, challenging the dominant understanding of individuals and events by telling the story from the perspective of the least powerful rather than, as is most often the case, the most powerful. Participatory action research provides a concrete method of giving voice to these stories and of placing them within the context of existing social and economic inequality. The researcher's interpretations are legitimate as one way of understanding a set of circumstances and events, but other interpretations are equally valid. This gets us away from the master narrative of the researcher telling the story to engage multiple voices. Obviously the writer writes, although literacy education has room for multiple writers. This disrupts the positivist, objective, master narrative to create more voices, more stories. As Delgado suggests, stories can be a constructive force: "But stories and counterstories can serve an equally important destructive function. They can show that what we believe is ridiculous, self-serving, or cruel. They can show us the way out of the trap of unjustified exclusion. They can help us understand when it is time to reallocate power. They are the other half—the destructive half—of the creative dialectic" (61).

Several postcolonial theorists, most notably Gayatri Spivak in her essay "Can the Subaltern Speak?" have raised a similar concern with issues of voice and agency. Spivak questions the possibility of intellectuals to represent, or even understand, the experiences and discourse of those outside the dominant culture without first translating it into terms comprehensible to the dominant culture. Such translation, according to Spivak, inevitably both alters the experiences and utterances of the subaltern and allows them to be used, even by well-intentioned intellectuals, for ends that support the dominant culture. As Cushman and Monberg remind us, the unexamined foundation of ethnography is in the colonial project of anthropology to examine and categorize indigenous and marginalized groups for the benefit of the dominant culture (173). For literacy ethnographers this raises the questions, as Patricia Sullivan asks:

> How can we conceive and reflect the "other," the not-us, in the process of inquiry such that we convey otherness in its own terms? How can we adequately transcribe and represent the lived experiences of others—inscribe an other's reality—in a text that is marked through and through by our own discursive presence? (97)

Even using a participatory action research approach, can we engage others about their desires, needs, and experiences without distorting them to serve our ends? The simple answer is, we cannot. To seek the pristine clarity of objectivity is not possible in such human interactions and Sullivan answers her own questions with a call for more multivoiced and dialogic ethnographic work. In participatory action research, however, the danger exists of not simply representing the "other" inaccurately, but also of speaking for community members' needs and desires rather than working with them to identify problems and work collaboratively toward change. For participatory action researchers, perhaps, the question is not only who can speak, but also can we listen? Can we adequately recognize the power that accompanies our privileged positions to reflect on the impact we have on the community members with whom we work? Spivak calls on intellectuals to interrogate their positions of power in relationship to marginalized members of society and, similarly, Cushman and Monberg argue that an essential element of social reflexivity is reflection about the power relationships and effects of the individual in contact with others.

All of these theoretical positions offer important tools for participatory action researchers to engage in critical reflection while working with community members. We urge that such reflection not be limited to the individual consciousness of the researcher, however. Such reflections and self-interrogations about power and privilege should be conducted overtly and collaboratively with members of the community. A more open and collaborative discussion of privilege, power, and the payoffs of the project for all involved create the opportunity for a more honest and ethical process. The stakes, including the risks, costs, and potential rewards, must be made clear for everyone involved in the project and available for ongoing discussion and negotiation as projects evolve. Of course such conversations do not stop us, or community members, from having certain aspects of power and privilege; but we can acknowledge these social forces. Open interrogation into the nature of power, and its uses and abuses, is part of the educational process for everyone involved in participatory action research. Such reflections need not create a paralysis that keeps the researcher from acting. Instead, when reflection of this kind is done openly with members of the community it can provide a richer, more open collaboration and reveal important structures of power and privilege to all involved.

THE IMPORTANCE OF ACTION

The fact that we cannot fully escape issues of inequitable power and concerns about representation should not be an excuse for inaction. The goal of participatory action research is to work with community members to begin a process of knowledge generation and action that can both result in tangible social change and outlive the scope of the initial project, which is the point. As many critics have noted, much critical pedagogy that ostensibly maintains as its goal the empowerment and liberation of marginalized groups remains, often, rigidly hierarchical and inflexible (Gallagher). Participatory action researchers, while equally troubled by the social inequities and injustices of contemporary society, begin with the deeply pragmatic and truly radical step of listening. There is more to enacting social change than writing another journal article or book review.

It is, however, important to recognize that journal articles, book reviews, and other publications are so often the coin of the realm in the academic world in terms not only of power and prestige, but more vitally in terms of individual livelihood. Participatory action research projects, because they do not conform to accepted, positivist ideas of knowledge generation and ownership, can present challenges for academics. The collaborative nature of such projects means that they often take much longer to develop than traditional ethnographies. Such work with marginalized communities can be particularly difficult to plan for and maintain as members face obligations of work, family, and survival that are certainly often more vital to them than the research project. Also, in the humanities and social sciences credit still accrues more to the single author and so heightens the professional risks of engaging in truly collaborative writing with community members, in which all writers receive appropriate credit. Such obstacles should not deter us from engaging in work in ways we find ethical and significant. We must, however, realize that there is educational work to be done within the academy to change the direction of entrenched thinking about ethnography and community literacy. Scholars involved in participatory action research should also reach out to one another for mutual moral and intellectual support.

We can continue to watch, to note, to analyze, and to critique. In doing so we will continue to have much to critique because not much will change. Or we can change the direction of our work, change the direction in which we expect knowledge and authority to flow, and change the direction of our field if we choose to act, to become engaged in efforts to challenge social inequality and economic disparity as they affect our classrooms and communities. Participatory action research reminds us, as scholars, of the need to make our work count in real and substantive ways in the daily lives of the people with whom we work and provides us both the theoretical framework and the concrete methods with which to do so.

WORKS CITED

Adams, Frank. *Unearthing Seeds of Fire: The Idea of Highlander*. Winston-Salem, NC: Blair, 1975.

Barton, David, and Mary Hamilton. "Literacy Practices." *Situated Literacies: Reading and Writing in Context*. Ed. David Barton, Mary Hamilton, and Roz Ivanic. London: Routledge, 2000. 7–15.

Bleich, David. "Ethnography and the Study of Literacy: Prospects for Socially Generous Research." *Into the Field: Sites of Composition Studies*. Ed. Anne Ruggles Gere. New York: MLA, 1993. 176–92.

Brydon-Miller, Mary. "Breaking Down Barriers: Accessibility Self-Advocacy in the Disabled Community." *Voices of Change: Participatory Research in the United States and Canada*. Ed. Peter Park, Mary Brydon-Miller, Budd Hall, and Ted Jackson. Westport, CT: Bergin and Garvey, 1993. 124–43.

——. "Education, Research, and Action: Theory and Methods of Participatory Action Research." *From Subjects to Subjectivities: A Handbook of Interpretive and Participatory Methods*. Ed. Deborah L. Tolman and Mary Brydon-Miller. New York: New York UP, 2001. 76–89.

——. "A Glimpse of a Lighthouse: Participatory Action Research, Postcolonial Theory, and Work with Refugee Communities." *Committee on Refugees and Immigration Selected Papers*. Vol. IX.2001. 254–76.

Clifford, James. "Introduction: Partial Truths." *Writing Culture: The Poetics and Politics of Ethnography*. Ed. James Clifford and George E. Marcus. Berkeley: U of California P, 1986. 1–21.

Comstock, Donald E., and Russell Fox. "Participatory Research as Critical Theory: The North Bonneville, USA, Experience." *Voices of Change: Participatory Research in the United States and Canada*. Ed. Peter Park, Mary Brydon-Miller, Budd Hall, and Ted Jackson. Westport, CT: Bergin and Garvey, 1993. 103–24.

Cushman, Ellen. *The Struggle and the Tools: Oral and Literate Strategies in an Inner City Community*. Albany: State U of New York P, 1998.

——. "The Rhetorician as an Agent of Social Change." *On Writing Research: The Braddock Essays 1975–1998*. Ed. Lisa Ede. Boston: Bedford/St. Martin's, 1999. 372–89.

Cushman, Ellen, and Terese Guinsatao Monberg. "Re-centering Authority: Social Reflexivity and Re-positioning in Composition Research." *Under Construction: Working at the Intersections of Composition, Theory, Research, and Practice*. Ed. Christine Farris and Chris M. Anson. Logan: Utah State UP, 1998. 166–80.

Delgado, Richard. "Storytelling for Oppositionists and Others: A Plea for Narrative." *Critical Race Theory: The Cutting Edge*. 2nd ed. Ed. Richard Delgado and Jean Stefancic. Philadelphia, PA: Temple UP, 2000. 60–70.

Dyson, Anne Haas. *Writing Superheroes: Contemporary Childhood, Popular Culture, and Classroom Literacy*. New York: Teachers College P, 1997.

Fals-Borda, Orlando. "Participatory (Action) Research in Social Theory: Origins and Challenges" *Handbook of Action Research: Participative Inquiry and Practice*. Ed. Peter Reason and Hilary Bradbury. London: Sage, 2001. 27–37.

Freire, Paulo. *Pedagogy of the Oppressed*. New York: Continuum, 1970.

Gallagher, Chris W. "'Just Give Them What They Need': Transforming the Transformative Intellectual." *Composition Studies* 28 (2000): 61–83.

Gaventa, John. "The Powerful, the Powerless, and the Experts: Knowledge Struggles in an Information Age." *Voices of Change: Participatory Research in the United States and Canada*. Ed. Peter Park, Mary Brydon-Miller, Budd Hall, and Ted Jackson. Westport, CT: Bergin and Garvey, 1993. 21–40.

Gregory, Eve, and Ann Williams. *City Literacies: Learning to Read across Generations and Cultures*. London: Routledge. 2000.

Herbert, Pat, and Clinton Robinson. "Another Language, Another Literacy? Practices in Northern Ghana." *Literacy and Development: Ethnographic Perspectives*. Ed. Brian V. Street. London: Routledge, 2001. 121–36.

Horton, Billy D. "The Appalachian Land Ownership Study: Research and Citizen Action in Appalachia." *Voices of Change: Participatory Research in the United States and Canada*. Ed. Peter Park, Mary Brydon-Miller, Budd Hall, and Ted Jackson. Westport, CT: Bergin and Garvey, 1993. 85–102.

Jones, Kathryn. "Becoming Just Another Alphanumeric Code: Farmers' Encounters with the Literacy and Discourse Practices of Agricultural Bureaucracy at the Livestock Auction." *Situated Literacies: Reading and Writing in Context*. Ed. David Barton, Mary Hamilton, and Roz Ivanic. London: Routledge, 2000. 70–90.

Kelly, James G., Lynne O. Mock, and S. Darius Tandon. "Collaborative Inquiry with African American Community Leaders: Comments on a Participatory Action Research Process." *Handbook of Action Research: Participative Inquiry and Practice*. Ed. Peter Reason and Hilary Bradbury. London: Sage, 2001. 348–55.

256   *Bronwyn T. Williams and Mary Brydon-Miller*

Kirsch, Gesa. "Reflecting on Collaboration in Feminist Empirical Research: Some Cautions." *Feminist Empirical Research: Emerging Perspectives on Qualitative and Teacher Research*. Ed. Joanne Addison and Sharon James McGee. Portsmouth, NH: Boynton/Cook, 1999. 158–62.

Lykes, M. Brinton. "Activist Participatory Research and the Arts with Rural Mayan Women: Interculturality and Situated Meaning Making." *From Subjects to Subjectivities: A Handbook of Interpretive and Participatory Methods*. Ed. Deborah L. Tolman and Mary Brydon-Miller. New York: New York UP, 2001. 183–99.

MacDonald, Susan Peck. "Voices of Research: Methodological Choices of a Disciplinary Community." *Under Construction: Working at the Intersections of Composition, Theory, Research, and Practice*. Ed. Christine Farris and Chris M. Anson. Logan: Utah State UP, 1998. 111–23

Maguire, Patricia. *Doing Participatory Research: A Feminist Approach*. Amherst: U of Massachusetts P, 1987.

———. "Uneven Ground: Feminisms and Action Research" *Handbook of Action Research: Participative Inquiry and Practice*. Ed. Peter Reason and Hilary Bradbury. London: Sage, 2001. 59–69.

McCarthy, Lucille Parkinson, and Stephen M. Fishman. "A Text for Many Voices: Representing Diversity in Reports of Naturalistic Research." *Ethics and Representation in Qualitative Studies of Literacy*. Ed. Peter Mortensen and Gesa Kirsch. Urbana, IL: NCTE, 1996. 155–76.

Merrifield, Juliet. "Putting Scientists in Their Place: Participatory Research in Environmental and Occupational Health." *Voices of Change: Participatory Research in the United States and Canada*. Ed. Peter Park, Mary Brydon-Miller, Budd Hall, and Ted Jackson. Westport, CT: Bergin and Garvey, 1993. 65–84

Moss, Beverly J. "Ethnography and Composition: Studying Language at Home." *Methods and Methodology in Composition Research*. Ed. Gesa Kirsch and Patricia A. Sullivan. Carbondale: Southern Illinois UP, 1992. 153–71.

Newkirk, Thomas. "Seduction and Betrayal in Qualitative Research." *Ethics and Representation in Qualitative Studies of Literacy*. Ed. Peter Mortensen and Gesa Kirsch. Urbana, IL: NCTE, 1996. 3–16.

Pitt, Kathy. "Family Literacy: A Pedagogy for the Future?" *Situated Literacies: Reading and Writing in Context*. Ed. David Barton, Mary Hamilton, and Roz Ivanic. London: Routledge, 2000. 108–24.

Ray, Ruth, and Ellen Barton. "Further Afield: Rethinking the Contributions of Research." *Under Construction: Working at the Intersections of Composition, Theory, Research, and Practice*. Ed. Christine Farris and Chris M. Anson. Logan: Utah State UP, 1998. 196–214.

Reardon, Ken, John Welsh, Brian Kreiswirth, and John Forester. "Participatory Action Research from the Inside: Community Development Practice in East St. Louis." *American Sociologist* 24 (1993): 69–91.

Robinson-Pant, Anna. "Women's Literacy and Health: Can an Ethnographic Researcher Find the Links?" *Literacy and Development: Ethnographic Perspectives.* Ed. Brian V. Street. London: Routledge, 2001. 152–70.

Rogers, Alan. "Afterword: Problematizing Literacy and Development." *Literacy and Development: Ethnographic Perspectives.* Ed. Brian V. Street. London: Routledge, 2001. 205–22.

Ronald, Kate, and Hephzibah Roskelly. "Untested Feasibility: Imagining the Pragmatic Possibility of Paulo Freire." *College English* 63 (2001): 612–32.

Samant, Ujwala. "Literacy and Social Change: From a Woman's Perspective." Proceedings of the 1996 World Conference on Literacy. Literacy Online. February 2, 2002. *http://litserver.literacy.upenn.edu/products/ili/pdf/ilprocus.pdf.*

Spivak, Gayatri Chakravorty. "Can the Subaltern Speak?" *Marxism and the Interpretation of Culture.* Ed. Carey Nelson and Lawrence Grossberg. Basingstoke: Macmillan, 1988. 271–313.

Street, Brian V. "Introduction." *Literacy and Development: Ethnographic Perspectives.* Ed. Brian V. Street. London: Routledge, 2001. 1–17

Sullivan, Patricia A. "Ethnography and the Problem of the 'Other'" *Ethics and Representation in Qualitative Studies of Literacy.* Ed. Peter Mortensen and Gesa Kirsch. Urbana, IL: NCTE, 1996. 97–115.

Swantz, Marja-Liisa, Elizabeth Ndedya, and Mwajuma Saiddy Masaiganah. "Participatory Action Research in Southern Tanzania, with Special Reference to Women." *Handbook of Action Research: Participative Inquiry and Practice.* Ed. Peter Reason and Hilary Bradbury. London: Sage, 2001. 386–95.

Tandon, Rajesh. "Participatory Research in the Empowerment of People." *Convergence* 14 (1981): 20–27.

14

Just What *Are* We Talking About?

Disciplinary Struggle and the Ethnographic Imaginary

LANCE MASSEY

Since the beginnings of composition as a field, we all have been struggling over how to define it, over its heart and soul.

—Gary Olson, "Death of Composition
as an Intellectual Discipline"

. . . I tried to show how a great transformation in our view of reality forms a background for the effort of composition to constitute itself reflectively as a unified discipline. The two decades in which we have striven toward that goal coincide with movements in many spheres of inquiry toward a contextualist understanding of knowledge, thought, and communication.

—Louise Wetherbee Phelps,
Composition as a Human Science

ETHNOGRAPHY IS A POWERFUL IMAGINARY, which is not to say that it does not exist. But establishing what "it" is, *is* a slippery venture. For some, ethnography is "naturalistic," whereas for others it is "phenomenological." For still others, it is both, and more: "The ethnographic mode, based in a cultural context, presents a *phenomenological* and *empirical* approach to research. It is *holistic* and *naturalistic*" (Bishop xvi, emphasis added).[1] I do not mean to suggest that these terms are mutually exclusive or even parallel, that phenomenological research cannot also be naturalistic, cannot also be holistic, and so forth. I do want to suggest, however, that each of these terms potentially evokes a (different) world of associations and ideas. In short, if we understand these words as authorized by and authorizing even subtly different discursive traditions, then we understand that such descriptions, far from pinpointing ethnography's essence, diffuse it exponentially. Complicating things further, some argue that what we do in composition cannot be called ethnography at all. Robert Brooke and John Hendricks argue that classroom research based in participant-observation is "often incorrectly called 'ethnographic' because of its reliance on anthropological ethnographic principles" (11). Keith Rhodes even offers a replacement term, suggesting that what is practiced in "exemplary composition 'ethnography'" is actually "psychography," because such research "does not explore cultures so much as it explores individual experience within closely defined cultural institutions" (31).[2] Finally, some appear to avoid such terminological messiness altogether. Ann M. Blakeslee, Caroline M. Cole, and Theresa Conefrey discuss the ethics of researcher/participant collaboration in "situated inquiry," a term they appear to use synonymously with ethnography, although, it seems, without the baggage. Attempts to define what ethnography is, then, imply that it has an essence, however diffuse, as do attempts to say what ethnography is not. And attempts to avoid the matter entirely suggest a real respect for the ambiguities and multivalences that inhere in definitions of ethnography. After all, the very volume of protests that ethnography is *this* and not *that* betrays its extreme malleability as a research method. Ethnography can be adapted, it seems, to numerous perspectives and ends.

In this chapter, then, I attempt to shed light on the question of *why* ethnography has been so difficult for compositionists to define by calling attention to both its discursive hybridity and its appeal to different disciplinary traditions. In this sense, I treat ethnography as emblematic of all such methodological constructs. Nobody, after all, would deny that methodologies such as composition historiography and rhetorical theory are also informed by diverse and even conflicting theories and discourses. Yet ethnography seems like a particularly visible and pertinent example, especially considering composition's arguable status as a "flexible social science" (MacDonald, "Voices" 111) that is nevertheless generally situated in traditionally humanist English departments. Ethnography thus comprises a complex discursive space that operates at the crux of one of composition's key disciplinary identity crises. Are we, to borrow Stephen North's terms, researchers or scholars (to say nothing of critics)? And how does an examination of ethnography in composition help us answer this question? Providing the start of just such an answer, I proceed from the position that the term *ethnography*, rather than denoting a

method or even a methodological orientation,[3] describes an imaginary construct through and around which compositionists order their disciplinary
experiences. Yet the construct does not itself represent an ideological or epistemological unity. The meaning of ethnography shifts with perspective.
Working from this premise, I explore ethnography as a site for playing out the
"hegemonic struggle" (Olson 39) between social science and humanism in
composition by examining the dynamic interaction and mingling of social scientific and humanist discourses in and on ethnography. I argue that, although
ethnographies of writing and literacy constitute (and are constituted by) a
complex discursive heterogeneity, displaying features of both humanist and
social scientific discourses, analyzing the reception of the contextualist
insights of antifoundational theory in social scientific and humanist research
reveals the workings of more stable, discrete disciplinary positions. Understood this way, then, ethnography not only becomes a kind of disciplinary
"contact zone," a space in which different disciplinary discourses "meet, clash,
and grapple with each other" (Pratt 34), but it also comprises a discursive
space in which otherwise divergent discourses might have one more reason to
engage each other.

INTERPRETIVE FRAME: RHETORIC AND RECEPTION

As an analysis of both rhetoric and reception, this chapter employs a form of
"rhetorical hermeneutics," which "attempts to move critical theory from general theories about interpretive process to rhetorical histories of specific
rhetorical acts" (Mailloux 61). As such, it "takes [historical acts] of interpretation . . . and attempts to do a rhetorical analysis of the cultural conversation
in which [those acts] participated" (61–62). Textual meaning, then, is only
useful insofar as it itself represents an act of reception (and, it follows,
response)—a reception whose author's interpretive frame is determined by a
complex function of her particular locations within cultural and social discourses as well as her perceived institutional and ideological affiliations.[4]
Implicit in this logic of reception is the notion that any act of meaning-making is predicated on a prior interpretation, and any interpretation is simultaneously an act of meaning-making.[5]

    This method of rhetorical analysis enables me to account for the fact that
compositionists continue to appeal to the explanatory power of paradigms, in
spite of Carl Herndl and Cynthia A. Nahrwold's argument that the concept
of paradigm is inadequate to describe the ways in which qualitative researchers
do their work. Aiming to move "beyond the relatively sterile notion of paradigms with their metaphysical debates about epistemology to describe qualitative research as a situated rhetorical practice," they argue that "a researcher's

commitments to specific forms of social action shape theoretical and philosophical commitments" and not vice versa (260). They assert that researchers' "prior social experiences and commitments drive" their "attachment to one theoretical position or another" (260). As an explanation of how researchers typically move from felt social commitment to study design, implementation, writing, and publication, Herndl and Nahrwold's argument is both reasonable and plausible. But their model represents only one sliver of time. If we understand coming to theory and developing social commitments to be ongoing, mutually informing activities, then we can say it is as true that "researchers' attachment to one theoretical position or another" influences their present and future "social experiences and commitments" as the other way around. In this very real sense, then, paradigms *do* help us understand and explain researchers' purposes and actions—all the more so if we consider Gary Olson's claim that "[in] every discipline there is hegemonic struggle over the identity of that discipline," that "one group of like-minded individuals attempts to further *its* vision of the field, while other groups do the same" (38). It is precisely the terms of this struggle that interest me here.

THE DISCURSIVE AMBIVALENCE OF ETHNOGRAPHY IN COMPOSITION

If composition is a hybrid discipline, then ethnography would seem to be its signature methodology. Just as scholars as diverse as Linda Brodkey, Ralph Cintron, Susan Peck MacDonald, and Gary Olson have posited the contributions of both humanistic and social scientific traditions to our discipline, ethnographic texts have followed suit, exhibiting a mix of humanistic and social scientific features that are often so finely interwoven that distinguishing them can be difficult. Indeed, ethnography most likely enjoys its popularity as both a methodology and an object of investigation precisely because it can satisfy compositionists' diverse tastes. Nevertheless, it is both useful and, to my mind, necessary to try to make precisely such distinctions if we want to develop a better understanding of how ethnography has been interpreted and deployed in composition.

According to Susan Peck MacDonald, social scientific writing is relatively compact, which means that it tends to operate within a more well-defined universe of disciplinary problems and questions than writing in the humanities (*Professional* 21–31). Writing in the social sciences tends to begin with conceptual questions, she says, seeking to explain these questions in general(izable) terms while employing an "epistemic" language that self-consciously calls attention to procedural and methodological operations as they relate to the larger field (*Professional* 32–50). Charles Bazerman also describes how social scientific rhetoric has moved from relying on "ordinary language terms" to specialized terms that "take on such narrow concrete meanings that they diverge from normal meaning" (274). Humanistic writing, on the other hand, tends to begin with texts, interpreting them on a fairly individual basis while employing a "phenomenal" language that focuses primarily on the text or object being studied (MacDonald, *Professional* 32–50). I do not want to rely too heavily on MacDonald's or Bazerman's descriptions. I eventually argue in this analysis that writing in the humanities, at least within composition ethnography circles, displays a strong sense of disciplinary self-awareness and can even be characterized by this quality. Nevertheless, the discourse of ethnography in composition reflects this taxonomy well, if, as I have said (and as MacDonald and Bazerman would no doubt agree), in a heterogeneous form.

Barbara Walvoord and Lucille McCarthy introduce the "Inquiry Paradigm and Research Assumptions" section of their 1990 "naturalistic" study of "thinking and writing in college" by stating that their initial research questions "were the general questions that [Clifford] Geertz says are traditionally asked by ethnographers facing new research scenes: 'What's going on here?' and 'What the devil do these people think they're up to?'" (19). Walvoord and McCarthy's citation of Geertz signals their allegiance to an explicitly interpretive, and therefore humanistic, sensibility.[6] They also profess an awareness that their "research findings were shaped by [their] perspectives," which led them, for example, to "focus on students' difficulties in meeting teachers' expectations and on those aspects of the classroom context . . . that were . . . most amenable to the teachers' influence" (20). On one hand, I would argue that Walvoord and McCarthy, by acknowledging that their research is influenced by their perspectives, make a "compacting" gesture. They implicitly define their "perspectives," after all, in terms of their disciplinary interests, suggesting that researchers of writing have already studied or articulated a need to study the discrepancies between teachers' demands and students' abilities to meet those demands. On the other hand, the reflexivity that gives rise to this gesture is based on the rationalist methods of critical theory, a tradition and body of work rooted in the humanist line.[7]

I would thus say that Walvoord and McCarthy's two statements fall on the side of humanism, if not unambiguously. Yet, in other ways, their text seems to be a strong example of social scientific writing. The thirty-three-page theory and methods chapter from which the previous statements were taken, for example, has forty-eight headings and subheadings, three tables, and seven bulleted or numbered lists. Such a high degree of categorization, together with the level of abstraction necessary to render qualitative data such as "characteristics of the classes in the study" into a quantitative table (18), suggests that the logic that informs this study, while perhaps interpretive, is also simultaneously powerfully analytical. Indeed, its body chapters, whose counterparts in other ethnographies often rely heavily on narrative, are even more subdivided than the theory and methods chapter. The forty-seven-page chapter reporting on "Sherman's Business Course" contains seventy-seven headings and subheadings.

Although I could say much more about Walvoord and McCarthy's study, I want to move on to two more recent examples. David Schaafsma's ethnographic study of a "community based . . . summer writing program in Detroit's inner city" (xv) and Victoria Purcell-Gates's ethnographic study of "a mother and son who are trying to learn to read and write" (10) appear to be based on a more narrative, humanistic sensibility than that of Walvoord and McCarthy.[8] Schaafsma opens with a journal entry recalling the events of a day in his study and moves directly into a narrative recounting the moments just after recording the entry: "I turned off the machine, walked into the kitchen and grabbed a beer. I was tired after another day in Detroit. Hot and tired. I took a long pull on the Labatts, stretched my back and neck and pressed them against the refrigerator, closed my eyes, and waited for the beer to ease into my arms. I kept my eyes closed and waited for the voices to be still" (4). Few things evoke the humanities—whose mantra arguably remains, even after postmodernism, "know-thyself"—the way such a personal narrative does, in this case with its knowingly (but not too knowingly) introspective tone, its hints of a wise sadness lurking in the mundane descriptions, and its figural, defamiliarizing image of beer easing into Schaafsma's arms. Purcell-Gates uses a similar personal narrative style in reporting her research. Recalling the time she informed Jenny, an adult woman she was teaching to read and write and a central figure of the study, that she "would learn to read by reading her own words," Purcell-Gates writes that Jenny:

> was stunned! She was disbelieving. She felt sorry for me, believing I had failed to understand her reports of her illiteracy. "Why, I ain't never read my *own* words before!" she explained softly. "See, I cain't write!"
>
> Doggedly pursuing my suggestion, I continued, "Well, I think you can write more than you think you can. The writing will come . . . as you start writing your own thoughts and your own feelings down, and not just copying somebody else's words."
>
> Jenny shook her head back and forth slowly as she acknowledged, "That's all I ever really did was copy stuff, you know, from a book." (102)

Taken out of context, this exchange between Purcell Gates and Jenny could easily be mistaken for a work of fiction, perhaps the consummate expression of a narrative sensibility. The emotive punctuation, the dialogue—this text wants to "take you there," to achieve mimesis. Both passages, then, would seem to exemplify claims that humanistic writing is "phenomenal," fixing its gaze on the text (or site) under study, with little if any attention to epistemic concerns.

On further inspection, however, both studies reveal a complex discursive heterogeneity. Schaafsma's study is not only based on narrative, but also on multiple narratives of and perspectives on the same event. Commenting on this rhetorical choice, Schaafsma writes that including "the voices of my colleagues helps me to work against the authoritarianism of certain kinds of educational discourse" (xxii). Schaafsma's multivocal text, then, enacts the humanist valuing of interpretation (and the humanist preoccupation with the politics of interpretation that recognizes the contingency of truth claims and the narrativity of knowledge—but I save that discussion for the next section). Taken together with the study's strong narrative base, we can conclude that, as published ethnographic accounts go, Schaafsma's is unusually strongly humanist in its forms and positions. Indeed, this is why I chose it: even Schaafsma's study is not without its discursive ambiguities. Let us consider, by way of explanation, his method of citation. What at first appears to be straightforward MLA (author-page number) style bears one curiously anomalous feature. In cases in which Schaafsma cites more than one work by the same author, he uses publication date rather than title of the work to distinguish the source. According to Diane Dowdey, the "prominence of the date" of a source in scholarship using APA (American Psychological Association) style "establishes recency as an important criterion for citation," and the importance of recency positions "knowledge as progress, as a process of accretion" (339).[9] This stylistic feature suggests a conceptual grounding, however tenuous, of the sort MacDonald attributes to social scientific writing, rendering Schaafsma's otherwise strongly humanist text discursively heterogeneous.

Purcell-Gates's study is also conceptual, even if the concepts are detailed in endnotes rather than in the body text. In the second note to her introduction, she writes that her work's sociocultural orientation:

> is most directly derived from the work of Judith Green (1990; Green and Harker, 1988; Green, Harker, and Golden, 1987; Green and Weade, 1986) and David Bloome (Bloome 1983, 1986, 1988; Bloome and Green, 1982). For a broad spectrum of approaches that situate literacy within social/cultural practice, see Cochran-Smith (1984); Cook-Gumperz (1986); Erickson and Schultz (1981); Ferdman (1990); Heath (1983); Ogbu (1974, 1978); and Szwed (1988). (213)

Here Purcell-Gates not only lays out a conceptual ground for her study, but she also uses epistemic language to refer to relevant contextualizing research in sociocultural literacy studies. Her use of the APA convention of stringing together multiple citations to provide a basis and context for understanding her project particularly reinforces the social scientific aspect of this passage. In fact, in the methodological appendix, Purcell-Gates almost explicitly announces her allegiance to (or, if you prefer, makes an explicit gesture to the convention of) a social scientific worldview when she invokes the practice of using multiple data-gathering "methods to minimize bias and strengthen the validity of the findings" (204). Even here, however, Purcell-Gates's language retains an element of ambiguity in her choice not to use the hard-sounding term *triangulation* to describe her data collection.

I could analyze even more recent examples of hybrid ethnographies—Karen Gallas's 2001 concept-based ethnography of literacy in her primary classroom that nevertheless acknowledges the role of the personal in disciplinary knowledge-making, or Laura Wilder's 2002 triangulated, conceptual study whose primary concept of interest is a theory situated explicitly in literary criticism—but I now want to focus on social scientific and humanistic discourses at work in and on ethnography separately. To many compositionists, after all, they represent (and, thus, become) fundamentally different ways of asking and answering disciplinary questions. To see how this difference has played out in composition research—how the paradigmatic constraints and possibilities of humanism and social science have been interpreted and deployed by compositionists—I examine the antifoundational turn toward context as it has manifested itself in social scientific and humanistic ethnographic practice and methodology in composition. In doing so, moreover, I question the "patterns of variation" in social scientific and humanist writing that informed the previous analysis, noting how, from a different viewpoint, social scientific discourse in composition could be said to focus relatively narrowly on the objects of its research, whereas humanistic discourse in composition would seem to have a well-developed disciplinary self-awareness.

CONTEXT: CONCEPT OR CRISIS?

Antifoundationalism represents a host of disciplinary movements, based in literary critical, postmodern, poststructural, rhetorical, and sociolinguistic theories that each somehow turn away from or express growing skepticism of the assurance of absolute foundations of knowledge and universal (decontextualized), stable semiotic/linguistic systems. My interest here is not to try to sort out these various disciplinary movements or to trace the convergences and divergences of these arguably distinct but overlapping theories. Rather, I mean to suggest that the insights generated by this broadly antifoundational movement have been taken up in different ways by social scientific and humanist research in composition. To demonstrate this point, I examine the concept of *context,* perhaps the one term common to and valorized across the range of these antifoundational movements, as it has been theorized and deployed in the discourses of social science and the humanities in composition. Antifoundationalism in social scientific composition research has manifested itself in the radical expansion of context's conceptual range as it operates within and informs empirical projects. Although this ever-expanding notion of context, moreover, has led social science in composition toward more and more ethnographic, context-sensitive methodologies and away from the more clinical methodologies many compositionists have associated with cognitivism, the deployment of these methodologies themselves has been accompanied by a continued, if implicit, positing of the potential for empirical observation to produce valid representations of subjects. On the other hand, the most visible consequence of antifoundationalism in humanist composition ethnography has been its almost overwhelming concern with epistemic questions—its radical questioning of the possibility of ever being able to produce valid representations (or foundational theories) of subjects (or the subject)—and that these questions have been directly or indirectly oriented around the crisis of representation that has prompted the recent ethical turn in composition.

Kantor, Kirby, and Goetz's 1981 description of "ethnographic studies in English education" offers a likely starting point for my examination of context in the social scientific discourse of composition ethnography because of its status as a landmark work signaling the arrival of ethnography on the scene of English studies. The authors include among the characteristics of ethnography "the importance of context" (296). Invoking sociolinguistic theory, they write that "language derives meaning from social context—the discourse topic, setting, and audience—and cultural values of language users" (296). They argue that these same categories are "crucial to composition and literature teaching as well" (296). Even more expansively, they note the importance of "the dynamic interplay among elements in the physical, natural, and sociocultural environments" in "understanding and explaining what people do" (296). Kantor, Kirby, and Goetz's characterizations are indicative of composition's attention to context in its emergent state. The categories that context encompasses—topic, setting, audience, cultural values, environment—are thus relatively imprecise by today's social scientific standards. Indeed, they resemble "diffuse disciplinary problems" (22), which Stephen Toulmin contends denote the "absence of a clearly defined, generally agreed reservoir of disciplinary problems" (qtd. in MacDonald *Professional* 22). We might read the subsequent history of this sociolinguistic, social scientific rendering of context, then, as a compacting process of both elaborating on these categories and honing them for conceptual precision.

By 1987 this compaction was well under way. Carolyn Piazza outlines the features of context as they have emerged in cognitivist writing research prior to her article. These features include "(1) the cumulation of experiences and knowledge in the writer's head, (2) the strategies writers use to make rhetorical decisions and language choice, (3) the constraints writers face in production and comprehension, and (4) the communicative situation as represented in the assignment or the text itself" (112). Although much narrower in scope than the "context" of Kantor, Kirby, and Goetz's article, this representation relies on a much more precise disciplinary vocabulary. Whether from the nominalizations ("production" and "comprehension" from producing and comprehending) or the quasitechnical language ("communicative situation"), this passage has an almost jargony feel. Certainly, it seems, some centripetal forces have been at work on the disciplinary language of context in composition. Having summarized the cognitivist understanding of context, Piazza nevertheless attempts to "move beyond the local and immediate considerations of writers, their task, and their text to broader contexts of the social and cultural settings in which writing is embedded" (112). Her message is that composition needs to take a "multidiscipline approach" so it can "provide a fuller richer account of a writer's competence, and develop a more comprehensive study of the complex communicative act, writing" (133). This approach is to be drawn from cognitive psychology, sociology, and anthropology, such that it "invokes a set of controls that ensures that a phenomenon is checked from a variety of perspectives" (133). Piazza's rendering of context in this essay suggests an intermediate phase between the apparently diffuse discipline of Kantor, Kirby, and Goetz and that of today (which I examine momentarily). She says that we need to make our theories of context more exact and that these theories need to be grounded in social scientific methods, but in making this call she also admits that we had not yet done so by 1987.

In the time since Piazza's article, social scientific conceptualizations of context have broadened their reach to cover almost every conceivable aspect of "social context," including "language learners' home, community, and public school environments" (Berkenkotter, Huckin, and Ackerman 1). Indeed, Elaine Chin's 1994 "redefinition" of context as "practice" includes even the most mundane, seemingly trivial aspects of context, calling our attention to "both the bodily experience of occupying spaces and times that constitute the material world from which writers compose as well as the meanings writers construct about what it means to inhabit such worlds and to do writing in them" (477). Chin makes good on the challenge Piazza issued by injecting context with the messiness of lived, embodied experience, so that it can finally account for "the complex network of trails, missteps, detours, backtracking, and sideways movements writers may actually make" (473). Moreover, in the very issue of *Written Communication* that contains Chin's article, Paul Prior appears to put Chin's call into practice in his attempt to complicate the notion of discourse community as a contextual factor in writing research. Basing his argument in part on a report of "an ethnographic study of writing and response in a sociology seminar at a major Midwestern university" ("Response" 489), Prior simultaneously advocates and practices "a dynamic, sociohistoric theory of disciplinary (discourse) communities" ("Response" 484). He employs a compact social scientific language as he draws a portrait of context in the process of "disciplinary enculturation" (as enacted by and in writing) no less sweeping in scope than Chin's. For Prior, "disciplinary enculturation is situated in streams of interpenetrated activity" that include "everyday and specialized discourses, sense-making practices, goal structures, [and] life experiences" ("Response" 521). According to Prior, then, any process of learning how to produce the discourse(s) of one's discipline—itself characterized by "nonlinear, discursively heterogeneous practices" ("Response" 483)—is shot through with residues of other discursive processes and other experiences. It is, as Mikhail Bakhtin might say, like so many "living utterance[s]," which, "having taken meaning and shape at a particular historical moment in a socially specific environment, cannot fail to brush up against the thousands of living dialogic threads, woven by socio-ideological consciousness around the given object of utterance" (276).

Ironically, the closer definitions of context move toward the sort of precision implied in a compact and discursively reflexive social scientific mode of writing, the more elusive the possibility that social scientific researchers can adequately account for it in their studies. One response to this phenomenon has been for compositionists working in a social scientific tradition to adopt ever more context-sensitive methods. Indeed, by the time Prior has published *Writing/Disciplinarity* in 1998, context continues to elude the easy grasp of the researcher. He recalls how his data-collection methods have developed over time, noting that he has "gone from no observation to observational note-taking to audiotaping," and that he "now [sees] the need to better capture activity in its embodied forms by videotaping" (*Writing* 274). As context has become more complicated for Prior (and social scientific research in composition), he has responded by moving toward data-collection methods that more fully capture "embodied" activity, and he has done so precisely because "[pursuing] the chronotopic laminations of writing and disciplinarity seems to lead inexorably into full cultural-historical lifeworlds of people and their communities of practice" (*Writing* 274).

We can now begin to see how conflating "method" and "methodology" is not completely inappropriate. We know that social scientific conceptions of context have grown increasingly complex since Kantor, Kirby, and Goetz. Furthermore, evidence suggests that, as a result, social scientific methods have shifted to become more context sensitive.[10] If this causal relationship exists, then, it must be predicated on a methodological commitment to the idea that research can and should strive to explain and represent the phenomena it investigates accurately—that validity is not only desirable, but also attainable, at least theoretically. That is, social scientific composition researchers such as Prior have chosen to take up the propositions that meaning is contextual, that context is almost infinitely complicated, and that identifying context's relevant factors is a function of interpretation, as conceptual insights that can help writing researchers investigate and represent the phenomena they investigate in more accurate ways than can the tenets of the "reified structural analysis" many of them work against (Prior *Writing* 308). And these insights have led social scientific research in composition to ethnographic methods that widen researchers' access to the context of the research site and all it implies.

The discourse of social science in composition, then, ultimately looks to standards of validity for authorization. It is in this sense that I was able to propose earlier that social science, as opposed to the humanities, trains its gaze on the research site: the source of the knowledge produced by social science research resides in the phenomena being investigated. Whereas, moreover, those phenomena must be interpreted, and whereas interpretive theory can thus be said to coevolve with the data it generates and orders, this coevolution's implicit teleological end is the total parity of phenomenon and interpretive theory, resulting in what I can only imagine would be a pure, dynamic simulacrum of the original research site and all of the dialogic threads woven into it—a sort of *Brainstorm* meets the holodeck. In short, the available discourses of and on ethnography have been received in social scientific composition circles primarily as tools for exploring writing with (and simultaneously developing) greater conceptual precision.

Whereas the primacy of context has led social scientific writing researchers into (and to imagine) ever more complex sites, it has, in humanistic work in composition, engendered the postmodern crisis of representation that has fueled the ethical turn in composition.[11] And, perhaps obviously, this difference can be accounted for by humanist discourse's implicit valuing of interpretation over analysis. That is, the humanist project has been to make sense out of the world and humanity by developing explanatory theories (more or less self-consciously) and by applying those theories to "texts" to be interpreted. It follows, then, that any theoretical statement that problematizes the relationship among reader, text, and world would force those who see interpretation as a mode of knowledge-making to examine both the worth and the propriety of their work and their disciplinary commitments.

One feature of the humanistic turn toward context in composition has thus been the injection of a reflexive awareness of one's methods and one's relationship to the research site into the ethnographic research narrative, what Elizabeth Chiseri-Strater calls "turning in upon ourselves" (115). She writes that reflexivity arises out of a need to "consider how positionality affects the entire ethnographic process" (120), and that "positionality" is "shaped by subjective-contextual factors such as personal life history and experiences" (116). A recognition that ethnographic knowledge is contextually determined, then, requires what James Clifford calls a "rigorous sense of partiality," which acts as "a source of representational tact" in writing ethnographic narratives (7). This turning inward, moreover, implies that the research site *per se* is not the sole font of knowledge, but the researcher's experience of the site as well. Thus, for ethnographers, "a major goal of the research process is self-reflexivity—what we learn about the self as a result of the study of the 'other'" (Chiseri-Strater 119).

Bearing this claim of ethnographic reflexivity out in a survey of ethnographies in composition is difficult, however. Although there has been much talk of autoethnography as a more and more important mode of research and representation, there has never been a mad rush to turn composition ethnography into a mode of autobiography. Yet this lack can be explained by a consideration of the institutional forces that enable and constrain disciplinary knowledge production in composition. In particular, it seems unlikely that this humanist tendency toward experimental forms arising out of epistemological and ethical crises would be able to find its fullest expression in conventional publishing forums. A quick look back at one of the ethnographies I examined earlier will clarify this point. I argued that, in an endnote, Purcell-Gates expresses her allegiance to a social scientific sensibility through the adoption of triangulation-like data-gathering methods. I noted in parentheses, however, that her statement could also be read as a kind of necessary gesture to social scientific conventionality. I want to foreground this reading here, suggesting that the overwhelmingly narrative body of Purcell-Gates's text does reflect a tendency toward humanism. Given this reading, we can assume that one reason Purcell-Gates included such endnotes was to conform to both the general disciplinary standards of situating one's research and the specific standards of Harvard University Press. The existence of such disciplinary inertia would seem to be supported, moreover, if we recognize that, whereas ethnographies are often studies done relatively early in one's career, "opportunities for such" experimental "writing tend to be confined to those who have already paid their professional dues" (Spigelman 68). If it takes clout to break the rules, then there have to be rules to break.

The "fullest expression" of humanism's antifoundational turn toward context in composition ethnography, then, is difficult to locate as ethnography. Its metatheoretical orientation and incompatibility with traditional research venues has led it into other forums, such as the metamethodological essay collections published by Kirsch and Sullivan, and Mortensen and Kirsch.[12] These collections include essays that report on research, but their primary function is to call attention to important methodological issues and problems. Although Kirsch and Sullivan include "chapters on some of the most commonly used research approaches in composition" (4), they want their collection "to contribute to a self-questioning stance . . . to cast into relief the issues that unite and separate us" (2). Mortensen and Kirsch, moreover, emphasize that their collection "is not so much a 'handbook' of qualitative research techniques as it is a book that illuminates the complex ethical and representational questions that are rarely discussed in research manuals" (xxii)—and, I would add, that can rarely be fully explored in research reports.

These and other such forums have been, not surprisingly, crucial sites for developing more autoethnographic, reflective, critical genres that allow compositionists to view researchers' experiences and the research process itself as potential sites of knowledge production (and, hence, for realizing the humanistic vision of context). One such genre is the postethnographic reflection,[13] in which researchers narrate and reflect on prior research experiences to illuminate ethical dilemmas or make theoretical contributions to ethnography in composition. Apropos of postmodern skepticism, this genre provides humanist composition ethnographers an opportunity to explore the limits of representation, the influence of the personal on "public" knowledge-making, and even to highlight mistakes and ethical missteps as opportunities to teach the field about ethics. Telling "a few stories that . . . illustrate some dilemmas" she encountered as an ethnographer (106), for example, Devan Cook recounts how her participants "assumed that the transcripts of their tapes, or selections from them, would be included" in her study and that she "said nothing to change their minds or to suggest that their stories would be more likely for inclusion if they illustrated one of my ideas . . . or if they said things in a colorful way" (109). In essence, Cook offers this moment in which her own ethical problems—her experience of the research site—provide an opportunity for reflection and, presumably, growth. The knowledge produced here is thus a product of her interaction with and experience of the research site and participants rather than simply her observation of them. Kathleen Blake Yancey summarizes this position, which she calls "reflective transfer": it "enables us to learn from and theorize our practice [and] requires . . . that we (1) observe and examine our own practice; (2) make hypotheses about successes and failures, as well as the reasons for each; and (3) shape the next iteration of similar experience according to what we have learned" (235).

Individual instances of this genre often blend, moreover, formal academic and intensely personal language. Helen Dale announces, in traditional academic style, her quite nontraditional intention of "using a first-person metanarrative to illustrate ethical dilemmas involved in [her] own work" (78). Illustrating this metanarrative form, however, Dale's language becomes more personal and reflective. Describing the pain she felt after a journal editor criticized actions she reported in research and that could have been seen as hampering students' educational experiences, Dale writes that "I reacted defensively. . . . But I knew that at the heart of things, the editor had a point. My responsibility to the students should have superseded my concerns about the 'integrity' of the research design" (90). This mingling of the academic and the personal—although most who write in this genre would reject that distinction in the first place—tends, then, to work its way around to affirming some principle of research in the antifoundational humanist research, as Dale's implicit argument that "integrity" of research design is a kind of fiction or, at least, less important than the researcher's responsibility to her participants.

These examples call attention to the fact that postmodern appropriations of context in humanist composition ethnography have never been and almost never are just postmodern. What I have been detailing for the last several paragraphs is a postmodern feminist perspective. Yet the most important reason to call attention to its feminist aspect has not surfaced until now. I have been describing context as having brought about an epistemological and methodological crisis for humanist ethnographers, and I have thus characterized this movement toward the personal in Chiseri-Strater's terms as a "turning inward." Charting the development of such a movement, then, we might expect postmodern humanist ethnography to have fallen into a solipsistic tailspin. And we can expect that outcome precisely because the development I have just described in humanist composition ethnography is, in fact, a conceptual movement of the sort attributed to social science earlier. Because humanist composition essentially seeks explanatory theories, it stands to reason that a rationally compelling theory questioning the viability of explanatory theories would result in the sort of discursive vertiginuity that has characterized the ethical turn as I have represented it so far. Yet there is a very real sense in which this movement toward metadiscourse has been an attempt to theorize theory more precisely and, thus, retain for the humanist project its explanatory potential. In short, the humanist contextualization of knowledge in composition has been an ontological response to the proposition that ontology is a fiction. Even in my description here one can see the potential for such discussions to enter endless feedback loops—the inevitable end, it would seem, for such projects.

Only the strong emphasis of feminism has kept humanist composition ethnography from this end because many recent feminist compositionists have forgone ontological questions in favor of an ethical vision. Adopting a pragmatic logic, many feminists in composition have chosen not to let theoretical conundrums divert them from the ethical goals of humanism as they have been implied in and reinterpreted by postmodernism. They have chosen instead to change the terms of disciplinary debate, asking not what sort of knowledge is produced by ethnography but, rather, what sort of good can be done with it. As Ralph Cintron writes, "it is important that self-reflexivity not undermine the pragmatic purposes of research. The critic who chooses the skeptical power of self-reflexivity needs to simultaneously choose an ethic of care, which . . . stops the analytic as downward spiral, for skepticism can undermine the fragile grounds of any commitment" (404). This infusion of feminist pragmatism, moreover, has enabled "postmodern" ethnography to become "critical" ethnography, which "[approaches] methodology not strictly in terms of its efficiency in producing or transmitting knowledge to inform subsequent (social) practice but in terms of its effects *as* a social practice" (Lu and Horner 257). In this description Lu and Horner expose the heart of the theoretical and methodological shift from a metaontological postmodern vision that wants to "inform subsequent practice" by developing an explanatory theory of theory to an ethical and pragmatic one that recognizes the need to act, to perform research that both benefits researcher and participant and attempts to "analyze how social, historical, and cultural factors shape the research site as well as participants' goals, values, and experiences" (Kirsch 5). Similarly, David Bleich advocates a "socially generous research" that "is no longer mainly a discovery project but, rather, an initiative that contributes to the empowerment of the subject community" (178). This pragmatic shift, then, repudiates anxiety, essentially changing the rules of the academic game from seeking explanatory accuracy to seeking empowerment.

Ellen Cushman's "activist methodology" exemplifies this repudiation of anxiety particularly well. Acknowledging but little regarding the crisis of representation, Cushman states that, in writing her ethnography, "I set pen to paper in the hope that I could do some small justice to my community members' struggles and tools" (21). I find her use of the phrase "do some small justice" particularly interesting in this passage because its ambivalence is that of pragmatic, critical ethnography. To do justice to something is, after all, to render it faithfully, to capture its essence. In fact, Cushman does not appear to feel a great deal of anxiety about the issue of representation. While she recognizes that the researcher/participant relationship is not one-way but, rather, "reciprocal," Cushman nevertheless assumes that she can learn "the process by which" her participants "hone and refine their oral and literate language skills" (26). On the other hand, to do justice is to make something right, to undo injustice. Read in this other way, then, the phrase indicates Cushman's desire to use her power as a researcher to change for the better all of the communities involved in her study, which she sees as a "method of intervention" related to "emancipatory pedagogy" (28). Perhaps Patricia Sullivan captures this duality best: "ethnography must be both an adequate account of the literate practices of others and accountable to those others. As we seek to understand and render the lived experience of others, our research should ultimately aim to benefit those whose voices, texts, and circumstances make such understanding possible" (98).

The humanist rendering of context, then, has undergone a powerful shift. As an attempt to develop a theory of theory, humanist postmodernism has sought to account for the uncertainties of context by formulating those uncer-

tainties as precisely as possible. In this very real sense, I can say that humanist ethnographic practices in composition have been based on the same sort of
reality principle as that implied by the empirical vision of social science. But
the pragmatic feminist response to the crisis of representation has made such
a summary judgment more difficult—although not impossible. Feminist
pragmatism seems to have changed the rules of the game, eschewing the anxiety of skepticism for an "ethic of care" (Kirsch and Ritchie 21; Cintron 404),
under the guidance of which research should be "a contribution to the welfare
of the community or society being studied" (Bleich 178).

But the rules have not been changed; they have only been ignored. The
same reality principle at work in what I have been calling ontological postmodernism is present in feminist pragmatism as well. Indeed, the very same
reflexive gesture that threatens to undermine political commitments when
deployed from a purely skeptical perspective has been preserved in the pragmatic shift as a "politics of location," in which researchers are urged to
"[acknowledge] our multiple positions" and "engage . . . in a rigorous on-going
exploration of *how* we do our research" (Kirsch and Ritchie 9). Kirsch and
Ritchie have not found any hard-and-fast solution to or way around the crises
of representation that such explorations can engender, however. Rather, they
choose not to let such crises keep them from doing research they see as important. They write that a "problematized 'politics of location' may seem to make
our task impossible; it may make us wonder if we can claim anything for our
research. But instead of falling into inaction and despair, we move forward
with the awareness that we can only approximate an understanding" of our
locations as researchers (10, emphasis added). Kirsch and Ritchie cannot characterize either the ethic of care or the politics of location, then, as having any
foundation in the sense that we, as academics, have come to understand the
term; they simply offer it instead of the alternative. There can be, it seems, no
theory of pragmatics as such: to be a pragmatist is always to be instead of, not
because of.

Can we say, then, that humanist composition research has come to ethnography in the same way that its social scientific counterpart has? We could only
say that, I think, if it had ended up as a radical form of autoethnography, which
it has not. In fact, although I have argued that the reality principle is present in
both social scientific and humanist treatments of context, I am still working
from an assumption of conflict between these two modes. Ultimately, however,
I do not think the question of how humanism in composition came to ethnography is as important as it is was for my examination of social science. Indeed,
much of my point has been that the most important ethnographic work has
taken place outside of research reports as such. More important here is what
ethnography now has to offer humanist compositionists. At its most basic level,
ethnography offers a site-based methodology—a prerequisite for studying (and,

thus, benefiting) communities—and a receptivity to reflexivity that fits the pragmatic feminist project as outlined in feminist critical ethnographic methodology. Again, then, humanist ethnographic methods seemingly cannot be separated from humanist ethnographic methodology.

CONCLUSION: CONFLICT AND CONVERGENCE

This chapter is based on an assumption of struggle. And although this struggle is not over life and death, it is there. As long as people choose to make knowledge in different ways and from different assumptions, this conflict will exist because new researchers who need to and undoubtedly will imprint on certain methodological and theoretical discourses are always entering the discipline. I do not want to suggest that this can never change, that we cannot reimprint, but I do want to suggest that there are such fundamental issues of identity, of who one is and how one sees the world, involved in such a change that one would need very strong motivation to do so. The "communities" of social science and the humanities in composition, then, are very likely to continue to appear to be communities to those of us in the field, irrespective of their arguable reality as "open, dynamic [bodies]" (Prior *Writing* 21).

As long as that is the case, methodologies such as ethnography will remain sites for playing out disciplinary struggle. Yet, because ethnography is a construct, it cannot ever be won or lost. Neither the humanities nor the social sciences will ever wrest ethnography from the grasp of the other. It is an imaginary, not a real, thing. But imagination has kept us in the academic language game in the first place. The clutches of skepticism are strong, and arguing with a skeptic a dangerous business. It does, indeed, seem to be turtles all the way down. The only way, then, we can suppose we are really communicating with each other is to imagine (or trust) that we are doing so. And, when we imagine that we write, or write about, ethnography, then—although we may be consciously or unconsciously committing ourselves to the disciplinary fray—we also call into being one of the very terms of our commonality.

NOTES

1. See also Lauer and Asher, who note that ethnography derives in part from phenomenology (39), and that it is holistic and naturalistic (46). We can further imply that the authors see ethnography as empirical because they include a discussion of it in their book *Composition Research*.

2. Rhodes, incidentally, sees just this kind of "methodological ambivalence" in Carrie Leverenz's description of her work at one point as "an ethnographic study" and at another as a "microanalysis" (29).

3. See Kirsch and Sullivan (2) and Sullivan and Porter (11), who both posit a distinction between "method" as technique and "methodology" or "methodological orientation" as "the underlying theory and analysis of how research does or should proceed" (Kirsch and Sullivan 2). I argue later in this piece, however, that the distinction is not as clear as it may seem.

4. In this careful sense I want to talk about "social scientific" and "humanistic" discourses in composition ethnography. These terms, rather than labeling phenomena that correspond to an objective reality, function as explanatory figures, tropes that we both interpret and deploy in constructing and representing our discipline.

5. Steven Mailloux writes, for example, that "interpretation functions repeatedly as a politically interested act of persuasion" (50). See also Michael Leff's extended discussion on the relationship between rhetorical production and interpretation in "The Idea of Rhetoric as Interpretive Practice."

6. Geertz is also known for employing traditionally humanist terms to describe ethnography, treating ethnographic writing as literature and anthropologists as authors. See, for example, his *Works and Lives.*

7. Although much critical theory actually articulates the terms of humanism's critique, it does so from within a line of rationalist thought that extends from the humanist tradition. For a discussion of the relationship between critical theory and humanism, see Baumlin, Jensen, and Massey. (More on this later.)

8. Again, I invoke the idea of reception, of how a work is received, as a basis for calling these works ethnographies. Gwen Gorzelsky, for example, implies that Schaafsma's study is an ethnography when she offers it as an instance of the type of critical ethnography Lu and Horner discuss in "The Problematic of Experience" (276). And, although the identity of the author is unclear, it is probably Purcell-Gates herself who refers to her study as "based on an ethnographic study of a nonliterate family" in "The Role of Qualitative and Ethnographic Research in Educational Policy."

9. For another such analysis, see Bazerman (273).

10. Wendy Bishop, for example, writes that to "study teachers as they moved from their pedagogy seminar to their own classrooms, I turned to ethnographic modes of inquiry," whose "hallmark . . . is a researcher's interest in studying the learning or educational process in a cultural context" (xv). Walvoord and McCarthy, moreover, cite the sociolinguistic proposition "that language processes must be understood in terms of the contexts in which they occur" as a key assumption informing their study (21).

11. At this point, I associate humanism with the developments of postmodern, poststructural, and critical theories in English departments. See Baumlin, Jensen, and Massey, who write that although many of these theories may appear to oppose humanist assumptions, they all "seek to explain the nature of the individual *in relation* to forces that influence and threaten to limit one's capacities, beliefs, and actions" (184). They also all seek to understand the possibilities for and conditions of knowing and knowledge, and they do so by the rational apparatus of theory building. Hence, they are all explicitly interpretive.

12. See also Kirklighter, Vincent, and Moxley as well as Farris and Anson for further examples of such collections.

13. This genre appears to be similar to Clifford's "self-reflexive 'fieldwork account,'" (14) although its unique location in composition's problems and conversations warrants an equally unique name.

WORKS CITED

Bakhtin, Mikhail. *The Dialogic Imagination: Four Essays by M. M. Bakhtin.* Trans. Caryl Emerson and Michael Holquist. Austin: U of Texas P, 1981.

Baumlin, James S., George H. Jensen, and Lance Massey. "Ethos, Ethical Argument, and *Ad Hominem* in Contemporary Theory." *Ethical Issues in College Writing.* Ed. Frederic G. Gale, Phillip Sipiora, and James L. Kinneavy. New York: Lang, 1999. 183–219.

Bazerman, Charles. *Shaping Written Knowledge: The Genre and Activity of the Experimental Article in Science.* Madison: U of Wisconsin P, 1988.

Berkenkotter, Carol, Thomas N. Huckin, and John Ackerman. "Social Context and Socially Constructed Texts: The Initiation of a Graduate Student into a Writing Research Community." Center for the Study of Writing Technical Report 33, 1989.

Bishop, Wendy. *Something Old, Something New: College Writing Teachers and Classroom Change.* Carbondale: Southern Illinois UP, 1990.

Blakeslee, Ann M., Caroline M. Cole, and Theresa Conefrey. "Constructing Voices in Writing Research: Developing Participatory Approaches to Situated Inquiry." *Ethics and Representation in Qualitative Studies of Literacy.* Ed. Peter Mortensen and Gesa E. Kirsch. Urbana, IL: NCTE, 1996. 134–54.

Bleich, David. "Ethnography and the Study of Literacy: Prospects for Socially Generous Research." *Into the Field: Sites of Composition Studies.* Ed. Anne Ruggles Gere. New York: MLA, 1993. 176–92.

Brodkey, Linda. "Writing Ethnographic Narratives." *Written Communication* 4 (1987): 25–50.

Brooke, Robert, and John Hendricks. *Audience Expectations and Teacher Demands.* Carbondale: Southern Illinois UP, 1989.

Chin, Elaine. "Redefining 'Context' in Research on Writing." *Written Communication* 11 (1994): 445–82.

Chiseri-Strater, Elizabeth. "Turning In upon Ourselves: Positionality, Subjectivity, and Reflexivity in Case Study and Ethnographic Research." *Ethics and Representation in Qualitative Studies of Literacy.* Ed. Peter Mortensen and Gesa E. Kirsch. Urbana, IL: NCTE, 1996. 115–33.

Cintron, Ralph. "Wearing a Pith Helmet at a Sly Angle: or, Can Writing Researchers Do Ethnography in a Postmodern Era?" *Written Communication* 10 (1993): 371–412.

Clifford, James. "Introduction: Partial Truths." *Writing Culture: The Poetics and Politics of Ethnography.* Ed. James Clifford and George E. Marcus. Berkeley: U of California P, 1986.

Cook, Devan. "Secrets and Ethics in Ethnographic Writing Research." *Foregrounding Ethical Awareness in Composition and English Studies.* Ed. Sheryl I. Fontaine and Susan M. Hunter. Portsmouth, NH: Boynton/Cook, 1998.

Cushman, Ellen. *The Struggle and the Tools: Oral and Literate Strategies in an Inner City Community.* Albany: State U of New York P, 1998.

Dale, Helen. "Dilemmas of Fidelity: Qualitative Research in the Classroom." *Ethics and Representation in Qualitative Studies of Literacy.* Ed. Peter Mortensen and Gesa E. Kirsch. Urbana, IL: NCTE, 1996. 77–94.

Dowdey, Diane. "Citation and Documentation across the Curriculum." *Constructing Rhetorical Education.* Ed. Marie Secor and Davida Charney. Carbondale: Southern Illinois UP, 1992. 330–52.

Farris, Christine, and Chris M. Anson, eds. *Under Construction: Working at the Intersections of Composition Theory, Research, and Practice.* Logan, UT: Utah State UP, 1998.

Gallas, Karen. "'Look, Karen, I'm Running Like Jell-O': Imagination as a Question, a Topic, a Tool for Literacy Research and Learning." *Research in the Teaching of English* 35 (2001): 457–92.

Geertz, Clifford. *Works and Lives: The Anthropologist as Author.* Stanford, CA: Stanford UP, 1988.

Gorzelsky, Gwen. "Reshaping Professionalization." *College Composition and Communication* 52 (2000): 273–78.

Herndl, Carl, and Cynthia A. Nahrwold. "Research as Social Practice: A Case Study of Research on Technical and Professional Communication." *Written Communication* 17 (2000): 258–96.

Kantor, Kenneth J., Dan R. Kirby, and Judith P. Goetz. "Research in Context: Ethnographic Studies in English Education." *Research in the Teaching of English* 15 (1981): 293–309.

Kirklighter, Cristina, Cloe Vincent, and Joseph M. Moxley, eds. *Voices and Visions: Refiguring Ethnography in Composition.* Portsmouth, NH: Boynton/Cook, 1997.

Kirsch, Gesa E. *Ethical Dilemmas in Feminist Research: The Politics of Location, Interpretation, and Publication.* Albany: State U of New York P, 1999.

Kirsch, Gesa E., and Joy S. Ritchie. "Beyond the Personal: Theorizing a Politics of Location in Composition." *College Composition and Communication* 46 (1995): 7–29.

Kirsch, Gesa, and Patricia A. Sullivan. *Methods and Methodology in Composition Research*. Carbondale: Southern Illinois UP, 1992.

Lauer, Janice M., and William Asher. *Composition Research: Empirical Designs*. New York: Oxford UP, 1988.

Leff, Michael. "The Idea of Rhetoric as Interpretive Practice: A Humanist's Response to Gaonkar." *Rhetorical Hermeneutics: Invention and Interpretation in the Age of Science*. Ed. Alan G. Gross and William M. Keith. Albany: State U of New York P, 1997. 89–100.

Lu, Min-Zhan, and Bruce Horner. "The Problematic of Experience: Redefining Critical Work in Ethnography and Pedagogy." *College English* 60 (1998): 257–77.

MacDonald, Susan Peck. *Professional Academic Writing in the Humanities and Social Sciences*. Carbondale: Southern Illinois UP, 1994.

———. "Voices of Research: Choices of a Methodological Community." *Under Construction: Working at the Intersections of Composition Theory, Research, and Practice*. Ed. Christine Farris and Chris M. Anson. Logan: Utah State UP, 1998. 111–23.

Mailloux, Steven. *Reception Histories: Rhetoric, Pragmatism, and American Cultural Politics*. Ithaca, NY: Cornell UP, 1998.

Mortensen, Peter, and Gesa E. Kirsch. *Ethics and Representation in Qualitative Studies of Literacy*. Urbana, IL: NCTE, 1996.

North, Stephen. *The Making of Knowledge in Composition: Portrait of an Emerging Field*. Portsmouth, NH: Boynton/Cook, 1987.

Olson, Gary. "The Death of Composition as an Intellectual Discipline." *Composition Studies* 28:2 (2000): 33–41.

Phelps, Louise Wetherbee. *Composition as a Human Science: Contributions to the Self-Understanding of a Discipline*. New York: Oxford UP, 1988.

Piazza, Carolyn L. "Identifying Context Variables in Research on Writing: A Review and Suggested Directions." *Written Communication* 9 (1987): 107–37.

Pratt, Mary Louise. "Arts of the Contact Zone." *Profession* 91: 33–40.

Prior, Paul A. "Response, Revision, Disciplinarity: A Microhistory of a Dissertation Prospectus in Sociology." *Written Communication* 11 (1994): 483–533.

———. *Writing/Disciplinarity: A Sociohistoric Account of Literate Activity in the Academy*. Mahwah, NJ: Erlbaum, 1998.

Purcell-Gates, Victoria. *Other People's Words: The Cycle of Low Literacy*. Cambridge, MA: Harvard UP, 1995.

———. "The Role of Qualitative and Ethnographic Research in Educational Policy." 2000. *http://www.readingonline.org/articles/purcell-gates/* (12 February 2002).

Rhodes, Keith. "Ethnography or Psychography? The Evolution and Ethics of a New Genre in Composition." *Voices and Visions: Refiguring Ethnography in Composition*. Ed. Cristina Kirklighter, Cloe Vincent, and Joseph M. Moxley. Portsmouth, NH: Boynton/Cook, 1997. 24–36.

Schaafsma, David. *Eating on the Street: Teaching Literacy in a Multicultural Society.* Pittsburgh: U of Pittsburgh P, 1993.

Spigelman, Candace. "Argument and Evidence in the Case of the Personal." *College English* 64 (2001): 63–87.

Sullivan, Patricia A. "Ethnography and the Problem of the 'Other.'" *Ethics and Representation in Qualitative Studies of Literacy.* Ed. Peter Mortensen and Gesa E. Kirsch. Urbana, IL: NCTE, 1996. 97–114.

Sullivan, Patricia, and James E. Porter. *Opening Spaces: Writing Technologies and Critical Research Practices.* Greenwich, CT: Ablex, 1997.

Walvoord, Barbara E., and Lucille P. McCarthy. *Thinking and Writing in College: A Naturalistic Study of Students in Four Disciplines.* Urbana, IL: NCTE, 1990.

Wilder, Laura. "'Get Comfortable with Uncertainty': A Study of the Conventional Values of Literary Analysis in an Undergraduate Literature Course." *Written Communication* 19 (2002): 175–221.

Yancey, Kathleen Blake. "Theory, Practice, and the Bridge Between: The Methods Course and Reflective Rhetoric." *Under Construction: Working at the Intersections of Composition Theory, Research, and Practice.* Ed. Christine Farris and Chris M. Anson. Logan: Utah State UP, 1990. 234–49.

PART V

Texts and (Con)Texts:
Intertextual Voices

15

The Ethics of Reading
Critical Ethnography

MIN-ZHAN LU

THE SO-CALLED ETHICAL TURN in composition has focused attention primarily on the responsibilities of researchers: how they interact with their informants and make use of the information they gather.[1] I'd like to argue here that it is important to consider the ethical responsibility of readers as well: how readers interpret and make use of ethnographic texts. Researchers are not the only ones faced with the need to become more self-reflexive about the politics of representation. Readers of ethnography, too, need to examine the politics of textual reception, the circulation of their reading of individual ethnographies, and the ways they intend to and actually use the knowledge they produce from their reading. We readers need to treat our own preferences for certain ethical turns—meanings as well as forms—as contingent and situated rather than as a set of autonomous and universal laws for ranking the ethical decisions of individual researchers.

As a reader of ethnography, I have an institutionally constructed preference for ethnographic texts embodying the following moves: texts that pay explicit attention to the asymmetrical power relations between researcher and informants and that treat the exchange between the researcher and the informants as having material consequences in the lives of both parties. In my effort to become a more responsible, ethical participant in the project a particular ethnographic text represents, the challenge I face is how to take seriously the different material conditions informing the words and actions of informants, researcher and writers, and individual readers such as myself. And it is with this challenge in mind that I read the pieces included in this collection.

As Bruce Horner argues in "Critical Ethnography, Ethics, and Work: Rearticulating Labor," instead of focusing energy on settling "what" sorts of meanings and forms make an ethnographic text "multivocal" or "self-reflexive," we need to approach issues of ethics in terms of the material social conditions, such as economic conditions and symbolic and physical resources, necessary to produce the kinds of labor involved in the reading as well as writing of such texts. Therefore, instead of treating these features as constituting a "requisite display" or as intrinsically "good," we need to consider not only who is writing but also who is reading and under what specific material social conditions and for what specific purposes (40, 41). Furthermore, Horner urges us to view readers as participants capable of "realizing meanings and values" that differ from those intended by the "author," sharing the responsibility with the writer by contributing to the writer's effort to reflect on the ideological limitations of the research and by locating and inserting alternative voices into their readings (42). We can read Horner's reminder to the writers of ethnography of the labor and agency of the readers of the texts they produce as also a reminder to the readers of ethnography of the reader's ethical responsibility to attend to not only the specific material conditions under which the writer of a specific text conducts field work and produces the text but also the purposes, uses, and audience the writer has in mind. Furthermore, we need to take the responsibility to situate our "dispositions"— taste or distaste—for "multivocal" and "self-reflexive" contents and forms in ethnographic writing within the specific material conditions informing our work as readers and in relation to the particular purposes and uses we intend for a individual ethnographic text. That is, we should become more reflective of the potential difference in material conditions shaping the labor of different participants—the researcher/writer, the informants, the reader—when producing and applying our knowledge concerning a specific subject matter, including the question of where, when, why, and how individual participants hope to use that knowledge.

Let me use Paul Rabinow's *Reflections on Fieldwork in Morocco* to illustrate the challenge I face when trying to become a more self-reflexive reader of ethnographic texts. I have found Rabinow's book gratifying on three accounts.[2] It presents the informant as well as the researcher as active agents negotiating differences and power at all stages of the research process. It presents ethnographic data as a product of such active negotiation rather than merely some sort of "rocks" to be picked up, shipped home, and analyzed in the laboratory. And it presents ethnographic research as having material consequences for the lives of the informants as well as the researcher. For instance, when helping Rabinow determine the range of socioeconomic variation in a village, one informant, Malik, had to do something he was not in the habit of doing: objectify his holdings by totaling up his possessions and making systematic and quantitative comparisons with his neighbors. In being forced to look at his life through the lens of the research objective, Malik realized that although he had perceived and presented himself as a spiritual man of relative poverty, a detailed listing of his possessions indicated that he had been doing quite well economically in recent years. Rabinow thus presents Malik as actively forming an understanding of himself and his village at the friction points of several discursive sites, Moroccan versus Western and village versus social scientific. Rabinow acknowledges the troubling effects his research can have on informants such as Malik, causing them the confusion and discomfort of seeing their naturalized self-knowledge or common-sense world destabilized.

In spite of my admiration for Rabinow's recognition of such ethical dilemmas, my interest in critical ethnography has also led me to expect researchers such as Rabinow to move beyond mere observation of these complications. I wanted to hear Rabinow engage Malik in examining the material consequences such moments of confusion might have on Malik's day-to-day life afterward, especially in terms of the changes in his understanding of himself in relation to his sociopolitical realities and in his participation in those realities. In short, I was disappointed to hear Rabinow claim that for his research in Morocco, observation but not participation and change had to be the governing term.

Consuming Rabinow's book within the ethical framework I value, Rabinow's decision to make observation the governing term might appear "traditional" or even somewhat ethically irresponsible. Yet, if we view ethics as a socially constructed concept rather than an autonomous essence, then it is my responsibility as a reader to contextualize Rabinow's choice of governing term, in the particular material conditions shaping Rabinow's research project. As Rabinow points out, except perhaps for teaching English to the people in the village, he had nothing to "offer" the community: he could not increase agricultural production, cure their diseases, nor get them work. Nothing he could have done to aid the villagers would have differed much from the kind of blatant interference in their affairs for which A.I.D. programs have been criticized. Furthermore, if he had been organizing or advocating antigovernment action, he would have been forced to leave the country or been thrown into jail. In other words, Rabinow's decision to make observation but not participation and change the governing term for his research is itself an ethical turn made in response to the complex, specific material, economic, and political conditions surrounding his project.

Contextualizing the ethical framework of the research can also help readers such as me become more reflexive about the particular subject positionings informing our interest in ethnographic projects that foreground participation and change. As Bruce Horner and I have argued in "The Problematic of

Experience," the kind of critical ethnography we value is particularly cogent for composition teachers interested in emancipatory goals. The educational contract between teachers and students is understood to involve the production of change. So, for composition teachers, the concern to gather information on the students and their educational experiences is inevitably interlocked with the concern for how to use such information to effect change not only in the ways in which students write but also in how they understand the structures of education and participate in them. Attention to the materiality of Rabinow's ethical decision can also work to caution readers like myself to become more vigilant toward our desire to see researchers like Rabinow acting like writing teachers to their informants and to treat an informant such as Malik as if he were a student in the kind of North American composition classrooms I am familiar and invested in. That is, it is my responsibility as a reader to become more self-reflexive toward the particular material conditions shaping my work as a teacher of composition and to not let the materiality of my own ethical concerns subsume the materiality of the researcher's ethical decisions. Rather, the question of how and why researchers such as Rabinow have not taken the ethical turn I value in critical ethnography must be explored in relation to not only the difference in the political goals of researchers but also the different working conditions surrounding the production and the reception of a particular project. We cannot lose sight of that difference when exploring the implications of Rabinow's work in Morocco for our effort to develop critical pedagogy in North American composition classrooms.

In the same spirit, I read many of the pieces in this collection for guidance on how to become more self-reflexive about the material conditions of our work as readers of critical ethnography when wrestling with issues of ethics. For instance, in "Just What Are we Talking About? Disciplinary Struggle and the Ethnographic Imaginary," Lance Massey poses one model of a responsible reading through his analysis of an endnote in a text by Victoria Purcell-Gates. Massey argues that the endnote demonstrates an "allegiance to a social scientific sensibility" (370). But he grounds his conclusion in not only Purcell-Gates's epistemological and ethical concerns but also the writer's need to negotiate disciplinary standards and the standards of publishers such as Harvard University Press (370). Massey then goes on to remind us that "it takes clout to break the rules" (371). Scholars in the early stages of their career do not have the same "opportunities" for conducting "experimental" writing as those who have already paid their professional dues (371). Massey thus reminds us of the ways in which institutional forces enable and constrain disciplinary knowledge production, a useful precaution for readers like myself when assessing the politics of ethnographic texts.

Likewise, Janet Alsup argues in "Protean Subjectivities" that when exploring the use of the personal in qualitative research texts, "it is important to understand not only the reasons for its inclusion but the arguments for its total exclusion from scholarly work" (16). For instance, given the existing structures of the academy, graduate students (and even untenured faculty members) still "developing a 'name' and a right to speak in the profession" risk having their work deemed biased, untrustworthy in analysis, or even sloppy in research design if they bring in a great deal of "personal information" (27). I read Alsup as joining Massey in reminding readers like myself that we have an ethical responsibility to acknowledge the writer's reasons for excluding as well as including "personal information" by considering the professional locations of the researcher/writer and the dispositions of the "prestigious" presses with power to make or break one's professional standing. More specifically, readers like myself need to acknowledge the privileged locations and conditions enabling us to contest "official" dispositions when dealing with such presses or to place our work with alternative presses more disposed toward multivocal, self-reflexive texts.

Christopher J. Keller argues in "Unsituating the Subject: 'Locating' Composition and Ethnography in Mobile Worlds" that instead of trying to fix the priorities of ethnographic work in terms of an either/or question, such as arguing whether the authority of the ethnographer "should" be informed by positivism or postpositivism; whether ethnography "should" be about the ethnographer, the research community, or the surrounding community; whether the ethnographer "should" act as a cultural worker or an objective scientist or whether ethnographers "can" tell the truth when doing so might reflect negatively on the community researched, we should ask "when" and "where" (and I'd add, "why" or "for what purposes") each of these different priorities is feasible, necessary, and needed (280–81). To explore the ethics of reading, we need to join Keller in acknowledging the fact that "certain contexts and research agendas call for certain forms of ethnography and ethnographic practices" (3).

Keller's argument brings to mind Deborah Brandt's argument that, as a researcher, she is interested in collecting life history accounts as a means for theorizing the history of literacy, and she is interested in protecting the privacy of informants willing to disclose their personal lives to a complete stranger in generous and unguarded ways (42–43). The ethical question Brandt wrestles with is the question of when the public's right to theorize literacy becomes an invasion of privacy. Brandt notices from sharing some of her raw interview material with colleagues and graduate students that readers tend to psychologize the informants, turning them into "characters to be analyzed and wondered about" (43). So, when presenting the information she has gathered from her informants, Brandt tries to find a methodology that "subvert[s] readers' psychologizing tendencies" (44). To counteract this tendency, she "break[s] the interview apart, changing it into scores and often hundreds of facts about the social structures and processes that bear on literacy" (43). She tries to "put descriptions of events and thoughts into historical currents of literacy, and from that . . . to build a theory of literacy worthy of the public interest" (43). In doing so, she departs from the concern among some ethnographers to "get the personal more responsibly into their published work" and tries instead to figure out "how responsibly to get [the personal] out" (43).

Deborah Brandt's argument points to another aspect of the material conditions of the production of knowledge we need to consider when exploring the question of how and why individual researchers have chosen to take certain ethical turns but not others. Researchers do not write in a vacuum. Rather, they write in response to very specific and socially constructed reader responses, including the dominant tendency among North American readers to psychologize informants. There is no essential ethical value to a researcher's decision to put the personal into ethnographic research or to get it out. Rather, the ethics of such decisions must be examined in relation to the particular conditions of work informing the research project, including the scale and goal of the project, the nature of the contract between the researcher and the informants, and the kinds of dominant modes of research methodology, textual representation, and reader response active on the social and historical horizon.

It is the responsibility of us as readers of ethnography to become more vigilant about our own situatedness as readers and of the ways in which our dispositions as readers inform the decisions of researcher-writers on how they meet or intervene with readers' likely responses, including the dominant tendency in North America to psychologize the informants. That is, as readers of ethnography, we need to see ourselves, in both our teaching and scholarship, as part of the research project rather than as impartial "readers" and evaluators of it.

I read Robert Brooke and Charlotte Hogg as joining Brandt in calling attention to the active roles readers play in research projects. Brooke and Hogg use Burke's concept of "consubstantiality" to pose two guiding questions for ethnographers in examining their relation to the studied contexts: (1) The identifications established between the ethnographer/participants, ethnographer/implied reader, or ethnographer/participants/implied reader; (2) The extent to which these processes of identification enable separate individuals or groups to "act together" for some common good (165–66). In his discussion of Charlotte's dissertation, Brooke notes her effort to identify with two sets of participants, the older rural Nebraska woman whose literacy practices Charlotte studies and Charlotte's imagined audience, such as feminists and compositionists. And he takes into account Charlotte's efforts to encourage identification between the participants and the implied audience (173). If we see the institutionalized disposition of readers—"compositionists" or "feminists"—as a force informing how the writer goes about initiating "consubstantiality," then vigilance toward how we contribute to—reinforce or revise—the standardized readerly dispositions is one direction for readers to labor over ethical issues. Furthermore, we need to see not only the ways we read that dissertation but also the ways we previously or subsequently interact with ethnographers such as Charlotte, her informants, and her projected audience—other feminists and compositionists—as practices with real effects on the form and content of the dissertation. When reading and in our interactions, we need to join the ethnographer in becoming more vigilant toward forms of "manipulative identifications" (8) that serve the interests of writers (and, I'd add, the readers) of ethnographic texts but not those of the informants. Conversely, we need to become more vigilant toward those standardized readerly dispositions that might interfere with our ability to join the identifications that indeed move us toward actions for the "common good."

The reader's ethical responsibility to function not only as a critical analyst of ethnographic texts but also an agent of change is embedded in Gwen Gorzelsky's "Shifting Figures: Rhetorical Ethnography," where she urges critical ethnographers to pay attention to figurative languages—especially the "embodied metaphors enacted by people [researcher and subjects] in the field," the "language-based metaphors used in the field," and the "figurative language that emerges" as the researcher writes the draft of the ethnographic text. Gorzelsky urges ethnographers to foreground the various sets of metaphors encountered not only by analyzing them but also by weaving them substantively into the narrative (124). Doing so, she argues, can help researchers take stock of how the researcher's and the informants' metaphorics "harmonize, conflict, or remain disconnected." This can enable the researcher to grasp limitations of the relational pattern—the narrow range of possible responses from the participants—resulting from the conflict between the researcher's metaphorics and those her informants (125). This can in turn motivate researchers to change their participation in the social situations they research (102). We can use Gorzelsky's mapping of the ethical concerns of the writer of ethnography to delineate a direction for the reader of such ethnographic texts. Readers need to increase attention to the potential harmony, conflict, or disconnection not only between the metaphorics of the researcher and informants but also between the researcher, informants, and the reader. And we need to increase awareness of not only the researcher and the informants' "foundational premises" (135) and their relational stances toward each other but also the reader's "foundational premises" and relational stances toward both the researcher and the informants. In subsequent readings and interactions, this could also motivate readers to shift and revise how they view, think, talk about, and interact with persons who hold similar values and who work in material circumstances similar to those of the researcher or informants.

The responsibility of the teacher as a reader of ethnographic texts by student writers is at the center of Sally Chandler's "Practicing What Critical Ethnography Teaches: Embracing Partial, Contradictory, Ephemeral Others." Using excerpts from papers written by her students for a community-based writing course, Chandler argues for the need to treat "shortcomings" in texts as information on the complex and conflicting relationships and material conditions informing the text's production. For instance, instead of faulting her student Brenda for "failing" to offer an overt and coherent critique of the American myth of the meritocracy when representing the life history of her writing partner, Dr. Ware, Chandler uses the "failure" to grasp the complex context informing Brenda's fieldwork and writing to probe the potential tension between the context of Brenda's work as a student researcher/writer and the context of Chandler's work as a teacher/researcher/reader. For instance, Chandler takes into consideration Brenda's multiple, partial, and shifting subject positions in respect to the stories of meritocracy embedded in the oral history Dr. Ware renders. And Chandler examines textual representations of Brenda's multiple positions in terms of Brenda's relationship with Dr. Ware, the composition of the course generating Brenda's project—course assignments, other students taking the course and the teacher (Chandler), and Brenda's lived experience as a younger woman and a college student. Then, Chandler takes the responsibility to reflect on her own implication in myths of the meritocracy as a single parent who sees herself as "setting an example for her children in terms of what women can do" (22). And she considers the impact her attitudes toward the myths might have on how she read and ought to read Brenda's paper. Chandler thus poses a method of reading that is reflexive of the materiality of textual production and reception, marking positionality and relationality as multiple, dynamic, and transformative.

In "Debating Ecology: Ethnographic Writing that 'Makes a Difference,'" Sharon McKenzie Stevens uses the concept of "diffraction" (Haraway) to call on ethnographers to "take a preexisting pattern of relationships and temporarily reconfigure it into something new" and to "enter into relationships and make something different out of them" (20). Stevens argues that by embracing diffraction, writers can acknowledge to themselves as well as their readers that they are involved in the creation of partial, situated knowledge. By becoming aware of the contingency and, thus, the politics of their writing, writers can bear fuller responsibility for their agency, treating the knowledge they produce as part of the system they are studying (21). This, Stevens points out, would entail attention to the relationship the writer establishes with the system she studies, with her informants, with the meanings they produce, and with the meanings and representations already current in the system studied. It would also require attention to the institutional and discursive power differentials informing and informed by these relationships. To join the ethnographer's effort to "diffract" along the direction Stevens has spelled out, a responsible reader would have to revise the institutional nervous system (that is, the official disposition of searching for definitive answers to "who" is speaking with or for "whom" about "what"). Instead, we too need to learn to focus attention on the actions and relationships of all participants in the research project. That focus, as Stevens points out, necessarily involves the relationship between ethnographer and the reader (21–22).

Stevens poses a list of questions for ethnographers to use while attending to their relationship with the reader: What meanings about the field site are already available to readers? How will those meanings shape how they interpret what the ethnographer writes? What genre do readers expect from an ethnographic writer? What does the writer hope will be the impact of the knowledge she produces? How can she work within the social constraints that will condition the reception for her work? How does she make the contingencies of her knowledge productions vulnerable to scrutiny (21–22)? These questions, posed for the ethnographer, can also be used by the reader of ethnography to reflect on his or her own implication in the system of meaning constraining the production of ethnographic texts and to reflect on his or her own participation in generating genre expectations and knowledge concerning research subjects. Furthermore, these questions can be used to motivate the reader to enact readings which "diffract"—go against the grain of the writer's projections of the field of reception—by highlighting where the writer tries to make a difference and subverting where the writer is trying to comply with the constraints.

Janet Alsup's call for researchers to recognize her own nonunitary subject positions, to disclose these positions for the purpose of improved communication with participants, and to recognize her participants' subjectivities as similarly complex is also likely to produce texts that would require responsible readers to reflect on and revise their institutionally constructed dispositions, such as the tendency to take an either/or approach toward issues of subjectivity. If, as Alsup argues, the researcher "must be mindful of a real or ideal audience and the multiple positionalities this audience might represent," then it is the responsibility of readers to participate actively in the project by treating the subject positionings of all involved, including the readers' own, as nonunitary and reciprocal. Such forms of reading can in turn shift the researcher's sense of audience and therefore affect how the researcher textualizes the fieldwork produced. For instance, such a reader would not only read John Sylvester Lofty's "State Standards in the United States and the National Curriculum in the United Kingdom: Political Siege Engines against Teacher Professionalism?" for "what" it says about the educational reform policies in the United States and the United Kingdom in relation to two schools (one in the industrial midlands of Derbyshire and the other in Maine). Such a reader would

also have to pay attention to the author's representation of his multiple positionings in relation to the informants, especially because such details in
Lofty's text are so subtly woven with the kinds of information—data and quo-
tations concerning the informants and their lives—frequently populating
"objective" studies. For instance, Lofty introduces the school in Derbyshire as
an "inner-city school that I attended myself in 1989" (183). A thick description of the material conditions of the neighborhood surrounding the Derbyshire school is offered along with details that call attention to the
researcher's current and past relation to the neighborhood, suggesting that the
data he offers is filtered through the lens of a researcher who walks from home
to the site of his fieldwork and holds memories of things heard "as a pupil"
when walking or riding a bus through that part of town (185). Lofty uses
materials gathered through interviews with Mary, a highly experienced
teacher at the Derbyshire school, to argue that quality control in assessments
results in harming the teacher's credibility and professionalism. In the midst
of this analysis, he briefly refers to his "struggle" to "visualize the actual details
of a time-consuming and painstaking process," thus calling attention to the
difference between the material conditions surrounding his own work and
that of teachers such as Mary (191). When using the school in Maine as a case
study to map out the kinds of conditions necessary for teachers to create a professional culture, Lofty weaves in such phrases as "they will need the practitioner knowledge that my own new teachers hungrily and rightly demand"
(216). He thus marks his knowledge of the required conditions as situated
within the context of his own current institutional location and role. A
responsible reader of such a text would have to work with the writer by treating these seemingly "peripheral" details as central information on the situatedness and partiality of the writer's data and conclusions, as knowledge
informed by a set of very specific lived experiences in the past and present.

In "Unsituating the Subject: Locating Composition and Ethnography in
Mobile Worlds," Christopher Keller likewise situates the content and form of
individual ethnographies in the contexts and research agendas of individual
projects. Keller's argument about the nature of ethnographic research on composition students can be used to map out the responsibility of the readers of
such research: instead of assuming that the priority of all ethnographic
research is to render a full account of the "whole culture," we need to consider
the specific contexts and research agendas of ethnography on composition
students and the feasibility and necessity for multisited case studies of individual writing students. That also entails that the reader would pay closer
attention to the extent to which individual research texts "allow us to recognize and emphasize the constant movement and mobility of subjects, identities, and contexts"—prying open sites, physical and nonphysical, for ethnographic investigation (287). For instance, instead of fixing students in

"classrooms," we need to treat representations of sites other than the "classroom" that the writing students "inhabit, dwell in, and move between" (295) as central to rather than irrelevant or peripheral to our understanding of the students' literacy practices. Instead of asking questions such as "what" is the "site" of research, we'll need to ask questions such as "how" are the research sites presented: as static and self-evident or as made, imagined, contested, and enforced by both teacher/researcher and students/informants? How does the research map new sites during fieldwork and in the text? How does the research make connections across the sites? Also, instead of paying attention only to representations of general, consistent connections, we need to treat them as critical representations of the "fleeting" connections (301). For instance, such a reader would take seriously accounts of how students "move" between the multiple sites they inhabit and dwell in, including nonphysical locations such as cyber environments (300) in relation to the constant flux of their sense of identity through these fleeting movements.

In "Changing Directions: Participatory-Action Research, Agency, and Representation," Bronwyn T. Williams and Mary Brydon-Miller argue that working in a responsible and thoughtful manner with informants necessitates that original conceptions of a project may change substantially, especially when community members are engaged in the process and reshape the issue in terms of their interests and values and when researchers see both sides as having knowledge to offer, goals to achieve, and concerns about how knowledge is used and represented (334). The research process and results, including access to and interaction with participants, is also constrained by the material conditions of the participants: "[T]heir obligations of work, family, survival are certainly often more vital to them than the research project" (346). This means that the reader of ethnography that treats informants as equal partners needs to pay serious attention to depictions (or lack of depictions) of the role of the informants. Specifically, the readers need to attend not only to the specific knowledge, goals, interests, and the material conditions enabling or constraining informants' participation in the research but also to the ways in which the researcher interacts with the informants during fieldwork as well as when writing the text. This in turn means becoming vigilant toward letting the reader's own knowledge, goals, interests, and material conditions of work overwrite the researcher's or the informants' when analyzing the ethics of research projects.

Likewise, to read the kind of "critical auto-ethnography" Susan Hanson poses in her article would require that the reader pay serious attention to not only "what" the writer has to say about the self, the informants, and about their shared "culture" but more important, to how the writer "bridges the chasm between the autobiographical Here and the ethnographical There." How does the writer interpret and present the dynamics of self-other engagement during fieldwork and textualization (259)? Furthermore, a reader of critical autoethnography by student writers needs to approach their writing also in terms of the pedagogical practices of the teacher: her assignments as well as her interactions with the student writers during class discussion, conferences, and through written comments on their papers. That is, we need to view the desire of the student/researcher, the teacher, or readers such as ourselves to know more about a particular culture as "interested desire," as situated in the specific material conditions of each participant's discursive practices (Spivak).

In short, the articles in this collection offer a full range of directions on how readers of ethnography might wrestle with issues of ethics when using such texts in teaching or research. Readers of ethnography have a responsibility to become more reflexive about their own situatedness as readers and of the ways in which the conditions of their own work construct their taste and distaste for certain kinds of ethical turns in ethnographic research. As teachers of composition, readers like myself need to be vigilant about how we analyze the ethical framework of a variety of ethnographic research projects conducted under conditions drastically different from the conditions of work with which we are most familiar and in which we are most interested in participating. And we need to sustain this vigilance when writing about and teaching these texts. Readers are neither outside nor above the challenges facing the researcher and informants. We need to take full responsibility for how we participate in the very research projects we "read about." How we labor as readers of ethnography matters.

NOTES

1. I use the word *informants* to highlight the active role participants play in forming and transforming their description of their life, action, thoughts, and feelings during their interaction with the researcher. For more detail, see Lu and Horner.

2. For a more detailed discussion of the book, see Lu and Horner.

WORKS CITED

Alsup, Janet. "Protean Subjectivities: Qualitative Research and the Inclusion of the Personal." *Ethnography Unbound: From Theory Shock to Critical Praxis*. Ed. Stephen G. Brown and Sidney I. Dobrin. Albany: State U of New York P, 2004.

Brandt, Deborah. "Protecting the Personal." "The Politics of the Personal: Storying Our Lives against the Grain." Symposium Collective. *College English* 64 (2001): 42–44.

Brooke, Robert, and Charlotte Hogg. "Open to Change: Ethos, Identification, and Critical Ethnography in Composition Studies." *Ethnography Unbound: From Theory Shock to Critical Praxis.* Ed. Stephen G. Brown and Sidney I. Dobrin. Albany: State U of New York P, 2004.

Chandler, Sally. "Practicing What Critical Ethnography Teaches: Embracing Partial, Contradictory, Ephemeral Others." (unpublished paper)

Gorzelsky, Gwen. "Shifting Figures: Rhetorical Ethnography." *Ethnography Unbound: From Theory Shock to Critical Praxis.* Ed. Stephen G. Brown and Sidney I. Dobrin. Albany: State U of New York P, 2004.

Haraway, Donna J. *Simians, Cyborgs, and Women: The Reinvention of Nature.* New York: Routledge, 1991.

Horner, Bruce. "Critical Ethnography, Ethics, and Work: Rearticulating Labor." *Ethnography Unbound: From Theory Shock to Critical Praxis.* Ed. Stephen G. Brown and Sidney I. Dobrin. Albany: State U of New York P, 2004.

Keller, Christopher J. "Unsituating the Subject: 'Locating' Composition and Ethnography in Mobile Worlds." *Ethnography Unbound: From Theory Shock to Critical Praxis.* Ed. Stephen G. Brown and Sidney I. Dobrin. Albany: State U of New York P, 2004.

Lofty, John. "State Standards in the United States and the National Curriculum in the United Kingdom: Political Siege Engines Against Teacher Professionalism." *Ethnography Unbound: From Theory Shock to Critical Praxis.* Ed. Stephen G. Brown and Sidney I. Dobrin. Albany: State U of New York P, 2004.

Lu, Min-Zhan, and Bruce Horner. "The Problematic of Experience: Redefining Critical Work in Ethnography and Pedagogy." *College English* 60 (1998): 257–77.

Massey, Lance. "Just What Are We Talking About? Disciplinary Struggle and the Ethnographic Imaginary." *Ethnography Unbound: From Theory Shock to Critical Praxis.* Ed. Stephen G. Brown and Sidney I. Dobrin. Albany: State U of New York P, 2004.

Rabinow, Paul. *Reflections on Fieldwork in Morocco.* Berkeley: U of California P, 1977.

Spivak, Gayatri. "Can the Subaltern Speak?" *Marxism and the Interpretation of Culture.* Ed. Cary Nelson and Lawrence Grossberg. Urbana: U of Illinois P, 1988. 271–313.

Stevens, Sharon M. "Debating Ecology: Ethnographic Writing that 'Makes a Difference.'" *Ethnography Unbound: From Theory Shock to Critical Praxis.* Ed. Stephen G. Brown and Sidney I. Dobrin. Albany: State U of New York P, 2004.

Williams, Bronwyn T. and Mary L. Brydon-Miller. "Changing Directions: Participatory Action Research, Agency, and Representation." *Ethnography Unbound: From Theory Shock to Critical Praxis.* Ed. Stephen G. Brown and Sidney I. Dobrin. Albany: State U of New York P, 2004.

16

Beyond Theory Shock

Ethos, Knowledge, and Power in Critical Ethnography

STEPHEN GILBERT BROWN

THIS CHAPTER THEORIZES VARIOUS aspects of the discursive power struggle between ethnographic research and the postmodern critique of it—an analysis with broader implications not only for pedagogies of cultural change but also for the dialectical relation between theory and practice in general. I review critical ethnography's strategic responses to the postmodern critique of traditional positivist ethnography, commencing with its countercritique of postmodern theory and concluding with an assessment of the implications for composition studies. I also map some of the new theoretical, rhetorical, and practical terrain critical ethnography occupies as it moves beyond postmodern criticism into a theoretically-informed critical praxis.

Critical ethnography is not a univocal, but a polyphonic discourse; it is not a unitary and fixed discourse as it was in its positivist incarnation, but multiple and shifting, characterized by what Juan Guerra describes as a "nomadic consciousness." It is deeply informed by the postmodern critique of its positivist predecessor; it is redefining if not reinventing itself, even as it moves beyond that critique into exciting, never before occupied, postpositivist terrains.

In the Crosshairs of the Theoretical Gaze:
The Postmodern Critique of Ethnography

As a discursive relic of a colonial era, it was simply a matter of time before the arcane epistemology of traditional ethnography fell under the critical postmodern gaze.

Postmodern theory found an object worthy of its attention when it turned its critical gaze to the largely unexamined goals, assumptions, and methods of traditional, positivist ethnography. Its critique was as incisive as it was comprehensive, as evidenced by a selective litany of its criticisms: the participant's voice was regularly, if not systematically, subsumed by the ethnographer's, was silenced throughout the research-to-publication process; the entire ethnographic project was univocal and hierarchical, foregrounding the interests of the researcher while ignoring the ambitions of the participant; the ethnographic endeavor unwittingly reinforced negative stereotypes of the exotic Other, who was reduced to object of study while serving the careerist goals of the ethnographer; field research thus often replicated the oppressive effects, if not the material conditions, of colonization, in which the Other found herself not only at the wrong end of a colonial gun but at the short end of an imperial pen; furthermore, the "material conditions of existence" were often omitted from the inquiry, or their inclusion in thick descriptions was unaccompanied by any concern for their transformation in an inquiry that privileged "scientific objectivity" over social progress and the acquisition of knowledge over the colonial effects of the knowledge-making process. Furthermore, the claims to objectivity of the positivist paradigm were called into question, as was its habitual practice of putting the ethnographic Self under erasure. Theory lamented and lambasted the purported "textual absence" of the ethnographer. As Brooke and Hogg observe in "Open to Change," "arrival in the field was followed by willed removal or withdrawal to a more distant 'scientific' stance." While purporting to be about the Other, positivist ethnography was in reality all about the ethnographic Self, which it nevertheless pretended to efface. Knowledge of the Other was but a means of asserting a narcissism of the ethnographic self, to produce writing that privileged the Self even in the act of representing the Other, that was self-serving in its careerist orientations and outcomes. Consequently, the Other was silenced even in the act of being represented, was put under erasure even while under study.

Postmodern theory has demonstrated that claims of scientific objectivity in the knowledge-making industry were as mythical as they were unethical. How, they ask, can an ethnographic Self ever definitively represent the Other, as implied by claims of epistemological authority? As Bruce Horner succinctly asserts in "Critical Ethnography, Ethics, and Work," the postmodern critique of traditional ethnography, "highlights the partiality and historicity of knowledge and experience." Postmodern theory invalidated not only the goals and methods, but one of the fundamental assumptions of ethnographic inquiry: that "knowledge" is a de facto, transcendent, a priori signified that can be discovered and possessed through observation. In contradistinction, postmodern critics theorize knowledge as something that is negotiated between knowledge-makers, that is not "found" but constructed, linguistically. Knowledge is language and language is social. Knowledge is not only the shadow of a sign, but also dwells in the shadows between signs, dwells in and between and beyond the signifying chains that can only always and forever represent it in its partiality. This view of the knowledge-making process undermines the ontological and epistemological claims of positivist ethnography, which asserts definitive and objective representations of the Other, which are in essence partial and subjective.

The effects of this postmodern critique have been pronounced, rendering traditional ethnography virtually impracticable and placing its practitioners in a bind from which they are struggling to liberate themselves. Postmodern theory has refocused the ethnographic gaze, not only toward the ethnographic Self, but toward the ethics of its means and the politics of its ends. Instead of knowledge about the Other, the ethics of the knowledge-making process has become the focus of ethnographic inquiry. Instead of being an end in itself, studying the Other is now merely the means to a greater political end: altering the material conditions of oppression.

The effect, as Sharon McKenzie Stevens observes, has been toward a more "ethical and self-aware ethnographic authority," which has altered "the possibilities of representation and knowledge production." Goals, methods, and assumptions have all been reconfigured. Stevens continues: the "old anthroppological ideal of definitively describing . . . a studied culture is now considered unobtainable," so thoroughly has the postmodern critique "altered our view of culture as a 'static system' that can be unproblematically objectified." This critique has exploded the positivist binary of observer-participant with theoretical claymores, calling into question not only the claims, but also the ethics of the positivist knowledge-taking apparatus.

Perhaps theory's most debilitating effect on ethnographic inquiry is the tyranny of a set of seemingly contradictory imperatives, one of which has produced a "crisis of representation." How can the ethnographer exist without representing the Other? Are representation of the Other and ethnographic inquiry mutually exclusive? Can the ethnographer foreground his or her presence without further marginalizing the Other? Or is such self-reflexivity inherently narcissistic and inevitably exclusionary? Ethnographers, consequently, find themselves trapped in the double bind of this imperative to acknowledge their own presence without further marginalizing participant voices. If each act of speaking is also an act of silencing, the question arises: can the ethnographer speak at all? This has produced an epidemic of "theoretical anxiety," or theory shock, amongst ethnographers. As Horner observes, the postmodern critique "has placed an impossible set of responsibilities on the shoulders of the critical ethnographer."

Ethnographers are evolving "alternate strategies for responding to this dilemma" (Horner). What is emerging from the rhetorical ruins of this critique is something altogether different, and yet the same. It still goes by the name of ethnography, although that is where the similarity ends. Ethnographers have abandoned the old goals, assumptions, and methods for new ones adapted to the rigorous ethical imperatives of the postpositivist moment. It is protean, renascent, and liberatory. It is ethical, political, and social. It has reestablished the vital link between theory and praxis, among ethos, knowledge, and power. A new dialectic is emerging between critical praxis and postmodern theory—one that revitalizes possibilities of altering material conditions and hierarchical, asymmetrical power relations through an emerging solidarity between ethnographer and participant.

ETHNOGRAPHY'S RESPONSE:
DIALECTICS, DISCOURSE, AND POWER

How critical ethnographers are reinventing their craft to meet the imperatives of postmodern theory is one of the most interesting and instructive struggles in composition studies. Their responses are as significant as they are diverse. They are, for instance, using theory to reinvent praxis even as theory was deployed to invalidate positivist practice. Additionally, critical ethnographers are countering postmodern criticism with criticisms of their own, calling into question the claims and assumptions of theory itself, critiquing its tendency toward rhetorical overkill, exposing its own contradictions and questionable ethics, articulating limits to the postmodern polemic. If theory brought an ax for chopping down ethnography, then critical ethnographers are setting about the work of reinventing it with the saws of signification, converting positivist practice into critical praxis: one in which the ethnographer is more reflexive, the process more dialogic, and the outcomes more political.

Critical ethnography is synthesizing the personal and the political. It has personalized and politicized ethnography in ways the positivist paradigm prevented. Further, it is generating antithetical tensions to the theses of the postmodern critique, and the result is an emerging hybrid of theory and praxis, of the personal and the political. The incompatibility of positivist practice and postmodern theory has given way to the reintegration of theory and praxis in critical ethnography, as it evolves out of theory a new praxis. Reacting to the postmodern critique, these researchers have personalized, socialized, and politicized ethnographic inquiry, creating a praxis that is informed by "collaboration, multi-vocality and self reflexivity" (Horner). Finally, new methods, goals, and assumptions require a new language. Consequently, critical ethnographers are adopting new signifying practices to define their praxis: a praxis informed by the theoretical imperatives of the postmodern critique, which gestures toward the social, the political, and the personal, and in which logos is infused with ethos.

In the aftermath of the postmodern assault, ethnography has undergone a discursive diaspora. It now flourishes under the sign of the fugitive, the exilic, the nomadic, the dispossessed and the repossessed. Its nascent, post-critical signifying practices are nothing if not strategies of Self possession—oriented toward the reclamation of an ethnographic Self evacuated by post-modern theory, toward the regeneration of a Self that is not theoretically determined, but linguistically and ethnographically protean. An element of mobility has always been associated with ethnography given the necessity of remote field sites. Now it is redefining the concept of "field site," broadening and configuring it to meet the imperatives of postmodern theory, to include linguistic sites and site-specific discourse communities within the country, the community, and the classroom.

Critical ethnography is confounding theory with its fugitive signs, even as it refocuses its critical gaze on the signifying practices of site-specific discourse communities, from the realms of labor and academe to corporate and rural America. As the chapters in this collection evidence, if postmodern theory has evacuated positivist ethnography of its content, of its goals, assumptions, and methods, then something vital and imperishable has escaped: a fugitive spore that, alas, has found fertile, if foreign, ground beyond the chains of postmodern signification. Ethnography in this postpositivist moment has foregrounded ethos in both the making of knowledge and the ends it serves, which inevitably involve the democratic redistribution of power through culture.

Critical ethnography is effectively waging a liberatory struggle of countercriticism against postmodern theory—talking back, as it were, to the theoretical discourse that would master it. In the process, it is liberating praxis from theory, as it takes possession of a new ethnographic Self that is in fact not one, but many selves, not a unified, fixed, autonomous Self, but a multiple, nomadic, dialogic Subject whose inquiries, as these chapters evince, are dispersed across a broad spectrum of field sites. Yet, of all ethnography's diverse responses to postmodern criticism, perhaps its own countercritique has had the most liberatory effect.

SIGN/COUNTERSIGN: ETHNOGRAPHY'S
CRITIQUE OF POSTMODERN THEORY

Power circulates in discourse and when power is possessed, it is wielded—as
it was by the postmodern critique of positivist ethnography, which by virtue
of its uncritically examined assumptions, methods, and aims was vulnerable to
such an overdue and systematic dismantling of its practice: one that not only
called into question the validity of ethnographic research, but threatened it
with extinction as well. The ethnographic response evidences the imperishable
impulse of resistance, the tendency of discourse to be always and forever
dialectical instead of absolutely dominant, as Giroux repeatedly and eloquently reminds us in *Theory and Resistance in Education* (recently revised and
expanded, 2001). Ethnography's "back talk" to postmodern theory evidences
the dialectical nature of all discourse, revealing the power dynamics between
residual, dominant, and emerging discourses. The operation of these three discourses is never absolute and disjoined, but dialectical and concomitant. They
are always in play with each other, as evidenced by the interplay of positivist
ethnographic discourse, the postmodern critique of it, and an emerging postpositivist, ethnographic discourse. Postcolonial discourse can be particularly
useful for understanding the dialectical tension between this postmodern critique and critical ethnography, which I am positing as a tension that is always
in play between dominant and emerging discourses. There is, moreover,
between competing discourses a struggle for power: between a tendency
toward the absolute power of a dominant discourse and a countertendency
toward the liberatory agency of an emerging discourse, which is not only
brought into existence by the dominance of the first, but also enervated by it.
This is evident in the emerging dialectic between critical ethnography and the
postmodern critique of traditional positivist ethnography.

Critical ethnography is deeply engaged in a discursive struggle for its own
agency, if not survival, as evidenced by the vitality and resourcefulness of its
countercriticism of postmodern theory. This countercriticism has finally contained the postmodern assault in the process facilitating its own liberatory
break out into new linguistic and research terrains. A discourse whose signs
were initially defined by the signs they countered is now emerging into the
autonomous and liberatory spaces of a new ethnographic Self, posited in dialogic relationship to research participants, oriented toward the liberatory
redistribution of power, often in new, rhetorically configured field sites. Before
proceeding, I would like to analyze the assertions of this countercritique,
which if not the first, is nevertheless one of the most significant responses of
critical ethnography to the mandates of postmodern theory.

As evidenced by the emerging arguments of its practitioners, critical
ethnography is rediscovering its own critical voice in dialectical engagement

with the polemics of postmodern discourse. At the leading edge of this countercritique are theorists such as Bruce Horner, who are calling into question some of the fundamental assumptions driving the postmodern critique, including its reliance on the Myth of the Lone Ethnographer. In contradistinction to the claims of postmodern critics, Horner asserts that all ethnography is collaborative in nature, particularly when viewed from a cultural materialist perspective. Ethnography, Horner avers, is no different from any other form of labor and no less social in nature. Like any labor, it does not occur in a social vacuum, but is the result of many collaborations at every phase of the production of knowledge, from its construction to its consumption. Horner posits the critical ethnographer as a laborer, and his work as a material practice "aimed at altering the physical and social environment."

Horner's countercritique provides a more nuanced view of the ethnographic Self than the reductive representations of the postmodern critique, which seek to contain all ethnographers under the misleading sign of the Lone Ethnographer operating in a social vacuum. Collaboration in the field is the means by which knowledge is constructed. Collaboration between writer, participants, editors, publishers, reviewers, and indirectly with the readers also characterizes the construction of knowledge in the post field-site phase. Throughout this knowledge-making process, meaning is made dialectically, through dialogue with others. It is less univocal than polyphonic. Its methods are inherently collaborative. In contrast to the reductive claims of the postmodern critique, Horner provides a nuanced problematic of the collaborative ideal that recuperates some of the epistemological and ontological terrain lost to the critique of positivist ethnography.

Horner's criticism exposes an egregious, if ironic, contradiction in the postmodern polemic. While calling into question the ethics of ethnographic representations of the Other, criticism ignores the reductive tendencies of its own representations of the Lone Ethnographer—engendering its own "crisis of representation." The question arises: should the critic and theorist be held to the same ethical imperative as the researcher—a point that Lu raises in "The Ethics of Reading Critical Ethnography." Are the representations of postmodern critics as guilty of reinforcing negative stereotypes as the signifying practices of the positivist ethnographer they criticize? Reductive representations such as the Lone Ethnographer reinscribe the signifying practices of colonizing discourses by assigning an economy of subject positions to the signified—in this instance, the ethnographic Self. All ethnographers are the Same, contained under the simplified and debilitating sign of the Lone Ethnographer. He who lives by the signifying sword sometimes dies by it. By exploding the myth of the Lone Ethnographer and exposing the underlying contradictions of the postmodern critique, Horner provides a more enabling view of the ethnographic Self.

The efficacy of these countercritiques is enabling critical ethnography to elucidate a radical episteme and a collaborative ontology that is at once informed by the ethical imperatives of theory even as it moves beyond the reductive limitations of it. The what, how, and why of ethnographic knowledge has been radically influenced by this postmodern polemic—and by ethnography's liberation from it: a liberation effected largely through signification. Countercritiques such as Horner's revise our assessment of the postmodern attack on ethnographic inquiry: instead of deterministic and absolute, that influence is proving to be protean and dialectical. Initially debilitating, it is now proving to be protean, as ethnography recovers from the "theory shock" of the postmodern assault, finds that it is still a viable mode of research, reconfigures its goals, methods, and assumptions to privilege cultural actions, dialogic processes, and constructed knowledges—across a broad spectrum of research sites, adjusts to the postmodern "crisis of representation" and assimilates into its methodologies and goals the implied ethical imperatives of postpositivist praxis.

In a word, ethnography is exposing the limitations of a critique that so effectively exposed its own. It is moving toward a more dialectic engagement with theory and a more dialogic solidarity with participants. These countercritiques are enabling insofar as they comprise a linguistic fire wall that frees critical ethnographers from the disabling imperatives of postmodern criticism, liberating them into new epistemological and ontological terrains. The evolution of this radical, postpositivist episteme begins with the reconfiguration of its ends.

BEGINNING AT THE END:
THE POLITICS OF CULTURAL CHANGE

In response to the ethical imperatives of criticism, critical ethnography has radically altered its goals. The desired outcomes have shifted from the career-oriented pursuit of knowledge about the Other to fostering political agency with the Other. The acquisition of knowledge about the Other is now yoked to the political empowerment of the Other. Knowledge, instead of being an end in itself, is now the means to a political end; instead of solely serving the interests of the ethnographer, it now serves the needs and interests of the participant. The study of the Other is only justified if it is somehow linked to the transformation of oppressive material conditions. In this context, the theories and praxis of Paulo Freire manifest their relevance to critical ethnographers. Critical ethnography is thus situated at the intersection of radical pedagogy and postmodern theory.

Praxis must be used as a tool for building freedoms not just as a means of extracting knowledge. It must become a "context-fortifying" discourse as opposed to a knowledge-extracting enterprise. It must forego its concern with extractable knowledges that it converts into books and articles to further its own ends, in favor of an interest in cultural change, in the liberatory redistribution of power. Knowledge should no longer be viewed as just another "extractable resource." As Bronwyn T. Williams and Mary Brydon-Miller assert, the focus of critical ethnography is "social inequality and economic disparity as they affect our classrooms and communities." It is, in the last analysis, enervated by a spirit of community activism. Its goal, as Brooke and Hogg assert, should be the development of "cultural action." The critical ethnographer seeks for ways to link ethnographic knowledge-making to political struggle, to position herself "within the complex of relations that constitute the cultural logics." The new aim, as Stevens asserts, is "analysis of cultural logics" and to "craft a more ethical and self-aware ethnographic authority." John Lofty endorses this political orientation, asserting that critical ethnography "explores key themes of power, resistance, identity politics and liberation," and represents ethnogrpahers as "researchers for change." Gwen Gorzelsky similarly asserts that critical ethnography is concerned with "cultivating systematic change."

Intervention in the uneven and undemocratic distribution of power is now posited as an ethical imperative of ethnographic inquiry. The aim, as Gorzelsky asserts is to "cultivate systematic change by using our work with others to better see and change ourselves." This dramatic reconfiguration of ethnographic goals has been accompanied by a transformation of the ethnographic process.

METHODS OUT OF MADNESS: TOWARD A DIALOGIC PRAXIS

Responding to the ethical imperatives of criticism that have raised a host of "metamethodological issues," critical ethnographers are reinventing the methods of their praxis (Massey). Their adjustments to criticism are altering the dynamics of the observer-participant relation, which is now less hierarchical, more dialogic. In contradistinction to its positivist tendencies, the ethnographic knowledge-making process is now characterized by an emergent and empowering reciprocity between participants and observer. Consequently, a new dialogic pragmatism is emerging, reflecting a fundamental shift in attitude toward participants as collaborators and coinvestigators, evidencing a commitment "to enact a dialogic encounter between researcher and subject" (Gorzelsky).

This new critical praxis is grounded in social solidarity with the Other, in the ethical concerns of cultural change. It uses knowledge not to advance the career of the knowledge-taker, but to transform the material conditions that degrade the lived reality of the participant. Here is where critical ethnography derives its ethical mandate, brings praxis, logos, and ethos together. As Horner asserts, ethnographers are responding to the "call for reimagining research practice as 'praxis' that is responsive to the local research site," that is "context fortifying" as opposed to knowledge-extracting in its orientation.

Critical ethnography is not only being influenced by postmodern criticism, but is being informed by "feminist pragmatism," by what Massey characterizes as an "ethics of care." The story of ethnography in this postpositivist moment is largely the story of "how humanism in composition came to ethnography"—and to its methodologies in particular. As Horner observes, "the Other can now speak in the text," can write collaboratively with the observer, who has broken away from the "univocality of research." If its methods are characterized by this "dialogic process," its goals are similarly to be achieved through "collaborative cultural action" (Brooke and Hogg).

This concern with yoking research to cultural action not only gestures toward Freirean praxis but is reflected in the signifying practices with which critical ethnographers are defining their praxis, as evidenced by descriptions such as "Participatory-Action Research" (Williams and Brydon-Miller). The construction of knowledge is not only assumed to be "relational," but also its outcomes political (Stevens). Knowledge is produced through dialogue between invested parties. This is "relationship conscious" ethnography. It is not an act of analysis but of interpenetration insofar as ethnographic inquiry is doubly sheathed in the experience of the ethnographer and in the lived reality of the participant, which are brought into dialectical contact in this knowledge-making process. Knowledge is, therefore, the outcome of a "web of relations": a collaborative effect that is a precondition for collaborative cultural action.

Furthermore, such a theoretical framework validates a project-oriented praxis as the primary means to the social construction of knowledge. The efficacy of such a community-based, project-oriented praxis is evidenced in the recent work of critical ethnographers such as Brooke and Hogg. They posit the "community project" as the ideal vehicle for realizing the ends of critical ethnography insofar as it privileges a methodology grounded in cooperation between participants and observer, as opposed to its positivist predecessor that reinscribed a master-slave dialectic by placing the observer in an active position and the participant in a passive position with respect to the knowledge-making process. In this reinscription of Freirean praxis, participants are engaged as collaborators and coinvestigators of community problems, the analysis and mitigation of which constitute termlong projects, wherein the field site is extended from the classroom into the community, where classroom and community are brought into dialectical contact. This is a project-oriented approach toward a problem posing, problem solving ethnographic inquiry.

Furthermore, it is a praxis with obvious implications and applications for the emerging discourse of ecoethnography, where students "examine the ecology" of a local place in historical, legal, and scientific contexts, intervening in disputes between conservationists and economic stakeholders over water rights, logging, fishing, the reintroduction of wolves, or the recreational use of wilderness areas (Stevens). Critical ethnography is, in the final analysis, a relationship-conscious and a "place-conscious" mode of inquiry.

REORGANIZING THE SELF IN THE FIELD

Critical ethnography has responded to this crisis of representation not only by politicizing its goals and by socializing its methods, but also by personalizing its narratological voice. Positivist ethnography has had virtually every aspect of its practice called into question by criticism, including its tendency to put the ethnographic self under erasure in the name of scientific objectivity. This critique has generated some fundamental questions among enthographers who wonder "what form of self reflexivity to adopt and to what purpose" (Stevens). The immediate effect of this criticism has been an overabundance of narratives foregrounding the personal experience of the ethnographer: a sort of narratological land rush in which ethnographers jumped aboard this bandwagon of the personal. This in turn has led to the additional, if somewhat contradictory, criticism that ethnography is now narcissistic in its self-reflexivity. By overreacting to criticism it has further marginalized or silenced the voice of the Other while foregrounding its own. Converting the absence of the ethnographic Self into a narratological presence has only amplified the absence of the Other. Criticism has thus placed critical ethnographers in a debilitating bind, creating a crisis of representation from which they are struggling to extract themselves. On the one hand they are criticized for putting the ethnographic Self under erasure; on the other they are attacked for foregrounding the experience of the ethnographer. Where to turn and what to do to escape this seeming critical bind?

Theory, criticism, and signification have enabled the critical ethnographer to escape this bind into a liberatory praxis. Criticized equally for omitting and including the Self in narratives, critical ethnographers have slipped the seeming noose of this double bind through countercriticisms of their own. Hanson, for example, argues that all writing is narcissistic, even non–self-reflexive discourse, proffering a more nuanced analysis than the reductive representations of the self-reflexive-ethnographer-as-narcissist proselytized by postmodern criticism, a complementary stereotype to the myth of the Lone Ethnographer. Countercritiques such as Hanson's liberate ethnographers from the seeming bind of self reflexive representations. If narcissism is a given of all writing, then the self-reflexive ethnographer is no more narcissistic than the postmodern critic.

Having effectively countered the criticism of self-reflexive narcissism, critical ethnography is adopting and developing narrative strategies that are openly, unapologetically, and partially self-reflexive. Forswearing all claims to objectivity, they are developing and deploying new signifiers that reflect their assumptions of a constructed knowledge. Ethnographers are, in the words of Hanson, acknowledging "that position affects perspective." Renouncing the positivist stance of the ethnographer as an objective determiner of knowledge, they have instead situated the ethnographic Self in a dialectic space that foregrounds theories of "positionality." Textual absence has given way to the "explicit presence of the ethnographer in representing practices" (Stevens). This is evidenced by the turn away from the objective and toward the subjective in general and by the proliferation of "arrival stories" and "autoethnographies" in particular.

Critical ethnographers are converting a false absence into an explicit presence under the sign of the personal, the subjective, and the autoethnographic, which adds another form of discourse to ethnography, creating a narrative which might be more usefully thought of as a "heteroglossic performance" (Hanson). Critical ethnographers are expanding the terrain of inquiry from the experiential and the political into the rhetorical, from the material into the symbolic, from the World into the Word, from the signified into the signifying, from a concern with the effects of analysis into the politics of representation. The ethnographic Self is now a sign that floats freely between the personal and the social, that lives and breathes in the dialectic space between the symbolic and the material, between the signified World of the Other and the signifying Word of the Self.

It has escaped the signifying shackles of a reductive criticism that contained it under the sign of the Lone Ethnographer, or "the objective scientist" into a free-floating, self-signifying agency across a spectrum of dialectic spaces it is discovering between the material and the symbolic. It is proliferating across a field of subject positions under the signs of "rhetorical ethnography" (Gorzelsky) ,"cultural materialist ethnography" (Horner), "autoethnography" (Hanson), "participatory-action research" (Williams and Brydon-Miller), "community-based, project-oriented ethnography" (Brooke and Hogg), "ecoethnography" (Stevens)—all converging under the sign of "critical ethnography." While talking back to criticism in its own tongue, it is simultaneously moving beyond the limits and constraints of postmodern theory into new dialectical terrain between the widely dispersed, yet inherently related signs of the personal and the political, the autonomous and the relational, privileging a relationship-driven, resistance-oriented research. It explores the dialectical tensions between the "lived textuality" of ethnographic writing and the "lived experience" of its participants, including the experience of the ethnographer (Reiff). Favoring a "politics of location" (Stevens), it constructs knowledges not as ends in themselves but as means to "social actions" (Reiff).

Furthermore, this tendency to foreground the explicit presence of the ethnographer has been accompanied by a similar tendency to privilege the presence of the participant. Thus, a Self-Other dyad formerly characterized respectively by a false and a genuine absence has been transformed into a relationship privileging a double presence. This has revolutionized the emerging discourse of critical ethnography. In the final analysis, ethnography has renounced an apolitical, scientific, hierarchical "objectivity" that never was for a more political, social, collaborative subjectivity oriented toward what might be.

Critical ethnography is therefore uniting the political and the personal, is tending toward political solidarity with the Other "without concealing what we learn about ourselves in the process." If it foregrounds the Other as a collaborator, it also seeks to "to locate the self as a subject," in the process discovering new spaces for itself in the field (Hanson). As evidenced by all these signifying strategies, critical ethnographers are occupying new narratological topoi.

In this postpositivist moment, the ethnographic Self has been reconstructed, if not reinvented. The ethical imperatives of criticism have generated a new organization of the Self in the field. It is a researching Self sensitive to the political interests of participants and committed to altering the material conditions that oppress participants. Furthermore, as the recent work of critical ethnographers shows, the ethnographic Self is not fixed and unitary but multiple and nomadic, proliferating across a continuum of research sites and occupying a broad spectrum of subject positions. In contradistinction to the reductive representations of the Lone Ethnographer and the "narcissistic ethnographer" imposed on them by theory, critical ethnographers are representing the ethnographic Self across a complex continuum of subject positions.

Ethnography's ability to signify itself not as one but as many is but one of the signifying strategies it has adopted to ensure its survival in the face of the postmodern assault on virtually every aspect of its assumptions, goals, and methods. It is, moreover, a strategy similar to that adopted by the Other when confronted by the reductive signifying practices of the dominant culture. Ethnography, by virtue of its inherent multiplicity and nomadism, has slipped the chains of postmodern signification. In the grasp of an essentializing postmodern discourse, (the Lone Ethnographer) ethnography has proven itself too slippery to be reductively contained. Like any subject, the critical ethnographer is endowed with a slippery multiplicity that resists reductive theoretical representations. What is emerging is a revised sense of the ethnographic Self, not as autonomous but as connected, not as detached from but as related to: a Self that is relational, dialogic, infused with a new, living dialectic between observer and participant, theory and practice, field site and classroom.

SIGNS OF STRUGGLE: THE REVOLUTION OF REPRESENTATION

Signification, as evidenced by the ethnographies of this collection, is playing a significant role in critical ethnography's liberatory struggle against postmodern theory. In this section I will selectively develop the implications of these signifying practices, which have transformed a deterministic theoretical monologue into a liberatory dialectic between theory and praxis. Signification is giving birth to a dialectic that is recuperating a measure of agency for critical ethnography. The word is liberating ethnography from the deterministic constraints of criticism into the protean spaces of praxis. Under a host of self-signifying signs, critical ethnography is transforming a crisis of representation into a revolution of representation, liberating new spaces for itself through a renascent dialectic between the material and the symbolic. A liberatory fusion of ethos, knowledge, and power is emerging from the dust of theoretical (con)fusion, ensuring the disciplinary survival, authority, and integrity of critical ethnography.

Signs of this struggle are evident in the struggle over "signs" in general, and over the sign of the "ethnographer" in particular, as postmodern theorists and critical ethnographers alike grapple over its meaning and usefulness in a linguistic contest to see who determines what ethnography means, how it is represented to the world, by whom, and for what purposes. Ethnographers are demanding a say in naming their own discursive terrain, as opposed to having it reductively represented for them by postmodern theory. Postmodern criticism has not been able to name absolutely the ethnographer nor tame the ethnographic tongue, now enunciating anew its own experience in a voice as critical as it is liberatory.

These signs of ethnography's liberatory struggle against the discourse of postmodern theory are evident in the proliferating signs it invents to "say its own world," in dialectic tension with the signs deployed to name and contain it by postmodern theory. In this discursive power struggle between theory and praxis, signification (whether proactive or reactive; accurate or reductive; hyperbolic or resistant; residual, dominant, or emergent) is a key player. The site of struggle is grounded in the rhetorical every bit as much as in the cultural or material.

Adapted to the rigors of new ethical imperatives, the critical ethnographic sign is emerging as a mobile, nomadic, politicized, and self-determining component of a dialectical praxis. Informed by the postmodern critique of objectivist claims to knowledge, critical ethnography is deploying a host of new signs to enunciate its reconfigured praxis and the repositioning of the ethnographic Self relative to knowledge. Under the self-reflexive signs of "diffraction" and "filter," critical ethnographers such as Hanson and Brooke and Hogg are acknowledging the deterministic effect of the ethnographic subject in the construction of knowledge. Under the sign of the "dialogic" and the "relational," critical ethnography is liberating the Self from a self-imposed isolation into a collaborative and transformative solidarity with the Other. Under the signs of the "political" and "cultural action," it is redefining its goals. Under the sign of the "nomadic," it is slipping the signifying chains of negative stereotypes such as the Lone Ethnographer. Under the sign of the "rhetorical," ethnography is expanding its concept of field site beyond the cultural and the material. As evidenced by all these signs, language and experience are converging to produce not only new texts but also new possibilities of lived reality, where the rhetorical, the cultural, and the political are usefully informing and altering one another. This is the protean vision that authorizes critical ethnography, and these are the generative signs with which it seeks to liberate itself into the world, and to bring forth the world from within itself, in a quest to narrow the gap between the possibilities and the realities of democracy.

CONCLUSION: IMPLICATIONS FOR COMPOSITION STUDIES

As the pieces in this collection evidence, critical ethnography is a resilient discourse with much to contribute to composition studies and to the liberatory struggle for cultural transformation. It has not only weathered the postmodern critique of traditional positivist ethnography, but also is contributing a sophisticated, nuanced, and liberatory critique of its own that has forced a reassessment of postmodern criticism, exposing its contradictions, challenging its assumptions, and identifying its limitations. The liberatory effects of this countercritique are evidenced in the critical praxis that is emerging: a praxis deeply informed by postmodern theory even as it moves beyond it into new rhetorical and material domains. This praxis privileges goals that are oriented toward liberatory ends, methods that are grounded in collaborative solidarity between ethnographers and participants, and is driven by epistemological and ontological assumptions that foreground the dialectic construction of knowledge, in which the personal and political, the rhetorical and the material, are conjoined. Critical praxis has liberated the ethnographic Self from the debilitating stereotype of the Lone Ethnographer into a free-floating signifier that nomadically occupies many ethnographic subject positions, under many signs, circulating between the dialectical poles of the personal and the social, the rhetorical and the cultural. Additionally, critical ethnography is inventing new signifying systems to liberate itself not only from the arcane constraints of positivist ethnography, but from the sometimes reductive, occasionally contradictory and often debilitating binds of postmodern theory. As these chapters evince, it is evolving a new ethnographic lexicon under the signs of the "nomadic," "autoethnography," "ecoethnography," "diffraction," "filter," "praxis," and "positionality," to name but a few. These signs were necessitated by and are adapted to the ethical imperatives of the postpositivist moment.

The decades-long silence of the Other by positivist ethnographic practice has finally been broken, a discursive spell whose passing we should all celebrate, and for the shattering of which we are indebted to postmodern theory. Critical ethnography owes an immeasurable debt to postmodern theory for problematizing positivist practice, for its liberatory effort to humanize, socialize, and politicize ethnographic inquiry, for its ethical resolve to rescue ethnography from the self-serving ends of science, to resituate it within the realm of the political, the cultural, and the rhetorical, to serve not the academic ends of knowledge but the political ends of cultural action. Ethnography cannot but be ennobled by this theoretical and pragmatic transformation of positivist practice into a critical praxis that is more reflexive, collaborative, and transformative, that has transformed a monologic discourse into a dialogic conversation whose ends are social and political. Lacking this active component, ethnography, like all education, devolves into an academic exercise with no impact on or connection to the problematic world beyond the classroom. It is now ready to play its part as a problem-posing, Freirean praxis in the broader liberatory struggle for social transformation and the democratic redistribution of power.

WORKS CITED

Brooke, Robert, and Charlotte Hogg. "Open to Change: Ethos, Identification, and Critical Ethnography in Composition Studies." *Ethnography Unbound: From Postmodern Theory Shock to Critical Praxis.* Ed. Stephen G. Brown and Sidney I. Dobrin. Albany: State U of New York P, 2004.

Giroux, Henry A. *Theory and Resistance in Education: Towards a Pedagy of Opposition.* Foreword by Paulo Freire. Westport, CT: Bergin & Garvey, 2000.

Gorzelsky, Gwen. "Shifting Figures: Rhetorical Form." Ed. Stephen G. Brown and Sidney I. Dobrin. Albany: State U of New York P, 2004.

Hanson, Susan S. "Critical Auto/Ethnography: A Constructive Approach to Research in the Composition Classroom." Ed. Stephen G. Brown and Sidney I. Dobrin. Albany: State U of New York P, 2004.

Horner, Bruce. "Critical Ethnography, Ethics, and Work: Rearticulating Labor." Ed. Stephen G. Brown and Sidney I. Dobrin. Albany: State U of New York P, 2004.

Lofty, John. "State Standards in the United States and the National Curriculum in the United Kingdom: Political Siege Engines against Teacher Professionalism?" Ed. Stephen G. Brown and Sidney I. Dobrin. Albany: State U of New York P, 2004.

Lu, Min-Zhan. "The Ethics of Reading Critical Ethnography." Ed. Stephen G. Brown and Sidney I. Dobrin. Albany: State U of New York P, 2004.

Massey, Lance. "Just What *Are* We Talking About? Disciplinary Struggle and the Ethnographic Imaginary." Ed. Stephen G. Brown and Sidney I. Dobrin. Albany: State U of New York P, 2004.

Reiff, Mary Jo. "Mediating Materiality and Discursivity: Critical Ethnography as Metageneric Learning." Ed. Stephen G. Brown and Sidney I. Dobrin. Albany: State U of New York P, 2004.

Stevens, Sharon M. "Debating Ecology: Ethnographic Writing that 'Makes a Difference.'" Ed. Stephen G. Brown and Sidney I. Dobrin. Albany: State U of New York P, 2004.

Williams, Bronwyn T., and Mary Brydon-Miller. "Changing Directions: Participatory-Action Research and Representation." Ed. Stephen G. Brown and Sidney I. Dobrin. Albany: State U of New York P, 2004.

CONTRIBUTORS

Janet Alsup is assistant professor of English education at Purdue University. She received her Ph.D. in English education from the University of Missouri-Columbia in 2000, and she specializes in teacher education, adolescent literacies, qualitative research, and young adult literature. She has published in *English Education* and *Pedagogy: Critical Approaches to Teaching Literature, Language, Composition, and Culture* and regularly presents at the National Council of Teachers of English convention and the Conference on College Composition and Communication. She is currently conducting a qualitative research study describing the professional identity development of student teachers in the English education program at Purdue.

Robert Brooke is professor of English at the University of Nebraska-Lincoln, where he directs the Nebraska Writing Project and edits the Studies in Writing and Rhetoric series. He has published more than thirty articles and three books in composition/rhetoric, including the Braddock Award article "Underlife and Writing Instruction." His fourth book, *Place-Conscious Writing: Writing Instruction for Community Involvement,* written with members of the Nebraska Writing Project Rural Voices, Country Schools team, is forthcoming from Columbia University's Teachers College Press.

Stephen Gilbert Brown is assistant professor and director of composition at the University of Nevada-Las Vegas. His book, *Words in the Wilderness: Critical Literacy in the Borderlands* won the W. Ross Winterowd Award (2000) as the outstanding book in composition theory. He has published articles in *Review of Education, JAC: A Journal of Composition Theory,* and *College Literature* on issues affecting the acquisition of literacy across cultures. His current interest is in the field of ecoethnography. Recently, he completed work on *The Gardens of Desire: Marcel Proust and the Fugitive Sublime,* SUNY Press (forthcoming).

317

Mary Brydon-Miller is an assistant professor in educational foundations and urban educational leadership at the College of Education at the University of Cincinnati. She has been engaged in developing the theory and practice of participatory action research for nearly twenty years and is co-editor of *From Subjects to Subjectivities: A Handbook of Interpretive and Participatory Methods* and *Voices of Change: Participatory Research in the United States and Canada.* She is currently working on a third edited volume, *Traveling Companions: Feminism and Participatory Action Research.* Her current research focuses on work with refugee communities.

Sidney I. Dobrin is director of writing programs and associate professor at the University of Florida where he teaches composition theory, technical and professional writing, ecocriticism, and environmental rhetoric. He also serves on the faculty for the College of Natural Resources and Environmental Studies at the University of Florida. He is author of *Constructing Knowledges: The Politics of Theory-Building and Pedagogy in Composition,* and is co-editor of *Composition Theory for the Postmodern Classroom* (with Gary A. Olson), *The Kinneavy Papers: Theory and the Study of Discourse* (with Gary A. Olson and Lynn Worsham), and *Ecocomposition: Theoretical and Pedagogical Approaches* (with Christian Weisser). He is also co-author of *Natural Discourse: Composition Studies and Environmental Theory* (with Christian Weisser). He has also recently published his first trade book, *Distance Casting: Words and Ways of the Saltwater Fishing Life.* His articles and essays cover a range of subjects about composition theory and writing and have appeared in a variety of journals and books. He is past co-editor of *JAC: A Journal of Composition Theory* and served for two years on the Conference on College Composition and Communication's Scholar for the Dream Award Committee. In 2002, he served as chair of the Conference on College Composition and Communication Nominating Committee.

Lynée Lewis Gaillet, director of Lower Division Studies at Georgia State University, teaches a wide range of undergraduate and graduate classes in composition theory and practice. She has published numerous chapters and articles concerning the history of rhetoric/composition practices and is the editor of *Scottish Rhetoric and Its Influences.* Her current research interests include civic rhetoric, writing program administration, and the professionalization of graduate students.

Gwen Gorzelsky is assistant professor in the composition program, Department of English, Wayne State University. With a group of colleagues, she is developing a graduate and undergraduate service-learning program that includes internships in community literacy and in public vocations for the humanities. She is writing a book, *Echoes Half Heard: Community Activists, Collective Movements,* on how literate practices help to advance personal and social change. Recent publications include "Ghosts: Liberal Education and Negotiated Authority" (*College English,* Jan. 2002) and "Writing Awareness" (*Journal of the Assembly for Expanded Perspectives on Learning,* Winter 2000–01). She is now beginning a study of metaphor's role in personal and collective change in community-university collaborative educational projects.

Susan S. Hanson is completing her Ph.D. in composition, ethnography, and folklore at Ohio State University where she holds an appointment as a graduate teaching associate, an opportunity that enabled her to hone the approach she discusses in this collection. She has an M.A. and B.A. in comparative studies from Ohio State University. Her research interests include performance theory, expressive culture, and autobiography. Her doctoral dissertation is on narratives of life in U.S. suburbs.

Charlotte Hogg is assistant professor at Texas Christian University where she teaches courses in writing, rhetoric, and literacies. Part of the research that contributes to this co-authored piece with Robert Brooke comes from a larger book project on the literacies of older women in western Nebraska entitled *Cultivating Identities and Literacies: Rural Women Writing Culture.* Other work drawing on this research appears in *Multiple Literacies for the 21st Century* and in *Western American Literature.*

Bruce Horner teaches composition and composition theory at the University of Wisconsin-Milwaukee, where he is professor of English and director of composition. His books include *Representing the "Other": Basic Writers and the Teaching of Basic Writing* (NCTE 1999), co-authored with Min-Zhan Lu, and *Terms of Work for Composition: A Materialist Critique* (SUNY 2000), winner of the W. Ross Winterowd Award for outstanding book on composition theory. His essays on composition have appeared in journals such as *College Composition and Communication, College English, JAC: A Journal of Composition Theory, Rhetoric Review,* and the *Journal of Basic Writing.*

Christopher Keller is assistant professor of English at the University of Hawaii at Hilo. He has written articles and reviews about composition studies, anthropology, and ethnography as well as ecocomposition and nature writing. He is currently finishing a book with Sid Dobrin entitled *Writing Environments: Rhetoric, Text, and the Construction of Nature* (SUNY Press, forthcoming), and he is also finishing a manuscript that examines connections between composition studies, cultural anthropology, and cultural geography, tentatively titled *Topographies of Power.*

John Sylvester Lofty is professor of English education at the University of New Hampshire, Durham, where he directs the program for English teaching majors. He has authored *Time to Write: The Influence of Time and Culture on Learning to Write* (SUNY Press, 1992). He is a former middle- and secondary-level classroom teacher originally from England. He is currently working on a book about the influence of standards on teacher professionalism in England and Maine.

Min-Zhan Lu is professor of English at the University of Wisconsin-Milwaukee, where she is currently coordinator of the graduate program in rhetoric and composition and teaches courses in composition pedagogy, life writing, and critical theory. She has published work on the constructive uses of cultural dissonance in the teaching and learning of writing and on theories and practices of life writing as social acts. Her books include *Shanghai Quartet: The Crossings of Four Women of China* (Duquesne UP, 2001), *Comp Tales: An Introduction to College Composition Through Its Stories* (Longman, 2000) with Richard Haswell, and *Representing the "Other": Basic Writers and the Teaching of Basic Writing* (NCTE, 1999) with Bruce Horner.

Lance Massey is a Ph.D. candidate and instructor of academic and business writing at the University of Illinois at Urbana-Champaign. He is currently writing his dissertation, entitled *Rhetoric, Reception, and Knowledge Production in Composition: The Disciplinary Dynamics of Author, Text, and Methodology*. He is also co-editor of *Feminism and Composition: A Critical Sourcebook* (Bedford/St. Martin's, forthcoming). His research interests include composition and rhetorical theories, feminism and composition, qualitative research methods, and disciplinarity.

Mary Jo Reiff is an assistant professor in the Department of English at the University of Tennessee, where she teaches a variety of courses in writing, rhetoric, and technical and professional communication. Her research has appeared in journals such as *JAC: A Journal of Composition Theory, Issues in Writing, Writing on the Edge,* and *WAC Journal.* She is currently writing a book on audience theory entitled *Approaches to Audience: An Overview of Perspectives* and is co-authoring (with Amy J. Devitt and Anis Bawarshi) a rhetoric entitled *Scenes of Writing: Genre Acts.*

Christopher Schroeder is an assistant professor of English at Northeastern Illinois University where he teaches undergraduate and graduate courses in composition and literature. His most recent publications include *ALT DIS: Alternative Discourses and the Academy,* which he proposed to and co-edited with Helen Fox and Patricia Bizzell, and *ReInventing the University: Literacies* *and Legitimacy in the Postmodern Academy*. In addition to other projects, he is currently collaborating on a social, political, and cultural analysis of web-authoring software.

Sharon McKenzie Stevens is a doctoral candidate in the rhetoric, composition, and Teaching of English program at the University of Arizona. Her research and teaching interests include the rhetoric of science and science studies, genre, writing across the curriculum, writing in the disciplines, identity theory, social movement studies, and ethnographic methodology. She is currently completing an ethnography-based dissertation about the role of language in public debates over whether to graze southern Arizona's desert grasslands. Within this dissertation, her primary emphases are the construction of politicized identities and science-based argumentation.

Bronwyn T. Williams is an assistant professor of English at the University of Louisville (Kentucky) and teaches and writes about issues of literacy, pedagogy, popular culture, and identity. His most recent book is *Tuned In: Television and the Teaching of Writing* (Boynton/Cook). He has also published his work in several anthologies and journals including *The Writing Instructor* and *College English*.

INDEX